Languages in Contact

Studies in Slavic and General Linguistics

Series Editors:

Peter Houtzagers · Janneke Kalsbeek · Jos Schaeken

Amsterdam - Atlanta, GA 2000

Studies in Slavic and General Linguistics, vol. 28

Languages in Contact

Edited by

Dicky Gilbers
John Nerbonne
Jos Schaeken

The paper on which this book is printed meets the requirements of "ISO 9706:1994, Information and documentation - Paper for documents - Requirements for permanence".

ISBN: 90-420-1322-2
©Editions Rodopi B.V., Amsterdam - Atlanta, GA 2000
Printed in the Netherlands

To honour Tjeerd de Graaf

An Editorial Note

In the summer of 1980, Adriaan Barentsen, Ben Groen and Rob Sprenger prepared a festschrift for Carl Ebeling, the Nestor of Slavic linguistics in the Netherlands. The collection of articles was given the title "Studies in Slavic and General Linguistics 1". At the time, Barentsen, Groen and Sprenger had no idea whether they would issue a second volume, not to mention founding a series. In the intervening twenty years, however, 28 volumes of *SSGL* have appeared and it has become the most important venue for Slavic linguistics in the Netherlands. The editors never strictly defined their profile nor did they schedule the issues at fixed intervals. Although *SSGL* appears to have developed into a well-established series in a somewhat haphazard way, Barentsen, Groen and Sprenger clearly succeeded in their goal to create an accessible and flexible journal for Dutch Slavists, one carefully prepared and widely disseminated. All Slavic linguists in the Netherlands are greatly indebted to the three editors. Special thanks go to Adriaan Barentsen, who carried most of the load and devoted an enormous amount of energy and time to *SSGL*.

In 1997, as a representative of the younger generation of Dutch Slavists, I was invited to join the editors. Now the time has come for other younger scholars to join me. It is my pleasure to welcome my colleagues Peter Houtzagers of the University of Groningen and Janneke Kalsbeek of the University of Amsterdam as joint editors of *SSGL*. The three of us shall try to carry on in the same spirit as the previous editors and to maintain their high standards.

Finally, also on behalf of Peter Houtzagers and Janneke Kalsbeek, I would like to welcome the members of the newly established Editorial Advisory Board. We look forward to cooperating in this collective enterprise.

Groningen, May 2000   *Jos Schaeken*

CONTENTS

CONTENTS

CONTENTS

Languages in Contact, edited by D.G. Gilbers, J. Nerbonne, and J. Schaeken (= *Studies in Slavic and General Linguistics*, vol. 28), 1-7. Amsterdam - Atlanta, GA: Rodopi, 2000.

INTRODUCTION

THE EDITORS

The present volume includes papers that were presented at the conference *Languages in Contact* at the University of Groningen (25-26 November 1999). The conference was held to celebrate the University of St. Petersburg's award of an honorary doctorate to TJEERD DE GRAAF of Groningen.

In general, the issues discussed in the articles involve pidgins and creoles, minorities and their languages, Diaspora situations, Sprachbund phenomena, extra-linguistic correlates of variety in contact situations, problems of endangered languages and the typology of these languages. Special attention is paid to contact phenomena between languages of the Russian Empire / USSR / Russian Federation, their survival and the influence of Russian.

In the following, we shall give a bird's-eye survey of the specific languages and topics that are treated in this volume. Starting off with Dutch we will travel eastward all around the world and cover Eurasia, the PACIFIC, the NEW WORLD, and, finally, Africa, thus returning to the OLD WORLD.[1]

1. The OLD WORLD I: Eurasia

In "Dutch-German Contact in and around Bentheim" WILBERT HEERINGA ET AL. investigate the influence of political borders on the Lower Saxon dialect continuum, in particular in the German county Bentheim and in the Dutch varieties which surround it on three sides. Pronunciations twenty-five years apart are examined. To measure the distance between dialects, "Levenshtein distance" is used. The results of comparison are analysed by clustering and multidimensional scaling. The historical development is examined by comparing the two sets of measurements, in particular the change in relative proximity to each other. Results show that the political border and the influence of standard languages are driving the Dutch and German dialects apart.

There are several more papers that deal with contact situations in which Germanic languages play a central role. Thus, JURIJ KUSMENKO AND MICHAEL RIESSLER discuss the most important isoglosses that are characteristic of the

---

[1] The terms OLD WORLD, PACIFIC, and NEW WORLD refer to linguistic macroareas as described by Johanna Nichols (*Linguistic diversity in space and time*. Chicago-London: The University of Chicago Press. 1992: 12-13, 26-27).

northern Scandinavian dialects. According to the authors, these isoglosses are the result of the Sámi-Scandinavian interference during the fourteenth through nineteenth centuries. WOUTER KUSTERS also concentrates on Scandinavian, but from a totally different perspective: he makes a typological comparison between the process of morphological simplification in Scandinavian languages and similar changes in Quechua languages (cf. below, section 3). The report by NINA VOLSKAYA AND ANNA GRIGORYAN describes the melodic patterns of Armenian intonation questions. Pitch patterns of intonation questions in English and Armenian in one-, two- and three-syllable words with different positions of the tonic syllable are compared and the results of the perceptual evaluation of the Armenian question intonation by English speakers are presented.

Two articles are devoted to language contact between German and different West Slavic neighbours. HANNA TOBY presents research that is devoted to a detailed diachronic investigation of a dialect area in Northeast Kashubia (in the northern part of Poland) in terms of different levels of interference with Low German. HÉLÈNE BRIJNEN addresses the question of German influence on the Sorbian aspect system. The use of verbal prefixes is analysed on the basis of historical evidence taken from writings of the peasant-writer Hanso Nepila (1761-1856).

Moving to the heart of Central Europe, we stop at Hidegség and Fertőhomok, two villages in the Northwest of Hungary where from the sixteenth century onward a Croatian (Kajkavian) migrant dialect has been spoken. In the previous volume of the present series, PETER HOUTZAGERS (1999) completed a monography on this dialect that is very rich in traces of both premigratory and postmigratory language contact, not only with Hungarian, but also with other varieties of Croatian and German. In his paper Houtzagers demonstrates the necessity and, at the same time, complexity of the distinctions between the various layers of borrowed language material.

In Southeast Europe we find the Balkan Sprachbund, "world's most famous contact situation" as cited by RONELLE ALEXANDER in her article on word order in Balkan languages. The recent historical change which produced the Balkan ordering would seem to be due to convergent change. According to Alexander, however, close analysis of dialectal data shows that the motivations of the change are Slavic in nature, and throws into question the parameters of the concept Sprachbund. A second article that is devoted to the Balkan Sprachbund is the one by JOUKO LINDSTEDT, who argues that difficulties in finding a source for the common grammatical innovations of the Balkan languages are not due to our limited knowledge of the history of the individual languages. The innovations have no source languages in the traditional sense: the linguistic contact situation itself has caused convergent changes that would not have occurred in *any* of the Balkan languages by internal drift only. This process, described by Lindstedt as "mutual reinforcement of change", does not lead to outright simplification, but it does favour explicit and analytic marking of syntactic functions.[2]

Before discussing the bulk of papers in which Russian is involved, we should first mention two articles that deal with matters of Yiddish. ANE KLEINE adds a new argument to the discussion of "Standard Yiddish" by distinguishing between two kinds of contact situation, the first being co-existence of different languages in one territory and the second being "intra-language contact". The latter means both the coming together of speakers from different dialectal backgrounds and also contact situations in which different social varieties meet. YURI KLEINER AND NATALIA SVETOZAROVA discuss the loss of quantity distinctions in the majority of the dialects of Yiddish. This must have been due to the influence of the Slavic languages, having the open syllable as the predominant type. The preservation of the quantity distinctions in the Mid-Eastern variety of Yiddish (Poland) may be accounted for by extra-linguistic factors.

Let us now turn to the language contact situations in which Russian plays a central role. Apart from the contribution by LARISSA NAIDITCH, who investigates the language of emigrants from Russia living in Israel and focuses on the influence of Hebrew on Russian on the lexical level, most articles deal with Russian as the dominant language within the Russian Empire / USSR / Russian Federation.

In more general terms, LIYA BONDARKO from the St. Petersburg Phonetics Department – an institution that has studied language contact for seventy years – stresses that the investigation of the phonetics of language contact presupposes the study of the phonetic systems of the individual languages involved. Data on Estonian, Lithuanian, Azerbaijani, Georgian, and other languages demonstrate different degrees of interaction with Russian. For Russian the problem of language contact is the problem of intra-language interference, which arises when the pronunciation norm interacts with stable dialectal features. PAVEL SKRELIN reports on two types of sound databases (sound archives and speech corpora) developed at the St. Petersburg Phonetics Department. They make it possible to process different types of sound material used in research on the interference between languages.

There are several case studies where Russian is involved. CORNELIUS HASSEL-BLATT addresses the question whether the often ascribed Russian influence on Estonian is historically founded or not. If not, Russian influence is asserted for political reasons without linguistic evidence. LARS JOHANSON deals with the complex language contact interaction of Russian, Finno-Ugric and Turkic in the Middle Volga area, where long-term contact-induced processes of mutual code-

---

[2] The Balkan Sprachbund is also discussed by Sarah Thomason.

copying have led to convergence of socially dominated and dominant codes and introduced new linguistic patterns, partly typical Sprachbund-phenomena.

Moving deeper into the territory of Siberia, we find a report by IRINA NEV-SKAJA who examines various Shor-Russian contact features. The Shors are an indigenous Turkic people. Until recently their language was neither written, nor taught at schools. Within the last thirty years the number of speakers has diminished, all of them are bilingual, language transmission to younger generations has almost stopped, and all the systems of the language appear to be open to influence of Russian. ALEKSANDR KRASOVICKY AND CHRISTIAN SAPPOK discuss the phonemic system of an isolated Russian dialect of the arctic Russian settlement Russkoye Ust'ye on the territory of Siberia. The dialect inherited and preserved features of ancient North Russian dialects and has greatly been influenced by the Tungusic language of the neighbouring Even. LENORE GRENOBLE, who conducted fieldwork in the Amur basin and Yakutia, examines changes which are taking place as the result of language contact between Evenki – a seriously endangered Tungusic language – and Russian, focusing on changes in word order, case, modal constructions and syntax. MARINA KHASANOVA provides us with examples of pidginized Russian, spoken in the Lower Amur region by native speakers of Tungusic languages and of Nivkh. The latter language – an isolate, usually classified as Paleosiberian – is also dealt with by EKATERINA GRUZDEVA, who investigates prescriptive and optative constructions with synthetic and analytical imperative forms. The imperative in Nivkh seems to have been affected considerably by the influence of the Russian grammatical system.

In geographical terms, PETER BAKKER's contribution constitutes a bridge between the OLD WORLD and the PACIFIC, in the sense that it mainly deals with Sri Lanka Portuguese and Sri Lanka Malay (Austronesian), two mixed languages of the "converted" type, being the result of a process called "convergence intertwining"; they have all grammatical and lexical elements from one language, but these elements have the functions, grammatical status, and structural positions of a different language. One might call them "transvestites".

2. The PACIFIC

Both articles that deal with languages within the PACIFIC macroarea concentrate on language contact on New Guinea.[3] In his paper BERNARD COMRIE refutes a particular combination of claims, namely that if words are recognizable as borrowings because of their near-identity in both borrowing and donating languages, then they will be restricted in semantic domain. Comrie uses evidence primarily from Haruai, a Papuan (i.e. non-Austronesian) language spoken in the Madang

---

[3] Cf. also Sarah Thomason's contribution, in which she outlines the Sepik River Basin Sprachbund in northern Papua New Guinea.

Province of Papua New Guinea, in order to show that there are indeed instances of such easily recognized borrowings that nonetheless cover a wide range of semantic domains within basic vocabulary.

On the Indonesian part of New Guinea (Irian Jaya), CECILIA ODÉ investigates the prosodic system of Mpur, an unwritten non-Austronesian language with three (possibly four) lexical tones spoken by approximately 5,000 speakers in the Northeast Bird's Head Area. The prosodic analysis shows that phenomena, characteristic of the Mpur oral tradition, can be expressed in Indonesian as it is in Mpur. Odé presents examples of prosodic loans in Indonesian from Mpur, and also of loans from Indonesian that are increasingly used in Mpur, as well as some Dutch loans.

3. The NEW WORLD

Travelling from North to South, first attention is payed to the Pacific Northwest of North America, one of the world's most extensive Sprachbunds which encompasses several controversial genetic phyla, including "Mosan" uniting Salishan, Wakashan, and Chimakuan.[4] In his paper DAVID BECK concentrates on Bella Coola, the most northerly of the coastal Salish languages within the Central Northwest language area. The Salishan outrider Bella Coola has gone even further than other Salish languages towards approximation to its Wakashan neighbours, and the novel features of this language illustrate both grammatical convergence and diversification.

In Southern Mexico LOUANNA FURBEE discusses narrative in the indigenous language Tojolab'al Maya, which incorporates Spanish both in terms of loan words and code switches. Furbee examines the less familiar loan vocabulary and longer code switches in twenty-six accounts of a miracle that occurred in 1994. The differences in the poetic usage of this loan vocabulary suggest different levels of vulnerability of the Tojolab'al shift toward Spanish.

The two remaining papers both deal with Quechua, one of the indigenous languages of the Andean countries in South America.[5] ELLEN COURTNEY discusses the development of Spanish word order in Quechua-speaking children and challenges the claim that the children have a transitional grammar with a non-adult phrase structure rule. Quechua, among other South American languages, is also discussed by PIETER MUYSKEN, who presents a tentative typology of linguistic areas. In this context Muysken considers areal features in the Andean/Amazonian transition area and offers relevant data on word order and agreement patterns, verb morphology, and case marking in the languages of the eastern slopes.

---

[4] Cf. also Sarah Thomason's paper.
[5] Cf. also Wouter Kuster's remarks on morphological simplification in Quechua and Peter Bakker's contribution, in which Media Lengua, a mixed Quechua-Spanish language in Ecuador, is used as an example of an "intertwined language".

4. The OLD WORLD II: Africa

PATRICK-ANDRÉ MATHER uses data primarly from West African L2 French in order to support the second language acquisition / gradualist model of creole genesis. Mather provides evidence from recent SLA studies and discusses features that are found both in creoles and in L2 varieties of European languages: the position of specifiers and adjectives within the noun phrase, the position of verbs, pronouns and full NP complements within the verb phrase, serial verb constructions, copula deletion, reduplication of adjectives, and others.

The Ethopian highlands are one of five linguistic areas that are outlined by SARAH GREY THOMASON. She argues that the existence of linguistic areas greatly complicates the work of the historical linguist. Sorting out the processes by which the languages in a linguistic area acquired their shared features ranges from difficult to impossible. Thomason examines the historical issues raised by five "representative" Sprachbunds that are geographically and historically diverse. Apart from the Ethiopian highlands these are the Balkan Sprachbund, the Sepik River Basin in Papua New Guinea, the Pacific Northwest of North America, and South Asia.

University of Groningen

A html-version (including hyperlinks) of the Introduction is also available on the Internet:
http://www.let.rug.nl/~schaeken/ssgl/ssgl28_intro.htm

Index to Map 1

1	Heeringa et al.	16	Johanson
2	Kusmenko and Rießler	17	Nevskaja
3	Kusters	18	Krasovicky and Sappok
4	Volskaya and Grigoryan	19	Grenoble
5	Toby	20	Khasanova
6	Brijnen	21	Gruzdeva
7	Houtzagers	22	Bakker
8	Alexander	23	Comrie
9	Lindstedt	24	Odé
10	Kleine	25	Beck
11	Kleiner and Svetozarova	26	Furbee
12	Naiditch	27	Courtney
13	Bondarko	28	Muysken
14	Skrelin	29	Mather
15	Hasselblatt	30	Thomason

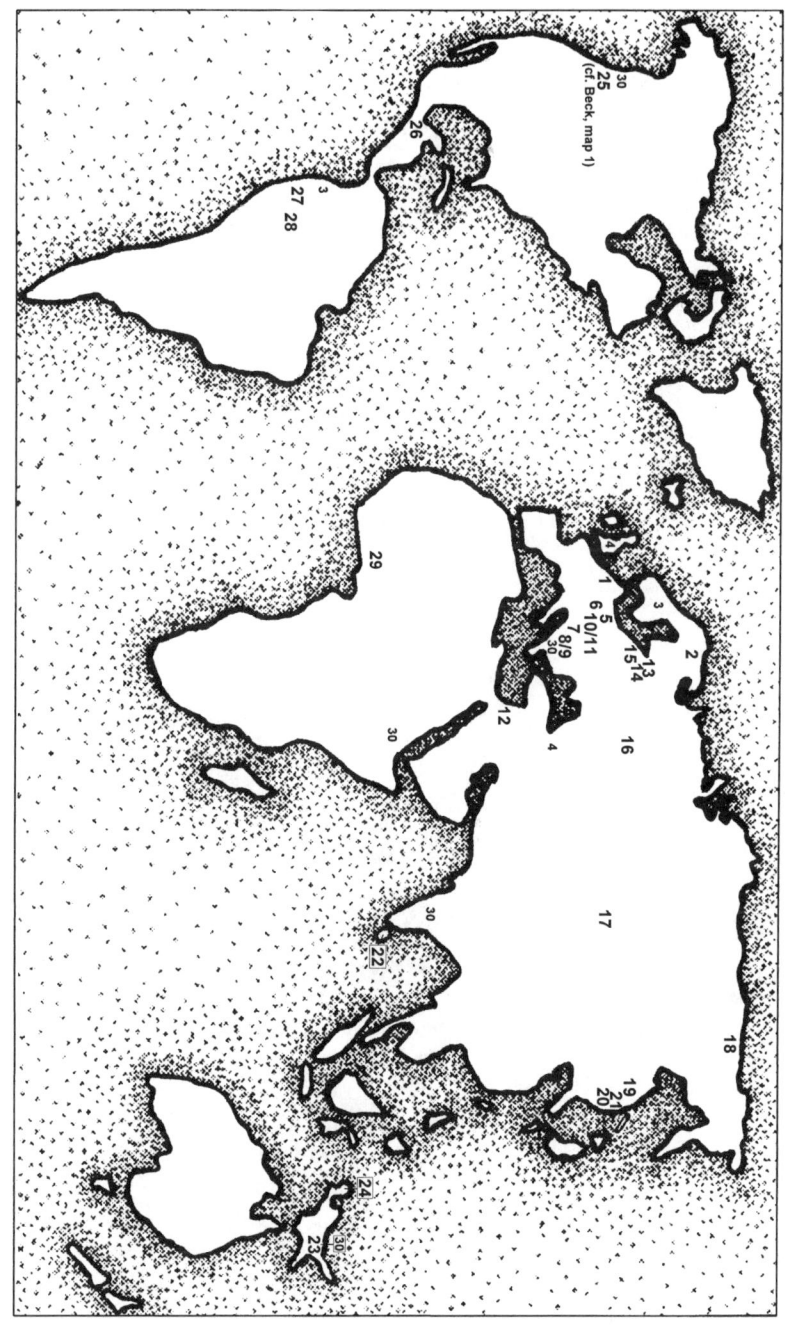

Map 1. The major languages and linguistic areas discussed in the present volume.

Languages in Contact, edited by D.G. Gilbers, J. Nerbonne, and J. Schaeken (= *Studies in Slavic and General Linguistics*, vol. 28), 9-27. Amsterdam - Atlanta, GA: Rodopi, 2000.

TRACKING SPRACHBUND BOUNDARIES:
WORD ORDER IN THE BALKANS[1]

RONELLE ALEXANDER

1. Introduction

As Thomason and Kaufman have noted in their classic survey, "Sprachbund situations are notoriously messy" (1988: 95). This is largely because in a situation of multilateral multilingualism, it is next to impossible to make an unambiguous determination, either in general or in any one particular instance, of either the source or the direction of interference. Often the best (and only thing) one can do is to list the shared features which could possibly be due to convergent change.

In the case of the "world's most famous contact situation" (ibid.), the Balkan Sprachbund, scholars have almost consistently ventured far beyond this cautiously stated boundary. Lists of shared features have been taken as an implicit claim (and even sometimes as clear proof) that contact phenomena are the source of the several language-specific changes which in each instance produced these shared features; this in turn has led to claims that a particular language has provided the source from which the others have borrowed. Not surprisingly, such claims are often made by linguists whose native language is the one claimed as source.[2]

Although it is relatively easy to counter most claims that one or another of the Balkan languages has provided the definitive model which others have followed (particularly when one is relatively free from the native's emotional attachment to his own language), it is much harder to differentiate between changes which are contact-induced and those which are motivated by each language's own internal structure. If, as would seem logical, most instances of individual language change within a Sprachbund area represent a combination of the two processes, it is even more difficult to determine the point at which the development of an internally motivated change becomes supported by the presence of a similar phenomenon in a neighboring language or, conversely, the point at which a borrowing initially

---

[1] I am grateful to Victor Friedman, Brian Joseph, Donca Steriade, Alan Timberlake and Willem Vermeer for discussion and comments.

[2] Of course this is not necessarily the case. The scholar generally recognized as the founder of the discipline, Kristian Sandfeld, felt that the striking similarities among Balkan languages were due to Greek influence (1930: 106). Sandfeld's native language was Danish.

adopted as a communicative variant then becomes sufficiently integrated into a language's structure such that it would then follow internally-motivated paths of development.

2. The role of Slavic within the Balkan Sprachbund

Due to the fortunate circumstance that one of the member language families of the Balkan Sprachbund, South Slavic, includes both Balkan and non-Balkan components, Sprachbund researchers have the possibility to conduct more focused comparative studies devoted to the distinction between changes that are presumed to be internal and those which are presumed to be contact-induced.

The complex of South Slavic languages (comprising Slovenian, Croatian, Bosnian, Serbian, Macedonian and Bulgarian) can be visualized as a continuum with its northwestern periphery in the Julian Alps and its southeastern periphery at the Black Sea. All Balkan linguists agree that the southeastern languages, Bulgarian and Macedonian, are central members of the Balkan Sprachbund, and that the northwesternmost, Slovenian, is not. The degree to which the other languages partake in the Balkan Sprachbund is less obvious, however.[3] Indeed, the term "language" itself is less than useful in an area where one standard language, Macedonian, came into being only in 1944 and another, Serbo-Croatian, went out of being in 1991. It is much more to the point to speak of South Slavic as a continuum of spoken dialects, especially as the convergence processes assumed to lie at the basis of the Balkan Sprachbund took place necessarily at the spoken level (first among peoples of the Byzantine Empire and then of the Ottoman Empire). The work of the South Slavic Balkanologist, therefore, consists in surveying the dialectal differentiation with respect to a particular linguistic feature, finding the point at which non-Balkan South Slavic shades into Balkan South Slavic, comparing the internal structures of the two basic South Slavic systems, and then comparing these with systems of contiguous non-Slavic Balkan languages.

The largely theoretical discussions of the Balkan Sprachbund can be given more solid grounding through the juxtaposition of concrete comparisons of linguistic systems which have a close genetic relationship to each other, with concrete comparisons of linguistic systems which bear only a distant genetic relationship to each other but which have been in close contact for a long time and have presumably undergone convergent change over a long period of time. Furthermore the choice of one particular structural element will give a clear focus to the discussion and set the model for further analysis of this sort.

---

[3] Schaller 1975 makes the useful distinction between languages of the Balkans (those situated on the Balkan peninsula) and Balkan languages (those which partake in the Balkan Sprachbund).

3. Balkan clitic ordering, basic facts

The particular structural element is the order of clitic pronouns. This facet of Indo-European languages has been studied much of late, often with reference to "Wackernagel's law" (Wackernagel 1892). This "law" makes two essential claims: first, clitics occur in a string whose internal order is strictly regulated; and second, this clitic string always occupies the second place in the utterance. South Slavic, which is already innovative with respect to the rest of Slavic in that it has significantly increased the inventory of clitics,[4] by and large conforms to both tenets of this rule. Balkan Slavic, however, deviates from this rule in two major instances, both of which find parallels in other Balkan languages. These two phenomena can thus be tentatively added to the list of "Balkanisms" – shared structural features which are potentially the result of convergent development, particularly inasmuch as one of them seems to be connected structurally with two well-known phenomena agreed by all to be classic "Balkanisms" – the loss of the infinitive and the development of a future construction marked by an invariant future particle derived from a verb of volition. A closer look at the facts, however, and especially at dialectal variation within South Slavic on this point, argues for greater caution.

South Slavic can have as many as six clitics in a row, though such utterances are cumbersome and rarely encountered unless elicited by the linguist. Sequences of three and four clitics are quite normal, however. The ordering of these clitics is usually quite rigid with respect to a number of factors, one of which is the position of the negative particle. If a non-Balkan Slavic verb with clitic pronoun objects is negated, the negative particle must precede the verb directly. Clitic objects take second position: either after the negated verb or after another stressed word (necessarily before the negated verb). Compare the following (where non-Balkan South Slavic is represented by standard Serbian and Croatian):

Serbian [non-Balkan] present indicative negative[5]

(1)   *Ne*   *dajem*   *mu*   *ga.*
       Neg.   verb.pres.   DAT   ACC
               1sg.   3sg.msc.   3sg.msc.
       'I don't give it to him.'

---

[4] See Cyxun 1968 for a thorough discussion of South Slavic clitics.

[5] Glosses in capital letters identify clitics, either pronoun objects (DAT, ACC, GEN) or the verbal auxiliary (AUX). Glosses in lower case letters identify accented words, using basic grammatical terms such as subject, verb tense forms or verbal participles (subj., verb.pres., verb.part.). Capitalized glosses identify words which are unaccented but which do not function as clitics, such as the negative particle (Neg.).

(2) | *Ja* | *mu* | *ga* | *ne* | *dajem.*[6] |
| --- | --- | --- | --- | --- |
| subj. | DAT | ACC | Neg. | verb.pres. |
| 1sg. | 3sg.msc. | 3sg.msc. | 1sg. | |

In Balkan South Slavic (here represented by standard Bulgarian), by contrast, the clitics must be placed between the negative particle and the verb. Compare:[7]

Bulgarian [Balkan] present indicative negative

(3) | *Ne* | *mu* | *go* | *davam.* |
| --- | --- | --- | --- |
| Neg. | DAT | ACC | verb.pres. |

(4) | *Az* | *ne* | *mu* | *go* | *davam.* |
| --- | --- | --- | --- | --- |
| subj. | Neg. | DAT | ACC | verb.pres. |

This order corresponds to that of the other Balkan languages.[8] Compare:

Albanian present indicative negative

(5) | *Nuk* | *i-* | *a* | *jap.* |
| --- | --- | --- | --- |
| Neg. | DAT | ACC | verb.pres. |

Modern Greek present indicative negative[9]

(6) | *Den* | *tu* | *ton* | *Dino.* |
| --- | --- | --- | --- |
| Neg. | GEN | ACC | verb.pres. |

Romanian present indicative negative

(7) | *Nu* | *i-* | *l* | *dau.* |
| --- | --- | --- | --- |
| Neg. | DAT | ACC | verb.pres. |

Comparative evidence, as well as that of early manuscripts, indicates that the non-Balkan order continues the original Slavic situation. Not only is the negative particle always written right before the verb, but in manuscripts which include accent

---

[6] The presence of the subject pronoun in (2) indicates emphasis; the neutral unemphatic expression is (1). As all languages to be discussed herein delete subject pronouns in unemphatic tensed clauses (i.e. are pro-drop languages), only the unemphatic variants will be cited henceforth unless special attention is being drawn to word order facts requiring the presence of an initial stressed element other than the verb.

[7] Subsequent examples will not be translated, unless the meaning is different from 'I [do not] give it to him' (adjusted for tense if necessary). Glosses will continue to identify category of speech but will not be marked for person, number or gender unless different from that in (1) or (2).

[8] The major non-Slavic Balkan languages are Greek, Albanian, and Romanian. For simplicity I cite forms from the standard languages. Dialectal material, such as that of Arvanitika in Greece or the Vlah dialects spoken in Greece and Macedonia, is obviously of great interest, and focus on such material is necessary for a full study of any one Balkan phenomenon. Because the standard languages also exhibit the phenomena discussed herein, and because of space constraints in the present volume, standard language forms are cited almost exclusively.

[9] The capital *D* denotes the Greek voiced interdental fricative.

marks (both South Slavic and North Slavic), the main word accent is often re-tracted onto the proclitic *ne*; furthermore, this accentuation is found also in mod-ern South Slavic. The order found in Balkan South Slavic, therefore, seems clearly to represent an innovation.

The other instance of innovation with respect to clitic ordering concerns the classic "second position" rule. Most of South Slavic, including most of Balkan Slavic, obeys this rule: clitics cannot stand in initial position but must occur after (at least) one stressed element of the utterance. Compare standard Serbian and Bulgarian:

Serbian present indicative affirmative
(8)	*Dajem*	*mu*	*ga.*
	verb.pres.	DAT	ACC

Bulgarian present indicative affirmative
(9)	*Davam*	*mu*	*go.*
	verb.pres.	DAT	ACC

In the southernmost areas of Balkan Slavic, however, clitics must precede the verb even if this requires them to occupy the first position in the utterance.[10] Compare standard Macedonian:

Macedonian present indicative affirmative
(10)	*Mu*	*go*	*davam.*
	DAT	ACC	verb.pres.

Again, this word order rule finds parallels in the other Balkan languages. Compare:

Albanian present indicative affirmative
(11)	*I-*	*a*	*jap.*
	DAT	ACC	verb.pres.

Modern Greek present indicative affirmative
(12)	*Tu*	*ton*	*Dino.*
	GEN	ACC	verb.pres.

Romanian present indicative affirmative
(13)	*I-*	*l*	*dau.*
	DAT	ACC	verb.pres.

Since the rule placing clitics in second position is documented in early Slavic manuscripts, and is posited for Indo-European, it seems clear that it represents the

---

[10] This rule holds only for finite verbs in Macedonian. Participles and imperatives require clitics to follow the verb.

archaic state, and that the word order of southernmost Balkan Slavic is innovative.[11]

The fact that both these innovations in word order are restricted to Slavic dialects spoken in areas agreed by all to be well within that of the Balkan Sprachbund, taken together with the existence of similar phenomena in the other three major Balkan languages, would suggest that these Balkan Slavic word order patterns are contact-induced, one of the many structural results of the long-term multilingualism of a convergence area. A closer look at the Slavic data, however, suggests that the historical changes in question concern more than just word order rules, and that the processes involved are an intrinsic part of Slavic phonology.

4. Clitics in negated verb phrases

Let us turn first to the question of negated verb phrases. As noted above, the Slavic negative particle *ne* was historically proclitic to the verb: the frequent shift of accent from the verb to this otherwise unaccented particle demonstrates that the unit "*ne* + verb" was a single prosodic word (the term "accentual unit" is also used with this meaning). The Balkan Slavic development, shifting the clitic string to a position after the negative particle and before the verb, splits this prosodic word asunder and thereby seems to destroy one of the basic inherited elements of Slavic prosody.

In fact, however, the same phenomenon is found in non-Balkan South Slavic as well, in the negated past tense. This tense is composed of the active participle and a verbal auxiliary. In affirmative utterances, word order is as in the present: the participle fills the slot of "verb", the auxiliary joins the clitic chain, and the clitic chain follows the first accented word (which often is the verb but can also be a subject). Compare the following, where standard Serbian is again taken as an example:

Serbian [non-Balkan] past indicative affirmative

(14) *Dala*   *sam*   *mu*   *ga.*
      verb.part. AUX-1sg.   DAT   ACC

(15) *Ja*   *sam*   *mu*   *ga*   *dala.*
      subj.   AUX-1sg.   DAT   ACC   verb.part.

When the past tense is negated, however, the negative particle appears to move to the head of the phrase, immediately preceding the clitic particles which themselves precede the verb. Furthermore, the negative particle fuses with the auxil-

---

[11] Dybo 1981 includes among his *formy enclinomena* (instances of unmarked accent appearing as stress retracted to the absolute initial [or final] syllable of a prosodic word) numerous examples of negated verbs.

iary to form a fully stressed word,[12] and it is this word which the clitics, again in second position, must follow. Compare:

Serbian [non-Balkan] past indicative negative[13]

(16)	*Nisam*	*mu*	*ga*	*dala.*
	neg.aux-1sg.	DAT	ACC	verb.part.

In Balkan Slavic, the tense which is parallel in form[14] is attested with exactly the same word order. Compare the Bulgarian past indefinite tense:

Bulgarian [Balkan] past indefinite negative

(17)	*Ne*	*sym*	*mu*	*go*	*dala.*
	Neg.	AUX-1sg.	DAT	ACC	verb.part.

When the word order of (17), the Bulgarian negative past indefinite, is compared with that of (3), the Bulgarian negative present (repeated below), it becomes clear that the Balkan Slavic innovation consists simply in the extension of the word order of the negative perfect to that of the negative present.

(3)	*Ne*	*mu*	*go*	*davam.*
	Neg.	DAT	ACC	verb.pres.

What is especially striking here is the parallelism in the prosodic structures of these utterances. In both Serbian (non-Balkan) and Bulgarian (Balkan), the affirmative string, composed of a verb and its clitics, constitutes a single prosodic domain and bears a single stress.[15] When negation is added, however, the unit is split into two prosodic domains, each with its own accent.

---

[12] Joseph (in press) has introduced the apposite term "negative fusion" to refer to this and other forms such as *nemoj* 'don't!' and *njamam* '[I do] not have'.

[13] If a pronoun subject is present, however, the negated auxiliary is placed *after* the pronoun objects, since (as a stressed word) it is no longer part of the clitic chain, while that chain continues to be required to take second position. Thus:

(i)	*Ja*	*mu*	*ga*	*nisam*	*dala.*
	subj.	DAT	ACC	neg.aux-1sg.	verb.part.

[14] The semantic scope of this tense is more limited in Balkan Slavic than it is in non-Balkan Slavic. This is because in both Macedonian and Bulgarian the unmarked narration of past events takes place in the simplex tenses, aorist and imperfect – tenses which exist only in highly marked speech in Serbian and Croatian. The compound tense illustrated in (17) is called the past indefinite in Bulgarian and the non-confirmative in Macedonian. Here and elsewhere the vowel *y* is used to transcribe the Bulgarian Cyrillic "er goljam", whose phonetic value is that of schwa.

[15] In these and following examples, all diacritics mark word accent. However, whereas the acute accent in Bulgarian denotes simply expiratory word stress, in Serbian it carries the additional information "long rising". The double grave in Serbian, by contrast, denotes word accent which is marked as "short falling".

(Serbian)	(Bulgarian)
Dála sam mu ga.	*Dála sym mu go.*

(Serbian)	(Bulgarian)
Nísam mu ga dála.	*Ne sým mu go dála.*

The implementation of the accents varies: in non-Balkan Slavic the negative auxiliary is a fully stressed word inflected for person and number (*nísam, nísi,* etc.) whereas in Balkan Slavic, the presence of negation before a pre-verbal clitic causes an accent to appear upon the immediately following clitic. The common point, however, is that negated phrases have two main accents while affirmative phrases have only one.

Non-Balkan Slavic exhibits this prosodic pattern only in the past tense. The innovation of Balkan Slavic is to extend it to *all* preverbal clitic strings, not just those whose first clitic is the auxiliary. Compare the following standard Bulgarian examples:

Bulgarian [Balkan] negative past indefinite indicative
(17)	*Ne*	*sým*	*mu*	*go*	*dála.*
	Neg.	AUX-1sg.	DAT	ACC	verb.part.

Bulgarian [Balkan] negative present indicative
(3)	*Ne*	*mú*	*go*	*dávam.*
	Neg.	DAT	ACC	verb.pres.

Bulgarian [Balkan] negative aorist indicative
(18)	*Ne*	*mú*	*go*	*dádox.*
	Neg.	DAT	ACC	verb.aor.

Bulgarian [Balkan] negative imperfect indicative
(19)	*Ne*	*mú*	*go*	*dávax.*
	Neg.	DAT	ACC	verb.impf.

Bulgarian [Balkan] negative imperative
(20)	*Ne*	*mú*	*go*	*dávaj!*
	Neg.	DAT	ACC	verb.imper.

The accentual pattern exemplified above is found in standard Bulgarian and in a wide range of its dialects. To the west and south, in many Macedonian dialects, accent is on the negative particle itself:

Macedonian dialectal [Balkan] negative present indicative
(21)	*Né*	*mu*	*go*	*dávam.*
	Neg.	DAT	ACC	verb.pres.

The pattern is the same, though. When verb phrases with clitic objects are negated, a second accentual unit is created which involves the negative particle; it is only the place of accent within this unit which varies.[16]

Dialectal differentiation throughout Balkan Slavic shows that this pattern is still evolving. Some areas have preserved the non-Balkan Slavic pattern in which only the compound past tense exhibits shifted word order; others show different degrees of spread.[17] The significant point is that the change combines syntax and prosody, and that whereas it has had a much broader effect on the grammar of Balkan Slavic, it is known in non-Balkan Slavic as well. Furthermore, it exemplifies an essentially Slavic phenomenon: the prosodic union of the negative particle and the form immediately following it.

Should one infer then that the word order change in Balkan Slavic is Slavic in nature rather than Balkan, and that its presence in Balkan Slavic has contributed to the rise of a similar pattern in the other Balkan languages?[18] Or should one rather infer that the change is Balkan in nature and that its spread into non-Balkan Slavic was aided by the ease with which it was integrated into the inherited prosodic structure of Slavic? Comparison with other Balkan languages contributes little information. In all non-Slavic Balkan languages, the word order is the same in both the affirmative and negative compound past tenses (the negative marker is simply prefixed to the clitic string), and in all instances the auxiliary is at the end of the string, immediately preceding the participle.[19] Furthermore, the auxiliary is

---

[16] In standard Macedonian, as well as in the southwestern dialects upon which it is based, accent is fixed with respect to word boundary. The accentuation of negated verbs in Macedonian will be discussed separately below, in section 6.

[17] For a preliminary survey of one compact dialectal area, see Alexander 1999.

[18] The fact that a fused form of the negative copula/auxiliary is found in the earliest written Slavic (Old Church Slavic) is proof that at least part of this construction is inherited.

[19] There is a limited point of comparison with South Slavic affirmative compound past tenses. There, the auxiliary marking 1st and 2nd singular and all three persons of the plural heads the clitic chain. The 3rd singular auxiliary, however, is placed at the end of the chain, yielding a word order more similar to that seen in the non-Slavic Balkan languages. This word order pattern is found in all South Slavic dialects, and is presumably archaic. Compare the following, both of which mean 'She gave it to him':
Serbian [non-Balkan] past affirmative
(ii)   *Ona*   *mu*   *ga*   *je*   *dala.*
       subj.   DAT   ACC   AUX-3sg.   verb.part.
Bulgarian [Balkan] past indefinite affirmative
(iii) *Tja*   *mu*   *go*   *e*   *dala.*
       subj.   DAT   ACC   AUX-3sg.   verb.part.
In the negative forms, Balkan Slavic differs from non-Balkan Slavic. Negative fusion, and the concomitant shift of the negated auxiliary to the head of the phrase, is characteristic of the latter, while in the former the place of the auxiliary is not affected by the presence of negation. Compare:

not a form of the verb 'be' as in Slavic but of 'have'.[20] As to accent, the negative particle bears a light accent in most non-Slavic Balkan languages, but in no case is this accent ever shifted to clitics.[21] Compare:

Albanian perfect indicative: affirmative (negative)

(22)	(nuk)	i-	a	kam	dhënë.
	Neg.	DAT	ACC	AUX-1sg.	verb.part.

Greek perfect indicative: affirmative (negative)

(23)	(Den)	tu	ton	exo	Dosi.
	Neg.	GEN	ACC	AUX-1sg.	verb.part.

Romanian perfect indicative: affirmative (negative)

(24)	(na)	i	l-	am	datu.
	Neg.	DAT	ACC	AUX-1sg.	verb.part.

5. Future constructions: a parallel instance?

A similar shift of word order with a concomitant prosodic restructuring is found in the non-Balkan Slavic future tense. In the affirmative future, a single accentual unit contains the verbal form (here, the infinitive) plus all attendant clitics (pronoun objects as well as the auxiliary). If an optional subject is present, it will function as a separate accented word, followed by the prosodic unit of clitics, and finally the verb form. In each case the clitic string is in second position. Compare the following (examples from standard Croatian):

Croatian [non-Balkan] affirmative future

(25)	Dàt	će	mu	ga.
	verb.inf.	FUT-3sg.	DAT	ACC
	'She will give it to him.'			

Serbian [non-Balkan] past negative

(iv)	Níje		mu	ga	dála.
	neg.aux.-3sg.		DAT	ACC	verb.part.

Bulgarian [Balkan] past indefinite negative

(v)	Ne	mú	go	e	dála.
	Neg.	DAT	ACC	AUX-3sg.	verb.part.

Furthermore, comparative Slavic evidence (and especially new data coming to light on the Old Russian vernacular of Novgorod, cf. Janin and Zaliznjak 1993: 282ff) suggests that all verbal auxiliary clitics formerly were placed at the end of the clitic chain. Further study is needed to establish the chronology of these word order changes in South Slavic; a more detailed study of dialectal differentiation on this point is in preparation.

[20] Compound past tenses with 'have' as an auxiliary are relatively widespread in Balkan Slavic, especially in Macedonian where they have taken on the primary function of the perfect tense (Friedman 1976). The auxiliary is always accented, however, and is not part of the clitic chain.

[21] Since the accentuation in non-Balkan Slavic is predictable (and therefore not immediately relevant to the discussion), these examples are given without word accent.

(26) *Óna*   *će*   *mu*   *ga*   *dàti.*
    subj.   FUT-3sg.   DAT   ACC   verb.inf.

When the negative particle is added, two accent groups are formed, one equal to the negated auxiliary and the other comprising the infinitive and dependent clitics (the example is again from Croatian):

Croatian [non-Balkan] affirmative future
(27) *Néće*   *mu*   *ga*   *dàti.*
    neg.fut-3sg.   DAT   ACC   verb.inf.

The negative future in Balkan Slavic is formed with an auxiliary meaning 'not have' combined with the subordinating conjunction *da* (which takes a finite verb form). This negative auxiliary is also a fully stressed word, and the prosodic structure can therefore be considered fully parallel to that of the non-Balkan Slavic negative future. Compare (the example is from Bulgarian):[22]

Bulgarian (Balkan) negative future
(28) *Njáma da*   *mu*   *go*   *dám.*
    neg.fut.Cnj.   DAT   ACC   verb.pres.

Balkan Slavic also has an alternative expression of the negative future, whose surface form is almost exactly parallel to the non-Balkan Slavic negative future seen in (27).[23] Compare Bulgarian:

Bulgarian [Balkan] negative future[24]
(29) *Ne*   *šté*   *mu*   *go*   *dám.*
    Neg.   Fut.   DAT   ACC   verb.pres.

The negative particle is followed by the future marker, the clitics, and finally the verb; furthermore whereas the affirmative future contains only one accentual unit, the negative future (at least in Bulgarian) contains two. However, this superficial similarity belies a much more fundamental difference, in that the non-Balkan Slavic future tense comprises a conjugated auxiliary and an infinitive, whereas the Balkan Slavic future is composed of an unchanging particle (historically derived from the 3rd singular auxiliary) and a present tense form which carries person marking. Furthermore, the Balkan Slavic future particle is functionally equivalent to the negative particle as concerns word order: both particles must stand immedi-

---

[22] The Macedonian negative future differs only in the phonetic shape of the auxiliary, which is *némam*.

[23] The phonetic correspondence seen here (Serbian/Croatian /ć/ ~ Bulgarian /št/ ~ Macedonian /ḱ/) is a regular one.

[24] Macedonian is similar in form, except that the future particle is *ḱe*. The accentual pattern of these negative utterances in Macedonian is different, however, and will be discussed below.

ately before pronoun clitic objects which in turn must stand immediately before the verb; if no subject is present, these particles of necessity begin the utterance. Compare (examples from Bulgarian):

Bulgarian [Balkan] negative present indicative
(30) *Ne*   *mú*   *go*   *dávam.*
     Neg.   DAT   ACC   verb.pres.

Bulgarian [Balkan] affirmative future indicative
(31) *Šte*   *mu*   *go*   *dám.*
     Fut.   DAT   ACC   verb.pres.

Because the word order rules of Bulgarian do not allow clitics in initial position, most grammarians now call the future marker a "particle" which can occupy utterance-initial position. This far-reaching syntactic change finds direct parallels in the other Balkan languages, all of which express the future by a sequence containing an unchanging particle derived from the verb meaning 'want, will', an optional subordinating conjunction,[25] and the present tense of the verb. Along with the loss of the infinitive and of declensional endings, the so-called "analytic future" is one of the central syntactic features defining the Balkan Sprachbund. Compare:

Albanian negative present indicative; affirmative future indicative
(32) *Nuk*   *i-*   *a*   *jap.*
     Neg.   DAT   ACC   verb.pres.

(33) *Do*   *t'*   *i-*   *a*   *jap.*
     Fut.   Cnj.   DAT   ACC   verb.pres.

Modern Greek negative present indicative; affirmative future indicative
(34) *Den*   *tu*   *ton*   *Dino.*
     Neg.   GEN   ACC   verb.pres.

(35) *Tha*   *tu*   *ton*   *Doso.*
     Fut.   GEN   ACC   verb.pres.

Romanian negative present indicative; affirmative future indicative
(36) *Nu*   *i-*   *l*   *dau.*
     Neg.   DAT   ACC   verb.pres.

(37) *O*   *să*   *i-*   *l*   *dau.*
     Fut.   Cnj.   DAT   ACC   verb.pres.

---

[25] The conjunction is present in in Albanian and Romanian, and though it is now absent in modern Greek, Bulgarian and Macedonian, there is ample dialectal and comparative evidence that it was present earlier (in both Slavic and Greek) and was lost quite recently.

Yet non-Balkan South Slavic also participates in this change, in two ways. The first is lexical: throughout nearly this entire region, the future auxiliary is from the same verbal root, meaning 'want, will', as opposed to the rest of Slavic, where the future auxiliary is from the verb meaning 'be'.[26] The second is syntactic and to a limited extent prosodic: at least one expression of the future tense (the negative future) requires the formation of an independent, utterance-initial unit. Again the query is whether one should infer a Balkan-based change which has spread into non-Balkan Slavic, or a Slavic-based change which has seen a far-reaching spread throughout other Balkan languages. The former interpretation – that the analytic future is primarily due to convergent development – stands as one of the central tenets of Balkan linguistics. Yet one should not dismiss lightly the data of non-Balkan Slavic, especially as concerns the syntactic and prosodic similarities between the negative future and the negative perfect.

6. Clitics in second position

In the majority of South Slavic dialects, Balkan and non-Balkan alike, clitics are barred from utterance-initial position. Only in Macedonian (and there only in conjunction with finite verbs) do they occupy initial position. Given the presence of similar word order rules in the other Balkan languages, together with the geographical and demographic distribution according to which Macedonia may be perceived as the very center of the convergence area, it seems reasonable to infer a process of convergent change on this point. Yet here too, the facts internal to Slavic warrant closer examination.

Examples (1) through (4) all seem to exhibit the same word order: if the verb begins the utterance it is followed directly by the clitic string, and if some other word begins the utterance, it is followed directly by a unit composed of the clitic string and the verb. These simplified examples belie a fundamental difference between Balkan Slavic and non-Balkan Slavic, however: in the former the clitics are head-dependent (bound to their syntactic host) whereas in the latter they are clause-dependent (bound to the second position in the clause). The presence of additional words (such as adverbs) in the utterance serves clearly to disambiguate the two types. Compare the following, in which standard Bulgarian represents Balkan Slavic and standard Serbian represents non-Balkan Slavic:

Bulgarian [Balkan]
(38)   *Az*   *često*   *mu*   *go*   *davam.*
        subj.   adv.   DAT   ACC   verb.pres.
        'I often give it to him.'

---

[26] In South Slavic, the future auxiliary is 'want' everywhere except in kajkavian and central dialects of Slovenian; in East Slavic, the future auxiliary is 'have' in a number of Ukrainian dialects.

(39) *Ti*   *včera*   *si*   *mu*   *go*   *dala.*
      subj.   adv.   AUX-2sg.   DAT   ACC   verb.part.
      'You gave it to him yesterday.'

Serbian [non-Balkan]
(40) *Ja*   *mu*   *ga*   *često*   *dajem.*
      subj.   DAT   ACC   adv.   verb.pres.
      'I often give it to him.'

(41) *Juče*   *si*   *mu*   *ga*   *ti*   *dala.*
      adv.   AUX-2sg.   DAT   ACC   emph.subj.   verb.part.
      'It was you who gave it to him yesterday.'

In Balkan Slavic, the clitics must occur directly adjacent to the verb, regardless of the position of the verb in the sentence. In non-Balkan Slavic, clitics must come in second position, regardless of whether or not this separates them from the verb on which they are syntactically dependent. Sentences with the ordering rules of (38) and (39) would be ungrammatical in Serbian, and those with the ordering rules of (40) and (41) would be ungrammatical in Bulgarian. This distinction, between head-dependent (as in Bulgarian) and clause-dependent (as in Serbian), which happens to coincide with the division of South Slavic into Balkan and non-Balkan, is in fact a purely Slavic one, and apparently a prosodic one at that. As Jakobson has noted (1933/1971: 18-19), clitics in Slavic languages with free, expiratory stress have become head-dependent as opposed to all other Slavic languages, which still follow the second-position rule.[27]

Even the most recent innovation in Macedonian, which appears to annul the second-position limitation and which seems to be shared by other Balkan languages, can be seen in terms of the internal Slavic change towards head-dependency. To see this, let us examine briefly the prosodic rules of standard Macedonian (as well as the southwestern dialects upon which this standard is based). Word accent is fixed on the third syllable from the end of the word, and the prosodic word according to which accent placement is determined sometimes includes clitics. Clitics following the verb are always included in this prosodic word, but clitics preceding the verb are included in it only if some other element in turn precedes them. For example:

non-finite verb (clitics follow): Macedonian [Balkan] imperative
(42) *Dónesi!*
      verb.imper.
      'Bring [it]!'

---

[27] For further discussion of South Slavic and West Slavic on this point, see Alexander 1993 and Rappaport 1988, respectively.

(43) Donési   mi!
     verb.imper.   DAT
     'Bring [it] to me!'

(44) Donesí   mi   go!
     verb.imper.   DAT   ACC
     'Bring it to me!'

finite verb (clitics precede): Macedonian [Balkan] negative present indicative

(45) Ne   gó   gledam.
     Neg.   ACC   verb.pres.
     'I don't see him.'

(46) Zošto   gó   gledaš?
     Q-word   ACC   verb.pres.
     'Why are you looking at him?'

(47) Go   glédam.
     ACC   verb.pres.
     'I see him.'

Thus, although clitics are required to precede finite verbs even if this places them in sentence initial position, they may bear a shifted accent only if some other element precedes them, i.e. if they are once again in second position. The change in word order rules in Macedonian appears to represent the final stage of head-dependency, in that pre-verbal position outweighs all other requirements. But the prosodic rules of Macedonian demonstrate that second position is still relevant.[28] None of the other Balkan languages in which clitics now stand in initial position exhibit any variation with respect to accent. The common feature is that clitics precede the verb directly (unless the verb form is an imperative or a participle), even if this places them in sentence-initial position.

7. Correlations between the two word order patterns

Indeed, it is possible to view both word order changes in terms of a head-dependence which has become more strictly defined according to internal Slavic developments. In earlier stages of South Slavic, word order rules required clitics either to follow or precede the fused unit of "negation + verb" in all instances, and to

---

[28] That this is a prosodic rule and not a syntactic one (despite the statements in all grammars that the shift occurs in negative and interrogative utterances but not in affirmative ones) is seen when a pronoun object occupies initial position in a question marked by the interrogative particle li:
(vi)   Go   glédaš   li?
        ACC   verb.pres.   INT
See Alexander 1995 for a more detailed exposition of this point.

stand after the first accented word of the utterance in all instances. These rules then underwent several changes. According to a common South Slavic change, the negation of a compound verb (future or perfect tense) required that clitics follow the negative particle and precede the main verb. In the southernmost portions of South Slavic, this rule was extended to *all* negated verbs. According to a different sort of change, common to all Slavic dialects which had lost tonal oppositions, clitics were required to precede the verb in all instances except when a verb began the sentence. In the southwesternmost portions of South Slavic, this rule was generalized further: clitics were required to precede all finite verbs regardless of position in the sentence; however they could not bear accent unless another word preceded them.

Both these changes have reached their greatest extent in the south-(west)ernmost portions of South Slavic, those areas which are located in the center of the Balkan Sprachbund. This fact, plus the existence of similar word order rules in the other Balkan languages, might lead one to suppose that they are "Balkanisms", due at least in part to multilingual interference within a contact area. In both cases, however, internal Slavic factors are clearly at work, provoking one to ask whether the changes are Slavic in origin (which have spread to other Balkan languages) or Balkan in origin, which, because of their congruence with Slavic structural changes, have accelerated the rate of these internal Slavic changes.

8. Concluding remarks

The question of causation posed immediately above (and at earlier points throughout this presentation) was stated in artificial, "black and white" terms. It is clear to all who have worked in Balkan linguistics, however, that questions phrased in terms of polar opposites can never be answered in any reasoned manner: the only possible alternative is to view everything in more or less delicate shades of gray. That is, practically every instance of a shared Balkan structural trait represents a change which can be at least partially described in terms of structural developments internal to each of the separate languages; at the same time it is intuitively obvious from the striking similarities in surface structures that convergence processes must have played a major role in all of these changes. The particular balance of the two factors in the description of any one change can probably never be recovered, and it is perhaps fruitless to try.

Yet this by no means suggests that one should abandon research efforts in Balkan linguistics. The above two syntactic phenomena were chosen as an example not only because the surface similarities (among Balkan languages) are so striking, but because they are so closely tied up with complex structural facts internal to Slavic. Furthermore, the exposition was presented in such a manner as to highlight the fact that practically all Balkan linguists work from the standpoint of a considerably greater familiarity with one of the four major language families, and that this state of affairs unavoidably slants their perspective on the issue in question. In the present instance, it is obvious that specialists in the history and dialectology of Albanian, Greek or Balkan Romance would have treated these parallels differently. Similarly, the issue also would have been treated differently by a Slavicist who was not particularly interested in Balkan linguistics.

For instance, the interpretation presented herein has suggested that the prosodic and syntactic rules connected with the non-Balkan South Slavic negated auxiliary, a fused form which has taken on the status of a fully accented word, have given rise to the innovative prosody and syntax found in Balkan Slavic negated verb phrases. A non-Balkanist Slavicist would immediately note that the fused form of the negated copula is very old (it is clearly attested in Old Church Slavic), and would consequently focus attention not on the fact of fusion (which is demonstrably archaic), but on the development and spread of the perfect tense in Slavic, the tense which eventually replaced the inherited primary past tenses in all branches of Slavic other than Balkan Slavic. The incorporation of this negated copula into the perfect tense in non-Balkan South Slavic, the relation of this copula to other full and reduced forms of the copula, and the reformulation of this system in West Slavic, where the copula has been retained in 1st and 2nd persons but completely lost in the 3rd person (as well as the fact of the ongoing loss of the 3rd person copula in various areas of South Slavic), constitute the issues of interest to Slavic historical linguistics. To such a Slavicist, primary focus on surface facts of prosody and syntax (the approach taken in the present contribution) might seem a disruption of the balance in a discussion of language change.

By contrast, a Balkan linguist with primary interest in a language family other than Slavic would note those surface structure facts about Balkan Slavic that present striking parallels to the surface structure of his "own" Balkan language, and would tend naturally to think in terms of similar if not common causes. The fact that the same descriptive terminology can be used successfully (and quite elegantly) to speak of facts which are similar on the surface (but often very disparate at a deeper level) presents a constant danger, particularly when, as is the norm in discussions of convergence phenomena, one begins by stating the similarities. Many Balkanists indeed feel that Balkan linguistics ought by right to focus solely on these similarities. To such a Balkanist, primary focus on facts internal to a single language (the approach taken in the present contribution), might similarly seem to be a disruption of the balance in a discussion of language contact.

The goal of Balkan linguistics (and of Sprachbund studies in general) consists precisely in finding the correct balance between these two extremes (and other positions not so extreme).[29] There is no one correct answer, no one completely

---

[29] Obviously, this is one of the goals of the present contribution. It takes part of its inspiration from Joseph 1983; for more discussion of these issues and an example of how surface similarities can be misleading, see Joseph (in press). In this respect, one should continually keep in mind Fried-

definable shade of gray. There are, however, two sharply delineated linguistic arenas within which change is taking place and within which linguists think and work. First, a Sprachbund is defined by a long list of striking structural parallels, all of which can be best stated in relatively surface terms, and all of which seem to owe at least part of their existence to contact phenomena. Second, each of the languages within a Sprachbund has a definable structure and history of its own, according to which any one surface phenomenon has both a long internal history and complex interactions with other structural facts internal to that language. The job of Sprachbund scholars is to bridge this gap between these two arenas, indeed two world views, in a responsible manner. As in any balancing act, this can only be done by continual, repeated, and disinterested adjustments on both sides.

University of California, Berkeley

REFERENCES

Alexander, Ronelle
    1993   "Remarks on the evolution of South Slavic prosodic systems", in: Robert Maguire and Alan Timberlake (eds.), *American contributions to the Eleventh international Congress of Slavists*, 181-201. Columbus: Slavica.
    1995   "The Balkanization of Wackernagel's law", *Indiana Slavic studies* 7, 1-8.
    1999   "Word order and prosody in Balkan Slavic dialects, the case of Thrace", in: V. Radeva et al. (eds.), *Dialektologija i lingvistična geografija*, 61-73. Sofia: Universitetsko izdatelstvo "Sv. Kliment Ohridski".
Cyxun, G.A.
    1968   *Sintaksis mestoimennyx klitik v južnoslavjanskix jazykax, balkanoslavjanskaja model'*. Minsk: Nauka i texnika.
Dybo, V.A.
    1981   *Slavjanskaja akcentologija, opyt rekonstrukcii sistemy akcentnyx paradigm v praslavjanskom*. Moskva: Izdatel'stvo Nauka.
Friedman, Victor
    1976   "Dialectal synchrony and diachronic syntax, The Macedonian perfect", in: S. Steever et al. (eds.), *Papers from the Parasession on Diachronic Syntax*, 96-104. Chicago: Chicago Linguistic Society.
    1983   "Grammatical categories and a comparative Balkan grammar", in: Norbert Reiter (ed.), *Ziele und Wege der Balkanlinguistik (Balkanologische Veröffentlichungen* 8), 81-98. Berlin-Wiesbaden: Otto Harrassowitz.
Jakobson, Roman
    1933/1971 "Les enclitiques slaves", in: *Selected writings* 2: *word and language*, 16-22. The Hague-Paris: Mouton.

---

man's admonition to his Balkanist colleagues (1983: 93): "Our goals must include the comparison of the divergent as well as the convergent".

Janin, V.P., and A.A. Zaliznjak
1993   *Novgorodskie gramoty na bereste (iz raskopok 1984-1989 gg.)*. Moskva: Nauka.

Joseph, Brian
1983   *The synchrony and diachrony of the Balkan infinitive, a study in areal, general and historical linguistics*. Cambridge: Cambridge University Press.
In press "Is a Balkan comparative syntax possible?", to appear in: M. Rivero and A. Ralli (eds.), *Comparative Balkan syntax*. Oxford: Oxford University Press.

Rappaport, Gilbert
1988   "On the relationship between prosodic and syntactic properties of pronouns in the Slavic languages", in: Alexander Schenker (ed.), *American contributions to the Tenth international congress of Slavists*. 1: *Linguistics*, 301-327. Columbus: Slavica.

Sandfeld, Kristian
1930   *Linguistique balkanique, problèmes et résultats*. Paris: Honoré Champion.

Schaller, Helmut
1975   *Die Balkansprachen, eine Einführung in die Balkanphilologie*. Heidelberg: Carl Winter.

Thomason, Sarah, and Terence J. Kaufman
1988   *Language contact, creolization, and genetic linguistics*. Berkeley: University of California Press.

Wackernagel, Jacob
1892   "Über ein Gesetz der indogermanischen Wortstellung", *Indogermanische Forschungen* 1, 333-436.

Languages in Contact, edited by D.G. Gilbers, J. Nerbonne, and J. Schaeken (= *Studies in Slavic and General Linguistics*, vol. 28), 29-35. Amsterdam - Atlanta, GA: Rodopi, 2000.

CONVERGENCE INTERTWINING: AN ALTERNATIVE WAY TOWARDS THE GENESIS OF MIXED LANGUAGES

PETER BAKKER

1. Introduction

In this brief paper I will discuss two types of mixed languages. The first type constitutes what has been called INTERTWINED LANGUAGES (Bakker and Muysken 1995) or BILINGUAL MIXTURES (Thomason 1997). The process which leads to these languages is called INTERTWINING and they have also been claimed to be the result of 'extreme borrowing', a 'matrix language turnover' in codeswitching or 'relexification'. A sentence in such a language typically has content words from one language and bound morphemes from another, with some crosslinguistic variation as to the origin of free grammatical markers such as pronouns, demonstratives and the like. One typically finds overt morphemes from two languages in even a single sentence.

The other type of mixed language has not yet been identified as a distinct type. I propose to call them here CONVERTED LANGUAGES. They are the result of extreme convergence, which may take place rapidly. They show semantic, phonological, morphological and syntactic patterns of one language, but all of the morphemes (both content and grammatical morphemes) are from another language. Typically these languages are both unrecognizable and unintelligible for those people whose vocabulary is found in the language.

Even though the term 'mixed language' has been incorrectly applied in the past to all kinds of languages with some visible influence from other languages, one should limit its use to those cases where genetic classification is no longer possible. This classification takes place on the basis of both the basic lexicon and the grammatical system. In almost all languages these are from the same source, even in a language like English which has remained a Germanic language despite pervasive influences from other languages, most notably French. Only if the grammatical system and the basic lexicon of a language are of different origin, OR if both of these components are roughly equally from different language sources can one speak of a mixed language. Mixed languages cannot be placed in a genetic tree, since they have more than one parent language, with some components from one language and some components from a different language.

Converted languages and intertwined languages are two types where the mixture is systematic. These are not the only two types of mixed languages. In some other cases both the grammatical system and the basic lexicon show dual origins, but we will not discuss those.

In what follows I will discuss both types in more detail.

2. Intertwined languages

A few dozen mixed languages have been documented which show a dichotomy between the language of origin of the lexicon and the language of origin of the grammatical system (Bakker, forthc.). The vocabulary is from language A, and the phonology, morphology, syntax from language B. Prototypical examples of such mixed languages are Media Lengua (Spanish vocabulary, Quechua grammatical system), Ma'a (Cushitic lexicon, Bantu grammar) and Angloromani (English grammar, Romani lexicon). It is only in recent years that these languages have been considered a type in themselves – perhaps not a homogeneous one, but certainly a type –, clearly different from pidgins and creoles (cf. Bakker and Mous 1994, Bakker 1997: ch. 7, Thomason 1997). Some examples of these 'intertwined languages' or 'bilingual mixtures' are:

(1) Media Lengua, Ecuador (Quechua grammar, Spanish lexicon)

miza despwesitu	*kaza-**mu***	*i-**naku-ndu-ga**,*	
miza k'ipa	*wasi-**mu***	*ri-**naku-pi-ga**,*	
mass after	house-to	go-PL-SUB-TOP	
*ahí-**bi***	*buda*	*da-**naku-n***	(Media Lengua)
*chi-**bi***	*buda*	*ku-**naku-n***	(Quechua)
there-LOC	feast	give-PL-3	

yendo a la casa después de la Misa, ahí dan una boda (Spanish)
'going home after mass, they then give a feast here'

(2) Angloromani (English grammar, Romani lexicon)

mo:	*roke,*	**you**	*dıv,*	**the**	*goje's*	*shun-**in'***	(Angloromani)
NEG	speak	you	fool	the	non-Gypsy-is	listen-PROG	

'don't speak, you fool, the non-Gypsy is listening'
(Romani *ma* 'don't', *raker-* 'speak', *dilo* 'crazy', *Gadžo* 'non-Gypsy', *šun-* 'listen')

(3) Caló (Andalusian Spanish grammar, Romani lexicon)

*Gill**ate***	*de*	*mi*	*que no*	*te*	*pueda*	*indic**ar***
go-IMPER.PL	from	me	that not	you	can-1.SUBJ	see-INF

'Get out of my sight'
(Romani *geljum* 'I went', *dikh-* 'see')

The genesis of these language has been the subject of debate in recent years, ranging from massive relexification, language death, purposeful mixture, to the result of the genesis of a new, mixed ethnic group.

3. Converted languages

The other type of mixed language is very different from these. I tentatively call the process by which they come about CONVERGENCE INTERTWINING, and the resulting languages 'converted languages'. The mixed languages which are the result of this process have all grammatical and lexical elements from one language (call it A), but they have the functions, the grammatical status and the structural positions of a different language, call it B. The almost total absence of lexical borrowings (basic or non-basic) from language B in these converted languages is prototypical. Such languages are syntactically and semantically virtually identical to language B, but all the overt morphemes are from language A, be it often with a different function. Often it can be established that such a language was originally language A, but it has been restructured radically. These are languages which changed their typological make-up radically under the influence from another language, often from isolational to agglutinative.

An example of such a language is Sri Lanka Portuguese. Sri Lanka is a clear example of a Sprachbund, which itself is part of the wider South Asian Sprachbund (cf. Emeneau 1956, Masica 1976). Languages from at least five families are spoken on Sri Lanka. Tamil (Dravidian) and Singhalese (Indic, Indo-European) are spoken by 99% of the population, but there is also a considerable community of Malay (Austronesian) speakers (Adelaar 1991) and a small minority of Portuguese speakers (Romance). Vedda, the aboriginal language, which may be extinct by now, seems to be an isolate, but it is influenced by Singhalese to such an extent that some consider the language to be a dialect of Singhalese. The grammatical system may indeed be very close to Singhalese, but the basic lexicon is unlike anything else (Dharmadasa 1974, De Silva 1972).

I will focus here on Sri Lanka Malay and Sri Lanka Portuguese. Both languages have been present on the island for at least three or four centuries. Both languages were documented in the early part of the last century and in both cases it is clear that the languages were creolized at that point in time: they lost all person inflection, almost all derivation, and all morphological irregularities. Instead these languages appeared to have preverbal markers for tense, mood and aspect, a system which can be considered typical for creole languages (Holm 1988). Word order is rather rigid SVO and the languages are typologically close to isolational. In short, they look prototypically creole. This, however, is true only for older stages of these languages.

Modern Sri Lanka Malay (SLM) and Modern Sri Lanka Portuguese (SLP), as documented from the 1960s onwards, show very different patterns. Both languages have become morphologically complex. Both languages now have a case marking system. The case markers are not identical in form to those of Tamil, but instead derived from Portuguese and Malay prepositions. At the same time SLP and SLM have changed a great number of other properties as well. They are now rigidly verb-final languages instead of verb-medial languages, the semantics of the tense-mood-aspect system has been radically changed, relative clause contruction is radically different now (from postnominal to prenominal), etc. Even though they were rather typical creoles, modern SLM and SLP have none of the typical creole properties left (for SLP see Smith 1979a, 1979b, 1984). Here are some example sentences in Sri Lanka Portuguese:

(4) e:w eli-pə   diñe:ru   ja:-dá: (SL Portuguese)
    na:n avan-ukku calli-ya   kúTu-tt-an   (SL Tamil)
    I   him-DAT   money-ACC PAS-give-PAS-CNC
    'I gave him the money'.
    (Portuguese: (Eu) dei o dinheiro para/a ele)

(5) əkə-ntu   fu:lə pə-bota: na:-poy   na: (SL Portuguese)
    that-LOC flower INF-put   NEGPOT-can   TAG
    at-ila   pu: po:T-a   e:l-a:t   e: (SL Tamil)
    that-LOC flower put-INF   can-NEGPOT   TAG
    '[You] can't embroider [lit. put flowers] on that [sewing machine], can you?'
    (Portuguese: Naquilo não se pode bordar, não é)

Table 1 lists the case markers of both SLM and SLP together of those of Tamil. It is clear that they have the same case inventory, but the case markers are all derived from Malay and Portuguese elements. Apparently there was such a strong pressure from Tamil that a case system developed, using native rather than Tamil material.

	SL Portuguese	SL Malay	SL Tamil
NOM	ø	ø	ø
ACC	ø/-pə < P. pera/para 'for'	-na (H, A) < M. nya 'the', 'that' ??	ø/-a(y)
DAT	-pə < P. para, id.	-pe(i) (H, A) < M. punya 'of'	-(u)kku
GEN	-su(wə) < P. sua, seu 'his, her, its'	-pe (H, A) < M. punya 'of'	-Ra
LOC	-(u)ntu < P. junto 'together'	-ka (H, A) < M. dekat 'near'	(i)la(y)/ -(i)TTa(y)
ASSOC	N ju:ntu < P. junto	-samma (H) < M. sama 'with'	-o:Ta(y)
INSTR	N wɔndə < P. banda 'side'?	-dari (H) < M. dari 'from'	-a:la(y)

Table 1: Nominal case marking in Tamil, Sri Lanka Malay and SL Portuguese
(H = Hussainmiya, A = Adelaar in SL Malay column)

I have no room here to discuss details, but I want to mention that the semantics of verb markers (even though preverbal in SLM and SLP) is virtually identical to that of Tamil. Furthermore a set of evidentials and quotative markers emerged based on Tamil.

4. Converted languages and Sprachbund

SLP and SLM show pervasive grammatical influence from Tamil, but no lexical influence. This is a phenomenon also reported from some linguistics areas (Sprachbund). Sri Lanka is a Sprachbund. For those other areas, if scholars were at all willing to take language contact as a possible cause in this matter, it is usually said that such processes were caused by an earlier substrate of a Sprachbund (e.g. for the Balkan), or they are taken as evidence for a genetic link (e.g. Africa and North America).

In many of the documented cases it is indeed not clear how much time it took for these languages to develop. Some people have suggested long-term influence. Languages which seem to have changed in such as way may be Armenian (towards Turkish?) and Asia Minor Greek (towards Turkish), which were in contact for many centuries. Further one can think of a number of radical language areas (Sprachbund) such as the Vaupes (Columbia-Brazil), parts of New Guinea (Central New Guinea) and Irian Jaya (Bird's Head), parts of Middle America, where languages share little or no lexicon, but almost all of their grammatical systems. The history of these areas is not well known, however, so that the direction of influence cannot be established with certainty in these cases.

In some documented cases, however, it can be shown that the whole process took place in one or two generations. Sri Lanka Portuguese (Portuguese with Tamil agglutination) and Sri Lanka Malay (Malay with Tamil agglutination) clearly have been Tamilized in a very short time span.

5. Conclusions

The two converted languages from Sri Lanka discussed here, could be called TRANSVESTITES, since they appear different on the inside than on the outside – and one can argue about which of these languages would be the 'outside' language and which ones the 'inside'. They constitute a type of mixed language different from intertwined languages, creoles, and pidgins. The deviating result must be linked to different social circumstances.

Institute for Linguistics, Aarhus University, Denmark

REFERENCES

Adelaar, K.A.
1991   "Some notes on Sri Lanka Malay", in: H. Steinhauer (ed.), *Papers in Austrone-
            sian Linguistics* 1 (*Pacific Linguistics*, Series A-81), 23-37. Canberra Research
            School of Pacific Studies.
Bakker, Peter
1996   "Language intertwining and convergence: typological aspects of the genesis of
            mixed languages", in: Nicole Nau and Martin Haase (eds*.), Sprachkontakt und
            Grammatikalisierung* (Special Issue of *STUF. Sprachtypologie und Universali-
            enforschung* 49/1), 9-20. Berlin: Akademie Verlag.
1997   *"A Language of our Own". The genesis of Michif – the mixed Cree-French
            language of the Canadian Métis.* New York: Oxford University Press.
forthc.   *Language intertwining. Structure and genesis of mixed languages.*
Bakker, Peter, and Maarten Mous (eds.)
1994   *Mixed languages. 15 case studies in language intertwining.* Amsterdam: IFOTT
            (Distribution: The Hague: Holland Academic Graphics).
Bakker, Peter, and Pieter Muysken
1994.   "Mixed languages and language intertwining", in: J. Arends, P. Muysken, and
            Norval Smith (eds.), *Pidgins and Creoles*, 41-52. Amsterdam: J. Benjamins.
De Silva, M.W. Sugathapala
1972   *Vedda language of Ceylon (Texts and lexicon) (Münchener Studien zur
            Sprachwissenschaft*, Beiheft 7, Neue Folge). München: R. Kitzinger.
Dharmadasa, K.N.O.
1974   "The creolization of an aboriginal language: the case of Vedda in Sri Lanka
            (Ceylon)", *Anthropological Linguistics* 16/2, 79-106.
Emeneau, M.B.
1956   "India as a linguistic area", *Language* 23, 3-16. (Reprinted in: Anwar S. Dil
            (ed.), *Language and Linguistic Area. Essays by Murray B. Emeneau*, 105-125.
            Stanford: Stanford University Press, 1980.)
Holm, John
1988   *Pidgins and Creoles* (2 Vols). Cambridge: Cambridge University Press.
Hussainmiya, B.A.
1987   "'Melayu Bahasa': some preliminary observations on the Malay creole of Sri
            Lanka", in: B.A. Hussainmiya (ed.), *Lost cousins: the Malays of Sri Lanka.
            Malaysia*, 153-172. Universiti Kebangsaan.
Masica, Colin P.
1976   *Defining a linguistic area: India.* Chicago: University of Chicago Press.
Muysken, Pieter
1981   "Halfway between Quechua and Spanish: The case for relexification", in: A.
            Highfield and A. Valdman (eds.), *Historicity and variation in Creole studies*,
            52-78. Ann Arbor: Karoma.
Smith, Ian R.
1979a   "Convergence in South Asia: a Creole example", *Lingua* 48, 193-222.
1979b   "Substrata versus universals in the formation of Sri Lanka Portuguese", *Papers
            in Pidgin and Creole Linguistics* 2, 183-200.
1984   "The development of morphosyntax in Sri Lanka Creole Portuguese", in: M.
            Sebba and L. Todd (eds.), *Papers from the Creole Conference, York University*,
            291-301. York: York University, Dept. of Language.

Thomason, Sarah Grey (ed.)
 1997   *Contact Languages. A wider perspective*. Amsterdam: J. Benjamins.

Languages in Contact, edited by D.G. Gilbers, J. Nerbonne, and J. Schaeken (= *Studies in Slavic and General Linguistics*, vol. 28), 37-53. Amsterdam - Atlanta, GA: Rodopi, 2000.

BELLA COOLA AND NORTH WAKASHAN: CONVERGENCE AND DIVERSITY IN THE NORTHWEST COAST SPRACHBUND[1]

DAVID BECK

1. Grammatical approximation in Bella Coola and North Wakashan

The Pacific Northwest of North America is home to one of the most geographically extensive Sprachbunds in the world, stretching from the north of California to southern Alaska and extending at its widest point as far east as the Rocky Mountains of Alberta and Montana. Within this area is found a diverse set of languages belonging to a wide range of families and phyla, many of which have come to resemble each other in typological terms to a remarkable degree. Unfortunately, while extensive trade, intermarriage, and bilingualism in the region seem likely, we can only speculate about the extent and the nature of the contact between the various language groups in prehistoric times. There is, however, at least one example of substantial grammatical approximation within the Central Northwest group of languages (see Map 1) which has taken place at a manageable time-depth and which might allow us to build a model of language interaction that reflects one type of contact situation found in the NWC Sprachbund as a whole. The case in point is Bella Coola, the most northerly of the coastal Salish languages; in its modern range Bella Coola is completely cut off from its relatives, being bounded on three sides by the Wakashan languages Haisla, Heiltsuk, and Oowekyala, and to the east by two languages of the Athapaskan family, Carrier and Chilcotin. According to McIlwraith (1948), the Bella Coola held the Wakashan in some esteem and admired their superior knowledge of ceremonial lore and rituals. The Bella Coola believe many of their rites to have originated with the Wakashan peoples, particularly the Bella Bella (Heiltsuk). McIlwraith reports intimate contact, including trade and intermarriage, between the two groups, and, judging by the nature and direction of lexical borrowings, the Bella Coola seem to

[1] Thanks are owed to Alana Johns, Bill Lewis, Keren Rice, and a number of anonymous reviewers for some excellent commentary and thought-provoking questions, and to Jack Chambers for quiet but useful advice throughout. I would also like to acknowledge the help of Emmon Bach, Thom Hess, William Jacobsen, and Dale Kinkade, as well as the efforts of these and other fieldworkers and their consultants in compiling the dozens of texts, articles, and grammars without which the present study would have been impossible. This research was supported by Doctoral Fellowship 752-96-1718 from the Social Sciences and Humanities Research Council of Canada.

have adapted themselves culturally to their Wakashan neighbours. The relative unidirectionality of the lexical borrowing, like the Bella Coola perception of the neighbouring cultures as prestigious, seems consistent with a contact situation which would foster extensive bilingualism and frequent cultural and economic exchange, key factors in the spread of linguistic patterns.[2]

Linguistically, the net result of the intimate contact between the Bella Coola and their Wakashan neighbours has been a process whereby Bella Coola has undergone a series of changes away from typically Salishan features towards structures and grammatical patterns more typical of the nearby Wakashan languages. Even in the absence of written records of the original Bella Coola language, the grammatical shifts which have taken place may be detectable by comparing the modern form of Bella Coola with other Salish languages: at least in those cases where the shift has set Bella Coola apart from other members of the family, it may be possible to use such comparisons to enumerate the extent and the types of changes that have taken place under Wakashan influence. This comparison may then allow us to infer the processes which have led to the divergent features observed in Bella Coola and, in turn, to exemplify those at work in the NWC Sprachbund as a whole. In some cases, particularly in the order of nominal actants in the matrix clause, the outcome of linguistic contact has been the grammatical convergence of Bella Coola with Northern Wakashan, whereas in other cases – most notably in the area of person-marking – the result has been the creation of a uniquely Bella Coola grammatical pattern. In this respect, the Bella Coola situation is of particular interest for models of language contact and grammatical diffusion in that it shows how the process of language convergence can lead, somewhat paradoxically, to linguistic diversity.

1.1 Word order in the matrix clause

The unmarked word order for the matrix clause in Central Northwest languages tends to be VSO. Within the Salishan family, however, there is some variation allowed, most commonly in the direction of VOS. Of all the Salishan languages, Bella Coola most rigidly holds to the VSO word-order and uses it as an interpretive device to identify subject and object – the leftmost of two NPs being the subject (Davis and Saunders 1997: 31). Similarly, in the Wakashan Heiltsuk, a strict subject-object-oblique order of NP actants is also observed, and in clauses with both third-person NP subjects and objects, the constituent-order in Heiltsuk appears to be rigid and to carry interpretive weight (Rath 1981: 85). The same is evidently true for Kʷakʷala (Boas 1969: 529), and so this may hold of Northern Wakashan in general. On the other hand, rather than using word order to mark the

---

[2] In addition to being largely unidirectional, the lexical borrowing in Bella Coola was also extensive. According to Nater (1984), "some 30% of the Bella Coola roots and stems with etymological counterparts on other Amerindian tongues are of Wakashan origin" (p. xvii).

syntactic roles of third-person subjects and objects, Salishan languages tend to use a process of topical NP-deletion in transitive clauses, leaving at most a single non-oblique actant whose syntactic role is determined by the morphology carried on the verb (Kinkade 1990).[3]

Another interesting feature of word-order in Bella Coola is the virtual abandonment of two important Central Northwest areal features – the use of the sentence-initial adverbial particle and the sentence-second clitic. Both of these innovations are tied to an overall shift in the Bella Coola strategy of predicate-modification away from the dual system of pre-predicate particle and predicate enclitics typical of Central Northwest languages in general towards a more restricted system making use only of sentence-second enclitics, a strategy that seems overall to be the preferred one in Wakashan. These patterns are exemplified for Salishan (S) by the Lushootseed sentence in (1a) and for Wakashan (W) by the Makah sentence in (1b):

Lushootseed (S)

(1a)   čkʷaqid=sixʷ   x̌ʷul´   ʔu+ʔəɬəd   tiʔəʔ   qawq́sʷ
        always=CONTEMPT   just   PNT+eat   D   raven
        'Raven is always just stuffing his face'

Makah (W)

(1b)   huuʔax̌i=ø=sii=cux̌   daac
        still=IND=1S=2S   see
        'I can still see you'
        (Jacobsen 1979: 132)

In Salishan languages other than Bella Coola, pre-predicate adverbs such as čkʷaqid 'always' are a common method of modifying sentence predicates. However, while they are also attested in Wakashan, they seem on the whole to be less common both in terms of textual frequency and the number of elements eligible to occupy the pre-predicate position.

Both language families also make use of predicate enclitics which occupy sentence-second position either immediately following the main verb or migrating leftward to follow a sentence-initial adverbial particle. In the Lushootseed sentence in (1a), for instance, the presence of čkʷaqid 'always' triggers the fronting

---

[3] In Lushootseed (Hess 1993; Beck, to appear) and possibly in Okanagan (Mattina 1996: 31), this deletion process has been grammaticalized to the point that syntactic subjects are obligatorily removed from transitive clauses; Kinkade (1983: 32) suggests that Lushootseed and Okanagan are conservative in this respect and that two-NP clauses have come into Salish under English influence. The identity of elided subjects is recoverable from their identification with the discourse topic (Kinkade 1990). For Kyuquot (Southern Wakashan) Rose (1981) notes that transitive verbs with a single NP are ambiguous as to whether the NP represents the subject or object. This is rarely the case in a contextualized Salishan sentence.

of the clitic $=six^w$ (expressing contempt on the part of the speaker), while in (1b) the Makah adverb *huu?aẋi* 'still' attracts the indicative marker (Ø in the third person) and person-morphology. In Salishan languages, these predicate enclitics are typically limited in number and tend to express "modal-aspectual notions" (van Eijk 1997: 199) and/or "the speaker's subjective relationship to the propositional content of the sentence" (Montler 1986: 200). In contrast, Wakashan predicate enclitics seem to be the preferred strategy for adverbial modification and constitute a large and varied class of morphemes. In Kʷak̓ʷala, for instance, Boas (1969: 451-2) offers a list of fifty-two "word-suffixes", and for Heiltsuk, Rath lists thirty-three "Category B suffixes" (*i.e.* predicate enclitics) which express a wide range of adverbial, evidential, and grammatical meanings. In neither of these languages does there seem to be more than a handful of pre-predicate particles.

Whereas Wakashan and most Salishan languages make some use of both pre-predicate adverbs and enclitics to modify sentence predicates, Bella Coola has abandoned the pre-predicate particle as a means of predicate modification in favour of post-predicate clitics, as in (2):

Bella Coola (S)

(2) $q^walls+am+ø=k^w=?it=alu=tu=ći=k$

hemlock·needles+INCH+3S=QTV=C-C=almost=now=PERF=C-C

'and now [it is said] he really almost became hemlock needles'

(Nater 1984: 131)

Like Wakashan predicate enclitics, these morphemes include a wide range of evidential, adverbial, and other meanings. In total, Nater (1984) lists thirty-three predicate enclitics, a number more comparable to those found in Heiltsuk and Kʷak̓ʷala than to those typical of Salish. This grammatical change in Bella Coola seems to be a clear example of what Heath (1978) refers to as "indirect diffusion", given that it involves the adoption of a grammatical pattern of one language by another without the actual transmission of a substantial number of actual morphemes.

An important consequence of the abandonment of the pre-predicate adverbial in Bella Coola has been the virtual loss of the clitic/suffix distinction which is so salient in other Central Northwest languages: given that predicate-modifiers are no longer particles and that Bella Coola has no true auxiliaries, this means that sentence-second position is the one immediately following the matrix verb. The only environment in which enclitics can still be identified as such is in the presence of the negative *?aẋw*, the only adverbial element in the language that is eligible to occupy sentence-initial position:

Bella Coola (S)

(3) $?aẋ=k^w=i=lu=k$ $ayk̓+m+i+s$ $ta+s+cx^w+lx+ulmx+tẋ$

NEG=QTV=C-C=EXP=C-C   long+MD+DIM+3S   D+NP+dark+INCH+earth+D

s+tuin+m+s=kʷ=lu=ć   *ta+nanmk̓+tx̌*
NP+appear+MD+3S=QTV=EXP=PERF   D+animal+D
'it wasn't long after dark that the animal showed up before expected'
(Davis and Saunders 1980: 8, line 33)

Here, the person-marker – the third-person intransitive suffix -*s* – has lost the clitic-like properties typical of person-markers in other Central Northwest languages and is attached to the matrix predicate, the negated verb *ʔayk̓* 'be long time', rather than to the sentence-initial *ʔax̌ʷ*. However, *ʔax̌ʷ* does play host to a string of evidentials – 'QUOTATIVE', =*lu* 'EXPECTATIVE', and =*(ʔ)i* ... =*k* 'CONTRASTIVE-CONJUNCTIVE' – which normally follow the matrix predicate when this appears at the beginning of the sentence (cf. the position of the evidentials =*kʷ*, =*lu*, and the aspectual clitic =*ć* 'PERFECTIVE' in the embedded clause *stuinmskʷluć tananmk̓tx̌* 'that the animal showed up').

Given the existence of sentence-initial adverbs in Wakashan, it is not clear that the loss of the pre-predicate particle (and the consequent loss of landing sites for sentence-second clitics) is the direct result of Bella Coola convergence with its Northern Wakashan neighbours; however, it is suggestive that of the two options for predicate-modification attested in the Salishan family, Bella Coola has opted for the strategy more strongly attested in the Wakashan languages – the use of predicate enclitics. One possible explanation for this is that the loss of pre-predicate particles is related to the Bella Coola adopting a rigid VSO word-order, a development which seems more certainly to be linked to the dynamics of language contact. Judging by the prevalent object-subject order of pronominals in Bella Coola and the rest of the Salishan family (see Section 1.3 below), VSO may not have been the predominant word-order in Proto-Salish, and certainly the widespread SO/OS variability reported for most Salishan languages suggests that the interpretive weight of SO order in Bella Coola is an innovation. The move towards a simpler, more rigid Wakashanized syntactic pattern for the matrix clause may have disfavoured the use of pre-verbal elements such as adverbs, which are marked in discourse terms and less frequent than unmodified predicates. This is especially true in contact situations where one of the two parties has less than perfect command of the other's language and so would provide, or have access to, a more restricted range of structures to use as a basis or model for templates. Alternatively, given the rather restricted number and frequency of sentence-initial adverbs in Northern Wakashan, it may be that the shift to a purely post-predicate system of verbal modification represents an overcompensation on the part of Bella Coola speakers emulating Wakashan linguistic patterns. Whatever its ultimate source, however, the loss of the pre-predicate adverbial particle and auxiliaries and the adoption of rigid VSO word-order in Bella Coola has resulted in a pattern where the unmarked matrix clause in this language resembles the most common type of matrix clause of its Wakashan neighbours. These two innovations have created a grammatical system which is uniquely Bella Coolan, setting this language apart from its relatives and neighbours in the Central Northwest language area.

1.2 Nominal Deixis

Another obvious way in which Bella Coola combines native Salishan traits with features borrowed from Wakashan is in its pattern of nominal deixis. Deictic systems marking NPs for spatial location with respect to the speech act are an important and well-known property of both Wakashan and Salishan grammars, but in spite of a large number of common semantic features, the deictic morphosyntax of the NP in the two families is highly distinct. In Salishan languages, deictic elements (often referred to as "determiners") are particles or clitics that appear immediately preceding an NP or other phrasal element which takes a nominal role in a sentence, as in (4):

Okanagan (S)
(4a) *ʕacənt+ís*   *i?*   *sənkɬćaʔsqáẍaʔ*
      tie+3S·ERG   D   horse
      'he tied the horse'
      (Mattina 1996: 30)

Squamish (S)
(4b) *ćáqʷ+anʼ=ɬkan*   *ni*   *ẍzúm+a*
      eat+DIR=1s   D   big+D
      'I ate the big one'
      (Matthewson and Davis 1995: 56)

Lushootseed (S)
(4c) *put*   *ƛ'u+bə+ʔitut*   *tiʔiɬ*   *ʔəs+dxʷ+pakʷ+ah+əb*
      only   HAB+ADD+sleep   D   STAT+DP+lie+ass+MD
      'this He-Lies-With-His-Ass-In-The-Air would only sleep'
      (Hess 1993: 183, line 57)

Nominal deictics (underlined) precede NPs and their modifiers as in (4a), introduce non-nominal elements used as nouns (4b), and can function as heads of relative clauses, creating syntactic nominals from finite clauses as in (4c).

Wakashan nominal deixis presents a completely different picture, making use of suffixation or encliticization, as illustrated in (5):

Makah (W)
(5a) *daasa=s*   *huktuub+iq*
      see=IND·1S   bird+D
      'I see the bird'
      (Jacobsen 1979: 125)

In both Salish (including Bella Coola) and Wakashan, the presence of nominal deixis is often the only way to identify an element – particularly a non-nominal element – as an actant rather than a predicate or a modifier.

In Bella Coola, nominal deixis blends the two patterns illustrated above: NPs bear both a proclitic and an enclitic, as in the example in (6):

Bella Coola (S)
(6) $k̓x+is$ $\underline{ti}+ʔimlk+\underline{tx}$ $\underline{ci}+xnas+\underline{cx}$
      see+3s·3s   D+man+D   Df+woman+Df
      'the man sees the woman'
      (Davis and Saunders 1978: 38)

In (6), the NP actants of the verb are marked with a circumclitic, in this case the masculine (non-feminine) and feminine proximal non-demonstratives (a full paradigm of these clitics is given in (9) below). This feature seems to be unique to Bella Coola, although Kʷakʷala demonstrative subject NPs appear bracketed between a deictic subject-marker attached to the verb stem and a demonstrative deictic suffix, giving a D-NP-D sequence reminiscent of the Bella Coola deictic circumclitic pattern, as in (7):

Kʷak̓ʷala (W)
(7) $k^háa\check{x}=ʔm+oo\check{x}$ $Wuláasəwʔ+ee\check{x}$
      come=TOP+D3·MIDDLE·SUBJ   Wuláasooʔ+D_MIDDLE·VISIBLE
      'Wuláasooʔ has come'
      (Boas 1969: 537)

Similarly, object NPs bear a deictic suffix and are preceded by a demonstrative morpheme which attaches phonologically to the preceding element in the sentence. We will return to this pattern in the context of the Kʷakʷala system of person-marking, discussed in more detail in 1.3 below.

In semantic terms, the Bella Coola deictic system also resembles the Wakashan one, particularly in its complexity. Wakashan systems of nominal deixis are highly developed and can encode up to seven different spatial categories; on the other hand, Salishan systems, which are still relatively complex compared to Indo-European, tend to be much simpler, although by and large they grow more complex as they approach the core Central Northwest area. A typical Salishan deictic system in terms of its complexity is that found in Upper Chehalis, which expresses three spatial degrees and a referential category of "indefinite":

(8)   Upper Chehalis nominal deictics

	proximal	middle	distal	indefinite
non-fem	tit	ʔit	tact	t
fem	tic, cic	ʔic	tac, cac	t

(Kinkade 1964: 258)

The feminine–non-feminine distinction is typical of coastal (as opposed to Coast) Salish languages running from Bella Coola in the north down to Tillamook in the south and is also a feature of Chinook and Chimakuan (Thompson and Kinkade 1990), but is not found in Wakashan.

In Bella Coola, nominal deixis is not only semantically more complex, but makes use of a large set of deictic enclitics that encode demonstrative–non-demonstrative and gender distinctions; these enclitics are distinctive for each spatial degree. In total, Bella Coola distinguishes three spatial categories, each subdivided into demonstrative and non-demonstrative classes, as in (9):

(9)   Bella Coola nominal deictic clitics

	proximal		middle		distal	
	demon	non-dem	demon	non-dem	demon	non-dem
non-fem	ti – táyx	ti – tx	ta – táx̌	ta – ɬ	ta – tix	ta – tx̌
fem	ci – ćayx	ci – cx	ʔiɬ – ʔiɬayɬ	ʔiɬ – ɬ	ʔiɬ – cix	ʔiɬ – ʔiɬ
plural	wa – ʔac	wa – c	ta – táx̌ʷ	ta – ɬ	ta – tax̌	ta – tx̌ʷ

(Davis and Saunders 1980: 254)

The Bella Coola paradigm shown here is not only remarkable for its complexity, but also for encoding an additional degree of plurality, an inflectional category which is unusual not only for Salishan but for languages of the area in general.[4]

While the plural inflection found in Bella Coola NPs is not typically Wakashan, the number of spatial categories is. Kʷakʷala distinguishes six spatial degrees – proximal, middle, and distal, each subdivided into visible and invisible. Heiltsuk has all of these plus the seventh category, 'ABSENT', used for something once present but currently removed from the speaker. The complete Heiltsuk system is given in (10):

---

[4] Thompson and Kinkade (1990) report that, aside from Bella Coola, in the area running roughly between the Alaska panhandle and the Washington-Oregon border, the Tsimshian languages are the only ones to consistently mark plurality.

(10)   Heiltsuk nominal deictic suffixes

proximal		middle		distal		absent
visible	invisible	visible	invisible	visible	invisible	–
-kʷa	-kʷacʰ	-iax̌	-iax̌cʰ	-ia	-iacʰ	-i

(Rath 1981: 77)

Given that the opposition demonstrative vs. non-demonstrative is semantically quite closely related to visible vs. invisible (visible things being most amenable to being pointed to and, hence, referred to demonstratively as "this" or "that"), the Heiltsuk deictic paradigm seems almost identical to the Bella Coola one, aside from the absence of the plural and gender categories. In addition, the Heiltsuk system appears to capture all three of the spatial degrees typically encoded in Salishan systems, while its fourth "non-spatial" category – 'ABSENT' – may correspond in some sense to the non-referential/indefinite/hypothetical category which is a component of many Salishan deictic systems. This may mean that Wakashan (or Central Northwest areal) influence on the Salishan deictic systems extends back into the realm of Proto-Salish, although it is equally possible that the various Salishan languages have borrowed only certain aspects of the complex nominal deictic system of their Wakashan neighbours, those languages closest to the Central Coast area showing the greatest influence.

1.3 Person-marking

Another area in which Bella Coola has become distinct from both Wakashan and other Salishan languages is in its person-marking, and – like nominal deixis – the person-marking system is a synthesis of features inherited from Salish and borrowed from Wakashan. In the Salishan family as a whole, the marking of subjects and objects is complex. In intransitive matrix clauses, Coast and Interior languages use clitics to mark first- and second-person plural and singular subjects, and the absence of a clitic pronoun indicates a third-person (singular or plural) subject. In most languages, these clitics follow the sentence-second pattern illustrated in the examples in (1) above. The same clitics are used for first- and second-person subjects of transitive clauses in Lillooet and Coast Salish languages, as illustrated in the Straits Salish (Lummi dialect) data in (11):

Straits (S)

(11a)   x̌či+t=sən
        know+TR=1S
        'I know it'

(11b) *x̌či +t=sxʷ*
know+TR=2S
'you know it'
(Jelinek and Demers 1983: 168)

Transitive clauses with a third-person subject take a suffix, -*s*. This suffix is morphologically bound to the verb stem, does not undergo sentence-second fronting, and can cooccur with an overt NP, as in (12):

Straits (S)
(12) *x̌či +t+s   cə   swəyʔqaʔ   cə   swiʔqoʔəɬ*
      know+TR+3   D   man   D   boy
      'the man knows the boy'
      (Jelinek and Demers 1983: 168)

In Interior languages other than Lillooet, subject-suffixes are used for all persons in transitive clauses (Kroeber 1991: 15). Again, these subject suffixes are bound elements rather than clitics and do not migrate to sentence-second position when the clause is introduced by pre-predicate particles.

Pronominal direct objects in Salishan languages are expressed by suffixes bound to the transitive verb stem, although – like third-person intransitive subjects – third-person objects are represented by a paradigmatic zero (that is, the absence of an object suffix signals a third-person object). In all Salishan languages in which the subject pronominals can follow the verb or in which they are suffixes, the required order of affixes/clitics is object – subject. Object suffixes are illustrated in (13):

Shuswap (S)
(13) *kuk+st+sécm+x*
      save+CAUS+1S·OBJ+2S·SUBJ
      'thank you' (lit. 'you saved me')
      (Demirdache *et al.* 1994: 154)

The Interior language Shuswap realizes both the first-person transitive object and the second-person subject with suffixes. Languages that mark transitive subjects with clitics show the same order of elements except in the presence of a sentence-initial adverb, in which case the subject clitic is fronted.

Person-marking in Wakashan in some ways resembles the general Salish pattern in that Wakashan languages also make use of sentence-second pronominal clitics, although these are used in both transitive and intransitive clauses and, at least in Southern Wakashan, are used for both subjects and objects. The order of pronominal actants, however, is subject-object rather than object-subject, as in the Southern Wakashan Makah:

Makah (W)
(14) *huuʔax̌i=ø=sii=cux̌ daac*
      still=IND=1S=2S   see
      'I can still see you'
      (Jacobsen 1979: 132)

Another similarity between the Southern Wakashan and Salishan subject-clitic paradigms is that third-persons are paradigmatic zeros, a pattern Haas (1969) reconstructs as being Proto-Nootkan. Paradigmatic zero subjects, however, do not seem to be a characteristic of Northern Wakashan, which has adopted the practice of using deictic or demonstrative enclitics as pronominals. In Kʷakʷ́ala, deictic elements may appear on their own but also obligatorily cooccur with third-person NP actants, which follow a rigid subject – object – oblique order:

Kʷakʷ́ala (W)
(15a) *kʰáax̌=kʰa*
       come=D$_{PROX·INVISIBLE·SUBJ}$
       'this one comes'
       (Boas 1969: 535)

(15b) *néex=la+ee*   *ćʰéećʰeskin+ee*
       say=QTV+D3$_{·DISTAL·SUBJ}$ Tseetseskin+D3$_{·DISTAL·VISIBLE}$
       'Tseetseskin said'
       (Boas 1969: 537)

(15c) *yóos+eeta*   *léelqʷʰalaɬʔʰ+aya+x̌a*
       eat·with·spoon+D3$_{·DISTAL·SUBJ}$ tribe+D3$_{·DISTAL·INVISIBLE}$+D3$_{·DISTAL·OBJ}$

       qʷáax̌nis+ee
       dog·salmon+D3$_{·DISTAL·VISIBLE}$
       'the tribes ate the dog salmon with spoons'
       (Boas 1969: 538)

In the first example here, a deictic person-clitic appears alone, acting as an anaphoric subject pronoun, while in (15b) a deictic clitic cooccurs with an overt third-person subject, which also bears a deictic suffix. As shown in (15c), deictics are also used with direct objects, although in this case they appear as enclitics on the preceding noun (if there is one) rather than affixed to the verb as we would expect were they inflectional agreement markers *per se*.

Syntactically, however, the deictic enclitics seem to form a constituent with the NP, leading to the mismatch between syntactic and phonological structure noted by Anderson (1992) wherein initial elements of NPs are incorporated phonologically to the preceding word. Pre-nominal deictic elements in this language thus seem more amenable to a syntactic treatment as part of the NP, which they mark for person and case; post-nominal elements distinguish visibility and the three primary spatial categories. As illustrated in data set (15), third-person deictics take different forms depending on whether they stand alone in the clause (1) or whether they precede (2) or follow (3) an NP. This gives us the following paradigm of Kʷakʷala deictic elements:

(16)   Kʷakʷala third-person-deictic markers[5]

		proximal		middle		distal	
		visible	invisible	visible	invisible	visible	invisible
1	SUBJ	=kʰ	=ka	=oox̌	=oo	=ooqʰ	=oo
	OBJ	-qʰekʰ	-x̌ka	-qʷʰ	-q́ʷ	-qʰ	-qʰee
	OBL	-seekʰ	-ska	-soox̌	-soo	-s	-see
2	SUBJ	-kata		-oox̌ta		-eeta	
	OBJ	-x̌kata		-x̌oox̌ta	-x̌ʷa	-x̌a	
	OBL	-skata		-soox̌ta	-sa	-sa	
3		- kʰ	-ka	-eex̌	-aax̌/-aq́	-ee	-aee

(based on Boas 1969: 532)

Aside from its case-marking function, the Kʷakʷala deictic system seems highly congruent, both structurally and functionally, with the Bella Coola system of deictic circumclitics in (9) above.

Unlike its sister languages, Bella Coola marks person exclusively with suffixes, as shown in (17):

Bella Coola (S)
(17)   *ksnmak+c*
        work+1s
        'I work'
        (based on Nater 1984: 36)

Even more remarkable is the fact that this language has developed a unique system of agreement to mark the person and number of actants in transitive clauses, using portmanteau object-subject agreement suffixes as in (18):

---

[5] The pre-nominal person-markers show alternations based on whether or not the following noun is a proper name, indefinite, or if it is possessed by a person other than the subject of the sentence. There are a wide variety of other morphophonological complications as well; the interested reader is referred to Boas (1969: 527 ff.).

Bella Coola (S)

(18a) *kɬ+is*   *ti+ʔimmllkii+tx*   *ti+tq́ɬa+tx*
drop+3s·3s   D+boy+D   D+knife+D
'the boy dropped the knife'
(Davis and Saunders 1997: 24)

(18b) *sṕ+tis*   *ti+ʔimml̩kii+tx*   *wa+wać+uk+sc*
hit+3P·3s   D+boy ǀ D   D+dog+PLURAL+D
'the boy is hitting the dogs'
(Davis and Saunders 1978: 38)

The most significant point to be made about the Bella Coola person-markers from an areal-typological perspective is the fact that the both transitive and intransitive paradigms represent a distinctive pattern of subject-verb agreement which has no exact counterpart in the other Central Northwest languages.

The closest thing to this type of agreement in the Salish family is the transitive subject marker (*-s* in the Lummi examples in (11)); however, these agree with NP subjects in person only and not in number, and in most Salishan languages there is a strong tendency to avoid overt NP subjects with this suffix (Kinkade 1990), making it seem rather the inverse of agreement. Intransitive subject-clitic paradigms in Salishan languages also seem not to be agreement in the traditional sense in that these have a Ø third-person which one might be hesitant to claim "cooccurs" with overt NP subjects. Bella Coola intransitive person-markers, on the other hand, cooccur freely with overt NPs or pronominals with whom they agree in person and number, the latter being unattested as an inflectional category in the third person in any other Central Northwest language. Just as there is no verbal agreement in number for third-person subjects in any Salishan language other than Bella Coola, there is no other Salishan language which shows (non-zero) agreement of any kind with third-person objects (cf. the Bella Coola sentences in (18)), illustrating once again that processes of grammatical convergence can result in the creation of linguistic diversity.

2. Convergence and diversity

Within the context of the larger NWC Sprachbund, the case of Bella Coola is an especially important one because of the example it offers of the various effects of language contact that can arise as a result of contrasting patterns of historical development and interaction. What is significant about Bella Coola is the fact that where the Salishan family, as a part of the Central Northwest areal grouping of languages, appears to have been on a path of mutual grammatical convergence with Wakashan, perhaps for millennia, Bella Coola has gone farther down this path, and veered further towards the Wakashan pattern, than any of its congener languages. That this is due to Bella Coola's particular historical and geographic circumstances is, in hindsight, obvious – but this fact is, in and of itself, of enormous importance for linguistic models of language contact and language change, particularly in residual zones. Given the millennia of contact not only in the Central Northwest area itself but in the NWC Sprachbund as a whole, both the amount of grammatical convergence and the amount of diversity are remarkable. Yet, by and large, our models of language contact in residual zones seem to have focused on borrowings and convergences, and might seem to predict a greater degree of homogeneity than what we actually do see. What Bella Coola teaches us is that each language exists, as it were, in its own micro-climate or ecological niche, and its pattern of convergences, borrowings, and innovations are uniquely conditioned by the nature and intensity of an individual language's contact with its relatives and neighbours, and by the number and particular set of neighbouring groups it comes into contact with. Thus, within the larger Sprachbund area, we find eddies or pockets of local variation amidst the larger current of typological convergences that unify the area in terms of a subset of the most widely distributed – and hence, by inference, the most readily transmissible – features. In the case of Central Northwest and some of the neighbouring languages, we see the latter type of feature in the predominant (VSO) word-order, whereas a number of other traits such as the marking of plurality and gender or the visible-invisible deictic distinction are less consistently distributed over the same area, and so are apparently more amenable to microcosmic conditions on their (retention or) spread. Such observations open the door to further studies of patterns of convergence and diversity aimed in particular at the dynamics of language contact in residual zones. Coupled with statistical studies of feature transmission and stability such as that of Nichols (1992), these should pave the way for the development of a better understanding of the conditions governing the spread of linguistic traits and the areal-historical development of human language.

University of Alberta

ABBREVIATIONS

=	sentence-second clitic	EXP	expectative	P	plural
1, 2, 3	first, second, third person	f	feminine	PERF	perfective
ADD	additive	HAB	habitual	PNT	punctual
C-C	contrastive-conjunctive	INCH	inchoative	QTV	quotative
CAUS	causative	IND	indicative	S	singular
D	deictic	MD	middle	SUBJ	subject
DIM	diminutive	NEG	negative	STAT	stative
DIR	directive	NP	nominalizer	TOP	topical/old information
DP	derivational prefix	OBJ	(direct) object	TR	transitivizer
ERG	ergative	OBL	oblique object		

Transcriptions have been standardized in an Americanist IPA and may differ in slight ways from those used in the original source.

REFERENCES

Anderson, Stephen R.
1992   *A-Morphous morphology* (*Cambridge Studies in Linguistics* 62). Cambridge: Cambridge University Press.

Beck, David
to appear   "Semantic agents, syntactic subjects, and discourse topics: How to locate Lushootseed sentences in space and time", *Studies in Language*.

Boas, Franz
1969   "Kwakiutl", in: Franz Boas (ed.), *The Handbook of American Indian Languages* 1, 423-557. Oosterhout: Anthropological Publications.

Davis, Philip W., and Ross Saunders
1978   "Bella Coola Syntax", in: Eung-Do Cook and Johnathan Kaye (eds.), *Linguistic Studies of Native Canada*, 37-65. Vancouver: UBC Press.
1980   *Bella Coola Texts*. Victoria: British Columbia Provincial Museum.
1997   *A Grammar of Bella Coola* (*University of Montana Occasional Papers in Linguistics* 13). Missoula: University of Montana.

Demirdache, Hamida, Dwight Gardiner, Peter Jacobs, and Lisa Matthewson
1994   "The Case for D-Quantification in Salish: 'All' in Stá̓imcets, Squamish, Secwepemctsín", in: *Papers for the 29th Conference on Salish and Neighbouring Languages*, 145-203. Pablo: Salish Kootenai College.

Haas, Mary
1969   "Internal Reconstruction of the Nootka-Nitinat Pronominal Suffixes", *International Journal of American Linguistics* 35, 108-24.

Heath, Jeffrey
1978   *Linguistic Diffusion in Arnhem Land*. Canberra: Australian Institute of Aboriginal Studies.

Hess, Thomas M.
1993   *Lushootseed Reader with Introductory Grammar* I (Four Stories from Edward Sam, revised edition). Victoria: Tulalip.

Jacobsen, William H.
1979   "Noun and Verb in Nootkan", in: Barbara Efrat (ed.), *The Victoria Conference on Northwestern Languages*, 83-153. Victoria: British Columbia Provincial Museum.

Jelinek, Eloise, and Richard A. Demers
1983   "The Agent Hierarchy and Voice in Some Coast Salish Languages", *International Journal of American Linguistics* 49, 167-85.
1994   "Predicates and Pronominal Arguments in Straits Salish", *Language* 70, 697-736.

Kinkade, M. Dale
1964   "Phonology and Morphology of Upper Chehalis IV", *International Journal of American Linguistics* 30, 251-60.
1983   "Salishan Evidence Against the Universality of 'Noun' and 'Verb'", *Lingua* 60, 25-39.
1990   "Sorting Out Third Persons in Salish Discourse", *International Journal of American Linguistics* 56, 341-60.

Kroeber, Paul D.
1991   *Comparative Syntax of Subordination in Salish*, volume 1. Doctoral dissertation, University of Chicago.

Matthewson, Lisa, and Henry Davis
1995   "The Structure of DP in Statimcets (Lillooet Salish)", in: *Papers for the 30th International Conference on Salish and Neighbouring Languages*, 55-68. Victoria: University of Victoria.
Mattina, Nancy
1996   *Aspect and Category in Okanagan Word Formation*. Doctoral dissertation, Simon Fraser University.
McIlwraith, Thomas F.
1948   *The Bella Coola Indians.* Toronto: University of Toronto Press.
Montler, Timothy
1986   *An Outline of the Morphology and Phonology of Saanich, North Straits Salish.* (*University of Montana Occasional Papers in Linguistics* 4). Missoula: University of Montana.
Nater, Hank
1984   *The Bella Coola Language*. Hull: National Museum of Man.
Nichols, Johanna
1992   *Linguistic Diversity in Space and Time*. Chicago: University of Chicago Press.
Rath, John C.
1981   *A Practical Heiltsuk-English Dictionary with a Grammatical Introduction*. Ottawa: National Museums of Canada.
Rose, Suzanne
1981   *Kyuquot Grammar*. Doctoral dissertation, University of Victoria.
Thompson, Laurence C., and M. Dale Kinkade
1990   "Languages", in: Wayne Suttles (ed.), *Handbook of the North American Indians*. 7: *Northwest Coast*, 30-51. Washington, D.C.: Smithsonian Institution.
van Eijk, Jan
1997   *The Lillooet Language: Phonology, Morphology, Syntax*. Vancouver: UBC Press.

MAP 1: THE CENTRAL NORTHWEST LANGUAGE AREA

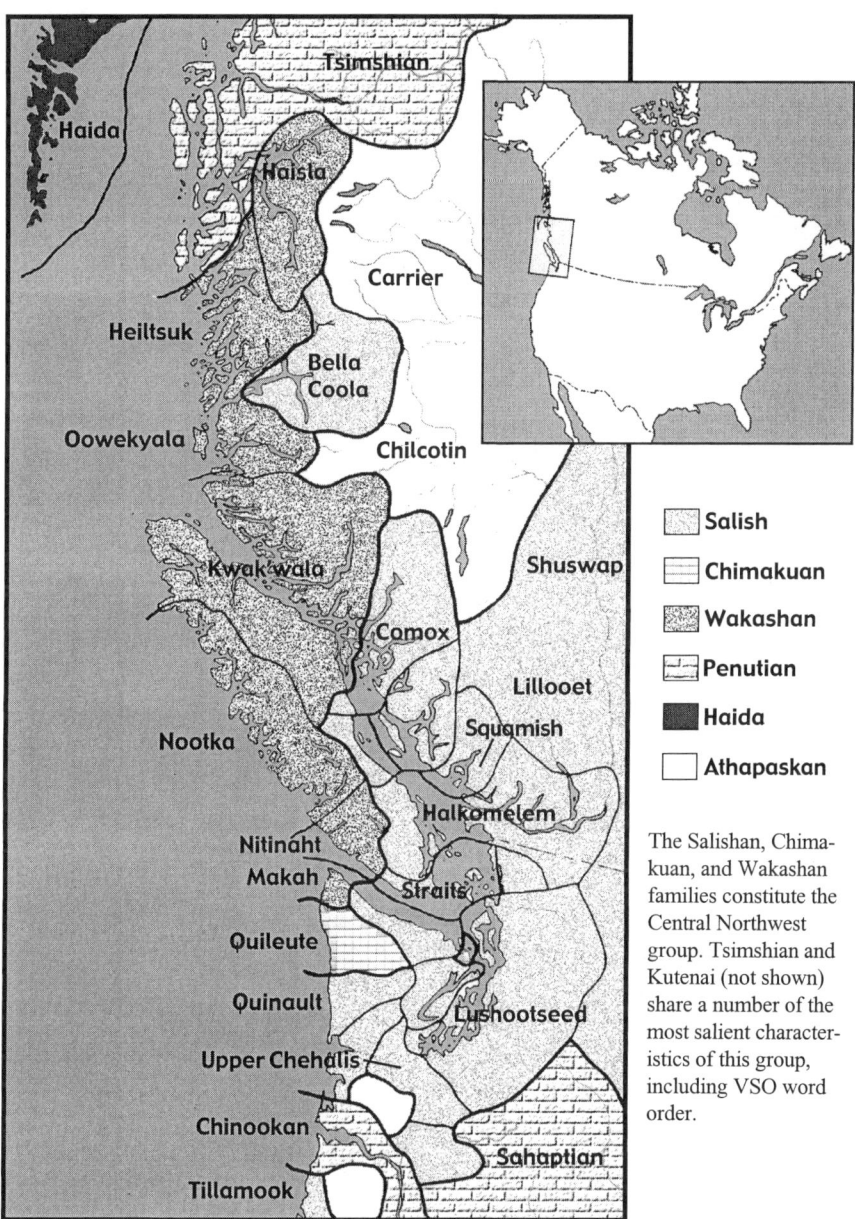

The Salishan, Chimakuan, and Wakashan families constitute the Central Northwest group. Tsimshian and Kutenai (not shown) share a number of the most salient characteristics of this group, including VSO word order.

Languages in Contact, edited by D.G. Gilbers, J. Nerbonne, and J. Schaeken (= *Studies in Slavic and General Linguistics*, vol. 28), 55-65. Amsterdam - Atlanta, GA: Rodopi, 2000.

LANGUAGE CONTACTS: PHONETIC ASPECTS

LIYA V. BONDARKO

Language contact is one of the main factors causing dramatic impact on a language system. Linguistic analysis of ancient extant manuscripts of comparable content such as early translations of the Bible into various languages gives distinct possibilities to reveal the changes that languages show in the process of interaction. The impact of such contacts on the sound systems can be inferred on the basis of comparison of the traditional methods of representing native linguistic units and the methods of representing in written form the so-called borrowed grammatical or lexical linguistic units. Unfortunately, this sort of evidence is utterly rare and should be regarded as an exception presenting only scanty information. In fact, the research into phonetic consequences of language contact became possible only with the appearance of reliable methods of speech sound registration.

The most common type of language contact is the situation when in a certain community two languages coexist on equal terms – the so-called mother tongue and the official language. Such a situation was characteristic of the republics of the former USSR and is still typical of the national republics of the Russian Federation as well as of the ex-colonies of Great Britain and France. The important thing is that the second (official) language is not only the language of official communication but is very often used as the mother tongue. It is well known that in many republics of the former USSR a good command of Russian was not only prestigious but natural, since Russian was often spoken at home in the family. Even today this natural bilingualism seems to remain in some now independent republics despite the nation-orientated official language policy. Without going into details about advantages and disadvantages of the language policy of the Soviet government, I would like to emphasize that a multi-national country like the USSR gives the possibility of systematic research into all types of inter-language interference, including phonetic interference (cf. Bondarko and Verbickaja 1987).

The contacts of the Russian language and the languages of the republics of the former USSR lead to obvious mutual influence. The Russian in the realization of the native population of national republics receives peculiar phonetic features resulting both from phonological and phonetic properties of the sound system of their mother tongue and transforms into a specific 'national' variant of the standard Russian language in its colloquial and sometimes official form (Zorina 1996).

This variant is characteristic not only of the native speakers of some other language, but also of the native speakers of Russian living in a non-native language environment. For example, the speech of Russians in Tbilisi, Georgia, can undoubtedly be viewed as one of such 'national variants'. There is much evidence to prove that its specific features are caused not by the Georgian language itself (if, say, Russian citizens of Tbilisi do not speak Georgian), but by the Russian speech of Georgians that can be heard in Tbilisi today.

The reverse tendency existent – namely the influence of the Russian language on the national languagès – presents a problem in itself. The influence of Russian on other contacting languages can be proved, for instance, by the so-called *borrowed phonemes* that come into national languages with lexical loans from Russian.

Another type of language contact leading to phonetic interference is the so-called intra-language interference. It emerges when the standard language and dialects in contact are bringing to life regional variants or forms of the standard language.

It is interesting that the criteria used for evaluating the results of inter-language interference and intra-language interference vary quite noticeably: for example, a glottalized realization of the Russian plosives /p, t, k/ in the speech of Georgians seems to be quite acceptable, which can be explained by the fact that such realization is restricted to a particular region and presents no threat of wide expansion into the standard literary language. On the other hand, a fricative realization of the voiced velar consonant in such words as *god*, *gramotnyj* is viewed as a dialectal feature and a source for spoiling the standard literary language.

The influence of the Russian standard literary language on the dialects is obvious and can be described as a destructive power continually pressing the sound systems of old Russian dialects to change.

The interaction of sound systems in the process of teaching foreign languages is of special interest for phoneticians from the point of view of both general phonetics and psycholinguistics (Bondarko and Lebedeva 1983).

Traditionally, speaking a foreign language in the situation of classroom bilingualism – the so-called classroom speech – is regarded as having a very narrow domain of functioning and a very limited importance in the general problem of interference since it shows no significant impact on any of the contacting languages. However, observations on the speech of young native speakers of Russian who know English reveal the possibility of a quite noticeable influence of some specific English features on the Russian speech of such people. Strange though it may seem, the system of intonation proves the most vulnerable in this case.

In the process of teaching Russian pronunciation to foreign students the inter-ference of sound systems presents as important a problem as other problems topi-cal for inter-language interference in general. The realization of the sound units of Russian by native speakers of other languages carries the information about both general phonetic features of the Russian speech and its specific characteristics that are subject to compulsory modification by all non-native speakers of Russian. The former imply the standard realization of these features, that is, common errors in pronunciation of non-native sounds, the latter include pronunciation difficulties in speaking Russian particularly because it is not a mother tongue. Of special inter-est is the type of interference which is caused by the sound system of the student's mother tongue, that is, when the mistake is connected not with the fact that something foreign is pronounced, but with similarities and dissimilarities of the two sound systems – that of Russian and the student's native language.

Of exceptional interest in the process of teaching a foreign language are bilin-gual students, for instance, the citizens of Russia for whom Russian is the second native language. It is important to study the dynamics of such bilingualism when a bilingual person studies a third, foreign, language. In the succession 'mother tongue – Russian language – foreign language' various combinations of the three elements are possible: a) mother tongue and Russian can be opposed to a foreign language, b) mother tongue is in opposition to two non-native languages, Russian and foreign, c) all the three function as totally independent systems.

The present report deals with the data on the character of interference emerg-ing in all the above-mentioned situations. The data were obtained at the Depart-ment of Phonetics and Methods of Teaching Foreign Languages at St. Petersburg State University, as a result of many years of systematic research into the prob-lem. Our attention has been focused on standard Russian pronunciation and its modifications in these situations of language contact. At different stages of the research the material and methodology varied, but on the whole we tried to obtain reliable data based on representative material using the methods of experimental phonetics.

The inter-language interference was studied as follows. The citizens of Tallinn, Baku, Tbilisi, Yerevan, Kishinyov, Riga, Vilnius, Minsk and some Ukrainian cities, including Kiev and L'viv (L'vov), were used as subjects. Native citizens of these cities aged 18 to 50 represented two levels of command of Russian, speak-ing with strong and slight accent. In each city, the speech of 20 people was stud-ied, 10 in each group. They all were asked to record the same text, which can conventionally be called phonetically balanced since it includes 200 of the most frequent syllables of the Russian speech. Before reading the text each subject re-corded his/her personal data (the year and place of birth, education, current place of residence, etc.) as samples of quasi-spontaneous speech. Thus the recordings of the same Russian text in the realisation of the speakers of Estonian, Azerbaijani,

Georgian, Armenian, Moldavian, Latvian, Lithuanian, Byelorussian and Ukrainian were analysed. The results of this research have been presented in a series of publications including a monograph (Bondarko and Verbickaja 1987). Some important issues are worth mentioning here.

All the groups of subjects, irrespective of their mother tongue and the Russian language competence, suffered strong influence of orthography when reading the text. It showed, for example, when in place of the vowels represented by the letter *o* in unstressed positions the vowel [o] was pronounced. The realization of final voiced consonants represented by respective letters can also be considered spelling pronunciation. As we will see later, the principles of Russian orthography (retaining the uniformity of the orthographic representation of a morpheme, even if it changes phonetically), noticeably complicates the process of acquiring a standard Russian pronunciation by foreign students.

Incorrect realization of soft consonants, labials and a fore-lingual sonorant trill, unavoidable for all the subjects, can be regarded as phonological errors proper. It is to be noted that this is typical not only of native speakers of languages where the opposition of soft and hard consonants is absent, but also of speakers of the typologically closely related languages Ukrainian and Byelorussian where the opposition is present on the phonological level, although the phonetic quality and the distribution of palatalized and velarized consonants is different. This fact also accounts for mistakes in realizations of vowels following palatalized consonants: they tend to be not enough front and not enough close. Impossibility to pronounce the Russian vowel /ɨ/ correctly is another universal mistake of all subjects.

These data is brought to life by the inherent properties of the Russian sound system, its specific phonological oppositions and specific phonetic realizations.

On the other hand, all our subjects, with the exception of Ukrainian and Byelorussian speakers, pronounce a lateral /l/ as non-velarized – a typical 'mid-European' realization. Though connected with the specific Russian articulation of the sonant, general phonetic features of most of the languages trigger this mispronunciation.

The influence of the subjects' native language is revealed in other cases, too, and it leads to mispronunciations that may be termed 'diagnostic'. For instance, absence of voiced and voiceless consonant opposition in Estonian triggers the pronunciation of Russian voiced consonants by Estonian speakers as half-voiced (lenis), that may be perceived by Russians as voiceless. Or, Estonian speakers of Russian may pronounce voiced consonants instead of voiceless ones. These mistakes are undoubtedly the result of the influence of the native sound system. The peculiar articulation of Russian /s/ and /š/ is due to the absence of the opposition of the two kinds of fricatives (those with a round narrowing and those with a long narrowing) in Estonian.

Error analysis of this kind can result in a fairly precise description of the influence of each of these languages on the Russian speech. Such descriptions can provide the basis not only for specific methods of teaching Russian as a foreign language, but for applied research in the fields of psychology and forensic phonetics as well.

Intra-language interference can be defined as deviation from the standard pronunciation of the educated urban native population under the influence of dialects bordering the urban areas. With the purpose of investigating the problem, we have performed a detailed analysis of speech peculiarities of natives of the cities of Vologda, Arkhangel'sk and Perm', lying in the North-Russian dialect area, Kursk, Ryazan' and Smolensk, lying in the South-Russian dialect area, Nizhniy Novgorod (Gorkiy), Pskov, Yaroslavl' and Volgograd, lying in the Mid-Russian dialect area, and Yekaterinburg (Sverdlovsk) and Chelyabinsk, having contacts with the Ural dialect areas. The analysis of intra-language interference can give an insight into the 'language memory' of the standard speakers who, being natives of the region, are in constant contact with dialect speakers or who retain in their own speech dialectal features characteristic of older speakers. As is to be expected, the analysis of such material yields data other than the analysis of inter-language interference. The most stable dialectal features are those that are the most typical (*Russkaja dialektologija* 1989).

Speaking about the standard Russian pronunciation, we can draw the following conclusions: South-Russian dialects mostly influence the realization of consonants and the North-Russian dialects mostly influence the realization of vowels. For instance, a velar voiced fricative is pronounced instead of a stop by 80% of Kursk and Ryazan' natives and by 70% of Smolensk natives, while mid-open vowels are pronounced as closer ones by 40% of Vologda natives, 100% Arkhangelsk and 80% Perm' natives. It should be noted that the dialectal features, although present in our subjects' speech, do not occur regularly and that some phonetic peculiarities are not substandard. Besides, spelling pronunciation was quite characteristic of near-standard subjects. We may conclude that the reading of orthographically correct texts may present a problem even for native speakers with good communication skills and leads to mistakes on the phonetic level.

Comparing intra-language and inter-language interference, it should be emphasized that the mechanisms of sound system interaction in these two cases are fundamentally different. In the case of intra-language interference, the speaker uses a familiar phoneme system and the dialect influence triggers either a misuse of a phoneme (an orthoepic mistake) or a wrong phoneme realization (an orthophonic mistake). In the case of inter-language interference, the speaker has to use a foreign phoneme system and foreign phonetic units. Speaking a foreign language, he or she has to construct the sound form of a word more or less anew (depending on his or her foreign language competence) or reconstruct it on the basis of a perceived sound sequence.

Phonetic mechanisms of both types of interference have to be investigated by themselves, since by analyzing speech with traces of language interference, we are dealing with the final result, and not with the process of sound system interaction. The difficulty of studying language interference on the sound level is due to the fact that sound units, having no meaning, function only within linguistic units of higher levels. So, the experimental analysis requires special methods that, on the one hand, can give all the linguistically relevant answers and, on the other hand, do not support the illusion that the subjects are capable of conscious evaluation of their speech behaviour on the phonetic level.

Mechanisms of foreign language speech production and perception are at the center of attention now, as well as they have been many years ago. The absence of complete symmetry between these two processes and the impossibility of making direct experiments has brought to life a whole range of roundabout methods of describing the processes.

There are two opposite views on human perceptual abilities. The traditional view for linguists claims that the perceptual space is analogous to the phonological space. L.V. Ščerba thought that a speaker could differentiate between as many vowel sounds as there are vowel phonemes in his or her language, and that other differences "do not lie in the lighted sphere of the linguistic consciousness". Later the idea of phonological conditioning of perceptual abilities has been reflected in various terms, such as 'phonological hearing' or 'phonological sieve', but it has always kept in agreement with Ščerba's words (Ščerba 1983).

The other view is the result of psychophysiological research into human aural perception. It claims that the ability to differentiate between various classes of speech sounds (for example, vowels) is universal, thus the perceptual space does not relate to the phonological system: apparently all people can perceive the same classes of sounds and use the same strategies (*Fiziologija sensornyx sistem* 1972).

Nowadays, the former viewpoint seems too categorical and too general. The latter is at variance with the numerous facts known both to phoneticians working in the field of perception, and to foreign language teachers, who from time to time face students unable to hear the difference between the sounds of their native tongue and those of the language they study.

A third view on human perceptual abilities can be formulated on the basis of the aforementioned experimental phonetic data (Bondarko 1981). We can ascertain that a speaker can differentiate between more sounds than there are phonemes in his native language, but ultimately this ability is conditioned by the phonological relations in the sound system. For instance, the fact that Russians are very sensitive to *i*-like transitions at the beginning and at the end of non-front vowels should be explained by the fact that this phonetic feature is used for the identification of soft consonants.

Studies of perceptual abilities of speakers of a given language are extremely important for both theoretical deductions and practical purposes: the perceptual relevance of a sound is often an indication of its functional independence, and comprehensive knowledge of peculiarities of perception in a sound system is necessary for the description of sound changes in contacting languages.

Here are some examples of various aspects of sound interference in different types of language contact. It is well known that similar phonetic features can have a different phonemic status in different languages. The influence it may have on perceptual abilities of speakers of these languages can be shown in experimental data derived from the analysis of perception of long and short vowels, nasalized and non-nasalized vowels and, finally, front and other than front vowels. In all the cases the vowels were taken from a natural context, and the subjects were native speakers of languages where the corresponding features have a different phonemic status.

In German and Kyrgyz – languages that are typologically very distant – vowel duration is phonologically relevant. While German long and short vowels differ in quality as well as in quantity, the difference between Kyrgyz long and short vowels is only quantitative (Bajterekova 1978). Apparently, this accounts for the fact that German vowels are actually twice as short as Kyrgyz vowels, so that the Kyrgyz subjects identify long German vowels only in 45% of the cases. Besides, the phonetic realization of Kyrgyz long vowels, unlike German ones, is often characterized by two intensity maxima (which is a relic of their origin from VCV sequences with a later consonant elision). The German subjects often perceived long Kyrgyz vowels as combinations of two vowels of the same kind or, if one of the intensity peaks was lacking, as short vowels, although their actual duration was about 100 ms and close to that of German long vowels. The fact that speakers of German mostly identify phonemically long vowels of their native tongue correctly and that they mostly identify long Kyrgyz vowels incorrectly (though the absolute vowel duration is comparable in both cases), shows that vowel quality serves as the main factor in the opposition of long and short vowels in German. Positive correlation of the absolute vowel duration and the correct identification by the Kyrgyz speakers proves that the main factor in this opposition in the Kyrgyz language is vowel duration.

The problem of perception of phonologically relevant features by speakers of different languages was dealt with in a study in which the perception of the Kazakh front rounded and unrounded vowels /ø/, /æ/ and English vowels /ɜː/, /æ/ were compared with the perception of the Russian vowels /a/ and /o/ in the context of palatalized consonants (Abuov 1978). The formant characteristics of all these vowels are very similar, but since their phonemic status is different, we could expect differences in the interpretation by speakers of different languages. The results of the study revealed that it is not always the case that vowels of the speaker's native language are perceived better than vowels of a foreign language. In the experiment, Russian subjects normally perceived Russian vowel allophones better than the vowels of English and Kazakh. English subjects adequately perceived a lack of labialization and frontness of the English /æ/, though in other cases, they had the same difficulties in categorizing English vowels as Russian and Kazakh subjects did.

It is interesting to note that some vowel features are perceived better than the vowel as a whole. The perception of one and the same stimulus (a synthesized vowel of the quality approximating one of the six natural speech vowels) depends on the rules of phonetic organization of the word form. Lower scores in the perceptual results of the Kazakh subjects witness principal differences with regard to the phonemic status of the vowel in their language, where vowel harmony plays the most important role in word formation.

In this context, studies of language interference that takes place in the situation of Kyrgyz students learning French are worth mentioning. It is well known that there is a phonological opposition of French half-open and half-close vowels which is absent in Kyrgyz, where open and close vowels are considered to be allophonic variations (Kasymova 1991). Thus, the Kyrgyz subjects are apt to perceive French vowels as closer vowels and to consider French open vowels to be more like vowels in Kyrgyz. It is interesting to note that the French subjects regarded the Kyrgyz vowels more like French close vowels.

The investigation of factors which influence the perception of sounds of one's native (as opposed to a foreign) language was carried out using synthesized vowels, which were presented to Russian, French and Georgian speakers (Ogorodnikova 1983). It turned out that the stimuli related to the *i-a-u* vowel triangle were perceived by all subjects as referring to the corresponding vowels of their native languages. When the formant values of the stimulus did not directly correspond to those of the allophone of a subject's native language, the accuracy of the subjects' responses were influenced by their knowledge of foreign languages. Thus, a native of Georgian who spoke French as a foreign language, was more precise in matching the properties of the synthesized stimulus with the transcription sign of the corresponding vowel. When the subjects were asked to imitate the synthesized stimulus, it turned out that some of them performed quite well and their pronunciation reflected the properties of the stimulus even if they were not characteristic of the subject's native language.

It should be mentioned that the study of perception and imitation of foreign language sounds and synthesized stimuli, which to various degrees resemble the allophones of the speaker's native language, was carried out in the former USSR in the situation of language contact of Russian with native languages and is continued nowadays, using the language material of multilingual Russia. These studies are both of theoretical and practical value, for the results can be applied in foreign language teaching. A mere enumeration of research projects carried out at the Department of Phonetics of St. Petersburg University would take up a few pages.

It is now possible to draw conclusions and discuss the results of the studies concerning the mechanisms of the interaction of sound systems at the level of speech communication of bilingual subjects or students, who learn a second or a third foreign language.

First of all, there is no doubt that the idea of the universal nature of distinctive features forming phonological oppositions, is not supported by experimental data: the perception of phonetic correlates of distinctive features is not governed by universal laws, but depends on actual phonetic characteristics of a given sound system. The second important conclusion is the necessity to introduce changes into our traditional knowledge about phonological perception. In sound perception the listener's judgments are not influenced exclusively by the phonological system of his own language, which induces him to classify the sounds he hears as phonemes of his native tongue. He is capable of making more subtle discriminations based on general principles of audio processing of speech signals, as well as on his knowledge of foreign languages and on his individual abilities as a listener. One of the most important properties of phonological perception is that it provides different mechanisms for the processing of native and non-native language sounds.

The influence of a speaker's native language on his ability to communicate in a foreign language (or his second native language) can be conditioned by a combination of his abilities both on the sensory and motor levels:

Sensory level	Motor level	Result
1. I can't hear it	I can't pronounce it correctly	A recurrent mistake on the perception level
2. I can hear it	I can't pronounce it	A recurrent mistake on the production level
3. I can hear it	I can pronounce it correctly	No phonetic conditions for mistakes
4. I can't hear it	I can pronounce it correctly	An irregular mistake

At first sight combinations No. 1 and No. 4 may evoke contradictions. The first one, 'I can't hear it, therefore I can't pronounce it' seems to contradict such conceptions as motor theory and analysis by synthesis theory, as it introduces the situation in the reverse order: from the point of view of these classical theories, the articulatory aspect is a means for simplification, re-coding the acoustic signal in the perception process, whereas in our case it is viewed as a subordinate, dependent on the sensoric aspect. Speech perception theories are all based on the speaker's behavior in the framework of his native language, when articulatory-acoustic links defined by his phonological system are established. In our case, we are dealing with a quite different situation: perception and production of foreign language sounds by the speaker whose perceptual abilities have already been formed within the framework of his native language. The combination No. 4 'I can't hear it, but I can pronounce it correctly', seems paradoxical only if we assume that acquisition (mastering) of the sound system of a foreign language takes place without the speaker's preliminary knowledge of it. As a rule, we observe quite the opposite: the speaker has some idea about the sound system of the foreign language he is going to master and tries to make his pronunciation as close to the original as possible. For example, students learning French, pronounce nasal vowels instead of oral ones, or people imitating Georgian accent, produce ejectives in contexts where they never occur.

In conclusion, I would like to point out that the situation of language contact characteristic of any society, calls for the investigation of both sociological and psychological aspects of the problem.

In Russia the long history of research into phonetic interference in the situation of language contact yielded invaluable data, and at the same time made the training of expert phoneticians – representing the mutilingual community of the former USSR and nowadays of Russia – more efficient (Bondarko 1995).

Department of Phonetics, St. Petersburg State University

REFERENCES

Abuov, Ž.
1978   *Vlijanie fonologičeskoj sistemy na vosprijatie fonetičeskix priznakov glasnyx.* Leningrad.
Bondarko, L.V.
1981   *Fonetičeskoe opisanie jazyka i fonologičeskoe opisanie reči.* Leningrad.
1995   *Fonetičeskij fond jazykov Rossii. Vozroždenie kul'tury Rossii: Jazyk i ètnos.* Sankt-Peterburg.
Bondarko, L.V., and G.N. Lebedeva
1983   "Opyt opisanija svojstv fonologičeskogo sluxa", *Voprosy jazykoznanija* 1983/2, 9-19.
Bondarko, L.V., and L.A. Verbickaja (eds.)
1987   *Interferencija zvukovyx sistem.* Leningrad.
Bajterekova, G.
1978   *Fonologičeskaja interpretacija fonetičeskix svojstv zvukov reči (èksperimental'no-fonetičeskoe issledovanie vosprijatija dlitel'nosti glasnyx v kirgizskom i nemeckom jazykax).* Leningrad.
Fiziologija sensornyx sistem
1972   G.V. Gezšuni (ed.), *Fiziologija sensornyx sistem* II. Leningrad.

Kasymova, B.
1991   *Issledovanie perceptivnoj bazy jazyka v uslovijax kirgizsko-russkogo dvujazy-
            čija*. Biškek.
Ogorodnikova, K.
1983   *Universal'noe i fonologičeskoe prostranstvo glasnyx*. Leningrad.
Russkaja dialektologija
1989   L.L. Kasatkin (ed.), *Russkaja dialektologija*. Moskva.
Ščerba, L.V.
1983   *Russkie glasnye v kačestvennom i količestvennom otnošenii*. Leningrad.
Zorina, Z.G.
1996   *Fonetičeskie osobennosti funkcionirovanija russkogo jazyka v uslovijax dvuja-
            zyčija*. Sankt-Peterburg.

Languages in Contact, edited by D.G. Gilbers, J. Nerbonne, and J. Schaeken (= *Studies in Slavic and General Linguistics*, vol. 28), 67-71. Amsterdam - Atlanta, GA: Rodopi, 2000.

GERMAN INFLUENCE ON SORBIAN ASPECT:
THE FUNCTION OF DIRECTIONAL ADVERBS

HÉLÈNE BRIJNEN

The Sorbian linguistic community has always been surrounded and dominated by speakers of German. Although in the 18th and 19th century many speakers of Sorbian were still monolingual, a clear German influence can already be detected in the writings of the peasant-writer Hanso Nepila (1761-1856) of the village of Rohne, Sorbian: *Rowne*, near Schleife/*Slěpe* in Saxony (formerly Lower Silesia). This influence is not only present in the lexicon and elsewhere, but also in the verbal morphosyntax.

In Sorbian, as in other Slavic languages, the aspect distinction plays a central role in verbal morphology. In this paper, I will address the question of German influence on the Sorbian aspect system, on the basis of evidence from Nepila's dialect, a transitional dialect between Upper and Lower Sorbian. I understand aspect in the restricted way as defined by Comrie 1976: 7. I will focus on one special case, the function of directional adverbs in combination with verbs expressing movement.

First, we shall briefly consider the Sorbian verbal system. In standard Upper Sorbian, as in other Slavic languages, we find imperfective (I) and perfective (P) verbs, which occur in pairs. Perfective verbs can be derived from imperfective simple verbs by means of prefixation, for instance, 'to drink' *pić* (I) - *wupić* (P). Such derived perfective verbs can again be turned into imperfective verbs by suffixation; in this case: *wupiwać* (I). Sorbian is a conservative language in the sense that it has preserved two synthetic past forms: the imperfect, formed from imperfective verbs, *pijach* 'I was drinking'; and the aorist, formed from perfective verbs, *wupich* 'I drank'. In addition, there are two analytic past forms, the perfect, *sym (wu)pił* (I/P) 'I drank, I have drunk'; and the pluperfect, *běch (wu)pił* (I/P) 'I drank, I had drunk'. The present tense is formed from imperfective verbs, *piju* 'I drink'. There are two future tense forms, a synthetic future, which is based on perfective verbs, *wupiju* 'I will drink'; and an analytic future, which is formed from imperfective verbs and the future of 'to be', *budu pić* 'I will drink'.

The description given for the standard language does not always reflect the spoken language. In many dialects, only the perfect past subsists. This is true of spoken Lower Sorbian, most of spoken Upper Sorbian, and the Slĕpe dialect as it is used today. Furthermore, in the whole Sorbian speaking area, it is quite common to form an analytic future tense from a perfective verb, *budu wupić* 'I will drink'. Whereas the loss of the synthetic past forms is a development that has taken place in many Slavic languages, the analytic perfective future appears to be a typically Sorbian phenomenon, attributed by most linguists to the influence of German.

Michalk (1959) clearly demonstrated, against Ščerba (1915) and Lötzsch (1956), that the category of aspect in Sorbian has by no means become obsolete, notwithstanding the occurrence of such an anomaly as an analytic perfective future. In order to express concrete present actions (the answer to the question "what are you doing there?"), only imperfective verbs can be used. The same holds for such actions when located in the past or in the future. Verbs conveying the meaning 'to start', 'to continue', 'to finish' must be combined with an imperfective infinitive. In the past tense, imperfective verbs express actions in progress, whereas perfectives express successive actions. In spite of his recognition of aspect as a contemporary grammatical category in Sorbian, Michalk also points to the influence of the German verbal system. As examples of such influence, he mentions not only the existence of an analytic perfective future, but also the combination of separate directional adverbs with motion verbs. The particular use of directional adverbs, such as *wen* (Upper Sorbian *won*) 'out', *fort* (Ger. 'fort') 'away', *prec* 'away', *nuć* 'in', was already observed for the Muskau dialect by Ščerba (1915: 118). In standard Sorbian, as in other Slavic languages, direction in combination with a motion verb is indicated by a prefix attached to the simple verb, which then generally becomes perfective, e.g. *wu-* 'out' + *hić* (I) 'to go' > *wuńć* (P) 'to go out'. In addition, direction is often indicated by means of a separate adverb, e.g. *won hić* 'to go out'. As is shown in this example, such directional adverbs may function as a replacement of the prefixes. An Upper Sorbian example of such use is 'to fall out' *won padać* (I), along with *wupadać* (P). In contrast to the prefixes, the adverbs do not alter the aspect of the verb they accompany.

According to Michalk, such combinations of an adverb and a non-derived imperfective verb are gradually replacing the imperfective verbs formed by secondary derivation. In this way, the number of aspectually paired verbs is reduced. It is one of the most far-reaching consequences of German influence on the Sorbian verb (Michalk 1959: 253).

In the dialect of Nepila's manuscripts, which date from the beginning of the 19th century, we still find an elaborate verbal system, in which both synthetic past tenses are preserved. In addition, an analytic future based on perfective verbs occurs frequently. Directional abverbs in combination with verbs expressing movement are also quite common. They can either precede or follow the verb form. Moreover, these directional adverbs can accompany verbs that contain prefixes, regardless of whether these verbs are perfective or imperfective; e.g. (the examples from Nepila are given in my transliteration):

...da io derrie chappiala sassei ten wogen wot togo gerrnyschka <u>wot</u>-sterkowaz <u>precz</u>... (p. 39)
then be.3P.SG.PR well begin(I).PERF.FEM again that.MASC.SG.ACC fire.MASC.SG.ACC from that.MASC.SG.GEN pot.MASC.SG.GEN PREF:away-push(I).INF away
'...then she began to push away the fire from the pot again...'

...aby io pak ten wogen <u>precz</u> <u>wot</u>-sterczylla... (p. 71)
whether be.3P.SG.PR again that.MASC.SG.ACC fire.MASC.SG.ACC away PREF:away-push (P).PERF.FEM
'...whether she once again had pushed away the fire...'

As a result of German influence (cf. *sie stieß weg* 'she pushed away', from *wegstoßen* 'to push away'), direction is clearly felt as something that has to be expressed separately from the verb, even when this leads to redundancy and to syntactic constructions not found in German itself. As a matter of fact, verbs containing directional prefixes rarely occur without an adverb. This also holds for Slěpe Sorbian as it is spoken today (1999):

a pón jo musał cakać, až su te rusy še <u>će</u>-ćĕhnuli ći nas <u>durich</u>...
(Marta Mrosk, age 86, Trebendorf / *Trjebin*)
and then be.3P.SG.PR must(I).PERF.MASC wait(I).INF, until be.3P.PL.PR those.PL.NOM Russians.PL.NOM all.PL.NOM PREF:through-move(P).PERF.PL at we.PRAEP through
'...and then he had to wait until all the Russians had moved through our place...'

Between the prefix and the adverb there are fixed correspondences, as, in this case, *će-* (< **pře-*) 'through' and *durich* (German *durch* 'through'). Apparently, the main function of the prefix in this modern example is to express result, whereas the directional meaning is underscored by the adverb. However, such an arrangement has not brought about the dissolution of the aspectual distinctions (*pace* Toops 1992: 12).

The verbs of motion strictly speaking ('to go', 'to carry', etc.) present a more complicated picture. In standard Upper Sorbian, as in other Slavic languages, they constitute a special case by presenting pairs of imperfective verbs, one determinate and one indeterminate; e.g., 'to go, walk', *hić* (I) (determinate: 'at the moment of speaking', 'in one direction') – *chodźić* (I) (indeterminate: 'not at a given moment', 'not in one direction'). Only from the determinate verb, a perfective can be derived by means of prefixation. An indeterminate verb to which a prefix is added remains imperfective.

In Nepila, we often find these verbs in combination with an adverb; e.g.,

...a dys ia som wotterry rass wen schel da io mi praiilla : to gorr to pissanie wosstaii a wen dzio...(p. 171)
and when I.NOM be.1P.SG.PR some.MASC.SG time.MASC.SG out go(I.DET).PERF.MASC
then be.3P.SG.PR I.DAT say(I/P).PERF.FEM that.NEUTR.SG.NOM really that.NEUTR.SG.
ACC write.VN.ACC leave(P).3P.SG and out go(I.DET).3P.SG.PR
'and, one time, as I went out, she said to me : «really, he leaves his writing and goes out»'

The verbs of motion exhibit a series of irregularities in relation to determinacy and aspect distinctions which deserve further investigation.

Nepila's manuscripts show that the use of directional adverbs in combination with verbs expressing movement is by no means the result of a recent development. Like the analytic perfective future, it is an old phenomenon that has been present in Slěpe Sorbian for at least 200 years. The long history of contact with German has brought about rearrangements of certain linguistic forms and their function. In the case of the directional adverbs (and also of the analytic perfective future), such rearrangements can be considered to be innovations, not signs of language loss.

University of Groningen

ABBREVIATIONS

(I)	imperfective	INF	infinitive	PR	present
(P)	perfective	MASC	masculine	PRAEP	prepositional
ACC	accusative	NEUTR	neuter	PREF	prefix
DAT	dative	NOM	nominative	SG	singular
DET	determinate	P	person	VN	verbal noun
FEM	feminine	PERF	perfect		
GEN	genitive	PL	plural		

REFERENCES

Brijnen, H.B.
1997   "An incipient literary tradition in Slěpe Sorbian: Nepila's manuscripts and their transcription by Handrik", in: B. Synak and T. Wicherkiewicz (eds.), *Language Minorities and Minority Languages in the Changing Europe*, 305-309. Gdańsk: Wydawnictwo Uniwersytetu Gdańskiego.
1999   "Rukopisy Hansa Nepile-Rowniskeho: eine unveröffentlichte Handschrift Nepilas", *Lětopis* 46, *Wosebity zešiwk*, 68-75.
Comrie, B.
1976   *Aspect*. Cambridge University Press.

Fasske, H.
1981 *Grammatik der obersorbischen Schriftsprache der Gegenwart. Morphologie.* Bautzen: Domowina.
Kretschmer, A.
1997 "Zum Verhältnis von Tempus und Aspekt in modernen slavischen Sprachen", *Lětopis* 44/1, 36-47.
Janaš, P.
1976 *Niedersorbische Grammatik.* Bautzen: Domowina.
Lötzsch, R.
1956 *Xarakter vlijanija nemeckogo jazyka na slovoizmenenie imeni i glagola verxnelužickogo jazyka.* Leningrad (diplomnaja rabota).
Michalk, S.
1958/59 "Der obersorbische Verbalaspekt im Spiegel der bisherigen Grammatiken", *Wissenschaftlicher Zeitschrift der Karl-Marx-Universität. Gesellschafts- und Sprachwissenschaftliche Reihe* 1, 159-164.
1959 "Über den Aspekt in der obersorbischen Volkssprache", *Zeitschrift für Slawistik* 4, 241-253.
1961 "Die sogenannten Doppelzeitwörter in der sorbischen Volkssprache", *Zeitschrift für Slawistik* 6, 1-42.
Muka E.
1965 [1891] *Historische und vergleichende Laut- und Formenlehre der niedersorbischen (niederlausitzisch-wendischen) Sprache.* Bautzen: Domowina.
Nepila, H.
Zapiski Hansa Nepile-Rowniskeho (1761-1856), 2. knižka, MS XXX 3C Restarchiv der Maćica Serbska, Sorbische Zentralbibliothek, Bautzen (unpublished manuscript).
Schuster-Šewc, H.
1968 *Gramatika hornjoserbskeje rěče.* 1. *zwjazk.* Bautzen: Domowina.
Smoler, J.E.
1859 "Přichodny čas serbskeho słowjesa", *Časopis Maćicy Serbskeje* XII/1, 7-14.
Ščerba, L.V.
1973 [1915] *Vostočnolužickoe narečie (Der ostniedersorbische Dialekt).* Bautzen: Domowina.
Toops, G.H.
1992 "Lexicalization of Upper Sorbian Preverbs: Temporal-Aspectual Ramifications and the Delimitation of German Influence", *Germano-Slavica* 7/2, 3-22.
Wornar, E.
1997 "Iteratiwnosć a distributiwne wašnje čina", *Lětopis* 44/1, 15-16.

Languages in Contact, edited by D.G. Gilbers, J. Nerbonne, and J. Schaeken (= *Studies in Slavic and General Linguistics*, vol. 28), 73-86. Amsterdam - Atlanta, GA: Rodopi, 2000.

LANGUAGE CONTACT, LEXICAL BORROWING, AND SEMANTIC FIELDS

BERNARD COMRIE

1. Introduction

In an important paper on genetic relationship, Greenberg (1957) notes that controversy can arise in determining whether lexical similarities between two languages are due to common ancestry or to contact, but argues that one test that can be applied is what I will call the semantic domains test. In clear cases of borrowing, the borrowed lexical items are often limited to particular semantic domains, while the rest of the vocabulary of the borrowing language shows no similarity to that of the donor. In this way one can, for instance, establish that Persian has borrowed from Arabic rather than being, like Arabic, a Semitic language, and that Thai has borrowed heavily from Chinese rather than being its close genetic relative. In this paper, I want to investigate these and related claims against the case of Haruai, a Papuan (i.e. non-Austronesian) language spoken in the southwest of Madang Province, Papua New Guinea.[1] I have already examined questions relating to the genetic affiliation of Haruai and its contacts with other languages in earlier work, in particular Comrie (1988; 1989). Although I will necessarily have to repeat some of the material that is contained in these earlier articles, my purpose in this article is to relate this material specifically to Greenberg's claim. In a sense, this is the least I can do, since in Comrie (1989) I made the perhaps rather unfair statement that Greenberg does not provide criteria that would enable a distinction to be made between lexical similarities due to common genetic origin and those due to contact. While my earlier claim is clearly not literally correct, given the reference to Greenberg's work that I have already made, I will argue that the criteria advanced by Greenberg do not in fact work as intended in the case of Haruai.

[1] This material is based upon work supported by the National Science Foundation under Grant BNS-8504293. I am grateful to the Madang Provincial Research Committee for permission to conduct this research and to the Summer Institute of Linguistics (Papua New Guinea Branch) for invaluable material aid. I am especially grateful to the Haruai people for their hospitality and enthusiastic support of my work on their language. My fieldwork on Haruai was carried out in 1985-86.

I will first introduce the languages that are going to play a role in what follows. The main protagonist will be the Haruai language, spoken by about 1000 speakers in the Schrader Ranges, on the northern fringe of the Highlands of Papua New Guinea. In some earlier literature, Haruai is referred to as Wiyaw, Waibuk, and even (confusingly, as will become immediately apparent) Kobon, but I will stick to the term Haruai, which is also the usual self-designation of the speakers. Haruai's neighbor to the east is Kobon, a completely different language from Haruai and not even remotely mutually intelligible with it; Kobon grammar is described comprehensively in Davies (1981), and I have also had access to John Davies's unpublished Kobon lexical materials. Further east still is Kalam, a language clearly genetically related to Kobon. Going even further to the east is Gants, apparently a more distant relative of Kobon and Kalam in what might be called the Kalamic family (named after its most populous member), although I have virtually no material on this language, and it will not figure in what follows.

Haruai's neighbor, or neighbors, to the west is a language which has come in the recent literature to be called Hagahai, although its speakers usually refer to themselves by more local designations, such as Aramo (the group contiguous with the Haruai) and Pinai; the speech of all these groups seems, however, to be mutually intelligible, while none of them are mutually intelligible with Haruai (or any language of the Kalamic family). Further still to the east is an uninhabited area, and beyond this the language Arafundi (Alfendio). The inclusion of Arafundi might seem rather strange, since Arafundi does not belong to the cultural area of the other languages and is basically not currently in contact with them, nor is it known to have been in contact with them recently. The reason for including Arafundi will become clear later.

Finally, one should note two other languages that have intruded into this region in the Schraders. One is Tok Pisin, a pidgin with a predominantly English lexical base that is the lingua franca of most of Papua New Guinea and which is widely spoken as a second or third language in this area. The other is English, which however plays a minimal role among the Haruai, or did so when I lived among them in the mid-1980s; English, other than in its contribution through Tok Pisin, will play little role in what follows.

The approximate distribution of the indigenous languages is as follows:

← To Arafundi	[Unin-habited]	Aramo Pinai	Haruai	Kobon	Kalam	Gants

Table 1

2. The genetic affiliation of Haruai

The first kinds of materials that were available for Haruai, as for many other languages of Papua New Guinea and elsewhere, were basic wordlists, in this area for the most part following a list worked out by the Summer Institute of Linguistics as being particularly suitable for New Guinea. Davies and Comrie (1984) present wordlists of this kind for Haruai and a number of other languages of the area, and calculate percentages of "look-alikes" among translation equivalents. It should be emphasized that the criterion was simply that of phonetic similarity; given that virtually nothing was known about some of the languages beyond these lists, and that the detailed reliability of some of the entries was questionable (most were impressionistic phonetic transcriptions), no attempt was made to do anything beyond this, e.g. to establish regular phonetic correspondences. The method, however, is essentially the same as that advocated by Greenberg. On the basis of similarities, a table of percentages of look-alikes for each pair of languages was compiled. The percentages for the languages that are most central to our discussion are reproduced in Table 2.[2]

	Pinai 1	Pinai 2	Aramo	Haruai	Kobon
Hagahai					
Nangenuwetan	75	82	63	29	16
Pinai 1		88	68	33	17
Pinai 2			70	36	18
Aramo				37	19
Haruai					35

Table 2

By inspection from this table of look-alikes, we can confirm that the three Hagahai varieties seem to be lexically very close, confirming the impression gained from their mutual intelligibility. Equally, one sees that Kobon is lexically quite distinct from the Hagahai varieties. But the interesting result is the position of Haruai. It shares roughly equal percentages of look-alikes with both Hagahai (29-37%) and with Kobon (35%). But if Hagahai and Kobon are not, by this evidence, closely genetically related, then how can one place Haruai, where the percentages might suggest that it is plausible to investigate genetic relations to either side?

Fortunately, a more detailed investigation of Haruai, and some investigation of the Hagahai variety Aramo, facilitates a ready solution to one part of the dilemma. Table 3 below gives the personal pronouns in four languages, in the leftmost two and the rightmost two columns.

---

[2] It should be noted that Arafundi and Kalam were, unfortunately, not included in this survey. Nangenuwetan is apparently another local variety of Hagahai. Pinai 1 and Pinai 2 refer to two locations where speakers identify themselves as Pinai.

		Haruai	Aramo	Proto-Piawi	Kobon	Kalam
Sg	1	n, nŋ, ngö	ŋgö	*n	yad	yad
	2	naŋ, nagö	naγö	*na	ne	nad
	3	nwŋʷ, nwgʷö	nöγwö	*nw	nipe	nwk
Du	1	= Pl	= Pl	= Pl	hol	ct
	2	= Pl	= Pl	= Pl	= Pl	nt
Pl	1	an, anŋ, angö	aŋgö	*an	hon	cn
	2	= 3	= 3	= 3	= 3	nb
	3	ñŋ, ñgö	ñeγö	*ñ	köl	kyk

Table 3

In all the languages, incidentally, the third person dual forms are identical to the third person plural. The Haruai and Aramo forms are very close to one another, indeed they are as similar as dialect variants in some pairs of speech varieties elsewhere in the world. The Haruai variant forms are all in use, with the longer forms being generally somewhat more emphatic than the shorter forms. Noting this fact and comparing the Haruai and Aramo forms, it is possible to reconstruct a plausible common ancestor for the pronominal forms in the two languages, and this is the middle column in Table 3; following a suggestion that predates Comrie (1988), I will refer to the family containing Haruai and Hagahai as Piawi. The Kobon and Kalam forms are certainly not as close to one another as are the Haruai and Aramo forms, and it is puzzling to find identical first person singular forms with a fair amount of diversity elsewhere, although even some of the diversity suggests possible sound correspondences, including the intriguing initial *h-c* one, given the phonetic difference between the two sounds. While these data might not in themselves clinch a genetic relation between Kobon and Kalam, they certainly do not contradict it. There are some intriguing similarities between either Kalam and Piawi (e.g. in the third person singular), or between Kobon and Piawi (e.g. the first person plural), but the only striking similarity across the whole set is in the second person singular. At any rate, the pronoun forms suggest that at the very least Haruai is much closer to Aramo, i.e. Hagahai, than it is to Kobon.

The striking similarity observed in Table 3 between Haruai and Aramo is repeated when we examine verb conjugation. (Haruai has, incidentally, virtually no noun morphology; only a few kinship terms have possessed forms, sometimes suppletive.) In Table 4 below are listed the three main tense forms, for each person-number combination, in Haruai and Aramo, based on Comrie (1988).[3] The

---

[3] For further discussion and slight reservations concerning the Aramo forms (which are here given some analysis parallel to that adopted for Haruai), reference should be made to Comrie (1988), but no significant effects affecting the general argument arise from the slight simplifi-

verb chosen is *w* 'go'. The two languages show striking similarities in their verb morphology, both for the indication of tense and for the indication of person-number (which, interestingly, shows virtually no similarity to the forms of the personal pronouns, i.e. is presumably ancient morphological material and not the result of recent grammaticalization). In both languages, in affirmative declarative clauses where the verb is sentence-final (the usual word order), a final -*a* is added to the verb form, before which a final vowel drops; the forms given here are thus those that would be found, for instance, in questions. Tense suffixes can be identified, but they are not the same for all person-numbers. Thus, in the present tense the first and second persons singular have -*l*, the third person singular -Ø, and the first person plural -*öl*; the second/third person plural forms seem to show Haruai -*öl*, Aramo -*l* (before palatalization; see below). In the past tense, both languages have -*m* except in the third person singular, where they diverge. The future has the suffix -*n* in first and second persons singular, -*ön* in third person singular and in second/third person plural, while the languages diverge in having Haruai -*n*, Aramo -*ön* in the first person plural; but even more strikingly, all the future forms involve palatalization of the stem-final consonant. The person-number suffix system is interesting in that most forms actually have no person-number suffix, but the person-number of the subject is nonetheless generally retrievable (somewhat less so in Aramo than in Haruai) from the variation in the form of the tense suffix. Both languages have consistently -*ö* for second person singular. Both languages consistently mark second/third person plural by means of palatalizing the word-final consonant (and here there is a similarity to the pronouns, cf. Table 3). Only the first plural suffix -*ŋ*, found in the past and future tenses only in Haruai, has no equivalent in Aramo.

		Haruai	Aramo
Present			
Sg	1	w-l	w-l
	2	w-l-ö	w-l-ö
	3	w	w
Pl	1	w-öl	w-öl
	2-3	w-öy	w-y

cation presented here. Note that in both languages, one form is used for second and third persons plural (as with the personal pronouns).

		Haruai	Aramo
Past			
Sg	1	w-m	w-m
	2	w-m-ö	w-m-ö
	3	w-öŋ	w̃-a
Pl	1	w-m-ŋ	w-m
	2-3	w-m̃	w-m̃
Future			
Sg	1	y-n	w̃-n
	2	y-n-ö	w̃-n-ö
	3	y-ön	w̃-ön
Pl	1	y-n-ŋ	w̃-ön
	2-3	y-öñ	w̃-öñ

Table 4

In sum, the verb morphologies of Haruai and Aramo are strikingly similar, involving a fair number of shared idiosyncrasies that are the very stuff of comparative linguistics. They are impressionistically at least as close to one another as, say, Spanish and Italian, and could hardly receive any interpretation other than genetic affiliation.

In Table 5 below some comparative information from Kobon and Kalam is added, though taking into account only person-number suffixes. The Haruai and Aramo columns simply repeat information given in Table 4. But what we note given this additional information is the striking similarity between the Kobon and Kalam forms. Indeed, these two languages also exhibit a degree of similarity that is at least as close impressionistically as that between Spanish and Italian. The forms are often identical;[4] many of those that are not provide further evidence for regular sound correspondences, e.g. between Kobon word-final *l* and Kalam word-final *t*, a correspondence we might already have suspected on the basis of the first person dual personal pronouns. But equally striking is the lack of any similarity between the Piawi languages on the one hand and the Kalamic languages on the other. Of course, both have zero in the third person singular, but this is a widespread phenomenon cross-linguistically, and certainly no basis for positing genetic relationships. Otherwise, the two languages are about as different as can be. To this we can add that the Kalamic languages have no equivalent of the variation in form of the tense suffix that is found in the Piawi languages.

---

[4] Note that the difference between Kobon *i* and Kalam *y*, and between Kobon *u* and Kalam *w*, is essentially transcriptional; the phonetic reality is the same.

		Haruai	Aramo	Kobon	Kalam
Sg	1	-Ø	-Ø	-in	-yn
	2	-ö	-ö	-an	-an
	3	-Ø	-Ø	-Ø	-Ø
Du	1	= Pl	= Pl	-ul	-wt
	2/3	= Pl	= Pl	-ɨl	-yt
Pl	1	-ŋ, -Ø	-Ø	-un	-wn
	2	= 3	= 3	-im	-m
	3	palatalization	palatalization	-al	-ay

Table 5

The above data on personal pronouns and especially on verb morphology are sufficient to demonstrate that, of the languages considered here, there are two groupings, one including the Piawi languages, the other including the Kalamic languages. While it cannot be conclusively disproven that these two groupings are genetically related to one another, there is certainly no verb morphology evidence that they are, and only minimal evidence from the personal pronouns that might be interpreted to point in the direction of a genetic affiliation. We may therefore summarize the genetic status of Haruai as follows.

Haruai and Hagahai are closely related languages, forming the Piawi family. Kobon and Kalam are closely related languages, forming (with Gants) the Kalamic family. There is no demonstrable genetic link between the Piawi and Kalamic language families. The question then arises of why Haruai shows a similar percentage of lexical look-alikes with Kobon as it does with Hagahai. The obvious solution would seem to be that, even if we allow for a small percentage of look-alikes between Haruai and Kobon as reflecting a distant genetic relationship, and a small percentage as being the result of chance, the bulk of the similarities are the result of borrowing. The direction of borrowing is clearly from Kobon into Haruai, since the borrowed words are shared by Kobon and Haruai but not in general by Hagahai. (Ideally, they should also be shared by Kalam, but I have not investigated this in detail.) This still leaves the problem of why there should be such a high percentage of loans, a question to which we return in section 4.

3. Indirect evidence

So far, all the evidence presented has been linguistic, and I would emphasize that this evidence is sufficient to justify the conclusions reached in section 2. However, there are other kinds of evidence that fit in well with the linguistic evidence presented in section 2, and moreover suggest the possibility of coming up with an even more specific hypothesis, much of which, however, is independent of the linguistic argumentation. There is nonlinguistic evidence that the Haruai, but not the Kobon, are relatively recent incomers to the part of the Highlands where they now live. According to medical evidence collected by Dr. Carol Jenkins of the Papua New Guinea Institute of Health, serogenetic evidence derived from HLA (human lymphocyte antigen) studies points clearly to Lowland affinities for both the Haruai and the Hagahai, even though most Haruai currently live at around 6,000 feet above sea level. Haruai are on average physically distinguishable from their Kobon neighbors by being taller – though it should be emphasized that this is a relative measure; no Haruai that I met matched even my 5 feet 6 inches/1.68 meters – and darker skinned; in general, darker pigmentation and taller stature correlate with lower altitude. There are also cultural differences: the traditional Haruai marriage is by elopement by mutual consent of bride and groom (see also section 4), whereas among the Kobon marriages are traditionally arranged by the families concerned (though requiring the final consent of bride and groom). All of this would suggest that the Haruai (and presumably the Hagahai) have moved from a more Lowland location to their present Highland one, and would thus fit in with the fact that their language is not demonstrably related to that of their neighbors the Kobon. To this we can add one piece of linguistic evidence. William A. Foley, of the University of Sydney, when shown my Haruai pronoun forms felt they bear nontrivial relations to those of Arafundi. Since the Arafundi are in a sense the neighbors of the Hagahai and Haruai, though now separated from them by uninhabited land and not in regular contact with them, the pieces add up to a consistent pattern of a more Lowland origin for the Haruai. But more work will need to be done to confirm the details – and indeed the general drift – of this hypothesis.

4. Word taboo

I will now return to the question of why Haruai has apparently borrowed so much of its vocabulary from Kobon, replacing more original vocabulary (given that these same concepts have denoting expressions in all languages of the area, including Hagahai). I will argue that the relevant motive force is that of word taboo, and it will therefore be necessary first of all to explain how word taboo works in Haruai, especially as there has been controversy with respect to other languages whether word taboo can lead to substantial, permanent lexical replacement across a community.

In Haruai society, one is not allowed to say the name of one's cross-cousin (i.e. one's father's sister's or one's mother's brother's children) or of one's in-laws. As with most other taboos in Haruai society, there is no explicit social sanction against violation of this word taboo – though children considered below the age of discretion will be warned, as part of their socialization – but adherence to the taboos is general because of beliefs that violation of taboos might cause one to become sick, might cause one's crops to fail, etc., all of which discourages experimentation.

Most personal names, both traditionally and in contemporary Haruai society, are also ordinary words. (Most Haruai also have nicknames, and many also have Christian names which they will usually present to Europeans, but all also have a real name, not considered particularly secret, but also not bandied about trivially.) Thus, if a person has a taboo relative whose name is identical to that of an ordinary lexical item, as will nearly always be the case, that person is also forbidden to use that lexical item, but must find a substitute. The taboo also applies to lexical morphemes contained within a word, but not to nonlexical morphemes. Thus, the taboo relatives of a man called *önöŋ-sö*, literally 'mountain-up', were forbidden to say *önöŋ*, but could freely use the demonstrative clitic *-sö*. In at least some cases, the taboo can extend to a homophone, as in one case known to me where a taboo against the indigenous lexical item *cöc* 'tobacco' was extended to the homophonous *cöc* 'church', a loan from English. Crucially, tabooed words must be replaced. Moreover, as far as I am aware tabooing is permanent. In other words, if I am not allowed to use a particular word because I have an elderly in-law called by that name, the subsequent death of that individual does not free up use of the word in question for me. This is different from what I take to be the usual situation reported in Australia, for instance, where a person's name and similar sounding words may be tabooed at that person's death, but after a certain period of time are allowed back into usage.

Since one has to replace tabooed lexical items, word taboo has clear linguistic repercussions. At present, most replacement seems to be done by borrowing the corresponding word from Kobon. Thus, one of my language consultants was forbidden by word taboo from using the word *wrap* 'medium-sized game mammal', and simply replaced it with the Kobon equivalent *wal*. Somewhat less commonly, words might be borrowed from Tok Pisin: for instance, the person referred to above who was not allowed to say *cöc* 'church' simply replaced it with the Tok Pisin equivalent *haus lotu*.[5]

Although I have presented word taboo so far as being the process of replacing a word once it becomes tabooed, this is actually a simplification. Especially given the traditional pattern of marriage by elopement by mutual consent, one could in principle be faced with the situation where one of one's close relatives, e.g. a brother, has run off and got married, and one is suddenly faced with an array of new in-laws expecting that their names will be tabooed. Of course, one imagines that the community would often have its suspicions about developing romantic attachments, but even during my year spent among the Haruai one such incident occurred where this was not the case. Given this, it is perhaps not surprising that for a large number of concepts Haruai speakers maintain synonyms, in the literal sense, i.e. words with exactly the same denotation but which can in principle be

---

[5] Tok Pisin *haus* is of course from English *house*; *lotu* is an Austronesian word meaning 'worship'.

used interchangeably. Typically, one is the traditional Haruai word, the other a loan from Kobon. Thus, some speakers I encountered alternated between Haruai *wöñö* and Kobon *kayn* 'dog' or between Haruai *nayö* and Kobon *sdö* 'sun'.[6] If one suddenly acquires a new taboo relative and requires replacement of one of these lexical items, the synonym is available as a substitute. Linguists have often argued over whether a language can have true synonyms. Haruai does have true synonyms, but they serve a clear function, namely as an escape hatch in cases of "acquired" word taboo.

One final observation is necessary concerning word taboo. The Haruai speech community is small, about 1000 people, so that a particular word taboo can potentially affect a significant proportion of the speech community. In sum, my hypothesis is that word taboo in Haruai has given rise to an accelerated rate of lexical replacement, this replacement taking place primarily by borrowing from Kobon; whence the current situation where the percentage of basic vocabulary from Kobon roughly matches the inherited vocabulary shared with Hagahai. Crucially, the objections that have been raised against word taboo as a factor in societal lexical replacement in other languages do not apply in the case of Haruai. The society is sufficiently small for such word taboo to affect a significant proportion of the speech community. The permanence of word taboo means that replacement is for ever for those affected. And the possibility of the sudden need to replace vocabulary has apparently led to the observed situation where the language harbors a large number of exact synonym pairs.

5. Word taboo, lexical replacement, and the methodology of comparative linguistics

It is now time to draw together the various strands that have been introduced so far in order to confront the question that started our discussion, namely whether the Haruai situation is consistent with the methodology set out by Greenberg (1957).

We can start with the question whether it is possible to establish the genetic affiliation of Haruai. I think that the answer to this is unequivocally affirmative, at least at the lower levels of the family tree. As I tried to show in section 2, the verb morphology of Haruai shows clearly that Haruai is closely related genetically to Hagahai, constituting the Piawi family, while Kobon is closely related genetically to Kalam, forming (part of) the Kalamic family; there is no clear evidence of genetic relationship between these two families. Thus, Haruai is unequivocally genetically much closer to Hagahai than it is to Kobon.

---

[6] The form *sdö* is actually the phonemic representation of the Haruai pronunciation; John Davies analyzes the Kobon form as *sɨdo*. Phonetically the two are effectively identical.

A second question is whether we can identify Kobon loans in Haruai, and the answer is again affirmative, or at least affirmative in a good proportion of the cases.[7] In clear cases, the word must be found in Kobon and Haruai, but not in Hagahai. (Note that a word found in all three presumably cannot be excluded as a loan, since it might have been borrowed further from Haruai into Hagahai; but it cannot serve as evidence of a loan, since the possibility of a more distant genetic relationship between the Piawi and Kalamic languages cannot be ruled out.) In the clearest cases, the Haruai form will be identical or virtually identical to the Kobon form, pace differences between the phoneme inventories of the two languages, thus suggesting that the similarities are indicative of borrowing rather than of a close genetic relationship (given that the pronoun and especially the morphological evidence excludes the possibility of a close genetic relationship). By discrepancies in phoneme systems I mean, for instance, the fact that Kobon distinguishes three laterals, whereas Haruai has only one; not surprisingly, the laterals are neutralized in loans. Beyond this, there are some substitutions that are frequently made in Kobon loans into Haruai but that are not absolutely required by the Haruai phoneme system. For instance, the Kobon vowel *a* is often replaced by the Kobon vowel *ö* (a low mid central vowel); here the motivation may be that *ö* is by far the most common Haruai vowel, whereas Haruai *a* is often derived from the fusion of two adjacent instances of *ö* in morphological structure. Finally, the pattern is strengthened if the Haruai and Kobon forms are (almost) identical but the Kalam form is more different (including completely different); given that Kalam and Kobon are genetically related languages, and Haruai is at best more distantly related, one would expect, other things being equal and in the absence of borrowing, that Kobon forms would be closer to Kalam forms than to Haruai forms.

We may now turn to the crucial question that motivated this article. Given all of the above, is it the case that loans from Kobon into Haruai are restricted to particular semantic domains? This is crucial because in particular cases the other criteria might not be available, for instance if we are investigating two languages neither of which has any close linguistic relatives. Let us therefore discuss the Haruai loans from Kobon from this viewpoint.

First, there are some semantic domains where Haruai seems particularly open to loans from Kobon, often going beyond those involved in word taboo. For instance, some items relating to the outside world have entered Haruai from Kobon, such as the Haruai word *brwd* 'white person, European'. In Haruai the word may

---

[7] One problem is that there is, alas, no dictionary of Hagahai. And although those working on Kalam, under the guidance of Andrew K. Pawley, formerly at the University of Auckland, now at the Australian National University, have shared with me extensive Kalam lexical materials, I have not yet been able to consult a comprehensive Kalam dictionary.

be unanalyzable,[8] but its Kobon etymon is simply *bɨ* 'person', *rud* 'white'. However, it should be noted that it is much more normal for such terms to be taken from Tok Pisin. The other identifiable semantic domain is kinship terms. While some Haruai-speakers have adopted a fair amount of Kobon kinship terminology, there are two Kobon terms that seem to be particularly widespread. One is Kobon *bane* 'wife's brother, sister's husband, husband's sister, brother's wife', rephonologized as *bönöy* in Haruai and used as a substitute for a number of indigenous in-law terms, including some that are not covered by the Kobon term (at least in the variety of Kobon investigated by John Davies); some younger speakers are even unsure of the denotations of the traditional Haruai terms. Kobon *bap* 'father', in the form *böp*, also seems to be beginning to replace Haruai *acö*. Of course, borrowing of kin terms is known from elsewhere – Maltese, for instance, has borrowed its word *missier* 'father' from Romance – but if one were trying to identify borrowing by identifying semantic domains, kin terms are probably not an obvious choice.

And of course the fact is that, outside this couple of domains, Haruai shows loans from Kobon that go across the whole of the lexicon divided into semantic domains. Indeed, as observed in section 2, lexical replacement has gone so far that Haruai has as much of its basic vocabulary in common with Kobon as it has with Hagahai. Examples of basic vocabulary items that are shared by Haruai and Kobon but not by Hagahai (on the basis of the lists in Davies and Comrie (1984)) include, for instance: Haruai *ram*, Kobon *ram* 'house'; Haruai *rmj*, Kobon *rɨmɨd* 'ear'; Haruai *hödal*, Kobon *hadal* 'wind (breeze)'. In general, in Haruai it is not possible to identify particular semantic domains that have been affected by borrowing from Kobon; such borrowing pervades the whole lexicon.

6. Conclusion

The methodology set out by Greenberg (1957) is clearly an important step in our understanding of the methodology of comparative linguistics, since it sets out clearly and explicitly a number of principles that have often been followed tacitly in trying to distinguish between similarities due to genetic affiliation and to language contact. What I have tried to show is that it is not possible to maintain all of these principles simultaneously, and more particularly I have tried to show in the case of Haruai that one must reject the claim that borrowing will always be identifiable through its restriction to particular semantic domains. But let me reiterate two important considerations.

---

[8] But I did note *mö rwd* 'white woman' from one speaker, where *mö* is the ordinary Haruai word for 'woman'. Note that *rwd* is not, to my knowledge, otherwise used for 'white' in Haruai; the normal word is *age*, also the name of a white species of cockatoo – I have no direct evidence which sense is original.

First, I do not think that there is any doubt about the immediate genetic affiliations of Haruai. Morphological evidence clearly points to Hagahai and away from Kobon and other Kalamic languages. But of course this is precisely what makes Haruai an important test case: Given that we can be reasonably sure of its genetic affiliation on the basis of certain criteria, we can test the validity of criteria whose basis is less solidly proven.

Second, the failure of the semantic domain criterion relates to a number of particular features of the Haruai situation, in particular of Haruai word taboo. The nature of Haruai word taboo means that a high proportion of the lexicon is likely to be targeted, irrespective of semantic domain.[9] The small size of the community means that taboo replacements are likely to affect considerable segments of Haruai society, rather than just isolated individuals. And finally, the permanence of the taboo means that for the affected individuals the replaced lexical item does not subsequently reappear: the replacement is for ever. It is this particular combination that makes the Haruai case so interesting. Not having studied word taboo as a general phenomenon or in a variety of other languages, I would not venture to say how typical the Haruai situation is. However, when we bear in mind that for most of human history our ancestors were small bands of hunter-gatherers, the possibility of such a situation as we find today in the sedentary agriculturalist Haruai certainly cannot be excluded as a widespread possibility in earlier periods.

Max Planck Institute for Evolutionary Anthropology

REFERENCES

Comrie, Bernard
1988   "Haruai verb structure and language classification in the Upper Yuat", *Language and Linguistics in Melanesia* 17, 140-160.
1989   "Genetic classification, contact, and variation", in: Thomas J. Walsh (ed.), *Synchronic and diachronic approaches to linguistic variation and change* (*Georgetown University Round Table on Languages and Linguistics* 1988), 81-93. Washington DC: Georgetown University Press.

Davies, John
1981   *Kobon* (*Lingua Descriptive Studies* 3). Amsterdam: North-Holland.

---

[9] Although the lexical items constituting or included in most Haruai speakers' personal names are nouns, I have encountered at least one case of a verb being tabooed because someone's name is a verb form. Haruai has, incidentally, a rather restricted set of basic verbs, with widespread use of serial verb constructions. The set of adjectives is also very restricted, and while I have not encountered anyone whose name is an adjective, there seems no principled reason why this should be excluded.

Davies, John, and Bernard Comrie
   1984   "A linguistic survey of the Upper Yuat", *Papers in New Guinea linguistics* 22, 275-312.
Greenberg, Joseph H.
   1957   "Genetic relationship among languages", in: Joseph H. Greenberg (ed.), *Essays in linguistics*, 35-45. Chicago: University of Chicago Press.

Languages in Contact, edited by D.G. Gilbers, J. Nerbonne, and J. Schaeken (= *Studies in Slavic and General Linguistics*, vol. 28), 87-98. Amsterdam - Atlanta, GA: Rodopi, 2000.

DUPLICATION IN THE L2 SPANISH PRODUCED BY QUECHUA-SPEAKING CHILDREN: TRANSFER OF A PRAGMATIC STRATEGY

ELLEN COURTNEY

Introduction

Quechua and Spanish, languages long in contact throughout the Andes, are particularly interesting partners in bilingual speech because the word order patterns of Quechua exactly mirror those of Spanish: while Quechua is uniformly left-branching for all maximal projections, Spanish is generally right-branching.[1] Hence, the canonical ordering of major constituents in Quechua is SOV, whereas, in Spanish, the basic surface order is SVO. The L2 Spanish produced by Quechua-speaking children in Peru has yielded intriguing observations of interlanguage phenomena, with corresponding speculation concerning early syntactic development in the second language. In work exploring the development of Spanish word order in young native speakers of Quechua (Minaya and Luján 1982; Luján, Minaya, and Sankoff 1984), for example, it was reported that children frequently produced "hybrid" (S)VOV structures. To account for these odd constructions, Minaya and Luján proposed that the children had a transitional grammar with a nonadult phrase structure rule: VP → VP V. They further maintained, in support of this proposal, that the pattern was idiosyncratic of the children's interlanguage, since it could not be derived from either of the participating languages, Quechua and Spanish.

This study presents a vigorous challenge to these claims. First, the reduplicative pattern is very much alive in the Quechua spoken by both adults and children, who duplicate, presumably for emphatic effect, not only verbs but also subjects, objects, adjunct expressions, negative forms – even entire phrases. It will thus be shown that the appearance of the VOV pattern in child L2 Spanish clearly represents transfer of a discourse-pragmatic strategy and not a transitional, nonadult, hybrid grammar.[2]

---

[1] Appreciation is extended to the Spencer Foundation and to Paul Bloom, recipient of the grant, for funding of the 1996 fieldwork undertaken for this study.

[2] In fairness to Minaya and Luján, the authors mentioned in their conclusion that purely pragmatic factors might be at work in the duplication of sentence elements; nevertheless, the thrust of their analysis, which constituted the body of their paper, was the hypothesized hybrid phrase structure.

The problem with the proposed grammatical rule is that it allows two identical Verb heads: VP → V (NP) V. Such a rule violates basic principles governing the syntax of all languages, no matter which analytic framework one might adopt. For example, the rule clashes with the Theta Criterion, a crucial principle in Government and Binding Theory (Chomsky 1981) that constrains the assignment of thematic roles by a Verb to its arguments. Accordingly, each Noun Phrase must receive one and only one thematic role from the Verb, and each thematic role must be assigned to one and only one Noun Phrase. The two-headed VP rule is at odds with this principle of one-to-one assignment of thematic roles. Which Verb assigns a thematic role to the direct object? If the first Verb theta-marks the direct object, what becomes of the thematic role the second Verb has to assign? The proposal is all the more alarming given the consensus among acquisition researchers that children do not exhibit "wild grammars"; that is, they do not violate universal constraints on the formation of sentences (Goodluck 1986). Nonetheless, Minaya and Luján attribute to the children a transitional grammatical rule which would be illicit for every language in the world. It is time to put their theory to rest.

The (1982) Minaya and Luján study

In the Minaya and Luján study, the corpus of Spanish utterances produced spontaneously by the Quechua-speaking children was divided into three sub-corpora according to age (5, 7, and 9 years), with each sub-corpus consisting of over 500 sentences. The VOV pattern appeared very frequently in the utterances produced by the five-year-olds (24.7%), and it gradually declined in frequency in the sentences produced by the older children (16.2% for the seven-year-olds; 7.5% for the nine-year-olds). In fact, on the basis of this outcome, the authors predicted that three-year-olds would produce the VOV pattern in 34% of their sentence. Among the utterances produced by the children, the following examples were reported, here renumbered as (1)-(3) for convenience.

(1)   *De Puno traemos hartas ocas traemos.*   V-O-V [280: (19)]
        From Puno we bring a lot of *ocas* we bring
        'We bring a lot of *ocas* from Puno.'

(2)   *Conozco los cabritos conozco.*   V-O-V [280: (20)]
        I know the little goats I know
        'I know the little goats.'

(3)   *En acá no más es su pensión en acá.*   Adv-V-S-Adv [284: (33)]
        In here no more is his *pension* in here
        'His *pension* is right here.'

As previously mentioned, the authors accounted for sentences such as these by allowing for the following two-headed configuration for the VP in the children's transitional grammar (285: 40c).

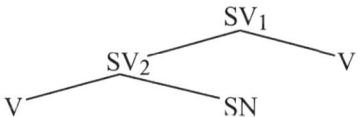

Even if such a configuration were plausible, it could account only for the Verb Phrases in (1) and (2) above, but not for the duplicated adverbial phrase in (3), which occurs after the postverbal Subject NP *su pensión* 'his pension'. Clearly, an exclusively syntactic account of the duplication phenomenon is elusive.

Missing from the Minaya and Luján account is any reference to possible processing factors in child production of duplicated forms. For example, several analyses have pointed to nonsyntactic factors in the occasional double-AUX errors produced by English-speaking children, e.g., *Can he can go?* (Menyuk 1969, Prideaux 1976, Mayer, Erreich and Valian 1978, Maratsos and Kuczaj 1978, Nakayama 1987). Nearly twenty years ago, Menyuk suggested that children may duplicate elements to ensure that the structures they are producing are fully understood. In a later study, Nakayama proposed the Syntactic Blends Hypothesis (SBH) to account for duplication errors. Accordingly, very young speakers of English may forget which of two competing forms they have selected for production, e.g., *Can he go* and *He can go*, consequently blending the two in an utterance with a duplicated auxiliary. Importantly, for Nakayama the error is a processing phenomenon which occurs when the demands of sentence production exceed children's processing capacity.

The SBH proposal would work for sentences such as (1) above, provided that the following two sentences were both acceptable in Spanish: *(De Puno) traemos hartas ocas* and *(De Puno) hartas ocas traemos.* The latter variant, with OV word order, is ill-formed in standard Spanish. However, Muysken (1984) provides evidence that sentences with OV word order are quite typical of vernacular varieties of Andean Spanish; in that case, both forms might be acceptable variants for the Peruvian children in the Minaya and Luján study. Nevertheless, there are two further considerations which lead one to abandon the SBH proposal as a plausible explanation. First, the incidence of the VOV pattern is very high; that is, the percentage of such errors in the Minaya and Luján corpus is probably too great to attribute to processing pressures during production. Second, the subjects in the study are much older than the three- to five-year-olds observed in the Nakayama study. Even though the Quechua-speaking children are producing sentences in a second language, their overall processing capacity is no doubt greater than that of younger children; moreover, the VOV pattern occurs in sentences which are not syntactically complex. Clearly, other factors must be involved: a good candidate for consideration is the pragmatic function of duplication in the first language, Quechua.

Reduplication phenomena in adult Quechua

Adult speakers of Quechua duplicate diverse elements utterance-finally for emphatic effect. This is illustrated in (4)-(8) below, all showing utterances produced spontaneously by Quechua-speaking adults living in the Department of Arequipa in southern Peru. The sentences were produced by different speakers with varying levels of proficiency in Spanish. They are examples from two corpora of naturalistic speech, one recorded on the outskirts of the city of Arequipa in 1993 and the second, in the rural community of Chalhuanca (Caylloma Province) in 1996.

(4) *Tarpu - nku papa, cebada, hawas, q'ala - n - pacha tarpu - nku.*
     Grow   3 pl   potatoes barley   fabas   everything   grow   3 pl
     'They grow potatoes, barley, faba beans – everything.'
     V-O-V

(5) *Uña - ta lliq chichi - rqu - nqa uña - ta.*
     Lamb   Acc all   hail   Exhort 3 fut lamb Acc
     'It will hail on the lamb(s).'
     O-V-O

In (4)-(5), we find that adult Quechua speakers duplicate not only the verb but also the direct object NP. Examples (6)-(7) below exhibit duplication of the quantifier *tawa* 'four' and the negative question form *manachu* 'won't?'. Each of the diverse duplicated elements in these sentences is highlighted through repetition at the very end of the utterance.

(6) *Tawa wawa - y   tawa.*
     Four   child   Poss 1 sg   four
     'I have four children.'

(7) *Paqarin manachu waqa - chi - ra - mu - sunki manachu?*
     Tomorrow Neg   cry   Caus Exhort Dir 3>2   Neg
     'Tomorrow won't they make you cry?'

(8) *Noqa huch'uy maq'ta - lla ka - rqa - ni huch'uy maq't - ito.*
     I   little   boy   Delim be Past 1 sg little boy Dim
     'I was just a little boy.'

In (8), it is the predicate complement NP which is highlighted in this way. This utterance is particularly interesting, for it reveals that the duplicated element may differ in form from the initial expression of the element; it is not necessarily an exact replicate. The head of the initial NP, *maq'ta* 'boy', bears the Delimitative suffix *-lla* 'just', whereas the duplicated noun root exhibits the Diminutive suffix *-ito*, a suffix borrowed from Spanish. In fact, the duplicated constituent may even be a synonym, altogether different in form from the initial constituent. It is also important to note that there is sometimes a phonological break before the final constituent; at other times, no break is detected.

The corpora of adult utterances also yield instances of duplicated elements occurring in Spanish sentences as well as in utterances with intrasentential codeswitching from Quechua to Spanish. Typical monolingual Spanish utterances are presented in (9)-(12).

(9)   *Te   vamos a matar-te.*
         You go-1 pl to kill   you
         'We're going to kill you.'

(10)   *Y   ya   no es   loco ya.*
         And now no be-3 sg crazy now
         'And he isn't crazy any more.'

(11)   *Mi mamá era   quechua legítima era.*
         My mom   be-Past-3 Quechua legitimate be-Past-3
         'My mom was a legitimate Quechua.'

(12)   *Más frío hace   alla, más frío hace.*
         More cold make-3 there, more cold make-3 sg
         'It's colder there.'

In these sentences, diverse elements are highlighted through repetition at the end: pronominal clitics (9), adverbs (10), verbs (11), and entire phrases (12). In (12), the repeated phrase, *más frío hace* 'it's colder', exhibits Quechua-like OV word order; the equivalent in standard Spanish would be *hace más frío*, with the Verb first. The adults who produced these utterances are bilingual speakers of long standing. In their daily routine as inhabitants of one of Peru's largest cities, they make use of Spanish constantly in different domains. Why, then, should they be producing Spanish utterances with Quechua-like patterns of word order and duplication? As Muysken has explained, it may well have to do with the variety of Spanish spoken within the bilingual speech community. The particular variety of Spanish acquired by these adults may itself have permanently acquired interlanguage features, including the transferred discourse-pragmatic strategy of highlighting elements through duplication (Muysken 1984: 102):

"As time goes on, the products of intermediate and advanced interlanguage grammars are incorporated into the native speech community, but most often as vernacular, nonstandard forms. Within a synchronic perspective, then, native speakers of the target vernacular produce outputs which seem like interlanguage outputs."

In the final two examples of adult utterances, we find duplication in intra-sentential code-switching. Example (13) shows equivalent forms meaning 'there are', while (14) exhibits a sentence-final Spanish version of utterance-initial *ni-* 'say'.

(13)   <u>*Hay*</u>   *bastantes   fiestas*   <u>*ka - n.*</u>
        There are   many   holidays   there are
        'There are many holidays.'

(14)   <u>*Ni - wa - q - ku*</u>   *te va a pagar plata*   <u>*dice.*</u>
        Say 1 obj Agt 3 pl   you go-3 to pay money   say-3
        'They'd say to me, "He's going to pay you money."'

Code-switches such as these, occurring when the language partners exhibit contrasting word order, have been described in the literature as portmanteau forms (e.g. Nishimura 1986 for Japanese-English; Park, Troike, and Park 1993 for Korean-English). It seems plausible, given the monolingual Quechua and Spanish utterances produced by these bilingual speakers, that the code-switches reveal yet another instance of final repetition for emphatic effect.

Reduplication in child Quechua

Having established that adult speakers of Quechua produce utterances with high-lighted elements duplicated at the very end, we now turn to the spontaneous production of very young children. If it can be shown that Quechua-speaking children also produce VOV and other duplication patterns for emphatic effect, the sentences in the Minaya and Luján corpus are readily explained: they represent transfer of a purely pragmatic strategy in the early production of L2 Spanish sentences.

In what follows, the discussion will center on utterances produced by three children acquiring Quechua as their first language. The naturalistic speech of these children, ranging in age from 2;5 years to 3;5 years, was recorded in their home community of Chalhuanca (Caylloma Province) in the Department of Arequipa, Peru. The recordings yielded a total corpus of 640 utterances with at least two of the three canonical constituents, i.e. subject, verb, and complement. (In the following discussion, the term "complement" is used very loosely to refer to any case-marked nominal constituent, including objects, directional expressions, and adjuncts.) The youngest child, Ana, was recorded for approximately eleven hours between the ages of 2;5 and 2;10 years, yielding 336 utterances. For the purpose of analysis, these utterances are considered in three groups distributed according to age: 2;5-2;6 years; 2;7-2;8 years; and 2;9-2;10 years. (This division serves to elucidate the rapid, dramatic changes observed in the speech produced by this child over the six-month recording period.) The two older children, Hilda (2;10 to 3;1 years) and Ines (3;2 to 3;5 years), were each recorded for approximately five hours. Recordings of these children yielded 145 utterances for Hilda and 159 utterances for Ines.

Analysis of the speech samples reveals that all three children highlighted utterance-initial elements by repeating them at the very end. They duplicated subjects, verbs, and different types of complements. Even the earliest utterances produced by Ana at ages 2;5 to 2;6 years exhibited duplicative emphasis of diverse constituent types. Examples (15)-(19) all show instances of duplicated subjects in the children's utterances.

(15)   Ana (2;5-2;6)   *Noqa   ma_cha-ku-sa_   noqa.*
                          I   fear   Refl 1 fut   I
                          'I am afraid.'

(16)   Ana (2;6-2;7)   *Lokacha   calle-pi   lokacha.*
                          Crazy   street-Loc   crazy
                          'The crazy one is in the street'

(17)   Ana (2;9-2;10)   *Awilita   mana ranti-pu-wa-n-chu   mamachi.*
                          Grandma Neg   buy Ben 1 obj 3 Neg   grandma
                          'Grandma didn't buy (it) for me.'

(18)   Hilda (2;10-3;1) *Chay - lla   saya - sha - n   chay - lla.*
                          That-Delim   stand   Prog   3   that-Delim
                          'Just that one is standing.'

(19)   Ines (3;2-3;5)   *Qan - qa   wayk'u - nki   qan - qa.*
                          You-Top   cook   2 sg   you-Top
                          'You will cook.'

Utterance (17) is intriguing, since the final element is actually a synonym of the first, rather than an exact replicate. Utterances such as these suggest that highlighting through end repetition is a purely pragmatic strategy, since there is no way to account for such synonymic duplication syntactically. In addition to subjects, all three children duplicated different types of complements. This is shown in (20)-(24).

(20)   Ana (2;5-2;6)   Duplication of Accusative Object:
                          Sara - ta   mama - y   apa - ku - sha - n   sara - ta.
                          corn   Acc   mom-1 poss   take   Refl Prog 3   corn   Acc
                          'My mom is taking the corn.'

(21)   Ana (2;7-2;8)   Duplication of Dative Object:
                         Tata - y - man toka - chi - saq   *tata - y - man.*
                         Dad 1 poss Dat   play   Caus   1 fut   dad 1 poss Dat
                         'I'll make my dad play (it).'

(22)   Ana (2;9-2;10)   Duplication of Directional Complement:
                         Chay *kay - ta*   hamu - sha - n   *kay - ta.*
                         That   this   Acc   come   Prog   3   this   Acc
                         'That is coming here.'

(23)   Hilda (2;10-3;1) Duplication of Accusative Object:
                         Pakocha - ta - n   ruwa - saq   *pakocha - ta.*
                         Alpaca   Acc   Ev   do   1 fut   alpaca   Acc
                         'I'll tend the alpacas.'

(24)   Ines (3;2-3;5)   Duplication of Infinitival Complement:
                         Graba-ku-y-ta   muna-ni kay-ta *graba-ku-y-ta*   ni-n.
                         Tape-Refl-Inf-Acc   want-1 sg   this-Acc tape-Refl-Inf-Acc   say-3
                         'He said, "I want to tape this."'

In this sequence, (24), produced by the oldest child, is especially interesting since
the duplicated infinitive occurs within the embedded sentential complement of the
verb *ni-* 'say'. All three children also highlighted verbs through duplication. The
utterances in (25)-(27) are among those produced by Ana at different ages.

(25)   Ana (2;5-2;6)   *Pasa - n* calli - pi   *pasa - n.*
                         Pass   3   street-Loc   pass   3
                         'He passes in the street.'

(26)   Ana (2;7-2;8)   *Puklla - sa*   noqa   *puklla - sa.*
                         Play   1 fut   I   play   1 fut
                         'I'll play.'

(27)   Ana (2;9-2;10)   *Qhawa-chi-sun* chay-ta-qa Aurora-man   *qhawa-chi-sun*
                         Look-Caus-1pl fut that-Acc-Top Aurora-Dat   look-Caus-1 pl fut
                         'Let's show that to Aurora.'

Finally, we find utterances produced by all three children with entire phrases duplicated at the end. These present an enormous challenge to syntactic accounts of
the duplication phenomenon, since it appears not to matter whether the subject or
the complement is paired with the verb for duplicative highlighting. That is, a
speaker might choose to emphasize either S-V or C-V, with the remaining, non-
duplicated constituent(s) relegated to the background. This is shown in (28)-(30)
below.

(28)   Ana (2;9-2;10)   *Qolqe-ta   qo-wa-n*   *mana*   *qolqe-ta   qo-wa-n*.
                          Money-Acc give-1obj-3 Neg   money-Acc give-1obj-3
                          'He doesn't give me money.'

(29)   Hilda (2;10-3;1) *Ahina ka - sqa*   *pakocha-qa*   *ahina ka - sqa*.
                          Thus be-Result   alpaca   Top   thus   be-Result
                          'The alpaca was that way.'

(30)   Ines (3;2-3;5)   *Oso puri-sha-n*   *carretera-nta*   *oso puri-sha-n*.
                          Bear walk-Prog-3   highway-along   bear walk-Prog-3
                          'The bear is walking along the highway.'

In (28), Ana has duplicated the entire Verb-Object complex, which she has attempted to negate by inserting the Negative form *mana*. In (29), it is the VP which Hilda has repeated; that is, the verb and its modifier, *ahina* 'thus'. Finally, in (30), Ines has duplicated Subject+Verb, without repeating the directional complement of the verb, *carreteranta* 'along the highway'. One wonders how Minaya and Luján's two-headed VP could account for utterances such as these. Indeed, how would *any* purely syntactic analysis explain this type of duplication?

Concluding remarks

The foregoing analysis establishes duplication as a pragmatic strategy available in Quechua discourse for highlighting a variety of sentence constituents. It then comes as no surprise that Quechua-speaking children should transfer this strategy to Spanish. First, there is ample evidence in the literature on second language acquisition that learners commonly transfer L1 discourse and pragmatic features to the second language (e.g. Rutherford 1983, Kasper 1992). Rutherford, for example, has asserted that Japanese learners of English transfer both topic prominence and pragmatic word order.[3] Second, we have seen that even very young Quechua speakers highlight elements through duplication, and they must wish to emphasize or focus constituents when they speak Spanish. The means available to Spanish speakers for focusing constituents are no doubt difficult to acquire: clefted structures and clitic doubling, for example, must require considerable morphosyntactic competence. Examples of clefting and clitic doubling are shown in (31) and (32), respectively.

---

[3] Preliminary reports from native-speaking informants of Japanese and Korean, both rigidly verb-final languages, suggest that a limited set of constituent types may be duplicated after the verb for emphasis in informal speech. A native speaker of Turkish, a verb-final language with flexible ordering of major constituents, has informed this writer that reduplication of varied constituent types occurs quite commonly in everyday Turkish speech.

(31)   *Es a Juan a quien yo quiero.*
        'It is JUAN that I love.'

        Es ese vestido que yo me voy a poner.
        'It is THAT DRESS that I'm going to put on.'

(32)   *Yo te quiero a ti.*
        'I love YOU.'

Before children acquire these devices, they may very well resort to the pragmatic strategies available to them in their native language, Quechua.

This is a felicitous outcome: it means abandoning the premise that children have a grammar that violates universal syntactic principles. The Minaya and Luján VP configuration, modified below in line with X-Bar Theory, clearly treads on accepted phrase structure principles.

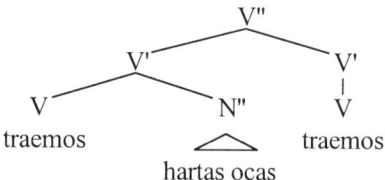

As mentioned earlier, within a GB approach, the configuration is unacceptable on a number of counts. In a minimalist framework (Chomsky 1995), the representation also falls short. Which verb adjoins to the head of a higher projection for checking of the Accusative Case feature on the direct object NP? Which verb moves up for the checking of tense features? Fortunately, we may now dispense with this representation altogether.[4]

---

[4] While repetition of constituents is a pragmatic strategy available to speakers of Quechua for emphasis, there may well be syntactic constraints on such reduplication, very worthy of future exploration. For example, both sentences below might be glossed 'I want Juan to BUY potatoes' (lit: '[Juan potatoes <u>buy</u>] want-1 sg <u>buy</u>.'):

(a)   *[Juan papa-ta <u>ranti-na-n-ta</u>] muna-sha-ni <u>ranti-na-n-ta</u>.*
(b)   *[[Juan papa-ta <u>ranti-nqa</u>] chay-ta] muna-sha-ni * <u>ranti-nqa</u>.*

Informants assert that duplication of the lower verb *ranti-* 'buy' is possible only in (a), where the verb occurs in nominalized form. In (b), the verb is inflected in 3rd person singular, future tense, and it occurs within a finite clause ending in *chay*. Following Lefebvre and Muysken (1988), *chay* is a complementizer which blocks extraction from the lower finite clause. It may be that duplication of constituents occurring within embedded CPs is also blocked.

Clearly, as one examines the interlanguage produced by speakers of languages in contact, one must carefully consider native language phenomena before attributing to L2 learners wild grammars based on "interdeterminacy" in word order.

East Carolina University
Greenville, North Carolina

REFERENCES

Chomsky, N.
1981   *Lectures on Government and Binding.* Dordrecht: Foris.
1995   "A Minimalist Program for Linguistic Theory", in: *The Minimalist Program*, 167-217. Cambridge, Massachusetts: The MIT Press.

Goodluck, H.
1986   "Language acquisition and linguistic theory", in: P. Fletcher and M. Garman (eds.), *Language Acquisition*, 49-68. Cambridge, UK: Cambridge University Press (2nd ed.).

Kasper, G.
1992   "Pragmatic transfer", *Second Language Research* 8, 203-231.

Lefebvre, C., and P. Muysken
1988   *Mixed Categories: Nominalizations in Quechua.* Dordrecht: Kluwer Academic Publishers.

Luján, M., L. Minaya, and D. Sankoff
1984   "The Universal Consistency Hypothesis and the prediction of word order acquisition stages in the speech of bilingual children", *Language* 60:2, 343-371.

Maratsos, M.P., and S.A. Kuczaj
1978   "Against the transformationalist account: a simpler analysis of auxiliary over-markings", *Journal of Child Language* 5, 337-345.

Mayer, J.W., A. Erreich, and V. Valian
1978   "Transformations, basic operations, and language acquisition", *Cognition* 6, 1-13.

Menyuk, P.
1969   *Sentences Children Use.* Cambridge, Massachusetts: The MIT Press.

Minaya, L., and M. Luján
1982   "Un patrón sintáctico híbrido en el habla de los niños bilingües en quechua y español", *Lexis* 6:2, 271-293.

Muysken, P.
1984   "The Spanish that Quechua speakers learn: L2 learning as norm-governed behavior", in: R.W. Andersen (ed.), *Second Languages: A Cross-Linguistic Perspective*, 101-119. Rowley, Massachusetts: Newbury House.

Nakayama, M.
1987   "Performance factors in subject-auxiliary inversion by children", *Journal of Child Language* 14, 113-125.

Nishimura, M.
1986   "Intrasentential code-switching: The case of language assignment", in: J. Vaid (ed.), *Language Processing in Bilinguals: Psycholinguistic and Neuropsychological Perspectives*, 123-143. New Jersey: Lawrence Erlbaum.

Park, J-E., R.C. Troike, and M.-R. Park
    1993   "Constraints in Korean-English code-switching: A preliminary study", *Journal of the Applied Linguistics Association of Korea* 6, 115-133.
Prideaux. G.
    1976   "A functional analysis of English question acquisition: a response to Hurford", *Journal of Child Language* 3, 417-422.
Rutherford, W.
    1983   "Language typology and language transfer", in: S. Gass and L. Selinker (eds.), *Language Transfer in Language Learning*, 358-374. Rowley, Massachusetts: Newbury House.

Languages in Contact, edited by D.G. Gilbers, J. Nerbonne, and J. Schaeken (= *Studies in Slavic and General Linguistics*, vol. 28), 99-103. Amsterdam - Atlanta, GA: Rodopi, 2000.

PRESTIGE, POWER, AND POTENTIAL FOR LANGUAGE SHIFT: THE INTRUSION OF SPANISH INTO TOJOLAB'AL MAYA

N. LOUANNA FURBEE

Narrative in Tojolab'al Maya, an indigenous language of Southern Mexico, incorporates Spanish as both loan words and code switches. Some loans are longstanding and well integrated grammatically, e.g. borrowed conjunctions (*i* 'and', *kwando* 'when') (Brody 1989), but others are less firmly embedded in the vocabulary and grammar. The latter often signal a speaker's attitude toward the participants or the information being conveyed in a discourse. I here examine the loan vocabulary and longer code switches in terms of their placement and poetic function in a narrative genre (*lo 'il*). It finds that the differing degrees of usage of this vocabulary suggest differing levels of vulnerability of the indigenous Tojolab'al to shift toward Spanish, as well as greater acceptance of Mexican national goals. It supports earlier findings (Garcia-Martinez 1997, Furbee 1997) that increased use of such vocabulary suggests early stages of language shift.

Examples derive from a corpus of 26 accounts in Tojolab'al of a miracle experienced in 1994 by a woman in the Tojolab'al community of Lomantán. These narratives come from the woman herself and from persons in other Tojolab'al villages, so they represent different degrees of closeness to and certainty about the miracle. Some communities are known to be progovernment, and some are less supportive of federal policies and more favorable to the goals of the revolt embodied by the Zapatista movement (Ross 1995). Speakers' attitudes toward the Lomantán miracle, which is itself a religious reflection of the revolt (Furbee 1998), can be interpreted as also reflecting the speakers' political stances with respect to Mexican federal government.

Spanish Intrusion

Use of Spanish loan words in these narratives varies, although knowledge of Spanish vocabulary does not. The inventory of loans is similar in all versions, but a greater or lesser employ of this vocabulary can be seen. Sociolinguistic and political causes seem to underlie this difference – those more favorable to the Federal government appear to use more Spanish in their Tojolab'al than do those more sympathetic to the EZLN (Garcia-Martinez 1997), suggesting a potential for language shift driven by political circumstances (Dorian 1992). I have also seen a specific use of Spanish associated with the authoritativeness of the speaker. I have two theses:

First, distinguishing well-integrated Spanish loan words from less well-integrated ones, which I call CRYSTALLIZED, I argue that crystallized Spanish loans in Tojolab'al characterize a more authoritative speaker's usage. Second, I claim that such use of crystallized Spanish represents use of a POWER dimension (Brown and Gilman 1960) in which power accrues to the Tojolab'al speaker not at the expense of Spanish speakers or the Spanish language but by association with it.

Taking the first thesis, it is possible to identify a route by which Spanish words, especially nouns, integrate into Tojolab'al. Even crystallized loan words may be involved in all manner of tropes; for example, in the structural parallelism mentioned above. Doña Dominga, who as the person that experienced the miracle is the most authoritative narrator, was at pains to tell me that she spoke no Spanish. Yet, her Tojolab'al is full of Spanish expressions, many integrated into structural tropes. She says in speaking about the flowers in her visions:

ti wax kila,	I suppose, there I saw it,
ja wax kila,	that which I saw,
b'a jardin jumasa b'utel ja rosa'i,	there in the gardens bloomed roses,
puro rosa waxjwaychini:	pure roses I dreamed:
ay blanko	There are white (*blanko*) ones,
ay chak	there are red ones,
ay rosado	there are pink (*rosado*) ones,
ay sb'i'il cho morado.	there are, its name is, purple (*morado*) ones.
oxe' kolora ja rosa waxjwaychini,	Three colors of roses I dreamed of,
oxe' kolora yojol jardin jawi.	three colors inside that garden.
ti b'i ay a chotik sakal choyol,	They say, there are white (*sakal*) choyal,

She knows the Tojolab'al word for white (*sak*). In the very next stanza, she uses its adjectival form (*sakal*). But her speech has more force when she speaks of *blanko*, *rosado*, and *morado* (of which she is unsure of the definition or name).

As words enter the language, they may be used without involvement in the morphological processes and remain unlabeled by definite or indefinite markers. But as they intrude more, they become subject to inflection, e.g. the well integrated loan words *lugar/slugar* 'place/its place', *lado/slado* 'side/its side', *diyos/jtatik diyos* 'God/Our Father God', and *ninyo/alaninyo* 'child/little child'.

Often Doña Dominga and others understandably use Spanish for ecclesiastical objects and concepts: *iglesia, kandela, krus, bela, diyos, berjin, resa, senya,* and so on. These are mostly well integrated loans, as evidenced by their participation in parallel structures and their acceptance of the Tojolab'al morphological apparatus (e.g., *skrus* 'its cross'). The following give another example from Doña

Dominga's version of the story, where the Spanish loan *diyos* is specified with the *ja....i* frame and the loan *seguro* 'sure, certain' accepts also the specifying *-iti* preceded by the first *ja*, making a cleft sentence (Brody 1984):

ja jtatik ja diyosi es seguro'iti.   That it is God the Father is certain.

As they further integrate, these loan words participate in compounds; e.g. *k'ulanperdon* 'to forgive' and *k'ulanresar* 'to say the rosary', from *k'ulan* 'to make, do, cause' plus the loans *perdon* 'pardon' and *resar* 'to say the rosary'. The loan *bwelta* 'time, occurrence, turn' compounds similarly with *i'a* 'to take':

"ela jawi kalatata!	"Come out, my dear Father!
ki'abwelta,	I will turn back,
ki'abwelta.	I will reform.
wajiyon,	I go,
wajiyon,	I go on,
pwes, laniki'abwelta", lachijiyon.	look, I really will be good", I said.

The rare use of the quotative verb *chij* in first person (*lachijiyon*) also makes this utterance by Doña Dominga special and elevated. Even more powerful are quoted Spanish phrases and sentences. Here Doña Dominga quotes God Himself, who speaks Spanish as befits his status as premier *swinkil* 'Ladino (non-Indian) patron'.

"Yo soy la resurrección y la vida. El que crea a mi se salvará", schij.
"I am the resurrection and the life. He that believe in me will be saved", he said.

Nothing can be less integrated, or more crystallized, hence powerful, than full sentence quotations from God. Such quotations cannot participate in ordinary poetic figures except as structural markers of arresting importance. They also lie at the end point of the power to solidarity continuum (Brown and Gilman 1960), whereas the long integrated *kwando* 'when' and *i* 'and' are far on the non-power end, so nativized that they have probably shaped and altered Tojolab'al syntax from an appositional frame using inalienably possessed relational nouns to introduce subordinate relations to a type that employs many conjunctions to express subordination. The conjunctions now carry a Tojolab'alness, comfortable and familiar, that conveys solidarity. Well integrated nouns like *bwelta* 'time, occurrence, turn', *gusto* 'liking, pleasure', *gana* 'want, desire', *diyos* 'God', *lugar* 'place', and *kristiano* 'person', also nestle close to the solidarity end of the continuum. Less well integrated loans like *adorno* 'adornment', and even *iglesia* 'church' (in place of the earlier and better integrated *ermita*), signal greater power and less solidarity. It is with the latter group that more instances occur of the reportative *b'i* 'they say' and the quotative *chij* 'to say':

ay b'i mi jna'a	There are, they say, I'm not familiar with
jaye' ja iglesia,	a lot of churches, but
waxkila tsamal ta ja b'a adorno	I've seen beautiful adornments
ochel ja b'a iglesia.	put there into the church.

Spanish phrases and sentences that are completely crystallized and independent of Tojolab'al are the most powerful of all, as seen in the quotations from God the Father that appear in Doña Dominga's story. These are limited in their participation in poetic figures, because as crystallized entities they are far removed from the morphosyntactic apparatus that creates poetic devices. However, they do have a poetic role to play at the organizational level of discourse.

In her paper and website, Hill (1997) identifies many examples of Spanish use by non-Spanish speaking North Americans, which she terms "Mock Spanish". In this collection, are examples that express solidarity with the Hispanic American world, but they are very few when compared with usage that is negative. Most Mock Spanish derogates Spanish speakers, Mexicans in particular, even though the derogation is largely out of the awareness of speakers. Hill includes media examples as diverse as the pronouncements of the Taco Bell Chihuahua and Exterminator II. In such instances, the speaker achieves power by using Mock Spanish at the expense of Spanish and its speakers. Tojolab'al uses of Spanish can be interpreted along the same power and solidarity dimensions. Again, the use of Spanish marks the speaker's authority, but it does not denote a hegemony over Spanish. Spanish in Tojolabal, especially CRYSTALLIZED loans, takes no power away from the Spanish speaker. Rather, it imbues the user with the POWER inherent in the dominant linguistic code. The transitivity of the power expression is reversed when compared with the Mock Spanish use of English speakers.

Conclusions

The paper argues two theses: First, Spanish loans into Tojolab'al fall along a continuum of integration to nonintegration (or CRYSTALLIZATION) with the more crystallized being the more powerful. Placement on this continuum can be judged according to the morphosyntactic involvement of a loan word or phrase, and by the potential of a loan to participate in the poetic structures and functions of Tojolab'al discourse, especially in parallelism and ambiguity. Second, use of Spanish, especially crystallized loan words, contributes POWER to the speaker. It does so without denigrating Spanish or its speakers. These findings suggest concern for the continued vitality of Tojolab'al Maya, even though the absorption of Spanish loans into Tojolab'al in itself is not threatening. After all, adopting vocabulary from diverse sources is a sign of a language that is alive and at work. Since, however, the Spanish usage appears to imbue power upon the speaker, and since it also is more prevalent in the narratives of persons who favor Federal policy and are more likely to ally themselves with national goals, it may be that Spanish is becoming a power laden code as well as a source of power laden loans. In that case, it could actually begin to be adopted as a prestige language by Tojolab'al communities that are orienting themselves toward integration with national aims.[1]

University of Missouri-Columbia

REFERENCES

Brody, M. Jill
    1987   "Particles borrowed from Spanish as discourse markers in Mayan languages", *Anthropological Linguistics* 29: 4, 507-521.
    1988   "Discourse genres in Tojolabal", in: M. Jill Brody and John Steven Thomas (eds.), *Tojolabal Maya: Ethnographic and linguistic approaches*, 55-66. Baton Rouge: Department of Geography & Anthropology.
Brown, Roger, and A. Gilman
    1960   "Pronouns of power and solidarity", in: Thomas A. Sebeok (ed.), *Style in Language*, 253-276. Cambridge, MA: The Technology Press.
Dorian, Nancy C. (ed.)
    1992   *Investigating Obsolescence: Studies in Language Contraction and Death.* Cambridge, England: Cambridge University Press.
Furbee, N. Louanna
    1988   "To ask one holy thing: Petition as a Tojolabal Maya speech genre", in: M. Jill Brody and John Steven Thomas (eds.), *Tojolabal Maya: Ethnographic and linguistic approaches*, 39-53. Baton Rouge: Department of Geography & Anthropology.
    1998   "The persistence of metaphor: Revolution and revolt in Chiapas" (paper presented at Conference on Maya Culture at the Millennium, Buffalo, NY, April 25, 1998).
Garcia-Martinez, Antonio
    1997   *Adios and lek ay* (B.A. Honors Paper in Anthropology). Department of Anthropology, University of Missouri-Columbia.
Hill, Jane
    1997   "Mock Spanish" (Third Annual James A. and Margaret S. Gavan Lecture in Anthropology, Columbia, Missouri, April 1997), Internet site *http://www.language-culture.org/colloquia/symposia/hill-jane/.*
Ross, John
    1995   *Rebellion from the roots: Indian uprising in Chiapas.* Monroe, ME: Common Courage Press.

[1] This paper derives from an earlier one presented at the Annual Meetings, American Anthropological Association, Philadelphia, 1998. I am grateful to the organizer of the symposium, Anne S. Dowd, and its discussant Dennis Tedlock, and to Paul Friedrich, who provided useful materials. This research was supported by grants from the Wenner-Gren Foundation for Anthropological Research, Inc., and the Faculty Research Council of the University of Missouri-Columbia, and by a Research Leave from the same university.

Languages in Contact, edited by D.G. Gilbers, J. Nerbonne, and J. Schaeken (= *Studies in Slavic and General Linguistics*, vol. 28), 105-120. Amsterdam - Atlanta, GA: Rodopi, 2000.

MORPHOSYNTACTIC CHANGE:
THE IMPACT OF RUSSIAN ON EVENKI

LENORE A. GRENOBLE

Evenki is a Tungusic language spoken throughout Siberia. Russian-Evenki contact dates back several centuries, and the Evenki people have long-standing contact with a number other groups of people as well, including Yakuts, Buryats and other Tungus people. Throughout their history, Evenki have often been bi- or multilingual, yet language *loss* is currently occurring at a rapid rate, with at least 2/3 of the population speaking a language other than Evenki: Bulatova (1994) estimates a total population of under 30,000, with less than 9000 speakers.

This paper discusses the linguistic impact of Russian on the Evenki language, focusing on morphosyntactic changes, as these have received less attention in the linguistic literature than have phonological changes. Findings are based primarily on my own fieldwork in the Amur basin and Sakha (Yakutia), supplemented by published descriptions.[1] The Evenki language is characterized by widespread dialectical variation, and 51 distinct dialects have been identified.[2] These are traditionally divided into three major dialect groups on the basis of the distribution of [s]/[h]: the Southern group, which shows phonetic [s] both word-initially and internally; Northern group, with [h] word-initially and internally; and the Eastern group, with [s] word-initially and [h] intervocalic position. These dialects show not only phonetic and lexical differences, but also morphosyntactic ones, including differences in the number of cases, the possessive pronouns, and in verbal morphology (see Atkine 1997 for a brief summary). The present paper focuses on changes occurring in several of the Eastern dialects; conclusions are based on work with speakers from the villages of Bomnak, Pervomayskoye, and Ust'-Nyukzha (Amurskaya Oblast') and the village of Iyengra (Sakha, Yakutia), and may not be true of all other dialects. Recent work on other dialects, such as Nedjalkov (1997), together with anecdotal kinds of evidence supplied by natives

---

[1] Research on this project was supported by NSF grant SBR-9710091. Unless otherwise noted, examples cited in the paper are taken from field recordings made by myself and Nadežda Bulatova; Russianisms are underlined.

[2] I suspect that some of these dialects are no longer spoken, due to language attrition. This does not affect the arguments presented here.

speakers, suggest that by and large the claims made here can be held to be true for most Evenki dialects.

Russian influence can be documented in all linguistic areas (phonological, lexical, morphological, and syntactic), as summarized here. Some changes are the direct result of Russian contact, while others are more the result of an indirect influence, i.e., they may be due to language loss, and not specifically Russian induced. The morphosyntactic changes, taken together, suggest an overall change in the Evenki linguistic system, a trend away from Tungusic syntax toward a more Indo-European system.

Long-standing contact and bilingualism has led to heavy lexical borrowing. Russian borrowings into Evenki predominate, although historically some Evenki words (such as specialized hunting/fishing terminology, or local flora and fauna) were borrowed into Russian. The last few decades, however, the nature of lexical borrowing has shifted in two important ways. First, borrowings are currently only unidirectional, from Russian into Evenki. Second, in contrast to borrowings from the early Communist era when there was a massive influx of new lexical items for new political and technical concepts brought by the Revolution, more recent borrowings from Russian have replaced native Tungusic words, sometimes at the core cultural level of reindeer husbandry and daily life, as seen in such borrowings as *tajga* 'taiga' (for Ev *agi:*) or *stada* (< R *stado* 'herd', versus Ev *aβdu*). Furthermore, earlier borrowings from Russian were adapted to Evenki phonotactics which do not allow word-initial consonant clusters (e.g. *ispička* < R *spička* 'match'; *kolob* < R *xleb* 'bread') or word-initial [r] (e.g. *urbaska* < R *rubaška* 'shirt'). In contrast, more recent borrowings do not conform to Evenki phonotactics but are adopted wholesale in their Russian form (e. g. *stado* < R *stado* 'herd').[3] This is indicative of a larger change, a change from an earlier pattern of borrowing from Russian, with the borrowing limited almost exclusively to the lexicon, to a situation of language shift. The Evenki language is affected in all spheres, i.e., not just the lexicon shows Russian influence, but also and primarily phonology, morphology and syntax are affected. This is presumably the direct result of heavy Russian-Evenki contact, coupled with major economic and social changes which have restructured Evenki society and severely limited the spheres of Evenki language usage. Crucially, from a linguistic standpoint, the scope and direction of language change in Evenki very much follow the predictions made by Thomason and Kaufman (1988) for situations of language shift.

As with any study of language change, it can be difficult to determine which changes are the direct result of superstratum contact, which are the result of lan-

---

[3] In bilingual speech communities, it can be difficult to distinguish borrowings from codeswitching. For the purposes of this paper I will consider Russian lexemes used with Evenki morphology to be borrowed terms (e.g. *stado-du:* 'in the herd', Ev dative *-du:*) and Russian lexemes with Russian morphology to be instances of codeswitching (*v stade* 'in the herd', R prepositional *-e*).

guage attrition, and which are more internally motivated changes. In the Evenki case, we are fortunate to have a comparison group of Tungusic languages spoken on Chinese territory whose speakers have had little to no contact with Russian speakers. At least one of these Tungusic varieties (Oroqen) is linguistically so close to Evenki that it has been classified as a dialect of Evenki, although I have argued against that view (Whaley et al. 1999). Lacking complete diachronic evidence for Evenki, Oroqen can provide important comparison data for the study of the impact of Russian on Evenki. This too is not without its problems, as the Tungusic languages in China are united by certain features which separate them from those in Siberia (see Atkine 1997 for an overview). These features may in part result from language contact with other linguistic groups.

Word order

Evenki is traditionally described as following SOV word order. Lacking a clear understanding of just how rigid verb-final word order was prior to contact, it is somewhat difficult to make a truly definitive statement on the impact of Russian word order on Evenki. In Modern Evenki, the verb can be found in non-final position for discourse purposes such as focus or emphasis (Kolesnikova 1966: 177). Nedjalkov (1997: 129-130) claims that although SOV is the neutral word order, all six possible word order variants do occur, although any sequence other than SOV or SVO requires contextual support. Yet Nedjalkov also points out that SOV is more frequent in folklore, suggesting that it is the more archaic pattern. Clearly, work is needed on Evenki discourse to determine word order patterns and their discourse functions. Nonetheless, following Nedjalkov we can draw conclusions on basic, neutral Evenki word order by looking at traditional formulaic texts, such as folklore and ballads, and by turning to other Tungusic languages, in particular, those Tungusic languages whose speakers have not had contact with Russian speakers. In such languages as Oroqen, Manchu, Solon, Xibe, word order is rigidly SOV.

In Modern Evenki there are certain instances where word order is predictably not SOV. These are: (1) in the imperative; (2) in questions, in particular in those cases where the verb (and not an interrogative pronoun) carries the interrogative force; and (3) when the main predicate is a converb or participle. It should be stressed that the clause-final position for the predicate is also possible in all of these cases. My own field recordings of spontaneous speech show violations of SOV word order even when these conditions do not hold; the verb can be found before other constituents in all sentence types. This is most likely due to Russian influence, although it may be internally motivated as well; this Russian influence was identified as early as Kolesnikova (1966). This results in sentences like the following, where the object follows the verb:

(1)   *Amin-mi*   *ičə-rə-n*   *udʒa-l-ba:-n.*
       father-POSS.1SG   see-AOR-3SG   track-PL-ACC-POSS.3SG
       'My father saw its [the bear's] tracks.'

Although the majority of clauses in my corpus follow SOV word order, every
speaker I have worked with produces VO word order as in (1). This is true with
speakers of all age groups, and predominates for many but the oldest speakers.
Yet age is not always a reliable indicator of linguistic competence, and the strongest predictor for word order changes is fluency in Russian: the more fluent a
speaker in Russian, the more likely the word order changes are to occur.[4] Furthermore, even for speakers who maintain verb-final word order in the majority of
sentences, there is a strong tendency for the verb to not be final if the speaker uses
Russian words, as borrowings or code-switches, in even a nearby clause. In other
words, like code-switching itself, word order changes appear to be at least in part
contextually (or situationally) motivated.

   Word order changes can be found at the phrase level as well as at the clause
level. Possessive constructions provide an example. There are a number of morphosyntactic means for marking possession in Evenki. One of the most frequent is
suffixation, with a possessive suffix which signals the person and number of the
possessor. The use of such suffixes is obligatory, as is the marking of case and
number. Possession is head-marked: the possessive suffix is on (the NP signaling)
the possessee; the head follows the dependent:

(2)   Evenki   *ətirkə:n*   *orortin*
                 old.man   deer-PL-POSS.3PL
                 'the old man's deer'

In contrast, in Russian possession is dependent marked with the genitive case on
the possessor, and the head precedes the dependent:

(3)   Russian   *olen-i*   *starika*
                  deer-PL   old.man-GEN
                  'the old man's deer'

Under Russian influence, a number of changes are occurring in modern Evenki.
One of these is a word order change from possessor-possessee to possessee-pos-
sessor, following the Russian model, as illustrated in (4):

(4)   Evenki   *orortin*   *ətirkə:n*
                 deer-PL-POSS.3PL   old.man

---

[4] Word order may be influenced by the Russian competence of the interlocutor as well. This requires further testing.

Note that here there has been no change in morphology: the possessive suffix is still used on the head.

Another change is represented in the following example, where the possessor-possessee word order is maintained, but Russian morphology is used:

(5) *ŋi:*   *bi-dʒəŋə:-n*   <u>*xolodil'nik-a*</u>   *ičəčiβun*
     who   be-FUT-3SG   refrigerator-GEN   watchman
     'someone will be there watching over the refrigerator'

Possessive case marking is on the dependent (R genitive), according to the norm for Russian. The head follows the dependent, as expected in Evenki. In this particular example, use of the Russian case marking might have occurred under the influence of the R lexeme *xolodil'nik* 'refrigerator'. Yet this alone cannot account for the case marking, as R borrowings may readily take Evenki case (for example with R lexemes: <u>*kolxos-tu:*</u> 'in the kolxoz', Ev dative *-tu:*; <u>*vunu:k-il-bi:*</u> 'my grandchildren', Ev plural (*-l*) and possessive (*-bi:*), and so on). This is an isolated example, but highly suggestive, given the other changes seen in possessive constructions. Taken together, these changes and inconsistencies in the word order, case marking, and head versus dependent marking suggests a high degree of Russian interference specifically in the marking of possession. This, combined with general language attrition, results in a collapse of the systematic marking of possession.

To summarize, there have been changes both in terms of basic constituent order, with a change from a rigid verb-final order to a less rigid pattern, with the verb frequently found in non-final position. There have been changes in the order of constituents in possessive phrases. Neither of these changes has been grammaticized to be obligatory; rather they are patterns that are emerging as the language changes or becomes lost.

Case marking

The exact number of cases in Evenki varies among the dialects, with a range of 11-13 cases. Standard accounts of literary Evenki place it at 13 cases, if the comitative is considered a case (see Kilby 1980 for discussion of the status of the comitative). Two changes appear to be underway in the Evenki case system: one is a reduction in the number of cases actively used, and the other is a reanalysis of some case functions.

Changes in case functions can be more directly linked to Russian influence. In the passive voice, the agent is regularly marked in the dative case in Evenki. Under Russian influence, there is an increasing tendency for it to occur in the instrumental. With verbs of speech, there is an increasing tendency to mark the addressee in the dative case, at the exclusion of the allative case, or of the accusative case in some dialects. Russian uses only the dative with speech verbs.

It is difficult to determine whether the reduction in the active use of case forms is in any way related to Russian influence. In my own fieldwork, speakers recognized all cases but did not produce them all with frequency. Two cases, the allative-locative (*-klV:*)[5] and the allative-prolative (*-kli:*), are not used by speakers of these dialects. The elative (*-git*) was used only very rarely. These dialects are characterized by a widespread use of the accusative indefinite, although it has been lost in a number of other dialects This reduction in the number of cases could conceivably be the result of language-internal changes, and it should be noted that the Tungusic languages spoken in China are characterized by considerably fewer cases than those in Siberia. However, one of the explanations put forth to account for this very geographic distribution is an areal one: Kilby (1980) demonstrates that a number of Siberian languages (Mongolian and Turkic), and not just Siberian Tungusic, have a relatively large inventory of cases. So it may be that the areal influence is breaking down with the widespread impact of Russian or that the Russian case system, with only six cases, is affecting the case system more directly. Finally, a loss of case morphology may also be the direct result of language attrition, and semi-speakers do in fact tend to use the locative where more fluent speakers would use the allative, and the ablative instead of the expected elative, as their functions are closely related. I see no way of determining this, and suspect that the changes in the Evenki case system stem from a combination of factors.

Mood

Evenki has an extensive system of moods. In addition, mood is regularly marked on participles and converbs, leading to a large number of morphological and semantic possibilities. However, a borrowed modal construction, based on the impersonal modal *na:da* (< R *nado* 'it is necessary') is frequently used. This modal is adapted to Evenki phonology (with vocalic length on what is the stressed syllable in Russian), and conforms to the rules of Evenki vowel harmony. It is also adapted to Evenki morphology. In Russian it is used with an infinitive form of the verb; the logical subject or experiencer, when overt, is in the dative case. In colloquial Russian it is also used with noun phrases, where the object needed is the nominative subject and the experiencer is again in the dative. In Evenki, *na:da* can be used in three basic constructions: (1) in a verbal construction, analogous to the standard Russian *nado* + infinitive; (2) in combination with noun phrases; (3) as a substantivized noun. In the verbal construction it is most frequently used in

---

[5] V is used to represent any of the vowels which are found in a suffix according to the rules of vowel harmony.

combination with the purposive personal converb (CVP).[6] This construction is used both in the positive (6) and in the negative (7), with the CVP:

(6) *tar*   *oronmo*   *ajat*   *ičət-tə:-s*   *na:da*
     that   deer-ACC   well   look.after-CVP-2SG   nado
     'You have to look after that deer well'

(7) *axi:*   *urgəxi:*   *bimi:,*   *ma:ut-pa,*   *uhi:-βə*   *ə-də:-n*
     woman   heavy   being   lasso-ACC   bridle-ACC   NEG-CVP-3SG
     olo:-ra   *na:da*
     step-PRT   nado
     'A pregnant woman must not step on a lasso or on a bridle'

The CVP, unlike the R infinitive, is marked for person and number; the experiencer here is the nominative subject. (This is in contrast to the Russian construction, where the experiencer is in the dative.) The Evenki analog to the Russian *nado* construction can be used impersonally, with no overt experiencer; the Evenki correlate to this impersonal construction is to use 2nd person singular morphology on the CVP, with no pronominal subject. Thus the Evenki *na:da* construction is an adaptation of the Russian, not a wholesale borrowing of the construction in its entirety.

It is difficult to quantify the frequency with which such constructions are used. However, my own field recordings show an overwhelming preference for the borrowed *na:da* construction in conversation and in narratives, with only rare instances of native deontic modal forms. All speakers of all ages, and with all levels of fluency, used the *na:da* construction.

In addition to its use as a verbal modal, *na:da* is also used to signal that an object is needed. Here the Evenki construction is a calque of Russian syntax:

(8) R   *čto*   *tebe*   *nado/nužno?*
          what-NOM   2SG.DAT   need
     Ev   *e:kun*   *sin-du:*   *na:da?*
          what-NOM   2SG-DAT   need
          'What do you need?'

In both Evenki and Russian, the person who needs something is in the dative case, and the needed thing is the nominative subject.

---

[6] A complete list of abbreviations used here is supplied at the end of the paper. For a more complete description of the use of converbs, see Bulatova and Grenoble (1999) or Nedjalkov (1997).

Although I was able to elicit the *na:da* construction with a few other verb forms, only the CVP was used in spontaneous speech. It is used with such frequency to the exclusion of all forms which I elicited that I question their actual use.

(9) R *Mne*   *nužno*   *mjaso.*   *Mne*   *nužna*   *ryba.*
       1SG-DAT   need   meat   1SG-DAT   need   fish
    Ev *Min-du:* *ullə*   *na:da.*   *Min-du:* *ollo*   *na:da.*
       1SG-DAT   meat   need   1SG-DAT   fish   need
       'I need meat.'   'I need fish.'

Here *na:da* is used predicatively. Tense, other than present, is marked on the auxiliary *bi-* which agrees in person and number with the grammatical subject, the needed object. While I was able to elicit this construction with the auxiliary in a full range of tenses, in my corpus of spontaneous uses it occurs only in the present tense without *bi-*, as in (9).

When *na:da* occurs in combination with a personal converb, the person/experiencer is not marked in the dative case, but is a nominative subject:

(10) *I-lə:*   *si:*   *huru-da-s*   *na:da?*
      where-ALL   2SG   go-CVP-2SG   need
      'Where are you supposed to go?' or 'Where do you need to go?'

This construction differs significantly from those listed in (9), which calque Russian syntax. Instead, the construction in (10) uses native Evenki strategies.

In addition, the lexeme *na:da* has become substantivized and may function as a noun in Evenki, taking full number, case and possessive morphology:[7]

(11) *bi:*   *na:da-β*
      1SG   nado-POSS.1SG
      'my necessity'

(12) *Nuŋan*   *na:da-l-βa-n*   *o-kal.*
      3SG   nado-PL-ACC-POSS.3SG   make-IMPER.2SG
      'Make the things that s/he needs.'

The fact that it can be used in this substantivized form underscores the extent to which it has entered the Evenki linguistic system. Evenki is characterized by a relatively weak division of parts of speech, and it is common for a single lexeme to be used with different morphology to form different parts of speech. In (4)-(5), with nominal morphology, it functions as a noun.

We have seen that the lexeme *na:da* is used in three basic constructions in Evenki: (1) as a predicative modal adverbial, in conjunction with a purposive converb; (2) as a predicative modal adverbial, in conjunction with a noun phrase; and (3) as a noun phrase. There are two probable motivations for the borrowing of *na:da*: dialectical variation in the morphological marking of deontic modality and lexical gaps.

---

[7] I am grateful to Nadežda Bulatova for bringing this to my attention.

There is widespread variation in the morphological marking of deontic modality. There are two deontic modal suffixes in Evenki, -*mačin* and -*ŋat*. The first of these, -*mačin*, is found in the literary language, and in some northern and southern dialects. It is difficult to determine how widespread its current usage actually is. Both Konstantinova (1964: 186-188) and Nedjalkov (1997: 263-264) cite it as the morphological marker of the deontic mood, but neither discusses geographic nor dialectical distribution. Vasil'evič (1958: 772) cites -*mačin* as a marker of deontic modality in the Podkamenno-Tungus dialects only; she sees it as marking a hypothetical mood in two southern dialect groups (Podkamenno-Tungus and the Nepa) and in two northern dialect groups (Erbogochen and Ilimpiy).[8]

In the same vein, the suffix -*ŋat* is also subject to dialect variation. Vasil'evič (1958: 779) cites it as being used for deontic mood in at least one southern dialect group (the Sym group) and in several eastern dialect groups, where I have also recorded its use. (See also Romanova and Myreeva 1962, 1964 and Vasil'evič 1948, all of which provide examples of -*ŋat* in Eastern dialects). It is used synthetically in the non-past, taking personal suffixes, and analytically in the past, with the auxiliary *bi:*- 'be' which takes the personal suffixes.

In addition to its synthetic use with personal suffixes signaling grammatical subject, the suffix -*mačin* can be found in an analytic construction with the verb *bi*- 'be'. In this latter construction -*mačin* occurs in an uninflected participial form: tense and person are marked on the auxiliary:

baka-mači-m	*baka-mačin*	*bi-čə:-β*
find-DEO-1SG	find-DEO	bi-PST-1SG
'I should find'	'I should have found'	

The analytic construction is possible in a full range of tenses (e.g. the future: *baka-mačin bi-si-m* 'I will be supposed to find').

The question is further complicated by the fact that speakers of the Eastern dialects do not use the suffix -*mačin* at all. Instead they use the suffix -*ŋat*. (This suffix is described as marking an optative in some dialects by both Konstantinova 1964 and Nedjalkov 1997, but it is quite clearly signals a deontic mood in the dialects I have worked with, and can be elicited through translation of the Russian deontic modal *dolžen* 'should'.) It is not used in some dialects at all (Konstantinova 1964: 189). In the villages where I have worked speakers used only the morpheme -*ŋat* and the *na:da* construction; speakers did not recognize forms in -*mačin*, neither as isolated verbs nor in context. Thus one possible motivation for the extensive borrowing of *na:da* is simply to avoid confusion: given that differ-

---

[8] The dialect distribution is significant in that first the Podkamenno-Tungus and then the Nepa dialect groups formed the basis of the literary language, where -*mačin* is the prescribed form for deontic modality.

ent dialects use different native strategies for marking modality, *na:da* provides a form that cuts across dialects and is understood by all.

A second motivation for the borrowing of *na:da* is that it fills in a lexical gap: there is no native Tungusic word for 'necessity', and borrowing of the Russian term is cited in a number of Tungusic languages whose speakers have heavy contact with Russian. Cincius (1975: 578) notes that it has been borrowed in Even, Negidal, and Orok in addition to Evenki, and cites it as also occurring in Yakut (Turkic). There is no evidence that the Tungusic languages spoken in China where there has been no contact with Russian have any word for 'necessity'. This gap may be explained language-internally: throughout Tungusic, modal meanings are expressed morphologically, not lexically.[9] In contrast, Russian has only three grammatical moods (indicative, imperative, and conditional) and expresses deontic and epistemic modal meanings lexically, or lexico-syntactically, relying chiefly on modal adverbs. Perhaps the closest Evenki equivalent to a Russian modal adverb such as *naverno* 'probably', *verojatno* 'probably' is the 3SG future finite verb form *bidʒəŋən* 'will be', used as a separate clause. In dialects whose speakers have heavy contact with Yakut, the word *bagar*, or *ba:r* 'probably', is found (< Yakut *baɣar-* 'want', *baɣa* 'desire'), and *badaga* 'possibly', 'seems' (< Yakut *badaɣa* 'probably', or 'it seems', 'should be'). Both of these are found in my recordings of spontaneous speech (taken in Iengra, Sakha, where Yakut is the majority language), along with the native Evenki *bidʒəŋən*. This borrowing from Yakut supports the hypothesis of a lexical gap.

Syntax

Native Evenki syntax is highly paratactic. Straight parataxis is the unmarked sentence structure for all Tungusic languages; it is still the most widespread sentence structure in the speech of fluent speakers. Evenki does have a few conjunctions, and a few particles which are used conjunctively. The conjunction *taduk* 'then' is by far the most frequently used; it is sometimes used with a clear sequential meaning (first X, then Y) and sometimes for straight conjunction. The particle *=də* is also used to join together clauses, although less frequently. As a clitic, it is found after the first word in the clause. However, fluent speakers for whom

---

[9] There is some disagreement among Evenki scholars as to what should be properly classified as a mood. Konstantinova (1964) lists seven grammatical moods, all marked inflectionally; Nedjalkov (1997: 259) points to the distinction between mood and modality; the former is an obligatory category and marked inflectionally, while the latter is indicated with verbal suffixes such as *-mu* 'want' and *-ssa* 'try' and either a mood morpheme or a participial or converbal morpheme. Although the details of Evenki moods are disputed, they do not affect the larger point here about the systematic differences between Evenki and Russian mood and modal systems.

Evenki is a first language show a strong preference for parataxis; example (13) is representative:

(13)   *Guni-βki-l*   *min-du:*   *hurup-kul,*   *gənnə:-kəl*   *ukumni-βə.*
      Say-PA.HAB-PL   1SG-DAT   go-IMP.2SG   bring-IMP.2SG   milk-ACC
      Bi: *huru-ŋnu-m,*   *əmuβu-ŋnə-m,*   *Saska-du:*   *bu-dʒə:-m.*
      1SG   go-A.HAB-1SG   bring-A.HAB-1SG   Sasha-DAT   give-A.IMPR-1SG
      Saska   *kortik*   *o:da:-n.*
      Sasha   whipped.milk   make-3SG
      'They say to me: "Go and bring the milk." I go, bring it, give it to Sasha. Sasha makes whipped milk.'

Here there is a lack of coordination, clauses are joined paratactically only. Connections between clauses are made through context, and by relying on intonation and clause ordering, such that so that sentential event order matches real-world event order.

Conjunctions comprise a distinct set of words that have been borrowed. In free speech, the use of such Russian conjunctions as *zatem* 'then', *potom* 'then', *opjat'* 'again', *posle ètogo* 'after this', and *i* 'and' is very frequent. Even the most fluent of speakers make use of these conjunctions:

(14)   <u>*potom*</u>   *ilan*   *anŋani:-βa*   *təgə-t-tin*
      then   three   year-ACC   sit-PST-3PL
      'Then they sat [in prison] for three years'

This, I would argue, is not so much a lexical borrowing as a syntactic one: borrowing of the conjoining syntax. It is admittedly difficult to determine to what extent it is the syntax that has been borrowed and to what extent Russian conjunctions are simply replacing Evenki ones, i.e. that there is no more involved than lexical borrowing. However, several factors point to a more general syntactic shift away from parataxis to coordination under Russian influence.

First, the pan-Tungusic pattern shows limited use of conjunctions, with events isomorphically mapped in real-world order, and loosely linked by intonation, as was illustrated in (13). In contrast, younger speakers in particular show a strong tendency to join serial events with the conjunction *taduk*, as in (15):

(15)   *Bi:*   *bira-la*   *huru-ŋnu-m,*   *taduk*   *təxi:-ŋnə-m.*
      1SG   river-LOC   go-A.HAB-1SG   then   clean-A.HAB-1SG
      Taduk   *banka-βa*   *ga-dʒaŋa:-m*   *ollo-βo*   *nə:-dʒə:-m*
      then   jar-ACC   take-FUT-1SG   fish-ACC   put-FUT-1SG
      taduk   *turukə-dʒəŋə:-m.*
      then   salt-FUT-1SG
      'I go to the river, then I clean [them]. Then I'll take a jar, put the fish in, then salt them.'

Second, although the amount of conjunction used seems to be fairly idiosyncratic, for some speakers conjunction is more likely to be found in sentences with Russian lexical borrowings, in particular in the same clause as code-switches. A good example is the following:

(16)   *Bi:*   *haβali-ŋki-m*   *arasnoj*   *haβaβi:*
       1SG   work-PST.HAB-1SG   various   job-REFL
       Olenevod-ta:nə-kət.   *Taduk*   *sel'sove:t-tu:*
       deer.herder-EMPH-PRC   then   city.council-E.DAT
       sekretar'   *bihi-m.*   *Potom*   *predsedatel-em.*
       secretary   be-1SG   Then   chair-R.INST

   'I have worked various jobs. As a reindeer herder. Then in the city council as an administrative secretary. And then as chair.'

The example is interesting in that the lexicon, morphology and syntax become increasingly Russian as the speaker talks. In line 1 *arasnoj* is a borrowing from R *raznyj* 'various'; note that it is used in conformance with Evenki phonotactics which do not permit word-initial [r]. In line 2 both Russian borrowings occur with Evenki morphology; clauses are linked with Ev *taduk*, but in line 3 the noun R *predsedatel'* is used with Russian morphology, and the conjunction *potom* is also Russian. The use of Russian here is not remarkable, in that the content involves Russian (or rather Soviet) culture. Not all examples of the use of R *potom* are this clearly linked to code-switching, and many speakers simply use the Russian conjunction instead of Ev *taduk*. (See also Comrie 1996, who discusses a similar influx of Russian conjunctions into Western Kamchadal.)

A third factor which is indicative of a general syntactic shift is that Russian conjunctions are now being used in environments where one would not anticipate any conjunction, given native syntactic patterns. Converbs and participles are the predominate means of marking subordination in Evenki (Nedjalkov 1997: 23). Converbs link a clause to a main predicate, with the tense of the main predicate functioning as a temporal origo, the event predicated by the converb is deictically linked as being anterior, posterior, or simultaneous to it. Thus temporal connections between the matrix clause and the converb clause are made by the converb, and not by temporal adverbials. Consider (17), taken from a folktale as recorded by Kèptukè (1991: 33):

(17)   *dʒə*   *səβəki*   *gunnə-βə-n*   *doldiksa,*   *əxə-t*
       PRC   god   say-ACC-POSS-3SG   hear   bear-POSS-1PL
       soŋo-ll-o-n   *soŋo-dʒo-no*   *soŋo-dʒo-βki,*   *soŋo-ro-n*
       cry-INCEP-3SG   cry-IMF-CV.SIM   cry-IMF-P.HABT   cry-PFT-3SG
       soŋo-ro-n,   *eha-l-in*   *tijə-ldə-lətin*   *soŋoron.*
       cry-PFT-3SG   eye-PL-POSS-3SG   narrow-COM-INCEP-3PL   cry-PFT-3SG

'And hearing God's words, our bear began to cry. Crying away while crying, he cried and cried. He cried until his eyes narrowed together.'

There is no conjunction between the clause in line 1 and those in lines 2-3. The interpretation of the converb in line 2 is in part dependent upon context. A similar examples is provided by Evenki participles, which can be used attributively, substantivally and predicatively, depending on the participle (see Bulatova and Grenoble 1999: 40-47; Nedjalkov 1997, 1977). These participles may be used to create links between two clauses. So, in example (13), the habitual participle *hurupki* 'leaving' is used here for a repeated, habitual action, concurrent to that of the main predicate *ilatčaŋnam* 'light'. Participles of all kinds and converbs are often most felicitously translated into English and Russian with temporal adverbials and finite verb forms. Even in examples like (13) and (17), the causal and temporal connections between clauses are made inferentially; the exact nature of the relationship being determined by discourse factors as well as the grammatical structure of the sentence itself (see especially Nedjalkov 1995).

In contrast, although Russian does use converbs, their use is considerably more restricted than in Evenki, and Russian participles are not used predicatively. In colloquial Russian in particular, temporal connections between clauses are created not only with tense/aspect, but also by relying heavily on temporal adverbials. One general shift in modern Evenki is that speakers are replacing converbs and participial constructions with Russian conjunctions and temporal adverbials. An illustrative example is the borrowing of the Russian preposition *posle* 'after' which requires a complement in the genitive case. Evenki does not have a genitive case; in my corpus the preposition occurs both with a complement in the Russian genitive (18) and without a complement, as a conjunction (20):

(18) *posle èt-ogo*   *əspədi:sija-l*   *oro-r-di:*   *haβali-ŋki-tin.*
      after this-R.GEN   expeditions-PL   deer-PL-INST   work-PST-3PL

      posle vojn-y,   *əhitkə:n*   *əhi:lə*   *redko,*   *vertolet-it,*
      after war-R.GEN   now   now   rarely   helicopter-Ev.INST

      oro-r ači-r.
      deer-PL neg-PL

      'After this, expeditions worked [riding] on reindeer. After the war, now only rarely, by helicopter, there are no deer.'

In (18) *posle* is used as required by Russian syntax, while in (19) its use is unacceptable in Russian:

(19) *ča:stu:*   *obettəni-ŋnə-rə-β,*   *ča:stu:*   *lečeniyə*
      hour-DAT   lunch-A.HABT-PRS.P-1SG   hour-DAT   treatment

      taduk exi:lə vanna, posle əmə-xə:
      then   further bath   after come-CV.ANT

kak-to   _tizalo_   _večer-om_   _o:ran._
somehow   hard   evening-R.INST   became
'I would have lunch for an hour, then treatment for an hour, and then next a bath. After coming [home], it was rather difficult in the evening.'

This construction is ungrammatical in Russian, which would require either a full clause, with a genitive complement and finite verb, or a perfective converb (_pridja_ 'having come') without the use of the preposition _posle_.

Perhaps even more striking is that this example comes from the speech of a seventy-year-old woman. This excerpt would suggest that she is a semi-fluent Evenki speaker, but in actuality Evenki is her first language. I conducted three interviews with her, lasting several hours, over the course of two separate field trips. The heavy use of Russian in this excerpt is situationally triggered: the course of treatment which she received in the city would have been with Russian doctors, in an all Russian environment. The frequency of Russian interference is often situationally motivated: when a speaker talks about an event that occurred in Russian setting, or reports a conversation that took place in Russian, there is a strong tendency to use borrowed terms, code-switches, word order changes and an increased usage of conjunctions. This is true of all speakers, regardless of age and fluency.

One last syntactic point to be made is the use of interrogative pronouns as subordinating pronouns in Evenki, as in (20), where the interrogative _idu_ 'where' is part of the subordinate clause:

(20)   _gu-kəllu,_   _idu_   _tar_   _kniga_   _bisi-n._
       say-IMPER.2PL   where   this   book   is
       'Tell [me] where this book is.' (Lebedeva et al. 1985: 216)

This construction again parallels a construction found in Russian; its usage appears to be restricted to Evenki among the Tungusic languages (Tsumagari 1997: 182-183), although further research on syntax might uncover its use elsewhere in Tungusic.

This paper has documented a number of changes in the structure of Evenki. While lexical changes can often be clearly traced to the impact of a contact language, other changes – such as changes in nominal case morphology and usage – are less unambiguously the result of contact, and quite arguably the result of language attrition. Interpreting the source of phonological changes can be equally difficult. Some, such as the velarization of what is historically described as a pharyngeal [ħ], are at least possibly due to Russian influence, since Russian has a velar fricative [x] but no pharyngeal. Changes in the vowel harmony system are equally difficult to interpret. These range from a reduction in the environments for which vowel harmony applies, to a complete or nearly complete loss of the system for some speakers, and may result from Russian contact, or they may be the result of attrition. (Although changes in vowel harmony are quite probably part of the natural process of language change, the accelerated rate of these changes, seen over the last few decades, almost certainly stems from attrition.) The source of morphosyntactic changes can be equally difficult to determine. Regardless of the impetus, the morphosyntactic changes analyzed here, taken together with corresponding phonological and lexical changes, indicate a fundamental restructuring of Evenki. This restructuring shows a move toward a more Indo-European type, with a tendency toward SVO word order, conjoined clauses, and a greatly reduced case system. These kinds of changes are indicative of what happens in cases of language attrition, rather than more stable language contact situations.

Dartmouth College

ABBREVIATIONS

ABL	ablative	EMPH	emphatic	PA	participle
A	aspect	FUT	future	PL	plural
ACC	accusative	GEN	genitive	POSS	possessive
ALL	allative	HAB	habitual	PRC	particle
ANT	anteriority	H.ASP	habitual sub-aspect	PRT	participle
COM	comitative	IMF	imperfective	PST	past
COND	conditional	IMP	imperative	REFL	reflexive
CV	converb	INCEP	inceptive sub-aspect	R	Russian
D	derivational	INST	instrumental	SG	singular
DAT	dative	NEG	negative auxiliary	SIM	simultaneous
DEO	deontic mood	NOM	nominative		
Ev	Evenki	P	purposive		

REFERENCES

Atkine, Viktor
    1997   "The Evenki language from the Yenisey to Sakhalin", in: H. Shoji and J. Janhunen (eds.), *Northern Minority Languages: Problems of Survival* (*Senri Ethnological Studies* 44), 109-121. Osaka: National Museum of Ethnology.
Bulatova, N.Ja.
    1994   "Èvenkijskij jazyk", in: V.P. Neroznak (ed.), *Krasnaja kniga jazykov narodov Rossii*, 68-70. Moskva: Akademija.
Bulatova, N.Ja., and Lenore A. Grenoble
    1999   *Evenki* (*Languages of the World, Materials* 141). München: LINCOM.
Cincilus, V.I.
    1975/1977 *Sravnitel'nyj slovar' tunguso-man'čžurskix jazykov*. Leningrad: Nauka.
Comrie, Bernard
    1996   "Language contact in northeastern Siberia (Chukotka and Kamchatka)", in: Ernst Hakon Jahr and Ingvild Broch (eds.), *Language Contact in the Arctic: Northern Pidgins and Contact Languages*, 33-45. Berlin: Mouton de Gruyter.

Kėptukė, G.I.
1991   *Dėgi xokton.* Jakutsk: Rozovaja čajka.
Kilby, David
1980   "Universals and particulars of the Evenki case system", *International Review of Slavic Linguistics* 5, 45-74.
Kolesnikova, V.D.
1966   *Sintaksis èvenkijskogo jazyka.* Moskva-Leningrad: Nauka.
Konstantinova, O.A.
1964   *Èvenkijskij jazyk.* Moskva-Leningrad: Nauka.
Lebedeva, E., O. Konstantinova, and I. Monaxova
1985   *Èvenkijskij jazyk. Učebnoe posobie dlja pedagogičeskix učilišč.* Leningrad: Prosveščenie.
Nedjalkov, Igor
1997   *Evenki.* London: Routledge.
1995   "Converbs: Control and interpretation", *Journal of Pragmatics* 24, 433-450.
1977   *Pričastija v tunguso-man'čžurskix jazykax* (Avtoreferat kandidatskoj dissertacii). Leningrad: Akademija Nauk.
Romanoval, A.V., and A. N. Myreeva
1962   *Očerki tokkinskogo i tommotskogo govorov.* Moskva-Leningrad: Nauka.
1964   *Očerki učurskogo, majskogo i tottinskogo govorov.* Moskva-Leningrad: Nauka.
Thomason, Sarah Grey, and Terrence Kaufman
1988   *Language Contact, Creolization, and Genetic Linguistics.* Berkeley: University of California Press.
Tsumagari, Toshiro
1997   "Linguistic diversity and national borders of Tungusic", in: H. Shoji and J. Janhunen (eds.), *Northern Minority Languages: Problems of Survival* (*Senri Ethnological Studies* 44), 175-186. Osaka: National Museum of Ethnology.
Vasil'evič, G.M.
1958   *Èvenkijsko-russkij slovar'.* Moskva: Izdatel'stvo inostrannyx i nacional'nyx slovarej.
1948   *Očerki dialektov èvenkijskogo (tungusskogo) jazyka.* Leningrad: Učpedgiz.
Whaley, Lindsay J., Lenore A. Grenoble, and Fengxiang Li
1999   "Revisiting Tungusic classification from the bottom up: A comparison of Evenki and Oroqen", *Language* 75/2, 286-321.

Languages in Contact, edited by D.G. Gilbers, J. Nerbonne, and J. Schaeken (= Studies in Slavic and General Linguistics, vol. 28), 121-134. Amsterdam - Atlanta, GA: Rodopi, 2000.

ASPECTS OF RUSSIAN-NIVKH GRAMMATICAL INTERFERENCE: THE NIVKH IMPERATIVE

EKATERINA GRUZDEVA

1. Introduction

The paper discusses the various ways in which Nivkh grammar has been affected during the last years as a result of interaction between Russian and Nivkh, focusing on the changes that have occurred in the realm of the Nivkh imperative. It may be supposed that such phenomena as the development of number opposition of synthetic third person imperative forms, the emergence of analytical first person singular imperative forms, the appearance of redundant third person imperative markers, the rise of new polite imperative forms, as well as some other language changes which have taken place in different areas of Nivkh grammar, were caused not only by intralinguistic and evolutionary tendencies, but also by possible influence of the Russian grammatical system.

Nivkh is spoken on Sakhalin Island and in the Amur region of Russia. Being a language isolate, not genetically connected with any other languages spoken in the area or elsewhere, it is traditionally classified as a Paleosiberian language. Typologically, Nivkh is an agglutinating synthetic language with SOV word order. There are four dialects in Nivkh, i.e. the Amur, the East Sakhalin, the North Sakhalin, and the South Sakhalin dialects. The paper deals with the data of the Amur (hereafter, Niv.A) and East Sakhalin (hereafter, Niv.S) dialects. Grammatical information and examples fixing the state of Nivkh at the turn and in the first half of the twentieth century come from Šternberg (1908), Krejnovič (1934), Austerlitz (1958), Panfilov (1962, 1965), Savel'eva and Taksami (1970). Facts of present-day Nivkh are taken mainly from the data collected during my field work on Sakhalin Island (Nogliki, Katangli, Čir-Unvd) in 1989 and 1991.

According to the data of the 1989 general Census of the population, there were 4,681 Nivkh people in Russia, of whom 2,008 lived on Sakhalin (*Nacional'nyj...* 1991).

Historically, the Nivkh people have undergone varying degrees of contact and influence from the Tungus-Manchu tribes, namely, the Orochs (Uiltas), the Nanays, the Evenkis etc., on the Amur, and the Orochs and the Evenkis on Sakhalin. Moreover, the Sakhalin Nivkh people have been living for a long time in close touch with the Ainu people, especially with those who lived in the south of the island. The historical ties with the Russians have been established since the mid-nineteenth century, when they began to settle in the Far East of Asia and on Sa-khalin. During the same period the Sakhalin Nivkh people were in contact with the Japanese.

At the turn of the twentieth century, the language situation in the area of the Nivkh people's residence was characterized by an active multilingualism. However, Nivkh has had little effect on neighbouring languages. It is often contended that the indigenous neighbours of the Nivkh people easily acquired a knowledge of all the other local languages in use, except Nivkh. That is why the Nivkh people had to express themselves in Ainu, Oroch etc., not in their own language, in their relations with their neighbours. A general rule that characterized the contacts between the native people and the immigrants was communication in the language of the latter. Though the original population was dominated by stronger nationalities, in particular by Russians and the Japanese, due to their isolated life as hunters and fishers, they could keep their native language and culture for a long time (Gruzdeva 1996).

In the 1960-70s an active process of massive russification of the indigenous peoples was set in motion, completely changing the language situation. At present, all the Nivkh people who know their native language are bilingual and speak fluent Russian as well. It is mainly linguistic peculiarities of the speakers' language that are taken as the object for the study of different interference processes. Nivkh does not have any official status and, as a whole, has a low retention rate. Only 23.3% of the Nivkh population regard Nivkh as their mother tongue. For all the others Russian is the mother tongue. The selected sociolinguistic inspection (315 persons) carried out in the town of Nogliki (Sakhalin Island) in 1989 demonstrates that approximately 75 persons (the youngest were at that time 40 years old; now they are 50 years), i.e. 23.8%, know and use Nivkh (Gruzdeva and Leonova 1990).

In spite of Russian being the second (non-native) language for all bilingual Nivkh people, at present, owing to various social and cultural reasons (cf., e.g. De Graaf 1992), Russian undoubtedly dominates. In conditions of Nivkh-Russian bilingualism Russian is a source of innovations that can be traced on different linguistic levels of Nivkh.

2. The outlines of grammatical interference

2.1 Pluralization of nouns

Nivkh noun distinguishes two numbers, i.e. the unmarked singular and the plural with the suffix Niv.A *-ku / -ɣu / -gu / -xu*, Niv.S *-kun / -ɣun / -gun / -xun*.

2.1.1 Nouns denoting dual objects

Nivkh nouns denoting dual objects, such as Niv.A *tymk*, Niv.S *tamk* 'hand, hands', Niv.A *ŋyt'x*, Niv.S *ŋat'x* 'leg, legs' etc., are generally used in the singular. Depending on the context, they may denote either a separate part of a dual object or a dual object as a whole. Occurring in the plural, such nouns refer mostly to several pairs of dual objects, cf. Niv.A *tymk-xu*, Niv.S *tamk-xun* 'hands (of several persons)', Niv.A *ŋyt'x-xu*, Niv.S *ŋat'x-xun* 'legs (of several persons)'.

However, nowadays, there is a clear tendency to attach the plural suffix to the stems of nouns also in cases when they refer to a single pair of objects, which can be attributed to the disturbance of Russian, where nouns designating dual objects always occur in the plural, cf. Rus. *ruk-i* {hand-F:PL:NOM} 'hands', Rus. *nog-i* {leg-F:PL:NOM} 'legs'.

2.1.2 Nouns in counting phrases

According to Nivkh grammatical rules, a counted noun does not require a plural suffix in the counting phrases, cf. Niv.A *xerrt'uɣr t'ex* {match-[SG-NOM] three} 'three matches'.

Consider, nevertheless, the plural form of the noun Niv.A *ķan-gu* in the counting phrase *ķan-gu meķř* {dog-PL-[NOM] two} 'two dogs', which clearly calques the plural form of the Russian noun *sobak-i* 'dogs' in the corresponding Russian counting phrase *dv-e sobak-i* {two-F:NOM dog-F:PL:NOM} 'two dogs'.

2.2 Shift to obligatory subject-verb agreement

Basically, the indicative finite verb form in Niv.A *-d' / -t'*, Niv.S *-d / -nd / -nt* does not agree with any of its arguments in person, but the verb suffix identical to the noun plural suffix optionally codes the plural subject.

The verb may not agree in number with the subject in case the latter is expressed by a plural personal pronoun, cf. Niv.S *In vi-nd* {they-[NOM] go-FIN-[SG]} 'They go / went', or by a noun carrying the plural suffix, cf. Niv.S *Eɣlŋ-gun lu-nd* {child-PL-[NOM] sing-FIN-[SG]} 'The children sing / sang'. In its turn, the noun referring to several objects may occur in the singular provided that the plural suffix is attached to the verb, cf. Niv.A *Ķan yɣ-d'-ɣu* {dog-[SG-NOM] bark-FIN-PL} 'The dogs barked'.

Currently, following a widespread tendency among second-language speakers to acquire more regular rules (Trudgill 1986), Nivkh speakers tend to mark the plural number both on subjects and verbs, i.e. the subject-verb agreement in number has acquired an obligatory character, as is typical of Russian:

(1)　　Niv.S　*Ķanŋ-gun*　　*vavli-d-ɣun.*
　　　　　　　　dog-PL-[NOM]　　growl.at.each.other-FIN-PL
　　　　　　　　'The dogs growled at each other.'

Rus.	**Sobak-i**	**ryča-l-i**	*drug*	*na*	*druga.*
	dog-F:PL:NOM	growl-PAST-PL	each	at	other

2.3 Elimination of possessive markers in kinship terms

Formerly, Nivkh kinship terms were construed with obligatory grammatical indication to the possessor. If the latter refers to a singular person, it may be coded by a reduced form of the corresponding personal pronoun, which functions as a prefix, cf. Niv.S *ń-ytk* 'my father', Niv.S *č-ymk* 'your:SG mother'. In case the possessor refers to a dual or a plural person, a full form of the corresponding personal pronoun in preposition to the noun is used, cf. Niv.S *čin aķi* 'your:PL elder brother', Niv.S *in asķ* 'their junior brother'.

In modern Nivkh, the possessive markers in kinship terms are gradually vanishing, which may be explained by the influence of Russian, where the indication to the possessor in kinship terms is necessary only in the conditions of reference conflict.

2.4 Appearance of redundant markers in conditional sentences

The Nivkh conditional sentence contains at the minimum two verb forms, which is a converb with the suffix -*ğaj*, denoting a condition, and a finite verb form, denoting a consequence. There are neither a conditional nor other types of conjunctions in Nivkh.

However, apparently copying the structure of Russian conditional sentences, the most common variant of which includes the conjunction *esli* 'if', at present, the initial position of the Nivkh conditional sentence is often filled by the redundant word *aif*. The latter functions as an analogue of a conjunction 'if':

(2)	Niv.S	**Aif**	*ytk*		*ń-aχ*	**vi-gu-ğaj**		*ńi*
		if	father-[SG-NOM]		I-ACC	go-CAUS-CONV:COND		I-[NOM]
		ńa		*ŋaγ-n*			*vi-i-d-ra.*	
		seal-[SG-NOM]		look.for-CONV:MAN:1SG			go-FUT-FIN-[SG]-PTL	

'If [my] father permits me to go, I shall go hunting.'

	Rus.	**Esli**	*otec*		**razreš-it**	*mn-e*	*poj-ti,*
		if	father-[M:SG:NOM]		permit-FUT:3SG	I-DAT	go-INF
		ja	*pojd-u*	*na*	*oxot-u.*		
		I:NOM	go-FUT:1SG	to	hunt-F:SG:ACC		

2.5 Alternations in the word order

2.5.1 Word order in counting phrases

The syntactic peculiarity of Nivkh numerals up to five is that in counting phrases they are in postposition to the counted nouns, cf. Niv.S *pitŋŋ t'oķř* {book-[SG-NOM] five} 'five books', whereas all other numerals are always placed in preposition.

This rule, however, cannot be applied to the counting phrases comprising the nouns borrowed from Russian. In such cases, all the numerals, including numerals up to five, are used prepositionally, cf. Niv.S *t'oķř čas* {five hour-[SG-NOM]} 'five hours', which is the same as in the corresponding Russian counting phrases, cf. *pjat' čas-ov* {five-[NOM] hour-M:PL:GEN} 'five hours'.

2.5.2 Word order in single-predicate sentences

Nivkh canonic word order is SOV. The finite verb form closes the sentence, the attribute precedes the head word, temporal and locative adverbials usually come sentence-initially, cf. (3a-4a).

The tendency towards a freer word order (as it is in Russian), which is found in the speech of modern Nivkh speakers, first of all affects the positions of the subject and adverbials. Nowadays, they may occupy also non-standard linear positions, for instance, at the end of the sentence, i.e. with the OVS word order, cf. (3b), or with the traditional word order SOV, but with the shift of the adverbial to the final position of the sentence, cf. (4b).

(3) Niv.S a. *Nudvařklu*   *řaŋģ*   *urguř*   *ń-idy-d.*
         some   woman-[SG-NOM]   well   I-look-FIN-[SG]

        b. *Urguř*   *ń-idy-d*   *nudvařklu*   *řaŋķ.*
         well   I-look-FIN-[SG]   some   woman-[SG-NOM]
         'A woman was looking at me intently.'

     Rus.   *Na*   *men-ja*   *pristal'no*   *smotre-l-a*
         at   I-ACC   intently   look-PAST-F:SG
         kak-aja-to   *žentšin-a.*
         some-F:SG:NOM-PTL   woman-F:SG:NOM

(4) Niv.S a. *P'xi-ux*   *ķaṇṇ*   *ńin*   *vez-d.*
         forest-[SG]-LOC   dog-[SG-NOM]   we-[NOM]   rush-FIN-[SG]

        b. *Ķaṇṇ*   *ńin*   *vez-d*   *p'xi-ux.*
         dog-[SG-NOM]   we-[NOM]   rush-FIN-[SG]   forest-[SG]-LOC
         'In the forest, a dog rushed at us.'

     Rus.   *Sobak-a*   *brosi-l-a-s'*   *na*   *nas*
         dog-F:SG:NOM   rush-PAST-F:SG-REFL   at   we:ACC
         v   *les-u.*
         in   forest-M:SG:PREP

2.5.3 Word order in multiple-predicate sentences

A multiple-predicate sentence in Nivkh is traditionally represented as a predicate chain whose verb forms are connected with different semantic relations, i.e. tense, purpose, cause, condition, concession etc. The finite verb form occurs sentence-finally. Converbs occupy non-final positions and take the suffixes marking the type of semantic relations, cf. the standard location of the temporal converb *p'řy-ba* 'as soon as [he] come' in (5a).

The influence of Russian has caused a greater freedom of the linear organisation of multiple-predicate sentences. In particular, the sequence of converbs and finite verb forms becomes less rigid. Currently, the converb with its arguments may not only precede but also follow the finite verb form, as in (5b).

(5)   Niv.S   a.   ***Jaŋ***   ***nana***   ***p'řy-ba***   *ń-az-ja.*
                      he-[NOM]   just   come-CONV:TEMP   I-call-IMP:2SG
               b.   *Ń-az-ja*   ***jaŋ***   ***nana***   ***p'řy-ba.***
                      I-call-IMP:2SG   he-[NOM]   just   come-CONV:TEMP
                      'Call me as soon as he come.'
       Rus.   *Pozov-i*   *men-ja,*   ***kak tol'ko***   ***on***   ***prid-jot.***
                      call-IMP:2SG   I-ACC   as.soon.as   he: NOM   come-FUT:3SG

3. Contact-induced changes in the imperative

The imperative paradigm of the earlier Nivkh language contained five forms opposed by person and number. It should be noted that in Nivkh the differentiation of person (together with number) of the subject is found only in imperative verb forms and is not typical of indicative verb forms. Consider the imperative suffixes and the sample imperative forms:

(6)   Niv.S   2SG   *-ja*   *Vi-ja!* 'Go (you:SG)!'
                2PL   *-ve*   *Vi-ve!* 'Go (you:PL)!'
                1DU   *-nate*   *Vi-nate!* 'Let us (I & you:SG) go!'
                1PL   *-da*   *Vi-da!* 'Let us (I & you:PL) go!'
                3SG / PL   *-ğaro*   *Vi-ğaro!* 'Let him / her / them go!'

Nowadays, the first person dual imperative form with the corresponding first person dual personal pronoun *men* 'I & you:SG' has practically vanished, the first person plural imperative form and the personal pronoun being used instead. The loss of dual forms may be a case of radical interferential reduction (Thomason and Kaufman 1988) as the result of direct influence of the less elaborated pronoun system of Russian.

The other changes that have probably arisen from Russian interference are also found in the third person and the first person singular imperative forms (Gruzdeva 1992, 1998).

3.1 Development of number opposition of synthetic third person imperative forms

As seen in (6), the Niv.S imperative paradigm formerly included only a single third person form with the suffix *-ğaro* used both in the singular and in the plural.

However, contemporary Nivkh displays number opposition of the third person singular and the third person plural imperative forms. So the suffix -ğaro has been retained in the capacity of the third person singular marker:

(7) Niv.S *Jaŋ*   *nana*   *oz-ba*   *ińk*
            he-[NOM]   just   get.up-CONV:TEMP   meal-[SG-NOM]
            aj-ğaro.
            cook-IMP:3SG
            'As soon as he gets up, let him cook the meal.'
     Rus.   *Kak tol'ko*   *on*   *vstan-et,*   *pust'*
            as.soon.as   he:NOM   get.up-FUT:3SG   let
            ed-u   *gotov-it.*
            meal-F:SG:ACC cook-PRES:3SG

At the same time the reduplicated form of the third person singular imperative suffix -ğarğaro is currently used as the third person plural marker:

(8) Niv.S *In*   *nana*   *oz-ba*   *ińk*
            they-[NOM]   just   get.up-CONV:TEMP   meal-[SG-NOM]
            aj-ğarğaro.
            cook-IMP:3PL
            'As soon as they get up, let them cook the meal.'
     Rus.   *Kak tol'ko*   *on-i*   *vstan-ut,*   *pust'*
            as.soon.as   they-NOM   get.up-FUT:3PL   let
            ed-u   *gotov-jat.*
            meal-F:SG:ACC cook-PRES:3PL

Note, incidentally, that although formerly reduplication was quite a regular device of expressing plurality, in modern Nivkh it is practically not used for word formation.

The number opposition of the Nivkh third person imperative forms seems to have been developed under the influence of Russian, where as a result of the imperative paradigm evolution, the analytical third person imperative verb forms are nowadays opposed by number. Compare the third person singular form *pust' gotovit* 'let [him] cook' in example (7) and the third person plural form *pust' gotovjat* 'let [them] cook' in example (8).

3.2 Emergence of analytical first person singular imperative forms

As far as it is possible to follow the evolution of Nivkh, on the one hand, there is a clear tendency towards the elimination of analytical forms that were widespread at earlier stages of Nivkh. The oldest folklore texts (Šternberg 1908) contain a great number of complex forms with auxiliary verbs, many of which are not used now.

On the other hand, in modern Nivkh the reverse process of emergence of some rare analytical forms has been in action lately. For example, the analytical imperative forms have been formed according to new patterns structurally similar to those used in Russian. This phenomenon perfectly confirms the idea that the quickly developing bilingualism, irrespective of the grammatical systems of 'co-existing' languages, leads to the growth of analytism (Weinreich 1953).

The new analytical forms are found in the peripheral zone of the Nivkh imperative paradigm, namely in the first person singular form. Traditionally, neither synthetic nor analytical first person singular imperative forms were attested in the East Sakhalin dialect of Nivkh. An autoprescription was standardly expressed by synthetic future indicative forms:

(9)   Niv.S   *Ńi*   *čin*   *taf-toχ*   ***t'or-i-d-ra.***

             I-[NOM]   you:PL-[NOM]   house-[SG]-DAT   carry-FUT-FIN-[SG]-PTL

             '[Let] me take you to [your] house.'

In contemporary Nivkh, the same meaning can also be indicated by two complex forms, which by analogy with corresponding Russian imperative forms can be considered as analytical first person singular imperative forms. These analytical forms consist of the two components:

(i) Special petrified imperative forms *t'ana* {give:IMP:2SG} or *t'ana-ve* {give:IMP:2SG-IMP:2PL} which can also be used as independent imperative forms. For instance, in example (10), *t'ana* means 'give' addressing a single hearer, whereas in example (11), *t'anave* has the same meaning addressing more than one hearer. These words do not change, take no grammatical markers in the singular and traditionally occupy the final position of the imperative sentences.

(10)   Niv.S   *Ymk-a*   *χasaṇ*   *eɣguř*   ***t'ana!***

             mother-[SG]-VOC scissors-[SG-NOM]   quickly   give:IMP:2SG

             'Mother, give me the scissors quickly (you:SG)!'

(11)   Niv.A   *Ōla-ġo!*   *Ńe-rx*   *ńińak*   *als*

             child-PL:VOC   I-DAT   some   berry-[SG-NOM]

             t'ana-ve! (Panfilov 1965: 133)

             give:IMP:2SG-IMP:2PL

             'Children! Give me some berry (you:PL)!'

(ii) Regular second person imperative forms always containing the causative suffix *-gu- / -ku-*, which marks non-coreference of the hearer and the prescription executor. These forms are normally used when the speaker appeals to the hearer in order that the latter transfers the prescription to the executor of the action who does not participate in the speech act:

(12) Niv.S *In*   *xe-ř*   *in-aχ*   ***p' řy-gu-ja!***
              they-[NOM]   tell-CONV:MAN:2SG   they-ACC   come-CAUS-IMP:2SG
              'Tell them to come (you:SG)! (lit. Telling them, let them come!)'

As parts of analytical forms, *t'ana* and *t'anave* appear in the very beginning of the sentence, while imperative forms keep their sentence-final position. *T'ana* occurs in combination with the second person singular imperative form in *-ja*, as in (13), whereas *t'anave* combines with the second person plural imperative form in *-ve*, as in (14).

(13) Niv.S ***T'ana***   *ń-aχ*   ***lu-gu-ja!***
              give:IMP:2SG   I-ACC   sing-CAUS-IMP:2SG
              'Let me sing (you:SG)!'
      Rus.   *Daj*   *spo-ju!*
              give:IMP:2SG   sing-FUT:1SG

(14) Niv.S ***T'ana-ve***   *ń-aχ*   ***lu-gu-ve!***
              give:IMP:2SG-IMP:2PL I-ACC   sing-CAUS-IMP:2PL
              'Let me sing (you:PL)!'
      Rus.   *Daj-te*   *spo-ju!*
              give:IMP:2SG-IMP:2PL sing-FUT:1SG

As can be seen, such special analytical first person singular imperative forms are opposed according to the number of hearers. This is typical, for example, of Russian analytical first person singular imperative forms that are derived by singular and plural desemantized imperative forms of the verb *dat'* 'to give' and the first person singular future indicative form of the main verb (Birjulin and Xrakovskij 1992: 9). When addressing a single hearer, the verb *dat'* 'to give' is used in the second person singular imperative form *daj*, as in (13), whereas in case of more than one hearer the second person plural imperative form *dajte* occurs in the sentence, as in (14).

Note, however, the difference of the second components of Russian and Nivkh analytical forms under discussion. In Russian, the main verb, irrespective of the number of hearers, occurs in the same first person singular future form. The number opposition of hearers is therefore marked only by the first components of the analytical forms, that is by singular and plural desemantized imperative forms of the verb *dat'*. On the other hand, in Nivkh, the number of hearers is indicated not only by the words *t'ana* in singular and *t'anave* in plural, completely corresponding to *daj* and *dajte* in Russian, but also by singular and plural imperative forms of the main verb, that is by the second components of the analytical forms.

As can be observed, the Nivkh pattern does not directly mirror the Russian one since it is derived on the basis of its own construction.

3.3 Appearance of redundant third person imperative markers

As mentioned in section 3.1, in the modern East Sakhalin dialect of Nivkh, the prescription to the third person addressee is coded by the synthetic imperative forms with the suffixes -ǧaro (3SG) and -ǧarǧaro (3PL). Yet, at present, hortative sentences with special synthetic third person imperative forms are often completed by the particles Niv.S p'eγrdoχ 'let' and Niv.S haǧaro 'let', which are semantically redundant in this type of sentences.

According to a few examples from Savel'eva and Taksami (1970), the particle Niv.A p'eγazdoχ 'let' (cf. Niv.S p'eγrdoχ 'let') is normally used in combination with the indicative verb form and expresses the optative meaning:

(15)   Niv.A   *P'eγazdoχ*   *toγa-d'-ra.*   (Savel'eva and Taksami 1970: 283)
              let   be.so-FIN-[SG]-PTL
              'Let [it] be so.'

In the contemporary East Sakhalin dialect of Nivkh, the particle p'eγrdoχ 'let' occurs also in hortative sentences with synthetic third person imperative forms. It functions as an additional lexical nomination coding the prescriptive, see (16-17), or optative, see (18), meanings:

(16)   Niv.S   *Jaŋ*   *p'ŕy-in-aǧńi-ǧaj*   **p'eγrdoχ**   **p'ŕy-ǧaro**!
              he-[NOM]   come-MOD-want-CONV:COND   let   come-IMP:3SG
              'If he wants to come, let him come!'

       Rus.   *Esli*   *on*   *xoč-et*   *prij-ti,*   **pust'**   **prixod-it**!
              if   he:NOM   want-PRES:3SG   come-INF   let   come-PRES:3SG

(17)   Niv.S   *In*   *p'ŕy-in-aǧńi-ǧaj*   **p'eγrdoχ**   **p'ŕy-ǧarǧaro**!
              they-[NOM]   come-MOD-want-CONV:COND   let   come-IMP:3PL
              'If they want to come, let them come!'

       Rus.   *Esli*   *oni*   *xot-jat*   *prij-ti,*   **pust'**   **prixod-jat**!
              if   they:NOM   want-PRES:3PL   come-INF   let   come-PRES:3PL

(18)   Niv.S   **P'eγrdoχ**   *painŕak*   *k'eŋ*   **poj-ǧaro**!
              let   often   sun-[SG-NOM]   shine-IMP:3SG
              'Let the sun often shine!'

       Rus.   **Pust'**   *často*   **svet-it**   *solnc-e!*
              let   often   shine-PRES:3SG   sun-N:SG:NOM

As can be seen, the particle p'eγrdoχ may combine both with singular, see example (16), and plural, see example (17), imperative forms.

The particle haǧaro 'let', being derived from the verb ha- 'be' by means of the third singular imperative marker -ǧaro, is apparently used only in optative sentences:

(19) Niv.S **Hağaro**   *la*   **ur-katn-ğaro!**
              let   weather-[SG-NOM]   be.good-INT-IMP:3SG
              'Let the weather be very good!'

      Rus.   **Pust'**   *pogod-a*   **bud-et**   *očen'*   **xoroš-ej!**
              let   weather-F:SG:NOM   be-PRES:3SG   very   good-F:SG:INST

The appearance of the redundant markers in the hortative sentences, typical also of conditional ones (scc section 2.4), can be attributed to the direct influence of the corresponding Russian analytical third person imperative forms with the particle *pust'* 'let', cf. examples (16-19).

3.4 Rise of new polite imperative forms

Appealing to a single elder hearer, the Nivkh speaker may traditionally use a special polite imperative verb form, that is the second person plural imperative form in *-ve* containing the additional second plural iterative suffix *-na-*:

(20) Niv.S *Vi-na-ve!*
              go-ITER:2PL-IMP:2PL
              'Go [please] (you:SG)!'

Nowadays, a polite prescription may also be expressed by the standard second person plural imperative form without the iterative suffix, as it is in Russian:

(21) Niv.S *Vi-ve!*
              go-IMP:2PL
              'Go [please] (you:SG)!'

      Rus.   *Id-i-te!*
              go-IMP:2SG-IMP:2PL

Example (22) demonstrates the use of the Nivkh polite form *umġavrve* and the Russian polite form *ne serdites'* both meaning 'do not be angry (you:SG)':

(22) Niv.S *Andχ-a!*   **Um-ġavr-ve**   *ur-gu-n*
              guest-[SG]-VOC   be.angry-NEG-IMP:2PL   be.good-CAUS-CONV:MAN:1PL
              ņafk-xun   *vot'i-n*   *kerai-da!*
              friend-PL-[NOM] be.like-CONV:MAN:1PL   speak-IMP:1PL
              'Guest! Do not be angry (you:SG), let us speak as good friends!'

      Rus.   *Gost'!*   **Ne**   **serd-i-te-s',**   *pogovor-im*
              guest-[SG-NOM]   not   be.angry-IMP:2SG-IMP:2PL-REFL   speak-FUT:1PL
              kak   *xoroš-ie*   *druz'j-a!*
              as   good-PL:NOM   friend-M:PL:NOM

4. Conclusions

In this paper, a variety of data on contact-induced language change that has taken place in present-day Nivkh syntax and morphosyntax has been presented. The incorporation by native speakers of Russian grammatical features into Nivkh grammar refers to the process of "borrowing within language maintenance" (Thomason and Kaufman 1988: 37) or "recipient language agentivity" (van Coetsem 1988: 3), and includes language innovations which may be considered mostly as a complication of the Nivkh grammatical system adopting various shapes. One may recall, for instance, the pluralization of nouns, the shift to obligatory subject-verb agreement, the appearance of redundant markers in different types of sentences, and especially the changes that have occurred in the imperative. With respect to the topic of the present paper, the imperative is of particular interest since it demonstrates a number of striking examples of emergence of new forms and constructions obviously caused by Russian interference but on the basis of grammatical means originated from Nivkh itself.

On the whole, the general output of the Russian influence on Nivkh does not seem to be very considerable, probably due to the fact that it is not promoted by a general similarity of grammatical structures of contacting languages, which according to Weinreich (1953) should facilitate the interference. The impact of language contact does not show up so much in the proper linguistic interference as it does in the total domination of Russian in everyday communication. Besides the data of the Census cited in the introduction, it should be noted that even Nivkh bilinguals, who consider Nivkh as their mother tongue, nowadays prefer Russian, not Nivkh, even in routine situations. The knowledge of Nivkh remains a passive, rarely used reserve. It is most likely that in the future the expansion of Russian will continue and will lead to the gradual rejection of Nivkh, first of all by the younger generation, whose knowledge of Nivkh even now is considered by elder speakers as "not very good". In these circumstances, the present-day situation is a unique opportunity for studying Russian-Nivkh linguistic interference, the discussion of which has only barely begun.

Helsinki

ABBREVIATIONS

ACC	accusative case	INT	intensifying			NOM	nominative case
CAUS	causative	ITER	iterative			PAST	past tense
COND	conditional	LOC	locative case			PL	plural number
CONV	converb	M	masculine gender			PREP	prepositional case
DAT	dative case	MAN	manner			PRES	present tense
GEN	genitive case	MOD	modal			PTL	particle
F	feminine gender	N	neuter gender			REFL	reflexive
FIN	finite	NEG	negative			RES	resultative
FUT	future tense	Niv.A	the Amur dialect of			Rus.	Russian
IMP	imperative		Nivkh			SG	singular number
INF	infinitive	Niv.S	the East Sakhalin dialect			TEMP	temporal
INST	instrumental case		of Nivkh			VOC	vocative case

REFERENCES

Austerlitz, Robert
1958   "Vocatif et impératif en ghiliak", *Orbis* VII, 2, 477-481.
Birjulin, Leonid A., and Viktor S. Xrakovskij
1992   "Povelitel'nye predloženija: problemy teorii", in: Viktor S. Xrakovskij (ed.), *Tipologija imperativnyx konstrukcij*, 5-50. Sankt-Peterburg: Nauka.
Coetsem, Frans van
1988   *Loan phonology and the two transfer types in language contact.* Dordrecht: Foris.
Graaf, Tjeerd de
1992   "Small languages and small language communities: news, notes, and comments. 9: The small languages of Sakhalin", *International Journal of the Sociology of Language* 94, 185-200.
Gruzdeva, Ekaterina Ju.
1992   "Povelitel'nye predloženija v nivxskom jazyke", in: Viktor S. Xrakovskij (ed.), *Tipologija imperativnyx konstrukcij*, 55-63. Sankt-Peterburg: Nauka.
1996   "The Linguistic Situation on Sakhalin Island", in: Stephen A. Wurm, Peter Mühlhäusler, Darrell T. Tryon (eds.), *Atlas of Languages of Intercultural Communication in the Pacific, Asia, and the Americas* II, 2 (*Trends in Linguistics. Documentation* 13, 2), 1007-1012. Berlin-New York: Mouton de Gruyter.
1998   *Nivkh* (*Languages of the World: Materials* 111). München-Newcastle: LINCOM Europa.
Gruzdeva, Ekaterina Ju., and Julija V. Leonova
1990   "K izučeniju nivxsko-russkogo dvujazyčija v sociolingvist-českom aspekte", in: Nikolaj D. Andreev (ed.), *Lingvističeskie issledovanija 1990. Sistemnye otnošenija v sinxronii i diaxronii*, 48-55. Moskva: Institut jazykoznanija AN SSSR.
Krejnovič, Eruhim A.
1934   "Nivxskij (giljackij) jazyk", in: Eruhim A. Krejnovič (ed.), *Jazyki i pis'mennost' narodov Severa. III: Jazyki i pis'mennost' paleoaziatskix narodov*, 181-222. Moskva-Leningrad: Učpedgiz.
Nacional'nyj...
1991   *Nacional'nyj sostav naselenija SSSR. Po dannym Vsesojuznoj perepisi naselenija 1989 g.* Moskva.

Panfilov, Vladimir Z.
1962   *Grammatika nivxskogo jazyka* 1. Moskva-Leningrad: Nauka.
1965   *Grammatika nivxskogo jazyka* 2. Moskva-Leningrad: Nauka.
Savel'eva, Valentina N., and Čuner M. Taksami
1970   *Nivxsko-russkij slovar'*. Moskva: Sovetskaja enciklopedija.
Šternberg, Lev Ja.
1908   *Materialy po izučeniju giljackogo jazyka i fol'klora.* I: *Obrazcy narodnoj slo-vesnosti* I (*Izvestija imperatorskoj Akademii nauk* XXII). Sankt-Peterburg.
Thomason, Sarah Grey, and Terrence Kaufman
1988   *Language contact, creolization, and genetic linguistics*. Berkley: University of California Press.
Trudgill, Peter
1986   *Dialects in contact.* Oxford: Blackwell.
Weinreich, Uriel
1953   *Languages in contact. Findings and problems.* The Hague: Mouton.

Languages in Contact, edited by D.G. Gilbers, J. Nerbonne, and J. Schaeken (= *Studies in Slavic and General Linguistics*, vol. 28), 135-144. Amsterdam - Atlanta, GA: Rodopi, 2000.

ESTONIAN BETWEEN GERMAN AND RUSSIAN: FACTS AND FICTION ABOUT LANGUAGE INTERFERENCE

CORNELIUS HASSELBLATT

German and Russian are the most important contact languages for Estonian. While the German influence has been described at different levels in several monographs (e.g. Ariste 1940, Pauley 1980, Hinderling 1981, Hasselblatt 1990) and numerous articles, the Russian influence still lacks a profound analysis. Some work has been done in the field of loanwords (e.g. Mägiste 1962, Seppet 1983), but most of the work seems to lie before us.

Since the weakening of the Soviet/Russian political influence (ca. 1988) and the regaining of Estonian independence (1991) the Russian influence on Estonian has been dealt with by several Estonian scholars (cf. Hint 1990, 1990a, 1996, 1996a; Liivaku 1993 and 1994). The problem is, however, that some of the linguistic features characterized as Russian might be ascribed to other, i.e. mainly (Low) German influence, as this language was the most important contact language for Estonian for seven centuries: Estonia was conquered by Teutonic knights in the 13th century. This, and the embedding into the Hanseatic League led to a strong (Low) German influence which lasted until the beginnings of the 20th century when the German upper class finally lost its privileged position (1918) and left the country (1939). The Russian influence was intensified in the period of Russification beginning with emperor Alexander III (1881) but was interrupted during the first independence period (1918-1940). The Soviet period (1941/44-1991) strengthened the position of Russian again, leading to a demographic shift, resulting in the large Russian minority of Estonia today.

The problem, in short, is to weigh 700 years of (Low) German influence against 100 years of intense Russian influence. In what follows I will try to present a critical review of Russian influence in Estonian and ask whether Russian is, indeed, the only probable source for specific un-Estonian features in Estonian, or whether other source languages should also be considered. The following inventory is based mainly on Mati Hint (1990) but other sources are also taken into account. Hint 1990a is an English version of the first part of (the Estonian) Hint 1990.

1) Ideologization of word usage (Hint 1990: 1383-1387): It is true that in a centralized, totalitarian state language is an important instrument for rulers to steer the people. This certainly happened in Soviet Estonia as well as in Nazi-Germany and elsewhere. The specific position of Russian in the Soviet Union does indeed give the ideologization of word usage a Russian guise. Generally, however, ideologization of word usage is not confined to totalitarian states. Contemporary American 'political correctness' can also be a kind of ideologization as is any kind of prescribed euphemism: in German nuclear energy was originally called *Atomkraft* (e.g. Wahrig 1968: 454) but later replaced by *Kernkraft* (*Duden* 1993-1995: 271 refers from *Atomkraft* to *Kernkraft*) because *Kernkraft* lacks the negative connotation with the atomic bomb. So Hint's statement on ideologization of word usage should be modified: Due to the Russian rule the (normal) ideologization of word usage received a Russian guise.

2) Using reflexive (intransitive) verbs instead of transitive verbs or German *sich*-constructions (Hint 1990: 1388-1392): As Hint himself admits, the suffix *-u-* for reflexive or intransitive verbs is a common derivation suffix in Baltic-Finnic. The hypothesis that the use of this suffix has increased due to Russian influence can hardly be proved or disproved without larger-scale quantitative analysis. But there are some arguments which suggest that many *-u*-verbs are older than recent Russian influence could account for. One of Hint's examples – *sulguma* 'to close' – can be attested for the early 18th century (Vestring's unpublished dictionary, see Vestring 1998: 234) and cannot therefore exist due to recent Russian influence. Secondly, a look at Finland can prove useful: the pair *sisaldama* 'to contain' / *sisalduma* 'to be contained, be included' – the latter being one of Hint's examples for the spreading of *-u*-verbs – has an exact Finnish counterpart in *sisältää* and *sisältyä*. A comparable Russian influence on Finnish has, however, never been suggested, and the fact that in a frequency analysis the Finnish verbs do not range very far away from one another (*sisältää* has position 580, *sisältyä* position 712 in a sample of more than 40.000 lexems, cf. Saukkonen et al. 1979: 468) is a further argument for the 'normality' of this verb pair. Mägiste (1982-1983: 2823) even suggests that not only *sisaldama* – which is quite obvious (cf. Raun 1982: 158) – but even *sisalduma* is a 19th century Finnish loan. Finally, we find the pair already in a pre-war Estonian-German dictionary (Graf 1937: 534-535) which again makes recent Russian influence seem more unlikely.

3) Aspect (Hint 1990: 1392-1393): The category of aspect is sometimes believed to be a peculiarity of the Slavic languages (cf. Lewandowski 1994: 95), but it is actually found in most of the world's languages, though the means of realisation can be very different (Comrie 1976, Dahl 1985). The Baltic-Finnic languages originally show the uncommon feature of marking aspect with the nominal object, not with the verb. But this method is restricted to certain syntactical constructions – e.g. only transitive verbs can display aspectual meanings with the object – and

syntactical aspectual minimal pairs are extremely rare (cf. for Finnish Ground-stroem 1988: 10). In Estonian, such cases are even less frequent (Metslang 1997: 32). Nevertheless the category of aspect can be expressed, as Estonian has developed its own system of phrasal verbs which function mostly as aspect markers (Hasselblatt 1990; Metslang 1997). Although Hint (1990: 1392) admits that this aspectual system came into being mostly according to the German pattern (cf. G. *essen* vs. *aufessen*), he argues that the recent Russian influence has stimulated most of the contemporary phrasal verbs. This statement is insubstantial insofar as a large number of the phrasal verbs are considerably older than one hundred years. As Russian pressure was much weaker, or even non-existent, in previous centuries, a Russian loan translation is less likely than a German loan translation in case both possible source languages offer the same pattern. According to Hint (1990: 1393) Est. *välja ütlema* 'to speak out' (*välja* 'out' + *ütlema* 'to say') would be a recent (= Soviet) loan translation from Russ. *vy-skazat'sja* 'to speak out', but as this verb is found already in earlier sources (e.g. Wiedemann 1869: 1413), the German verb *aussprechen* might fit better as the source.

I have shown earlier (Hasselblatt 1999: 228-229) that the Russian influence Erelt and Metslang (1998: 665) suggested for some verbs is not very probable as these verbs could already be attested in earlier centuries. Another example is a newspaper column by Hint (1990b) where he says: "In order to reach exactly the grammatical structure of the Russian verb one uses means of expressions which have come into being by German influence", and he mentions several examples of verbs with the (redundant) aspect marker *ära*. In his opinion these verbs are constructed according to their Russian counterparts with the means and methods earlier German influence had created in Estonian. I state, however, that a considerable number of the phrasal verbs has already been formed long before the Russian influence strenghtened, as they can be attested in sources from the 17th and 18th century.

As the most common aspect marker is *ära* 'away, off' I will scrutinize the verb patterns with this particle. In an earlier corpus (Hasselblatt 1990) based on contemporary, 20th century, dictionaries I examined 266 phrasal verbs with *ära*. Of these verbs, 41.4 % could be attested in the 17th century, 15.8 % in the 18th century, 18.4 % in the 19th century, and only less than a quarter (24.4 %) had no earlier attestation. This corpus is based on bilingual dictionaries (cf. Hasselblatt 1990: 50-53) and is not at all all-inclusive. But the tendency is rather obvious: more than the half of the phrasal verbs with *ära* stems from, at least, the 17th and 18th century. Additional material from older dictionaries even shows that the number of phrasal verbs was still higher: Vestring's 18th century dictionary includes 76 phrasal verbs with *ära* which are not found in contemporary dictionaries.

The question is, of course, why is the particular vintage of any given syntagma an argument for German as opposed to Russian influence? The answer can only be given by consulting books on social and educational history. In their thorough study on the social and national situation in Tallinn in the Middle Ages, Johansen and von zur Mühlen (1973: 379) state: "Auffallend wenig wurde in Reval im Gegensatz zum Schwedischen das Russische gekonnt und gesprochen". Ariste (1981: 34), in writing about the 16th century, notes that there was a certain trilingualism in Tallinn which can even be found in historical documents, however, those three languages were Estonian, German, and Swedish – and not Russian. The first primary schools for Russian children were not founded until the 1780ies in Narva and Tallinn (Laul 1989: 257). The older a phenomenon is, the less probable Russian influence would appear to be, since Russian was simply not that visible in earlier times.

In general, the phenomenon of the phrasal verb can be found in a number of other Finno-Ugric languages (cf. Hasselblatt 1990: 46-48, and Bujnák 1928, recently Honti 1999), above all Hungarian (Soltész 1959, Schlachter and Pusztay 1983), and it is not absolutely clear whether it is due to foreign influence in all Finno-Ugric languages. On account of this fact and the earlier sources mentioned above, I do not estimate as particularly significant the Russian role in the development of the Estonian system of phrasal verbs. Russian played, at most, an auxiliary or supporting role concerning the very contemporary development, and no more.

4) Usage of periphrastical verb forms and negation (Hint 1990: 1394-1395): According to Hint the expression *ei saa jätta märkimata, et...* 'it cannot be left unmentioned that...' is Russian influenced as 'normal' Estonian would run *tuleb märkida, et...* 'you have to mention that...'. Double negation, however, is a common stylistic element in many languages to make speech more lively, and the literal English translation above is idiomatic as well as is the German translation 'man darf nicht unerwähnt lassen, dass...'. There is no reason to posit only Russian influence for this element of style; it is, at least, general Indo-European. The same element of style may already be found in letters from the 19th century. Lydia Koidula wrote in 1867 to Friedrich Reinhold Kreutzwald: '... siis ei või Teil mitte teadmata olla, ...' which is literally 'so it cannot be unknown to you' (Kreutzwald and Koidula 1910: 9). The correspondence of Kreutzwald and Koidula is, by the way, partly written in German, which means that German influence, if any, is most likely. Also in records from the early 18th century we find stylistic double (or even triple) negation (cf. Vestring 1998: 133). The tendency to express the opposite by double negation is older than recent Russian influence.

In general negation (cf. Honti 1997) differs in most Uralic languages from the Indo-European pattern, as instead of particle negation often a negation verb is applied. This is not the case in the Ugric languages: the Hungarian *nem* functions exactly as the German *nicht* or the Russian *ne*, i.e. in front of or after the finite verb form. Finnish, on the other hand, still has a fully conjugated negation verb with six different forms which is followed by the verb stem without personal suffixes. Estonian stands in between having reduced the negation verb to one form (*ei*, which is originally 3rd person singular) which functions as a particle like the above-mentioned *nem*, *nicht* or *ne*, but which still is followed – as in Finnish – only by the stem without personal suffixes. Additionally a second negation particle has arisen, *mitte* 'not'. Originally in literary Estonian the usage of *mitte* was excluded from the negation of a finite verb form and confined e.g. to the negation of infinitives or nouns or additionally used for emphasis.

In contemporary texts, as Hint (1990: 1394-1395) states, the negation with *mitte* followed by both finite and non-finite verb forms is gaining ground, but actually this topic has already been dealt with earlier (Kindlam 1976: 82-84). It is questionable for two reasons whether this happens only due to Russian influence: Firstly, in dialects we also find the *mitte*-negation with verbs and without *ei* (cf. Koit 1963: 143; Sang 1975: 156). Secondly, in certain constructions like the English 'not only ... but [also]' the negation with *mitte* is even preferable to the one with *ei* because the sentence is semantically positive and the case of the object has therefore to be the one normally applied in positive sentences, too. Using *ei* in those sentences would disturb this rule, cf.: **Ta ei kaotanud mitte ainult riideid* [partitive], *vaid ka dokumente* [partitive] **'She didn't only lose her clothes but also her documents' and *Ta kaotas mitte ainult riided* [nominative], *vaid ka dokumendid* [nominative] 'She lost not only her clothes but also her documents' (Sang 1983: 259-260). Aspectually the action is perfective, as clothes and documents are definitively lost, therefore the object has to be in the nominative. Using the partitive in the first part of the sentence could only be correct if the clothes were not lost. Similar examples are quoted by other authors, too (cf. Erelt 1977: 436).

The question of negation has been discussed thoroughly in Estonian linguistics, because the system is changing (cf. Finnish on the one hand and Hungarian on the other hand). The shift away from the negation verb to a more analytical particle negation has, in my opinion, roots older than recent Russian influence. Again, I think, Russian influence is but one possibility and maybe only an accelerating factor.

5) Tense (Hint 1990: 1395-1396): The Estonian tense system consists of four tenses (present, past, present perfect, past perfect), where Russian has only two (present and past). The general opinion is that Proto-Uralic had no compound tenses (as present perfect and past perfect in Baltic-Finnic today are) and that the Baltic-Finnic tense system developed either independently or due to the influence of the Baltic languages. Later the Germanic languages might also have played a part in this development (Laanest 1982: 235). The use of the tenses follows

roughly the same pattern as in English: *ta on töötanud* [present perfect] *meil juba hulk aega, aga keegi ei tunne teda õieti* 'she has worked with us already for a long time, but actually nobody knows her'. Hint (1990: 1395) states that in texts translated from Russian we also find the following form which is, literally translated into English, ungrammatical: *ta töötab* [present tense] *meil juba hulk aega, aga keegi ei tunne teda õieti* *'she works with us already for a long time, but actually nobody knows her'. Russian influence is here indeed rather probable, as this contact language has only two tenses. Also Metslang (1993: 34) mentions Russian influence in certain temporal constructions in Estonian. On the other hand one has to take into account that the German translation could only be in the present tense (*sie arbeitet hier schon eine geraume Zeit, aber niemand kennt sie eigentlich*, cf. **sie hat hier schon eine geraume Zeit gearbeitet, aber niemand kennt sie eigentlich*), though German has a present perfect as well (but cannot use it in this example). Without further investigation of old Estonian texts the source language is difficult to determine.

Morphologically, the future tense does not exist in Uralic (or is, if you like, a homomorph with the present tense), but Estonian has developed an analytical future with the verb *saama* 'to become' following the German *werden*-future. This was quite strongly, and successfully, banned by the language renewal movement at the beginning of this century. A lot of future constructions with *saama* can nevertheless be found in Estonian texts, which according to Hint (1990: 1396) copy the Russian construction with *budu* etc. But the situation is more complicated: Metslang (1994) shows the general need for a future form a written language has and states that the revival of the *saama*-future in Estonian can be ascribed to the growing importance of the press. She gives an internal explanation and does not even mention Russian influence. I cannot solve this question here but it can be mentioned that in the meantime another language with an analytical future – English – has become an important contact language for Estonian. Russian does not seem to be the only explanation.

6) Plural (Hint 1990, 1396-1400): Hint is certainly right when stating that plural use is rather limited in Uralic languages, and also in Estonian. He states that in the sentence *Lõppeval nädalal oli osal* [sg adessive] *saadikutest* [pl elative] *kohtumisi* 'at the end of the week a number [lit. "part"] of the delegates had meetings' we find the normal Estonian singular whereas the following sentence would display Russian plural use: *Lõppeval nädalal oli osadel* [pl adessive] *saadikutel* [pl adessive] *kohtumisi* 'at the end of the week some ["parts"] of the delegates had meetings'. On the other hand he admits that in the same Russian constructions no number agreement occurs (Hint 1990: 1398). In other words: Hint cannot prove direct Russian influence in this case either.

His second example is more convincing: indefinite pronouns and relative pronouns tend to apply the plural where the singular would be expected or 'normal'.

Elasime mitmeid aastaid [pl] *koos* 'we lived many years together' instead of the expected *Elasime mitu aastat* [sg] *koos* 'id.' The semantically understandable plural form is not genuine Estonian and follows an Indo-European or Russian pattern. The same semantic influence we find in the following sentences: *Enamik* [sg] *hääletab* [sg] *vastu* 'the majority votes against', and *Enamik* [sg] *hääletavad* [pl] *vastu* 'id.'. The 'danger' of applying the plural with a morphologically singular but semantically plural subject is inherent, I believe, to all languages, that is why I am not sure that the possible Russian pattern is the only solution.

7) Prepositions instead of postpositions (Hint 1990: 1400-1402): The original Uralic pattern is centripedal as is usual for agglutinative languages, which entails using postpositions instead of prepositions. In Baltic Finnic and Saamic, however, a number of postpositions are used as prepositions, too. This is generally believed to be Germanic or Slavic influence (Majtinskaja 1982: 17; Stoebke 1968: 3). Both contact languages, Russian and German, are prepositional, therefore the growing use of prepositions in Estonian is not particularly surprising. Ehala (1994) has examined the possible Russian influence thoroughly and comes to the conclusion "that the robust Russian influence explanation for this change in progress is oversimplified" (Ehala 1994: 177). He analysed texts from 1905, 1972 and 1992 and found out that the frequency of adpositions has fallen considerably during this century, but the frequency of prepostions has risen between 1905 and 1972 and fallen between 1972 and 1992. "This evidence has brought into question the belief that the rise of prepositions in Estonian has been caused by an increasing Russian influence in the second half of this century" (Ehala 1994: 191). Once again we have to admit that Russian influence is not the only possible explanation and that the problem is much more complex, and insoluble without further research.

Conclusion

Of the seven features ascribed to recent Russian influence and examined above, only one could more or less unequivocally be labelled as having undergone Russian influence (no. 1, ideologization of word usage). All the others were either somewhat doubtful (no. 2, reflexive verbs, partly no. 4, negation, no. 5, tense, no. 6, plural, no. 7, prepositions) or even improbable (no. 3, aspect, partly no. 4, negation). I would therefore hesitate to speak of an immense Russian influence as some scholars do. There are, of course, traces of Russian influence, but in hardly any case has this been the only possible source of innovation. Russian influence on Estonian is less strong than has often been assumed.

University of Groningen

REFERENCES

Ariste, Paul
1940   *Georg Mülleri saksa laensõnad* (*Acta et Commentationes Universitatis Tartuensis* B 46,1). Tartu.
1981   *Keelekontaktid* (*Eesti NSV TA Emakeele Seltsi Toimetised* 14). Tallinn: Valgus.
Bujnák, Pavel
1928   *Praefixa verbalia v jazykoch ugrofinských a zvlášte v maďarskom*. Praha: Fr. Řivnače.
Comrie, Bernard
1976   *Aspect. An introduction to the study of verbal aspect and related problems*. Cambridge: Cambridge University Press.
Dahl, Östen
1985   *Tense and aspect systems*. Oxford: Blackwell.
Duden
1993-1995   *Das große Wörterbuch der deutschen Sprache. 2., völlig neu bearbeitete und stark erweiterte Auflage*. Mannheim et al.: Dudenverlag.
Ehala, Martin
1994   "Russian influence and the change in progress in the Estonian adpositional system", *Linguistica Uralica* 30, 177-193.
Erelt, Mati
1977   "Ühest eitamise viisist", *Keel ja Kirjandus* 20, 435-436.
Erelt, Mati, and Helle Metslang
1998   "Oma või võõras?", *Keel ja Kirjandus* 41, 657-668.
Graf, A. E.
1937   *Estnisch-deutsches Wörterbuch*. Durchgesehen von Mag. Joh. Aavik. Tartu: Kool.
Groundstroem, Axel
1988   *Finnische Kasusstudien* (*Acta Universitatis Umensis. Umeå Studies in the Humanities* 87). Stockholm: Almqvist & Wiksell.
Hasselblatt, Cornelius
1990   *Das estnische Partikelverb als Lehnübersetzung aus dem Deutschen* (*Veröffentlichungen der Societas Uralo-Altaica* 31). Wiesbaden: Harrassowitz.
1999   "Kuhu tõttad, eesti keel? ("Muutuv keel")", *Keel ja Kirjandus* 42, 227-234.
Hinderling, Robert
1981   *Die deutsch-estnischen Lehnwortbeziehungen im Rahmen einer europäischen Lehnwortgeographie*. Wiesbaden: Harrassowitz.
Hint, Mati
1990   "Vene keele mõjud eesti keelele", *Akadeemia* 2, 1383-1404.
1990a   "Russian Influences in the Estonian Language", *Congressus Internationalis Fenno-Ugristarum* VII, Debrecen, 1A, 87-104.
1990b   "Keel ja kõne", *Reede* 23.III.1990, 5.
1996   "Indo-euroopa mallide lisandumine eesti keele analüütilises morfoloogias", *Congressus Internationalis Fenno-Ugristarum* VIII, Jyväskylä, 4, 183-185.
1996a   "Eesti keel okupatsiooni järel", *Keel ja Kirjandus* 39, 802-808.
Honti, László
1997   "Die Negation im Uralischen", *Linguistica Uralica* 33, 81-96, 161-176, 241-252.

1999   "Das Alter und die Entstehungsweise der 'Verbalpräfixe' in uralischen Sprachen (unter besonderer Berücksichtigung des Ungarischen) I", *Linguistica Uralica* 35, 81-97.

Johansen, Paul, and Heinz von zur Mühlen
1973   *Deutsch und undeutsch im mittelalterlichen und frühneuzeitlichen Reval.* Köln, Wien: Böhlau.

Kindlam, Ester
1976   *Meie igapäevane keel. Tema hoolet ja seadet.* Tallinn: Valgus.

Koit, E.
1963   *Eitus saarte murdes. Nonaginta (Emakeele Seltsi Toimetised* 6), 136-147. Tallinn: ENSV Teaduste Akadeemia.

Kreutzwald, Friedrich Reinhold, and Lydia Koidula
1910   *Kreutzwaldi ja Koidula kirjawahetus* I *(Eesti Kirjanduse Seltsi toimetused* 5,1). Tartu: Eesti Kirjanduse Selts.

Laanest, Arvo
1982   *Einführung in die ostseefinnischen Sprachen.* Hamburg: Buske.

Laul, E. (ed.)
1989   *Eesti kooli ajalugu. 1. köide: 13. sajandist 1860. aastateni.* Tallinn: Valgus.

Lewandowski, Theodor
1994   *Linguistisches Wörterbuch* 1-3. 6. Auflage *(UTB für Wissenschaft. Uni-Taschenbücher* 1518). Heidelberg: Quelle & Meyer.

Liivaku, Uno
1993   "Venepärane rajav kääne", *Keel ja Kirjandus* 36, 491-492.
1994   "Venepärasest võõrsõnatarvitusest", *Keel ja Kirjandus* 37, 40-41.

Mägiste, Julius
1962   *Äldre ryska lånord i estniskan särskilt i det gamla estniska skriftspråket (Lunds Universitets Årsskrift.* NF, Avd. 1, Bd. 55, Nr. 1). Lund.
1982-1983   *Estnisches etymologisches Wörterbuch.* 1-12. Helsinki: Suomalais-Ugrilainen Seura.

Majtinskaja, Klara
1982   *Služebnye slova v finno-ugorskix jazykax.* Moskva: Nauka.

Metslang, Helle
1993   "Viron aika – muoto, merkitys, ikonisuus", *Studia Comparativa Linguarum Orbis Maris Baltici* 1. *Tutkimuksia syntaksin ja pragmasyntaksin alalta.* Toim. V. *Yli-Vakkuri*, 24-40. Turku: Turun yliopisto.
1994   "Eesti ja soome – futuurumita keeled?", *Keel ja Kirjandus* 37, 534-547, 603-616.
1997   "Eesti prefiksaaladverbist *ära* soome keele taustal", *Lähivertailuja* 9. *Suomalais-virolainen kontrastiiviseminaari 3.-5.5.1996 Lammi. Toim. Riho Grünthal ja Reet Kasik*, 31-46 *(Castrenianumin Toimitteita* 53). Helsinki: Suomalais-Ugrilainen Seura.

Pauley, Douglas Ronald
1980   *German Loan Translations in Estonian, Finnish and Hungarian.* Ph.D. Indiana University.

Raun, Alo
1982   *Eesti keele etümoloogiline teatmik.* Rom, Toronto: Maarjamaa.

Sang, Joel
1975   "Eitus Kihnu murrakus", *Keel ja Kirjandus* 18, 155-162.
1983   "Eitus eesti keeles", Tallinn: Valgus.

Saukkonen, Pauli, Marjatta Haipus, Antero Niemikorpi, and Helena Sulkala
1979 *Suomen kielen taajuussanasto*. Porvoo et al.: Werner Söderström OY.

Schlachter, Wolfgang, and János Pusztay
1983 *Morpho-semantische Untersuchung des ungarischen Verbalpräfixes el- (A Magyar Nyelvtudományi társaság kiadványai 167)*. Budapest.

Seppet, Anita
1983 "Vene laenud tänapäeva eesti kirjakeeles (ÕS-i ainestiku ulatuses)", *Sõnasõel* 6, 75-92.

Soltész, Katalin
1959 *A ősi magyar igekötők (meg, el, ki, be, fel, le)*. Budapest: Akadémiai Kiadó.

Stoebke, Renate
1968 *Die Verhältniswörter in den ostseefinnischen Sprachen (Uralic and Altaic Series. University of Bloomington, Indiana 93)*. The Hague: Mouton.

Vestring, Salomo Heinrich
1998 *Lexicon esthonico germanicum. Tartu: Eesti Kirjandusmuuseum* (edition of the manuscript from the early 18th century).

Wahrig, Gerhard
1968 *Deutsches Wörterbuch* (einmalige Sonderausgabe 1971). Gütersloh: Bertelsmann.

Wiedemann, Ferdinand Johann
1869 *Ehstnisch-deutsches Wörterbuch*. St. Petersburg: Eggers & Co.

Languages in Contact, edited by D.G. Gilbers, J. Nerbonne, and J. Schaeken (= *Studies in Slavic and General Linguistics*, vol. 28), 145-156. Amsterdam - Atlanta, GA: Rodopi, 2000.

DUTCH-GERMAN CONTACT IN AND AROUND BENTHEIM

WILBERT HEERINGA, JOHN NERBONNE, HERMANN NIEBAUM, ROGIER NIEUWEBOER, PETER KLEIWEG

1. Introduction

Up to the middle of the 20th century, for people on both sides of the Dutch-German border, the border was no impediment for understanding each other. The Low Saxon dialects on both sides of the border formed a smooth continuum. Until the Second World War the use of the Dutch and German standard languages was restricted almost completely to school, the church and government circles. Especially since the Second World War, the use of standard languages has increased particularly in everyday communication, while the use of the dialect has increasingly been restricted to the private sphere. Furthermore, the dialects in Eastern Netherlands were becoming more Dutch while the dialects in North West Germany were becoming more German (cf. Auer and Hinskens 1996: 15-18 for the influence of political borders in Europa). On the one hand a number of everyday objects were no longer used, so words denoting them in both the Dutch and the German Low Saxon dialects disappeared. On the other hand, when new objects are introduced, the name is often borrowed from the standard language. Existing words were also replaced by words which are the same or similar to ones in the standard languages. The result is that the significance of the political border as dialect border is increasing (Kremer 1984, 1990, Niebaum 1990). The present paper examines the contemporary situation in order to find out whether the border continues to drive the dialects apart and to examine the effect of the standard languages. Remarkably, the effects are noticeable over a period of two to three generations.

Part 14 of the Reeks Nederlands(ch)e Dialectatlassen (RND) was compiled by H. Entjes and contains transcriptions of dialects in South Drenthe and North Overijssel (Entjes 1982). The transcriptions were made in 1974-1975. Besides Dutch dialects this part also contains eight dialects in the German county Bentheim. Entjes justified his choice by referring to the dissertation of Arnold Rakers: *Die Mundarten der alten Grafschaft Bentheim und ihrer reichsdeutschen und niederländischen Umgebung*, Oldenburg, 1944 (cf. also Rakers 1993). The dissertation mentions that the *Gildehäuser Schulchronik* reported that the first grade of the elementary school used Dutch as a language of instruction for the last time in April, 1902. In 1925 Laar was the last reformed church which sang psalms in Dutch in services. National Socialism completely eliminated the use of Dutch language only in 1933. But Dutch sacred writings and the Dutch *Statenbijbel* were still used for a long time.

In this paper we investigate the (changes in the) relation between the eight varieties in Bentheim, and nine Dutch dialects which form a ring around Bentheim (see Figure 1). We research the influence of political borders and language standardisation. For this purpose we use Levenshtein distance for measuring the phonetic distances between dialects. The distance measure is explained in Kruskal (1983) and was first applied to dialect data by Kessler (1995). Using Levenshtein distances two strings (two dialectal pronunciations of the same word) are compared by calculating the cost of (the least costly set of) operations mapping one phonetic transcription to another. The basic costs are those of insertions, deletions and substitutions. The basic procedures are made more sensitive by using bundles of features and weighting operation costs by phonetic similarity (realised in feature overlap).

On the basis of Levenshtein distances the dialects are classified by clustering (Jain and Dubes 1988) or multidimensional scaling (Kruskal and Wish 1984). The final result of clustering is a dendrogram which is a hierarchically structured tree in which the dialects are the leafs. The result of multidimensional scaling is a map, where the geographic distance between kindred dialects is small, and between different dialects great. Nerbonne et al. (1996), Nerbonne and Heeringa (1998) and Nerbonne et al. (1999) show the application of the comparison and classification methods on Dutch dialects.

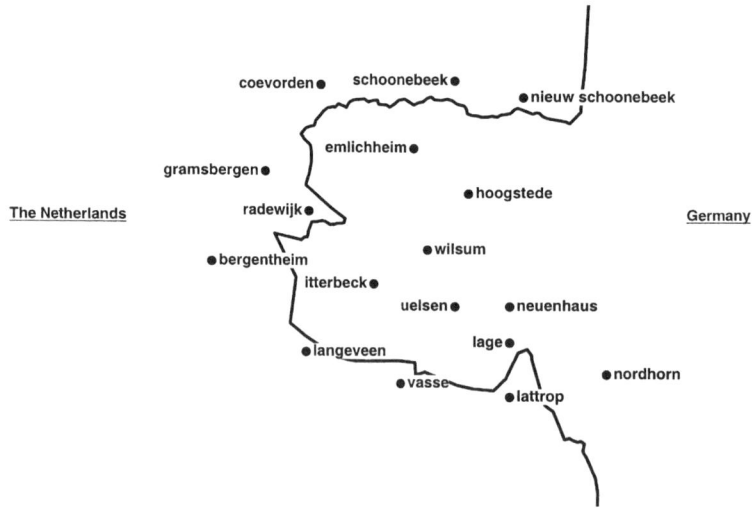

Figure 1. The locations of the Dutch and German dialects.

2. Data

2.1 Dialects

To examine changes in time we need comparable sources from different times. As mentioned above, the older source consisted of transcriptions in the RND, made in 1974-1975. We selected nine Dutch and eight German varieties, so we get a total of seventeen varieties. The average age of the informants of these varieties is 58. Per site, two informants were interviewed, except for Nieuw Schoonebeek and Wilsum, where three informants were interviewed. Entjes interviewed the informants mostly on the basis of a Dutch questionnaire. When this resulted in problems in connection with the German locations, he could almost always solve the problem by using his own dialect (dialect of Vroomshoop). In some cases, he could only solve the problem by using standard German.

A newer source was not available, so in 1999 we conducted new interviews and made transcriptions of the same dialects. To maximise the time span, we interviewed younger informants. Their average age is 39. Per site we interviewed one informant, except for Lattrop and Vasse where we interviewed two informants. For the Dutch dialects we used the questionnaire as given in part 14 of the RND. For the German dialects we made a German translation of the Dutch questionnaire and used that. The present inhabitants of Bentheim understand Dutch more poorly than the inhabitants in the past, so using a Dutch questionnaire would have resulted in a translation with a lot of echo forms.

When making transcriptions of the recordings, we took the old RND transcriptions as a basis, and made changes in it where we heard differences. We chose this procedure to guarantee maximal consistency of the new transcriptions with the old ones.

The complete RND questionnaire consists of 141 sentences. For our research, from these sentences we chose 100 words, which we think are representative for the range of sounds in the varieties. When making new recordings, we only recorded the sentences which contains one or more of the 100 words.

2.2 Standard languages

To examine the influence of the standard languages we need transcriptions of standard Dutch and standard German which are consistent with the dialect transcriptions. In deciding on transcription practice, we consistently avoid prejudicing the case for divergence. We provide details on our transcription practices in the following sections.

2.2.1 Standard Dutch

For the Dutch transcription we took the *Tekstboekje* of Blancquaert (1939) as a basis. The phonetic system used in it is the same as in the RND, with the exception of some extensions we will mention below. Using this 'textbook' we obtain a consistent word list because Blancquaert edited a great many parts of the RND, while other editors learned transcription from Blancquaert or worked with his outlines.

Transcriptions were taken from this textbook whenever the context was not significantly different from the RND questionnaire context. For words which could not be found there, transcriptions were made which are analogous to similar words in the source.

In the textbook, Blancquaert uses only [r], no [R]. However, in the RND the [R] is used. Because in Dutch both realisations are allowed, in the word list for each word containing one or more <r>'s, we also note a variant in which the <r>'s are pronounced as [R]. Further, Blancquaert transcribed both the labiodental and the bilabial <w> as [w]. In the RND a distinction is made between them. In our word list, at each place where a <w> appears at the beginning of a syllable, we note it as [ʋ]. If a <w> appears at the end of a syllable or after <u> (for example: <nieuwe>, <duwen>, <brouwer>), we note it as [w]. The [ɣ] is noted at the beginning of a syllable, the [x] at the end of a syllable. Blancquaert notes <tj> as [tj], for example: <tuintjes> is [tœ.ʸntjəs], <kindje> is [kɪntjə]. This is like the notation of the RND, with the exception of part 16 (Groningen and Noord-Drenthe) where <tj> is noted as [c]. If a word ends on the syllable <en> (for example: <komen>, <rozen>, <open>), Blancquaert always notes that syllable as <ən>. However, we always omit the final n (for example: [ko.mə], [ro:zə], [o.pə]). This is in accordance with the pronunciation given in CELEX and Paardekooper (1998). Blancquaert did not note which syllable is stressed. We also did not. Note that in both the textbook and the RND, the [ɔ] preceding the [m], [n] or [ŋ] is noted as [ʊ] (for example in: <bom>, <lont>, <honger>).

In the texts of Blancquaert, a distinction is made between [v] and [f], for example: <vier> is [vi.r] and <fier> is [fi:r]. It seems that both in the textbook and in the RND a [v] is transcribed if a <v> is noted and a [f] is transcribed if an <f> is noted. In the newer transcriptions we made, for most dialects only the [f] was heard and noted, even where in spelling a <v> would be spelled. But for present-day standard Dutch the same applies: both, the <v> and the <f> are pronounced as [f]. So we made a 1974 version of standard Dutch with distinction between [v] and [f], and a 1999 version of standard Dutch in which only the [f] is used. This prevents the results from unfairly showing that the 1999 dialects diverged from standard Dutch.

In the RND the [ç] is never used, although one should expect this sound in the transcriptions of Brabant and Limburg dialects. Instead of it the [x] was used. To keep the material consistent, we did the same for the new transcriptions, although sometimes the [ç] was heard in the recordings of the German dialects.

2.2.2 Standard German

For making a Standard German word list, we used the *Wörterbuch der deutschen Aussprache* (1969). Using this dictionary, one should be aware of the fact that IPA [ɑ] is noted as [a], while IPA [a] is noted as [ɑ]. The IPA [ʋ] is noted as [v]. Because the RND [ʋ] is not the same as the [ʋ] used in this dictionary, for German we used [u] instead of it.

In the dictionary the <r> is always noted as [r], never as [R]. However, in the RND the [R] is used. Because in German both realisations are allowed, in the word list for each word containing one or more <r>'s, we also note a variant in which the <r>'s are pronounced as [R].

As in the Blancquaert/RND notation, the [ɔ] preceding the [m], [n] or [ŋ] is noted as [ʋ]. The [x] was noted where the [ç] was given in the dictionary, and this procedure was carried over to the transcriptions of the 1999 varieties.

The dictionary uses only the [f]. The [v] represents the bilabial voiced sound which is usually noted as [ʋ] in Dutch transcriptions. Furthermore, only the [x] is used, the [ɣ] never appears.

In the dictionary, three diphthongs are mentioned: <au> transcribed as [ao], <eu> or <äu> transcribed as [ɔø], and <ei> or <ai> transcribed as [ae]. Below the two elements, an arch is noted. However, the notation of the diphthongs is not consistent with the RND notation. According to the dictionary the <ou> in Dutch <Gouda>, <Oosterhout> and <brouwer> is equal to the German <au>. Therefore we use the Blancquaert/RND notation for the German <au>: [ɔ.ᵘ]. Some people have the opinion that the German <au> is more open than the Dutch <ou> or <au>. The German <eu> or <äu> is equal to the Dutch <oi> as in <spoiler>. We note it as [ɔ.ⁱ]. The German <ei> or <ai> is equal to the Dutch <ai> as in <mais>. We note it as [ɑ.ⁱ].

According to Koenraads (1967), who uses the same notation as the *Wörterbuch der deutschen Aussprache*, German diphthongs are falling diphthongs. The first component is stressed more strongly than the second component. In Blancquaert and in the RND this is indicated by noting the first element half long and the second element smaller or in superscript. For reasons of consistency, we applied this notation to the German diphthongs as well.

In the dictionary it is mentioned that in words ending in <en> or the [ə] may be omitted after [f], [ʋ], [s], [z], [ʃ], [ʒ], [ç], [x], [pf] and [ts] in some situations (at fast rates of speech, in some phonological environments). However, in the diminutive ending <chen> the [ə] is always pronounced. In our transcription, after [f], [ʋ], [s], [z], [ʃ], [ʒ], [ç], [x], [pf] or [ts] we give a second variant in which [ən] is replaced by [n̩].

In words ending in <en> the [ə] may be omitted after [p], [b], [t], [d], [k] and [g]. This is not allowed in the endings <igen> and . In final syllable accumulations (for example <rettenden>) only the [ə] in the first <en> may be omitted. In our transcriptions, after [t] or [d] we give a second variant in which [ən] is replaced by [n̩], after [p] or [b] by [m̩], and after [k] or [g] by [ŋ].

In words ending in <el> (for example <Knüppel>) the [ə] may be omitted, except after [g], [l] and [r]. In our transcriptions we give a second variant in which [əl] is replaced by [l̩].

In words ending in <er> (for example <Lehrer>) the <er> should be pronounced as a mid vowel. We transcribe the syllable as [ə]. In words ending on <r> where the <r> is preceded by a long vowel (for example <vier>), the <r> should be pronounced as a dark mid vowel. We transcribe the <r> as [ə]. In words with one of the preliminarily syllables <er>, <her>, <ver> or <zer> (for example <Versuch>) the <r> should be pronounced as a dark mid vowel. We would transcribe the <r> as [ə], but in our word list such words do not occur.

3. Convergence and divergence with respect to standard languages

We calculated the mutual Levenshtein distances between the old variants, the mutual distances between the new dialects, and the distances between the old and the new variants. The correlation between the old phonetic distances and the geographic distances turned out to be equal to 0.6056, while the correlation between the new phonetic distances and the geographic distances is equal to 0.5228. This reduced value already points to a more abrupt phonetic map due to the effects of the border. Furthermore the correlation between the old and the new distances is equal to 0.8394. All correlation coefficients mentioned here are significant.

3.1 Dutch or German?

Goossens tries to answer the question: What are Dutch dialects? (1977: 11-30). Among other things he discusses the definition which recognizes a Dutch dialect as a variety which shows more characteristics of Dutch than of any other standard language. Goossens's objection against this definition is that applying it is not feasible. One has to know the complete vocabulary of all speakers of the dialect you want to research, and besides, the vocabulary of a speaker can change any time.

However, ignoring this objection, and assuming that the informants are representative of the dialects, and that the word list is representative of the vocabulary of the informants, we can determine if dialects are Dutch or German using Levenshtein distance. Applying this definition all dialects in 1974-1975 were Dutch, including those on German territory. In 1999, the dialects in the Netherlands are still Dutch, as are the Bentheim dialects of Lage and Wilsum, while the other Bentheim dialects were German.

3.2 Examining classification results

Clustering on the basis of the 1974-1975 dialects results in a main division consisting on the one hand of a group containing both standard languages and, on the other a group containing all dialects (see Figure 2a). We find that the southern Dutch varieties (Langeveen, Lattrop and Vasse) are more similar to the German varieties than to the rest of the Dutch dialects. Clustering the 1999 dialects we get a sharp division in Dutch varieties (including standard Dutch) and German varieties (including standard German) (see Figure 2b). Now the southern Dutch varieties are grouped among the other Dutch varieties, while the standard languages are grouped among the varieties of the countries they correspond with. Comparing the old and the new dendrograms shows that dialects have become more similar to their corresponding standard languages.

Having seventeen old dialects, seventeen new dialects, two old standard languages and two new standard languages, we get a total of 38 varieties. With multidimensional scaling we calculated on the basis of the mutual distances, two dimensional coordinates, one for each variety (see Figure 3). The result shows clearly that for each variety, the newer one is more closely located to its corresponding standard language than the older one.

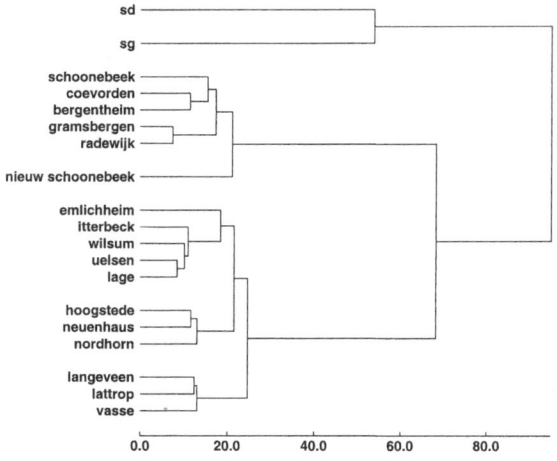

Figure 2a. The dendrogram on the basis of the 1974-1975 distances; 'sd' is the older standard Dutch, while 'sg' is standard German.

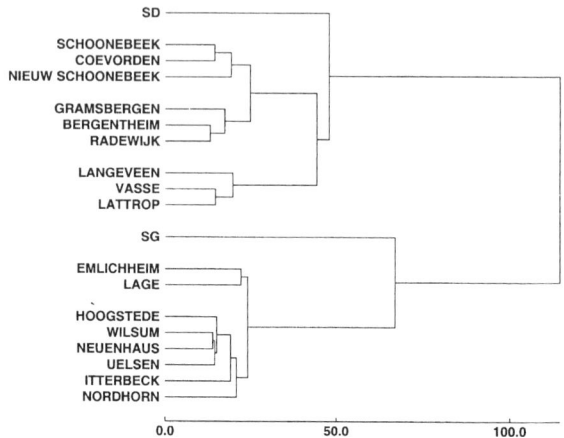

Figure 2b. The dendrogram on the basis of the 1999 distances; 'SD' is the newer standard Dutch, while 'SG' is standard German.

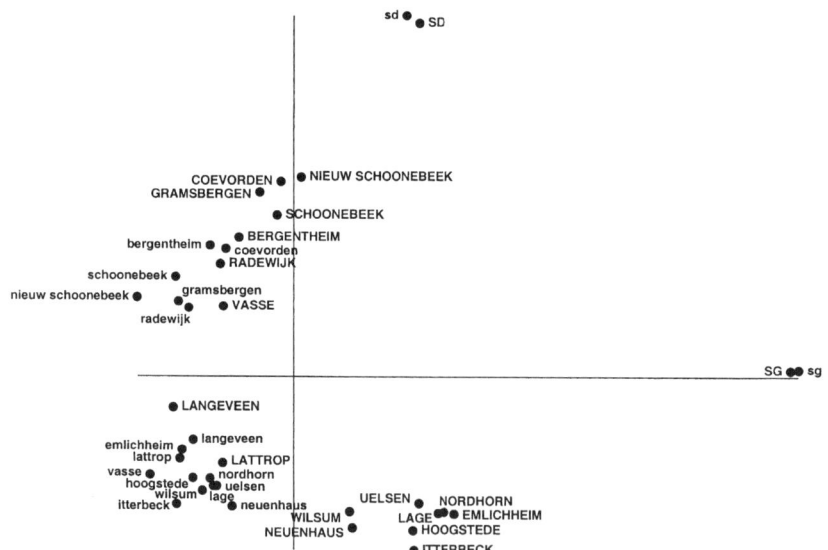

Figure 3. The multidimensional scaling plot on the basis of 38 varieties, containing seventeen old dialects, seventeen new dialects, two old standard languages and two new standard languages. Note the similarities to the geographic map. Also note that 1999 pronunciations (in CAPITALS) are consistently closer to the standard languages ('sd', 'SD', 'sg', 'SG').

3.3 Convergence and divergence

By subtracting the old distances from the new distances, we get negative and positive values. Negative values correspond with convergence, while positive values corresponds with divergence.

It turns out that all Dutch dialects converged toward standard Dutch, while all German dialects diverged from standard Dutch. All German dialects converged toward standard German. The Dutch dialects of Nieuw Schoonebeek, Schoonebeek, Coevorden, Gramsbergen, Vasse and Lattrop also showed some convergence toward standard German, while Radewijk, Bergentheim and Langeveen diverged from it.

Figure 4 gives an idea of the extent to which dialects converged (a) or diverged (b) with respect to their standard languages. Nieuw Schoonebeek, Schoonebeek and Vasse very strongly converged toward standard Dutch, just as all German dialects converged toward standard German. The extent to which other dialects converged or diverged is much smaller.

4. Conclusions

In the context of a book devoted to languages in contact, we should note the following. In the characterisation of Thomason and Kaufmann (1988), the situation we examine is clearly one of language *maintenance*: we have interviewed dialect speakers who have maintained local varieties in the face of encroaching standard languages. Although Thomason and Kaufmann caution that dialect contact situations are likely to be too complex to analyse neatly, they make the prediction that structured change may not occur without lexical borrowings from the standard languages, in accordance with the predictions of language contact theory.

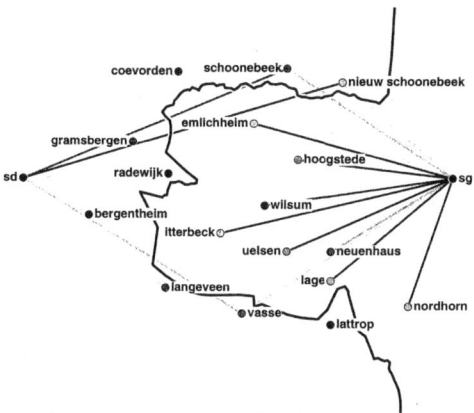

Figure 4a. The picture shows convergence. Darker lines show stronger convergence. The grey values of the dots represent distances between the old and the new variant. Whiter dots indicate greater distances.

Figure 4b. The picture shows divergence. Darker lines show stronger divergence. The grey values of the dots represent distances between the old and the new variant. Whiter dots indicate greater distances.

More importantly the research shows that some dialects in the German part of our area of interest, which could previously be regarded as Dutch Low Saxon dialects, are now German dialects. On the other hand, Dutch dialects which were previously grouped among German Low Saxon dialects, are now grouped among the other Dutch dialects. All Dutch dialects shifted towards standard Dutch while all German dialects shifted towards standard German. Some Dutch dialects strongly converged toward standard Dutch, just as all German dialects converged toward standard German. From these facts we may conclude that the political border has a significant influence on the graduality of the dialect continuum, acting as a separator between Dutch and German dialects.[1]

University of Groningen

REFERENCES

Auer, P., and F. Hinskens
    1996   "The convergence and divergence of dialects in Europe. New and not so new developments in an old area", in: U. Ammon, K.J. Mattheier, and P.H. Nelde (eds.), *Sociolinguistica, International Yearbook of European Sociolinguistics, Convergence and divergence of dialects in Europe*, 1-30. Tübingen: Max Niemeyer Verlag.

---

[1] We thank Jo Daan for giving copies of some pages of the *Tekstboekje* of Blancquaert (1939). We are also grateful to the native speaker respondents in the Bentheim area.

Blancquaert, E.
1939   *Tekstboekje (Nederlandse Fonoplaten van Blancquaert en van der Plaetse*, Eerste Reeks). Antwerpen: De Sikkel (2nd edition).
Entjes, H.
1982   *Dialektatlas van Zuid-Drenthe en Noord-Overijsel (Reeks Nederlands(ch)e Dialectatlassen* 14). Antwerpen: De Sikkel.
Goossens, J.
1977   *Inleiding tot de Nederlandse Dialectologie*. Groningen: Wolters-Noordhoff (2nd edition).
Jain, A.K., and R.C. Dubes
1988   *Algorithms for Clustering Data*. Englewood Cliffs, New Yersey: Prentice Hall.
Kessler, B.
1995   "Computational Dialectology in Irish Gaelic", in: *Proceedings of the European Association for Computational Linguistics* (EACL), 60-67. Dublin.
Koenraads, W.H.A.
1967   *Deutsche Laut- und Aussprachlehre für Niederländer*. Groningen: P. Noordhoff N.V.
Kremer, L.
1984   "Die niederländisch-deutsche Staatsgrenze als subjektive Dialektgrenze", *Driemaandelijkse Bladen* 36, 76-83.
1990   "Kontinuum oder Bruchstelle? Zur Entwicklung der Grenzdialekte zwischen Niederrhein und Vechtegebiet", in: L. Kremer and H. Niebaum (eds.), *Grenzdialekte. Studien zur Entwicklung kontinentalwestgermanischer Dialektkontinua*, 85-123. Hildesheim-Zürich-New York: Georg Olms Verlag.
Kruskal, J.B.
1983   "An overview of sequence comparison", in: D. Sankoff and J. Kruskal (eds.), *Time Warps, String Edits, and Macromolecules: The Theory and Practice of Sequence Comparison*, 1-40. Reading, Massachusetts: Addison-Wesley.
Kruskal, J.B., and M. Wish
1984   *Multidimensional Scaling*. Beverly Hills-London: Sage Publications.
Nerbonne, J., and W. Heeringa
1998   "Computationele Classificatie van Nederlandse Dialecten", *Taal en Tongval* 50/2, 164-193.
Nerbonne, J., W. Heeringa, E. van den Hout, P. van der Kooi, S. Otten, and W. van de Vis
1996   "Phonetic Distance between Dutch Dialects", in: G. Durieux, W. Daelemans, and S. Gillis (eds.), *CLIN VI, Papers from the sixth CLIN meeting*, 185-202. Antwerp: University of Antwerp, Center for Dutch Language and Speech.
Nerbonne, J., W.J. Heeringa, and P. Kleiweg
1999   "Edit distance and dialect proximity", in: D. Sankoff and J. Kruskal (eds.), *Time Warps, String Edits and Macromolecules: The Theory and Practice of Sequence Comparison*, v-xv. Stanford, CA: CSLI (2nd edtion).
Niebaum, H.
1990   "Staatsgrenze als Bruchstelle? Die Grenzdialekte zwischen Dollart und Vechtegebiet", in: L. Kremer and H. Niebaum (eds.), *Grenzdialekte. Studien zur Entwicklung kontinentalwestgermanischer Dialektkontinua*, 49-83. Hildesheim-Zürich-New York: Georg Olms Verlag.
Paardekooper, P.C.
1998   *ABN-uitspraakgids*. Den Haag: Sdu Uitgevers (3rd edition).

Rakers, A.
1993   *Mundartatlas der alten Grafschaft Bentheim* (edited and commented by H. Entjes and H. Niebaum). Sögel: Emsländische Landschaft.
Thomason, S.G., and T. Kaufmann
1988   *Language contact, creolization, and genetic linguistics.* Berkeley: University of California Press.
Wörterbuch der deutschen Aussprache
1969   *Wörterbuch der deutschen Aussprache.* München: Max Hueber Verlag.

Languages in Contact, edited by D.G. Gilbers, J. Nerbonne, and J. Schaeken (= *Studies in Slavic and General Linguistics*, vol. 28), 157-164. Amsterdam - Atlanta, GA: Rodopi, 2000.

EFFECTS OF LANGUAGE CONTACT AS A SOURCE OF (NON)INFORMATION: THE HISTORICAL RECONSTRUCTION OF BURGENLAND KAJKAVIAN

PETER HOUTZAGERS

1. Introduction

In the Austrian province of Burgenland and adjoining areas in Austria, Hungary and Slovakia there are approximately 80 villages where varieties of Croatian are spoken. The ancestors of this Croatian-speaking population for the most part settled there in the sixteenth and seventeenth century. Their original dwelling-places were those parts of Croatia and Slavonia that at that period suffered from Ottoman attacks.

Most of the dialects spoken in and around the Burgenland belong to the Štokavian or Čakavian dialect group. Only in two villages a representative of the third main group of Serbo-Croatian, viz. Kajkavian, is spoken. These are Hidegség and Fertőhomok (henceforth "Hi" and "Fe"), two neighbouring villages in the northwest of Hungary, near Sopron.

Although there is no hard evidence, there are strong indications from historical sources that in the early sixteenth century the ancestors of the inhabitants of Hi and Fe came from the area between Kutina and Novska in the westernmost part of Slavonia, somewhat to the east of the territory where Kajkavian dialects are spoken nowadays.[1] Moreover, it is the only surviving Kajkavian dialect that was separated from its original surroundings as early as the sixteenth century. Therefore the dialect is of interest for the dialectology of Serbo-Croatian, especially for the reconstruction of the history of Kajkavian and of the dialect picture as it was before it was dramatically changed by the mass migrations on the Balkans.

The dialect of Hi and Fe has understandably received relatively large amount of attention in the literature on Kajkavian. The attention of the various authors was especially drawn by the lack of certain characteristics that all Kajkavian dialects are believed to have in common and by the question of the origin of the dialect. Unfortunately however, the available data was small. I myself have been interested in Hi and Fe since 1985, when I visited them for the first time. In view of

---

[1] Today Kajkavian is spoken in a relatively compact area around Zagreb, the southeast corner of which is west of Novska.

the rapid extinction of the dialect, I gave priority to gathering a more or less complete picture of it on the basis of my own field-work and I recently published a synchronic description (1999). I think that now the issue of the history of the dialect can be addressed on a more solid basis than before. In the following I shall give a survey of the relevant questions and the problems that occur in answering them. Some of these problems are caused by loss of information due to intensive contacts with other languages and dialects through a very long period.

2. Questions to be answered

There are several ways in which the dialect material from Hi and Fe is of potential interest for the reconstruction of Kajkavian. First, it can give us information about where Kajkavian was spoken before the migrations. If it is true that the dialect came from the area indicated above, it can contribute to our knowledge of south-easternmost Kajkavian as it was around 1500. This part of Kajkavian disappeared shortly afterwards, together with its Štokavian and Čakavian neighbours and the transitional dialects in between.[2]

Second, the Hi and Fe material can be of help in reconstructing the development of Kajkavian as a whole or even of a larger part of western South-Slavic. For example, the fact that the dialect does not share all characteristics that are usually considered common Kajkavian can tell us something about the course of some of the oldest isoglosses in this part of Slavic. One of these is the isogloss of the so-called "neo-circumflex", a long falling accent that occurs under specific circumstances on a vowel that was short and rising in Proto-Slavic. Another example: the east of the Kajkavian dialect area is renowned for its accentual innovations, such as stress shifts in both directions. The Hi and Fe dialect does not show evidence of such innovations. This could be due to its peripheral location within Kajkavian, but also to the chronology of the innovations.

It is clear that if we want to use the Hi and Fe material as a source of information in the sense described above, we need to answer two questions:

1) Where did the dialect come from?[3]
2) What did it look like before the migration?

---

[2] The Štokavian and Čakavian neighbours referred to were to the east and south, respectively. The type of Štokavian spoken there at that period is also called Šćakavian. On the boundary between "real" southeastern Kajkavian and transitional dialects see Lončarić 1995: 96-98.

[3] It has often been suggested that the Hi and Fe dialect is the result of dialect mixture. (For a survey of the various opinions on the matter see Houtzagers 1999: 28-30). For methodological reasons, however, I prefer not to use the dialect mixture explanation (which can account for almost everything) until it is necessary to do so.

Ad 1

The historical indications on the provenance of the Hi and Fe people are not conclusive and, although the linguistic data do not seem to contradict the hypothesis
of the West Slavonian origin of the dialect, all of it is far from sufficient.[4] We
could say a lot more if we had:

- a less defective synchronic picture of Kajkavian as a whole, especially of its
  easternmost varieties. It is imaginable that a small number of characteristics of
  Hi and Fe Kajkavian would suffice to determine its place on the dialect map.
  For instance, it would be very interesting to know more about the geographic
  distribution of *sèstra* 'sister' and *čèkat* 'wait' and of the pronoun *vänî* 'what-
  d'ye-call-it' (see Ivić 1990: 205, Houtzagers 1999: 25, 111-112).[5] In *sèstra*
  and *čèkat* the vowel *e* is a non-etymological reflex of Proto-Slavic *ě/ь*.[6] The
  pronoun *vänî* is probably very rare. It is found neither in RHSJ 1880-1976,
  nor in Skok 1971-74, nor in the literature on the varieties of Croatian that surround Hi and Fe, but it is present in certain dialect descriptions (Fancev 1907
  and Lončarić 1986).
- a better impression of the Hi and Fe dialect as it was before the migration,
  which amounts to the same thing as question (2) above.

Ad 2

In the reconstruction of the premigratory picture of the dialect an important role is
played by hypotheses about language contacts:

- In the step-by-step reconstruction of parts of the system of the dialect, the
  moment when it came into contact with another language or dialect can be a
  terminus ante quem or *post quem*. For instance, in the development of the Hi
  and Fe vowel system there was a stage during which stressed long mid vowels
  developed from opening diphthongs to closing ones. In view of the phonetic
  realization of long mid vowels both in the Čakavian dialects and the variety of
  Hungarian that surround the dialect at its present location, it can be assumed
  that this process had been completed or was at least well on its way before the
  migration (see Houtzagers 1996: 127). On the other hand, the development of
  the unstressed vowels in Hi (not in Fe) suggests a strong influence from local
  Hungarian (see Houtzagers 1996: 132).

---

[4] For a discussion on the provenance of the inhabitants of Hi and Fe see Houtzagers 1999: 20-25.
[5] For technical reasons, the notation of the Hi and Fe vowels is somewhat different from the system used in Houtzagers 1999.
[6] In Hi and Fe we would expect *ä* (< *e*).

- For a proper premigratory picture we must identify those elements that were borrowed from other languages and dialects after the migration. As we shall see in the following, this is not an easy task.

3. Effects of language contacts

The dialect of Hi and Fe is rich in traces of language contact. A distinction must be made between (i) contacts with Hungarian (henceforth sometimes abbreviated "Hu") and (ii) contacts with other varieties of Croatian.[7] Both have been there before as well as after the migration.

However strange it may seem at first sight, it is not always simple to distinguish between the effects of (i) and (ii) above, and especially the distinction between premigratory and postmigratory linguistic influences presents difficulties. This is because the circumstances of linguistic contacts before and after the migration have been – to a certain extent – similar. In both periods the dialect was influenced strongly by Hungarian. Moreover, if before the migration the dialect was spoken in the south-east corner of Kajkavian, it probably had some of the same Štokavian and Čakavian neighbours it has now.

Another complicating factor is the fact that the borrowing relationships involved more than two parties, operated in several directions and lasted for a very long period of time. It is well-known that Hungarian at an earlier stage had borrowed a large number of words from Slavic. In the centuries preceding the migration, Croatian dialects spoken in Croatia and Slavonia – especially the Kajkavian ones – were strongly influenced by Hungarian (the language of the rulers) and non-Kajkavian dialects were influenced by Kajkavian, which also had a literary language. As a consequence, the non-Kajkavian Burgenland dialects also show a number of Kajkavian characteristics and those Burgenland dialects that are not spoken in Hungary also contain a number of Hungarian loan-words. After the migration, the northernmost Čakavian Burgenland dialects were sociolinguistically dominant and formed the basis for the development of a Burgenland Croatian literary language which, also through the church and the school, had a strong linguistic influence.[8]

---

[7] In contradistinction to most other Burgenland dialects, the influence of German was not great (see Houtzagers 1999: 28).

[8] Here are the most important sources on the matters discussed here. For a general outline of Burgenland Croatian see Neweklowsky 1978. On Hu influences on Serbo-Croatian see Hadrovics 1985. There are a number of old Kajkavian glossaries, the most famous of which are Belosztenecz 1740 (written for the most part in the 17th century) and Habdelić 1670. For a survey see Jonke 1949. Very important in this connection is Finka 1984-. For linguistic information from old Burgenland texts see Hadrovics 1974 and Nyomárkay 1996. On Kajkavian in general see Ivšić 1936 and Lončarić 1996. Synchronic Burgenland glossaries can be found in Koschat 1978, Hamm et al. 1982, Neweklowsky 1989, Tornow 1989, Finka et al. 1991 and Houtzagers 1999. Valuable

4. Hungarian elements

The most dramatic consequence of the contact with Hungarian for Hi and Fe Croatian is that, especially in the last few decades, the latter has rapidly retreated in favour of the former. Within the scope of this paper, however, we shall only be interested in those effects of language contact that influenced the dialect internally.[9] As may be expected, the dialect abounds in Hungarian loan-words. A few cxamples: *ajandìka* 'gift' (acc. sing., Hu *ajándék*), *lävägê* 'air' (Hu *levegő*). However, Hungarian also influenced the dialect in phonetic and syntactic respects. Examples: the phonetic realization of the low front vowel (*ä*) and, in Hi, the realization of long and short *a* is identical to that of the vowels that occupy comparable positions in the surrounding variety of Hungarian (*e, á, a*). Also the sentence intonation is very similar to that of Hungarian. The typically Hungarian use of antecedents before object sentences (e.g. *azt[1] mondja[2], hogy[3]* ... 'he[2] says[2] [it][1], that[3]) ...' is also present in Hi and Fe Croatian: *tò[1] su[2] mu[3] guvòrili[4], näka[5] ìdä[6] dumôm[7]* 'they[2] told[4] him[3] [it][1] that[5] he[6] should[6] go[6] home[7]'.

Distinguishing between premigratory and postmigratory effects of Hungarian influence is problematic. Also it is not easy to recognize whether one has to do with direct loans from Hungarian or with originally Hungarian words borrowed from other Croatian dialects. Diachronic phonology is seldom of any help. For instance, the root of the word *bätäžän* 'sick' (Hu *beteg* 'illness') could in principle have been borrowed and extended with the suffix *-än* at any period. Abundant attestation in Kajkavian sources suggests that it is an old loan from Hungarian (Hadrovics 1985: 143-145). On the other hand, it is also omnipresent in non-Kajkavian Burgenland Croatian and could have originated from there. This possibility is illustrated by the spread of such words as *hasnovat* 'use' (from Hu *haszon*), which is quite common in Burgenland Croatian but not used in Hi and Fe.

When diachronic phonology does provide a clue, it is usually not more than that. For instance, the word *bìruš* 'employee of the count' (Hi/Fe meaning) at first glance looks like an old loan: the suffix *-us* is an Old Hungarian predecessor of *-os* from before the lowering of *u* to *o*. Also, the word is well attested in old Kajkavian sources. However, the word is as popular in Burgenland Croatian as the word *bätäžän* that we just discussed. The substantive *bätäkšìga* '(gen. sing.) illness' (Hu *betegség*) is not as wide-spread in the Burgenland and reminds one of an older stage of Hungarian (before the lowering of *i* to *e*), but on the other hand *i*

---

sources of information are also Skok 1971-1974 and RHSJ 1880-1976, although in the latter Kajkavian is under-represented.

[9] Other effects of the contact with Hu that will not be discussed here are (a) those instances of variability and uncertainty in the linguistic competence of the speakers that are symptoms of the process of dialect death; (b) spontaneous borrowing from Hu as a consequence of the fact that all speakers of the dialect are bilingual.

is very often the regular vowel that in Hi and Fe corresponds with Hu *é*, also in loans that are probably not old, such as *šätämìnja* '(acc. sing.) pastry' and *ädìnjä* 'plates and dishes' from Hu *sütemény* and *edény*.[10] Of course there are evidently new borrowings, such as *räpülê* 'airplane' (Hu *repülő*), but for most Hu loans little can be said as to when and how they penetrated into Hi and Fe Croatian.

5. Influences from other varieties of Burgenland Croatian

Burgenland Croatian dialects show a lot of linguistic variety, which can be explained by their different places of origin prior to the migrations. Yet there are a consideral number of similarities. Neweklowsky (1969: 99-101) mentions 13 main "Burgenland croaticisms", i.e. characteristics that all or most Burgenland dialects have in common.[11] One of these consists of a large number of common lexical items, most of which are also found in Hi and Fe. In spite of its being the only Kajkavian dialect within Burgenland Croatian, the Hi and Fe dialect possesses only a small number of lexical items that it does not share with one or more other Burgenland dialects. The other 12 Burgenland croaticisms concern morphology and (synchronic and diachronic) phonology. Eight of them also apply (at least in part) to Hi and Fe. Examples: (a) the sandhi rule that makes voiceless obstruents voiced even before nondistinctively voiced phonemes (i.e. resonants and vowels), e.g. *tò jä vìdit ùš* 'that remains to be seen' → [vìdidùš], *nàmräm zàbit mujêga sîna* 'I can't forget my son' → [zàbidmujêga]; (b) the conditional auxiliary *bi* for every person in singular and plural; (c) the indeclinable possessive pronoun meaning 'her' (*njê* in Hi and Fe, similar forms elsewhere); (d) the genitive plural ending *-ov*, not only for masculine but often also for feminine nouns.

There is evidence that the other Burgenland dialects, especially those belonging to the three northernmost Čakavian groups, have influenced the Hi and Fe dialect from at least the 17th century till the present day (see Houtzagers 1999: 25-27). It seems to be clear that since the migration the Hi and Fe dialect has in principle been the "receiving" party in borrowing relationships.[12] Although some varieties of Burgenland Croatian were in all probability already neighbours before the migration, the common characteristics discussed here are so numerous and so wide-spread that we can safely assume that the majority of them penetrated the Hi and Fe dialect only after the migration. On the other hand, it is almost certain that some of them were already present: many lexical items that are common for Burgenland Croatian occur in the oldest Kajkavian glossaries (cf. Neweklowsky

---

[10] My assumption that these loans are not old is based on their meaning and on the fact that I did not find any attestations in the Burgenland Croatian and old Kajkavian sources that I checked. This assumption may be wrong.

[11] Of course, characteristics that are common Serbo-Croatian or otherwise shared by larger groups of Serbo-Croatian dialects are not included.

[12] Of course it is also possible that some of the shared elements are results of common innovations.

1982: 262-263).[13] The uncertainty about the distinction between premigratory and postmigratory linguistic influences remains.

6. Conclusion

In the above I have tried to show that for the moment many questions concerning the provenance and development of the Hi and Fe dialect must remain unanswered. The effects of language contacts do not contribute very much and one could even say that they caused the loss of much valuable information: the elements borrowed from other languages and dialects are not only of little help in the reconstruction, they also have taken the place of characteristics that kajkavologists would have been very interested in. I think, however, that we can end our account with a positive note. Part of the unclarity must be ascribed to our present state of knowledge in two fields that very much deserve to be studied in their own right. Progress in these domains will almost certainly contribute to the solution of the problems discussed here. I am referring to:

- the synchronic description of Kajkavian, especially its easternmost dialects;
- comparative analysis of Burgenland Croatian, also in contrast with the available synchronic and old data on Kajkavian.

There are already a number of reasonable hypotheses about the premigratory location of the various dialect groups within Burgenland Croatian (cf. Ivšić 1971: maps after page 798, Neweklowsky 1978: 264-281). Detailed study of the spread of every relevant characteristic will certainly bring more light into the matter.

University of Groningen

REFERENCES

Belosztenecz, J.
1740   *Gazophylacium, seu latino-illyricorum onomatum aerarium.* Zagreb. (Reprint in two volumes, 1972-73. Zagreb.)
Finka, B. (ed.)
1984-   *Rječnik hrvatskoga kajkavskoga književnoga jezika.* Zagreb.
Finka, B. et al. (ed.)
1991   *Gradišćanskohrvatsko-hrvatsko-nimški rječnik.* Zagreb-Eisenstadt.
Habdelić, J.
1670   *Diktionar, ili Reči slovenske zvekšega ukup zebrane....* Graz.

---

[13] There is one easily identifiable group of borrowings from surrounding Čakavian dialects. It is very small and consists of words that are clearly non-Kajkavian (in terms of reflexes of Proto-Slavic vowels) and appear only in Hi, which is geographically nearer to Čakavian than Fe. Examples: *lîp* 'beautiful' (Fe *lêp*), *ubìsit* 'hang up' (Fe *obèsit*; see also Houtzagers 1996: 121-123).

Hadrovics, L.
1974   *Schrifttum und Sprache der burgenländischen Kroaten im 18. und 19. Jahrhundert.* Wien-Budapest.
1985   *Ungarische Elemente im Serbokroatischen* (*Slavistische Forschungen* 48). Köln-Wien.
Hamm, J. (ed.)
1982   *Nimško-gradišćanskohrvatsko-hrvatski rječnik.* Eisenstadt-Zagreb.
Houtzagers, P.
1996   "The development of the Hidegség and Fertőhomok vowel system", *Studies in South Slavic and Balkan Linguistics* (*Studies in Slavic and General Linguistics* 23), 111-142. Amsterdam-Atlanta.
1999   *The Kajkavian dialect of Hidegség and Fertőhomok* (*Studies in Slavic and General Linguistics* 27). Amsterdam-Atlanta.
Ivić, P.
1990   "Prilog poznavanju govora kajkavskih naseljenika u okolini Šoprona", *Studia Slavica Hungarica* 36/1-4, 193-206.
Ivšić, S.
1936   "Jezik Hrvata kajkavaca", *Ljetopis JAZU* 48 (za godinu 1934-35), 47-88.
1971   "Hrvatska dijaspora u 16. stoljeću i jezik Hrvata Gradišćanaca", *Izabrana djela iz slavenske akcentuacije*, 723-798. München.
Jonke, Lj.
1949   "Dikcionar Adama Patačića", *Rad* 275, 71-175.
Koschat, H.
1978   *Die čakavische Mundart von Baumgarten im Burgenland.* Wien.
Lončarić, M.
1988   "Rani razvitak kajkavštine", *Rasprave Zavoda za jezik IFF* 14, 79-104.
1995   "Prostiranje kajkavštine u prošlosti", *Rasprave ZHJ* 21, 79-102.
1996   *Kajkavsko narječje.* Zagreb.
Neweklowsky, G.
1969   "Die kroatischen Mundarten im Burgenland. Überblick", *Wiener Slavistisches Jahrbuch* 15, 94-115.
1978   *Die kroatischen Dialekte des Burgenlandes und der angrenzenden Gebiete.* Wien.
1982   "O kajkavskim osobinama u nekajkavskim govorima Gradišća", *Hrvatski dijalektološki zbornik* 6, 257-263.
1989   *Der kroatische Dialekt von Stinatz. Wörterbuch* (*Wiener Slawistischer Almanach*, Sonderband 25). Wien.
Nyomárkay, I.
1996   *Sprachhistorisches Wörterbuch des Burgenlandkroatischen.* Szombathely.
RHSJ
1880-1976   *Rječnik hrvatskoga ili srpskoga jezika.* Zagreb (23 volumes).
Skok, P.
1971-1974   *Etimologijski rječnik hrvatskoga ili srpskoga jezika.* Zagreb (4 volumes).
Tornow, S.
1989   *Burgenländisches Dialektwörterbuch* (*Balkanologische Veröffentlichungen* 15). Berlin.

Languages in Contact, edited by D.G. Gilbers, J. Nerbonne, and J. Schaeken (= *Studies in Slavic and General Linguistics*, vol. 28), 165-178. Amsterdam - Atlanta, GA: Rodopi, 2000.

LINGUISTIC CONVERGENCE IN THE VOLGA AREA

LARS JOHANSON

The Middle Volga region presents a complex situation of language contacts. It is thought to be a convergence area in which different languages of adjacent speech communities have developed increasingly more common properties and thus come to resemble each other to a considerable degree. Contact-induced processes are supposed to have led to phenomena typical of a linguistic area in the sense of a so-called 'Sprachbund'.

The main protagonists in this drama belong to two genetic groups, Finno-Ugric and Turkic. The modern languages Mari (Cheremis), Udmurt (Votyak), and Mordva represent the Finno-Ugric side. Mari and Mordva belong to the Volgaic subgroup, though they are rather different from each other. Udmurt belongs to the Permic subgroup. On the Turkic side we find Tatar, Bashkir, and Chuvash. Tatar and Bashkir are closely related languages of the Kipchak branch of Turkic. Chuvash, the descendant of Volga Bulgar and the only living representative of the Bulgar branch of Turkic, deviates a good deal from other known kinds of Turkic. And there is of course a further protagonist, Russian, an Indo-European language that has dominated the area during the last centuries.

Adoption and imposition

We are confronted with many questions regarding this linguistic area. First, a few more languages, Komi (Komi-Zyryan), Nenets, and Kalmyk, are sometimes included into the relevant language complex (Décsy 1973). Secondly, the alleged 'Sprachbund' is based on varying criteria. Thirdly, numerous details concerning the interaction of the languages are obscure. How did the languages of the area acquire their shared features? To what extent are the observable similarities due to mutual influence, to common substrata or to original typological affinities?

It is my contention that there are no simple answers to these questions. The areal convergence is due to complex combinations of copying processes. Deeper and more detailed knowledge of the history of the languages concerned will help unravel the inter-tangled contact situations. We must reckon with the emergence of shared features that did not exist in any of the languages prior to the contacts between them, changes that would not have taken place in any of them without these contacts. But it would be a mystification to claim that there are no source languages for regional innovations of the 'Sprachbund' type, i.e. that a shared feature cannot be related to any triggering factor in the individual languages.

The similarities observed may have different backgrounds. Successful reconstructions largely depend upon correct analyses of so-called borrowing processes between languages, i.e. copying of elements from one code to another in two-language contact situations. One of the crucial distinctions necessary when discussing copying is the difference between ADOPTION and IMPOSITION. In the case of adoption, speakers of a primary code adopt (or 'take over') copies from a dominant code. This is traditionally referred to as 'borrowing' and 'calque'. In the case of imposition, speakers of a primary code insert (or 'carry over') copies of their own code into their variety of a dominant code. Imposition is observed in various kinds of bilingual situations and does not necessarily imply language shift in the sense of giving up the primary code. CODE SHIFT means that a primary code is not maintained, but given up in favor of a dominant one. This may in principle occur without any appreciable imposition. But if imposition does take place, the abandoned code remains operative as 'substratum influence'.

Adoption and imposition are thus unidirectional convergence phenomena of two different kinds. The distinction is important in order to determine the origin and development of shared features in linguistic areas. I will briefly discuss one highly problematic case of convergence, in which the distinction between adopting and imposing may have played a crucial role: the question of the widespread phonological lax vs. tense oppositions of vowels in the Volga region.

Lax vowels

So-called reduced vowels, which form oppositions with so-called full vowels, are claimed to be a shared feature of typological importance in the area. They are found in several languages, e.g. Kazan Tatar, Mishar Tatar, Mountain Bashkir, Lowland Bashkir, Chuvash, Mari, Moksha Mordva, and Khanty, an Ob'-Ugric language spoken in west Siberia. As a rule, the full vowels are ordinary vowels in terms of length, whereas reduced vowels are described as markedly short. The oppositions are mostly not purely quantitative. As may be expected, the tenseness differences are often combined with qualitative differences to the effect that the lax vowels are centralized. Thus, the 'front' ones are front-to-central; the 'back' ones are back-to-central. As a general rule, it may be claimed that the lax vowels are reduced in length, but not necessarily in quality.

For example, Tatar and Bashkir have the following vowel phonemes. The so-called mid vowels are the lax ones: a front unrounded ĕ, a front rounded ŏ̈, a back unrounded ĭ, and a back rounded ŏ.

	Front		Back	
High	i	ü	ï	u
Mid	ĕ	ŏ	ĭ	ŏ
Low	e		a	

As we will see, it is difficult to determine the origin of the areal phenomenon of lax vowels. Significant differences between the vowel systems will, however, show us that some features may have developed as a result of adaptation, whereas others can only be seen as products of imposition.

Distribution

Before discussing this and other problems, it is necessary to look at the distribution of languages in this multinational region. Note that the linguistic groups in question are never limited to the republics carrying their names, Bashkortostan, Tatarstan, Udmurtia, Mari El, Chuvashia, and Mordvinia. The Finno-Ugric languages are, as a rule, spoken in areas where Turkic dialects are also represented.

- Bashkir is the easternmost language, spoken from southern Ural area and westwards, mainly in the Kama basin. Bashkortostan borders on Tatarstan and Udmurtia.
- Tatar dialects are distributed over a huge territory in the middle of the European part of the Russian Federation. Tatarstan borders on Bashkortostan in the east, Mari El and Udmurtia in the north, and on Chuvashia in the west.
- Chuvash, the generally accepted descendant of Volga Bulgar, is spoken in Chuvashia, on the middle course of Volga, but also in Tatarstan, the Kuybyshev region, and Bashkortostan. Its main dialect groups are Upper Chuvash in the north of the republic and Lower Chuvash in the south and outside Chuvashia. Chuvashia borders on Tatarstan, Mordvinia, and Mari El.
- Mari is spoken in Mari El, on the middle course of Volga, by groups in the east of the Kama region, etc. One main variety is Hill Mari, spoken in the northwest of Mari El, on the right bank south of the Volga bend, in Upper Chuvash neighborhood, in northern Chuvashia, etc. Meadow Mari is the variety of the compact settlement area of Mari El, on the left Volga bank. Eastern Mari is spoken by groups in Bashkortostan, Tatarstan, Udmurtia, and other regions.
- Udmurt is spoken in Udmurtia, between Vyatka and Kama, but also in Tatarstan, Bashkortostan, Mari El, etc.
- Mordva is the westernmost language, spoken by scattered groups across a huge territory west and also east of Volga. Mordvinia borders on Chuvashia. The Moksha dialect is spoken mainly in the western part of Mordvinia, and the rather different Erzya dialect in the northeast and east.

Mutual influence

Different kinds of mutual influence have been suggested in earlier studies. The Finno-Ugric languages are claimed to be heavily influenced by Turkic. The impact on Udmurt vocabulary and syntax mainly comes from neighboring Tatar dialects. The contacts with Chuvash have been limited: Udmurt exhibits rather few Chuvash loanwords. The Turkic influence on Mordva also comes from neighboring Tatar dialects. Mordva, particularly the Erzya variety, contains numerous Tatar loanwords. Its contacts with Chuvash have been relatively unimportant.

The Turkic impact on Mari is considerable. Mari has a large number of Turkic loanwords, a number of copied bound morphemes, verb-final word order, extensive use of nonfinite verb forms, postverbial constructions (converbs + auxiliary verbs) to express actional modifications, an interrogative particle *mo*, etc. Large-scale copying has endowed Mari with a typological habitus similar to that of a Turkic language (Comrie 1981: 102).

The transformation is obviously due to widespread bilingualism of Mari groups in the contact areas. Meadow Mari dialects spoken in direct neighborhood of Tatar dialects have been subject to strong Tatar influences. The Volga Kipchak impact on Eastern Mari has been particularly heavy: lexical copying, phonetic influence, vowel harmony in closed syllables, copies of derivational suffixes, postpositions, the superlative particle *en* 'most', etc. On the other hand, there has been a massive Chuvash influence on western Mari dialects. Numerous lexical elements, word-formation suffixes, and syntactic patterns have been copied.

The Finno-Ugric influence on Turkic is usually exemplified by Mari influence on Chuvash. Mari has undoubtedly been of eminent importance for the development of Chuvash. The impact on Upper Chuvash is most evident. But there are less than 300 identified Mari loanwords in Chuvash, much less than the amount of Chuvash loanwords in Mari.

Volga Kipchak has not only exerted influence on Finno-Ugric dialects of the area, but also on Chuvash, most strongly on Lower Chuvash. For example, numerous Tatar loanwords have been adopted.

Finally, there is an immense and at the same time structurally superficial Russian influence on all varieties of the area. A flood of Russian words and international lexical elements mediated by Russian has affected the higher registers, in particular the styles of mass media and science. More importantly, Russian dominance has led numerous minority groups living among Russian majorities, e.g. many Mordva groups, to abandon their native language and shift to Russian as their primary code.

At first sight, then, the 'Sprachbund' issue seems to boil down to a strong Volga Kipchak influence on all varieties of the area plus a special Chuvash-Mari symbiosis. The Kipchak dominance is strongest in the Udmurt, Meadow Mari, and Erzya varieties spoken in the immediate Tatar neighborhood.

Varying dominance relations

However, simple enumeration of copied elements does not solve the problems involved in the convergence processes. In order to reconstruct the drama of convergence attention must be paid to the different situations of dominance: the varying roles the speaker groups have played in relation to each other. The social dominance relations between the codes can be indicators of what kinds of copying processes have taken place. The Volga-Kama area has experienced a complex interplay of adoption and imposition processes of socially dominated and dominant codes. The sociolinguistic role of most of the codes involved has changed from dominant to dominated.

The Finno-Ugric languages involved are regarded as autochthonous in the region. Though smaller Turkic-speaking groups may have arrived earlier, the first significant Turkic element entered in the 8th century, when Bulgar groups moved from the steppes and occupied both sides of the Volga north of the Samara bend (Zimonyi 1992). The Volga Bulgars came to dominate various Finno-Ugric tribes of the Volga-Kama region, e.g. the ancestors of the Mari, Mordva and Udmurt. The Mari settlements belonged to their sphere of influence from the 9th century on. At end of the 9th century they founded a strong empire which included vast territories: present-day Chuvashia, Mari El, Udmurtia, Tatarstan, western Bashkortostan, and further regions. Two points are important for the linguistic development: First, the Bulgar state was a strong and rich empire of high cultural prestige and with a socially dominant language. Secondly, up to the 13th century, Bulgar tribes seem to have assimilated several Finno-Ugric groups living among them.

The scene changed in the 13th century with the Mongol invasion, the fall of Volga Bulgaria and the establishment of the Golden Horde. Kipchak Turkic tribes had already lived in the Bulgar Empire, but now the role of the Kipchak groups became much more important since they constituted the main force of the victorious army. Kipchaks began to infiltrate the former Bulgar territories. One part of the Bulgars fled to the Russians, another part retired to today's Chuvashia, and the rest remained in their old settlements, where they were later assimilated. As for the Mari, the Meadow Mari region was part of the Golden Horde, whereas the Hill Mari, who in that period settled farther west and northwest, were more or less dependent on the Moscow principality.

After the disintegration of the Golden Horde in the early 15th century and the emergence of the Kazan Khanate, the population of the area was largely Kipchakized, i.e. acquired the language that later developed into Tatar and Bashkir. Kipchak gained ground among the peoples of the Volga region. Some groups, such as the Mordva, attempted to evade the Tatar by migrating. A merger of Kip-chaks, Bulgars, and Finno-Ugrians led to the emergence of the ethnic group of Kazan Tatars. Again, two points are important for the linguistic development: First, the Golden Horde and the Kazan Khanate were strong and rich states of high cultural prestige. Kipchak, which became its official language, had a socially dominant status, and Bulgar Turkic lost its former status. Secondly, Kazan and Misher Tatars assimilated ethnic minorities of the region: Kipchak groups of other origins, Volga Bulgars, and Finno-Ugric tribes. Kazan Tatars came to play the leading role in the region as the politically and economically dominant group. Kazan Tatar, the language of the central part of the former Volga Bulgaria, ex-erted a strong influence on Chuvash, Bashkir, Meadow Mari, Mordva, Udmurt and other languages.

The languages of the area got into contact with Russian at different times, de-pending on the distance of their territories to Moscow. The Russian influence is oldest and strongest in the west: in Mordva and Hill Mari. When the Khanate of Kazan fell in 1552, the whole Volga-Kama region was annexed to Russia. Rus-sian influence on Tatar, Chuvash, Mari, Mordva, Udmurt and other languages increased rapidly.

In the 17th and 18th centuries, the Russian colonization and the settlement of Russian peasants in the north and northwest split up the linguistic regions. For example, many Chuvash left their country in the 17th century. Some came to in-habit the southern regions of today's Chuvashia, and others went eastwards and thus came into contact with Tatar and Bashkir groups. The Mari were split up in the 18th century following the migration of Meadow Mari groups into the Ural region. The Mordva also attempted to escape Russian domination by migrating. The linguistic influence of Russian was relatively weak in pre-Revolutionary times. The massive lexical influence started in the Soviet era. The main linguistic result of the Russian dominance was language shift among many minorities.

Non-Kipchakized areas

What was the origin and early development of the Chuvash? Their ancestors lived on the right bank of Volga, in the northern part of today's Chuvashia, close to the Bulgar center on the other side of the Volga. It is obvious that Bulgar-speaking newcomers absorbed certain Mari groups in this region. A specific culture with Bulgar and Finno-Ugric elements developed, which also affected the neighboring Mordva, Mari, and Udmurt. After long processes of assimilation, a Chuvash eth-nic unity seems to have emerged by the 15th century. At this time, the Chuvash territory became a part of the Khanate of Kazan.

Large Mari groups had moved to the north and northeast. There is nothing to prove that the Mari inhabited their present-day homeland on the left Volga bank before the mid-13th century (Bereczki 1994: 14-16). After their settlement in this region, the dissolution of the ancient Mari unity and the dialectal differentiation began.

It is a remarkable fact that a Bulgar variety was preserved on the right Volga bank, whereas the Bulgars on the left bank were Kipchakized. Both under the Golden Horde and the Khanate of Kazan, Kipchak exerted a strong impact on Chuvash, but the Kipchak dominance did not lead to any code shift. The Chuvash escaped Kipchak assimilation. Neither were they converted to Islam. Though a Muslim mission had been active among the Finno-Ugric and early Kipchak tribes under Bulgar control, Islam had not reached all parts of the Volga-Kama area. Thus the Mari, Mordva, and Udmurt had remained pagans. The Bulgar-speaking ancestors of Chuvash obviously did not belong to the Bulgars who had adopted Islam. Later on, the Muslim culture of the Tatars gained ground among the Chuvash and the Finno-Ugric peoples of the region, but these peoples did not adopt Islam.

Kinds of copying

Certain conclusions can be drawn from these historical data. They suggest various asymmetrical relations between sociolinguistically dominated or 'weak' codes and dominant or 'strong' codes, i.e. fluctuating dominance relations in the course of the long-term contacts in the area.

First, Bulgar elements were adopted in Finno-Ugric varieties. Bulgar was not a substratum, whose features were imposed on them. There is a considerable stock of Bulgar loanwords in Mari. Udmurt and Mordva also have a larger number of Bulgar loanwords, whereas Komi (Zyryan) only displays two or three dozen words of Bulgar origin. Early Bulgar loanwords are found in both Meadow and Hill Mari; several hundred lexical items were copied up to the 13th century. It is important to note that they are typically words of material and social culture, as we would expect in the case of adoption from a prestigious code. After the 13th century the lexicon of Hill and Meadow Mari developed differently due to different language contacts. From this time on, Chuvash loanwords are mainly found in Hill Mari.

Secondly, Kipchak elements were adopted in practically all varieties of the area. Some were subject to a very strong Kipchak lexical and morphosyntactic influence. As regards Mari, the impact was strongest on Eastern Mari and Meadow Mari; as for Chuvash, it particularly affected Lower Chuvash.

Thirdly, Russian elements were adopted in all languages of the area. As in the first two cases, this influence was typically restricted to adoption of copies from a socially dominant code.

But we must also reckon with several cases of imposition, convergent changes due to complex processes of ethnolinguistic assimilation in the area. Thus early imposition of Finno-Ugric elements on Bulgar varieties is highly probable. There was also Bulgar and Finno-Ugric imposition on the Kipchak varieties that many groups shifted to from the 14th century on. Finally, elements of all varieties of the area were imposed on the respective local varieties of Russian, in particular with respect to pronunciation.

The prehistory of some Turkic varieties of the area is likely to have involved changes due to abrupt reorganization processes, when various ethnic groups using different codes were brought together to coexist in new confederations and other mixed speech communities with new social networks.

The Chuvash-Mari symbiosis

Chuvash and Mari present the most intriguing interactions in the area. The contacts between them have been extremely close, leading to a profound symbiosis. But the nature of their mutual copying processes is still far from clear. The 'direction of borrowing' is often problematic: it is difficult to identify shared features as copies from Mari in Chuvash or copies from Chuvash in Mari.

In what way has Chuvash been subject to the strong influence from Mari? Some problems appear less puzzling if we reckon with large-scale imposition of Mari elements in Chuvash as against the well-known adoption of Chuvash elements in Mari. This would imply that the Finno-Ugric influence on Chuvash is essentially a substratum influence due to assimilation of segments of a local Finno-Ugric population by Bulgar-speaking immigrants. The Finno-Ugric groups in question imposed features of their primary code on their variety of Bulgar – thus an example of transfer of structures in the course of second-language acquisition.

The Finno-Ugric substratum of Chuvash is obvious. The influence is typically strongest in Upper Chuvash, especially in the Sundyr dialect spoken in the northwestern part of Chuvashia, in immediate Mari neighborhood. As toponyms show, Upper Chuvash largely covers the area formerly inhabited by the Mari population. Russian 16th-century sources refer to both Chuvash and Hill Mari as 'the mountain people', since they settled in the hilly region along the right Volga bank. Until the end of the 18th century, the Chuvash were often called 'Cheremis', the old name for the Mari, or 'Cheremis Tatars'. Chuvash was long mistaken for a Finno-Ugric or a Turkicized Finno-Ugric language.

Lexical copies

It is not the aim of the present article to discuss the differences between adopted and imposed features in detail. With respect to loanwords, it may be enough to state that possible semantic constraints on lexical copying are likely to differ between adoption and imposition. In cases of adoption, speakers naturally tend to copy words that reflect the very aspects by which the culture of the dominant code is dominant. In cases of imposition, speakers prefer the basic vocabulary of semantic domains left untouched by these aspects. Typically, Mari loanwords in Chuvash are not items reflecting a prestigious social or material culture, but include basic every-day vocabulary such as *kătkă* 'ant', *lăk* 'corner', *lăm* 'dew, moisture', *lĕp* 'lukewarm', and *mĕlke* 'shadow'.

The origin of lax vowels

In order to illustrate the difference between adoption and imposition, let us take a brief look at the phenomenon of lax vowels, which is most instructive in this respect. We have already seen that Tatar and Bashkir have four of them. This is also the case in Upper Chuvash: *ĕ, ŏ, ă, ŏ*, though certain southern dialects lack *ŏ*. Lower Chuvash and Standard Chuvash only exhibit *ĕ* and *ă* due to delabialization of *ŏ* and *ŏ*. In some Tatar dialects, partly also in Kazan, *ŏ* and *ŏ* have developed to *ĕ* and *ĭ* similarly to Lower Chuvash. The northwestern dialects of Mari display, like Upper Chuvash, four lax vowels, a front unrounded *ĕ*, a front rounded *ŏ*, a back unrounded *ă*, and a back rounded *ŏ*. Hill Mari, like Lower Chuvash, only exhibits two lax vowels: one front unrounded *ĕ*, and one back unrounded *ă*. Most Meadow Mari dialects only have one lax vowel, a back unrounded *ă*. Moksha exhibits a centralized lax vowel that is absent in Erzya. The Vakh dialect of the west Siberian language Khanty has, again, four lax vowels: front unrounded, front rounded, back unrounded, and back rounded.

How did these lax vowels emerge? Several researchers have proposed a Finno-Ugric origin. Some have regarded the reduced vowels of Mari and Khanty as preserved properties of the Finno-Ugric proto-language (Steinitz 1944). Others have rejected the idea of a connection of the reduced vowels in Mari and Khanty with reduced vowels in first syllables in the proto-language. Some researchers have claimed that the reduced vowels in Mari are the result of inner development; others ascribe them to Turkic influence, since they mainly occur in Chuvash and Tatar loanwords, seldom in native words. On the other hand, it is claimed that the phonological system of Chuvash is strongly influenced by the neighboring Finno-Ugric languages. The vowel systems of Mari and Chuvash are very similar. Some researchers have even supposed an areal connection with the Russian *akan'e*, originally a typically Southern Russian innovation, e.g. reduction of unstressed *o* in words such as [vʌdá] *voda* 'water'. There have been attempts to explain this tendency as a Moksha influence (Stipa 1952). Some have reversed the direction of copying, suggesting that the reduction in Moksha might be due to influence from Russian as represented by the central dialect of the Moscow region.

Since the lax vs. tense oppositions are rather old in Volga Kipchak, some researchers have suggested a Kipchak origin. Thus the reduced vowels in initial syllables in Mari would be a result of Kipchak influence. Others assume a Bulgar origin, claiming that the point of departure was Volga Bulgar of the 13th and 14th centuries. From here, the phenomenon spread eastwards to Volga Kipchak.

Some scholars find it impossible to state anything certain about the origin of this feature, which is part of a sound change extending across a vast area. The phenomenon is simply claimed to be of 'areal' origin and typical of a 'Sprachbund', a shared areal property for which, as it were, none of the languages involved can be held responsible.

The question of origin will not be dealt with further here. Several facts point to a Bulgar origin, though the evidence is scarce. Volga Bulgar is a little known language to which various kinds of peculiar features may be attributed without much risk of falsification. The point I will make is different. It makes little sense to focus on the occurrence of individual lax vowels without considering their roles in the respective sound systems. And I will argue that Volga Kipchak and Chuvash represent two different cases with respect to the roles of lax vowels in the given systems.

The Volga Kipchak vowel shifts

It is a well-known and much discussed fact that the Turkic languages of the Volga-Kama area have undergone chain shifts of earlier high and non-high vowels. Here I limit the discussion to the situation in initial, primary stem syllables. The high and mid vowels of modern Tatar are likely to have emerged in the following way:

	Front		Back	
High	i	ü		u
	↑	↑		↑
	*e	*ö		*o
	*i	*ü	*ï	*u
	↓	↓	↓	↓
Mid	ĕ	ŏ	ї̆	ŏ

Most Turkic languages have preserved the asterisked vowels. The new Volga Kipchak system implies that a new opposition of lax vs. tense has replaced the earlier oppositions of high vs. mid. The old mid vowels rise; the old high vowels relax. The Turkic etymological relations are preserved, which means that there are regular correspondences between Tatar and other Common Turkic languages such as *it* vs. *et* 'meat', *kür-* vs. *kör-* 'see', *yul* vs. *yol* 'way', *bĕl-* vs. *bil-* 'know', *kŏl* vs. *kül* 'ashes', *qïš* vs. *qïš* 'winter', *qŏrt* vs. *qurt* 'worm'. For details, see, e.g. Berta 1989.

Note that the Volga Kipchak shift was not simply a switch in the sense of falling high vowels and rising mid vowels. The tense vowels in Tatar are not necessarily higher than the lax ones. It is true that *i* is higher than the high-mid *ĕ*, but *ü* and *u* are not higher than *ŏ* and *ŏ* (Bajčura 1959: 33-38).

I will not go into the long and controversial discussion on reasons for the vowel shifts, their possible origin, and their relative and absolute chronology. I will not discuss the impact of accent, the neutralization of the Proto-Turkic length distinctions in vowels, or the role of heterogeneous diphthongs, vowel glides with an audible change of quality (Johanson 1992). But let us suppose that it was Volga Bulgar that started the engine in the area. The effect was crucially different in Volga Kipchak and in Chuvash.

Whatever the origin and development of the Volga Kipchak system may be, the switch is regular and systematic. It preserves the inherited Turkic vowel correlations, albeit in a somewhat different garb. And it is clearly part of a natural cycle of the following type, exemplified here with unrounded front vowels in IPA notation:

high tense [i]	$\Rightarrow$	high lax [ɪ]
$\Uparrow$		$\Downarrow$
mid tense [ɛ]	$\Leftarrow$	mid lax [ə]

The common point of departure had been a phonetic approximation of high and mid vowels to the effect that the security distance between them became narrow. The distinction ±high, which is of crucial importance in Turkic phonology, was endangered. Volga Kipchak preserved the distinction by analogous, though materially different phonetic means. Phonological confusion was avoided. Old phonemes left their slots, but their neighbors moved in after them. The chain reaction gradually influenced the whole system in a clear-cut way: the old correlation, so essential in Turkic, was now reinterpreted and expressed by means of tense and lax vowels. The etymological relations largely remained intact. Thus the Volga Kipchak system is clearly motivated by internal principles of Turkic phonology.

The Chuvash vowel shifts

The situation is quite different in Chuvash, the supposed direct heir of Volga Bulgar. The developments of the vowels in Volga Kipchak and Chuvash are often described as basically identical. But the Chuvash deviations from the normal Turkic vowel system are very different from those in Tatar and Bashkir. If we assume a similar original vowel system as for the ancestor of Volga Kipchak, we find that both earlier high and mid vowels may be represented as high or as lax.

Some examples (with modern Common Turkic equivalents in brackets): *ăš* 'interior' (*ič*), *ĕś-* 'drink' (*ič-*), *kun* 'day' (*kün*), *kul-* 'laugh' (*kül-*), *kĕl* 'ashes' (*kül*), *xir* 'field' (*qïr*), *xĕr* 'girl' (*qïz*), *tit-* 'hold' (*tut-*), *păr* 'ice' (*buz*), *xurt* 'worm' (*qurt*), *kur-* 'see' (*kör-*), *vil-* 'die' (*öl-*), *kăk* 'root' (*kök*), *xur-* 'put' (*qoy-*), *tăxăr* 'nine' (*toquz*). The realization of primary stem vowels may also change according to the word structure, which is most unusual in Turkic, e.g. *vil-* 'die' (*öl-*) vs.

vĕler- 'kill' (*ölür-*) or *piś* 'boil' (*piš-*) vs. *pĕśer-* 'let boil, cook' (*pišir-*). See also Clark 1998. For details of the Common Turkic vowel system, see Johanson 1998.

The question how the Chuvash vowels have reached their present positions will not concern us here. There is rather little direct evidence of the Volga Bulgar vowel system. However, highly competent and trustworthy specialists in Turkic and Finno-Ugric historical linguistics have attempted to reconstruct older stages of the vowel systems of Chuvash and Mari on the basis of phonetic reflexes in loanwords (see, e.g., Róna-Tas 1982, Rédei and Róna-Tas 1983, Bereczki 1992, Agyagási 1997 and 1998). Rather complicated developments have been suggested, for Chuvash even changes such as raising followed by reduction of originally non-high vowels, e.g. **o > *u > ŏ*. All details of these interesting discussions must be omitted here.

The important point here is that the new system does not mirror the oppositions defining the earlier vowel system generally assumed for Turkic. If the latter was really the starting-point for the Chuvash development, this development has not been systematic in the way observed in practically all other Turkic languages. The old distinction high vs. non-high has not been preserved; and it has not been replaced by any analogous distinction. The tense vs. lax opposition does not serve the same phonological purpose as in Volga Kipchak. The diachronic transparency is blurred; the etymological connections are broken. The problem of coinciding old high and non-high vowels has become unimportant, the whole system being reorganized regardless of the old correlations.

Chuvash displays similar disloyalty with respect to old front vs. back relations. Many Turkic primary stems that are either front or back in a rather constant way from language to language are subject to class shift in Chuvash. There is thus a further dimension in which diachronic relations are disturbed and etymological connections blurred. Synchronically, however, the front versus back distinction still plays a crucial role, particularly in intersyllabic and intrasyllabic sound harmony.

Finno-Ugric imposition on Chuvash

The phonological comparison with the 'normal' Turkic languages Tatar and Bashkir is highly revealing. It is not enough to state that the vowel shifts in question are local phenomena that are also found in the Finno-Ugric languages of the region. In my opinion the deviations in Chuvash can only be explained by Finno-Ugric imposition. This means that speakers of ancient Mari (and probably also Permic) carried over their articulatory habits into their variety of Volga Bulgar. The phonological word structure of Turkic was alien to those speakers. Thus the tense vs. lax features were preserved or reorganized under Finno-Ugric substratum influence, i.e. distributed according to the position in the word and to non-Turkic accent patterns. Even if the tense vs. lax opposition originates in Volga

Bulgar, these specific realizations seem to be the effects of Finno-Ugric imposition. The opinion that Chuvash is a 'typically Turkic language' displaying only minor deviations from Common Turkic is as wrong as the old opposite opinion according to which Chuvash is a Turkicized Finno-Ugric language.

University of Mainz

REFERENCES

Agyagási, Klára
1997   "The theoretical possibilities of the chronological interpretation of Cheremiss loanwords in Chuvash", in: Árpád Berta (ed.), *Historical and linguistic interaction between Inner Asia and Europe* (*Studia Uralo-Altaica* 39), 1-10. Szeged: University Press.
1998   "On the characteristics of Cheremis linguistic interference on Chuvash", in: Lars Johanson (ed.), *The Mainz meeting* (*Turcologica* 32), 667-682. Wiesbaden: Harrassowitz.

Bajčura, Uzbek Š.
1959   *Zvukovoj stroj tatarskogo jazyka* 1. Kazan': Izdatel'stvo Kazanskogo Universiteta.

Bereczki, Gábor
1992   *Grundzüge der tscheremissischen Sprachgeschichte* 2 (*Studia Uralo-Altaica* 34). Szeged: University Press.
1994   *Grundzüge der tscheremissischen Sprachgeschichte* 1 (*Studia Uralo-Altaica* 35). Szeged: University Press.

Berta, Árpád
1989   *Lautgeschichte der tatarischen Dialekte* (*Studia Uralo-Altaica* 31). Szeged: University Press.

Clark, Larry
1998   "Chuvash", in: Lars Johanson and Éva Á. Csató (eds.), *The Turkic languages*, 434-452. London: Routledge.

Comrie, Bernard
1981   *The languages of the Soviet Union*. Cambridge: University Press.

Décsy, Gyula
1973   *Die linguistische Struktur Europas*. Wiesbaden: Harrassowitz.

Johanson, Lars
1992   "Zur Isochronie im Türkischen", in: Géza Bethlenfalvy et al. (eds.), *Altaic religious beliefs and practices*, 183-188. Budapest.
1998   "The history of Turkic", in: Lars Johanson and Éva Á. Csató (eds.), *The Turkic languages*, 81-125. London: Routledge.

Rédei, Károly, and András Róna-Tas
1983   "Early Bulgarian loanwords in the Permian languages", *Acta Orientalia Hungarica* 37, 3-41.

Róna-Tas, András
1982   "The periodization and sources in Chuvash linguistic history", *Asiatische Forschungen* 79, 113-70.

1988   "Turkic influence on the Uralic languages", in: Denis Sinor (ed.), *The Uralic Languages* (*Handbuch der Orientalistik* 8:1), 760-777. Leiden: Brill.

Steinitz, Wolfgang
1944   *Geschichte des finnisch-ugrischen Vokalismus* (*Acta Instituti Hungarici Universitas Holmiensis* B:2). Stockholm: Almqvist & Wiksell.

Stipa, Günter
1952   "Phonetische Wechselwirkungen zwischen Mokscha-Mordwinisch und Russisch", *Ural-Ataische Jahrbücher* 24, 59-64; 25, 28-51.

Zimonyi, István
1992   *The origins of the Volga Bulghars* (*Studia Uralo-Altaica* 32). Szeged: University Press.

Languages in Contact, edited by D.G. Gilbers, J. Nerbonne, and J. Schaeken (= *Studies in Slavic and General Linguistics*, vol. 28), 179-185. Amsterdam - Atlanta, GA: Rodopi, 2000.

THE LOWER AMUR LANGUAGES IN CONTACT WITH RUSSIAN

MARINA KHASANOVA

The Russian Far East is a large territory that stretches from the Arctic up to the Japan Sea. The Amur River basin is one of the most interesting places in the Far East. The area is rich in animals, fish, minerals, and timber. Besides, the Amur is the largest river of the Russian Far East. Its source is in the Amurskaya Oblast' and it flows to the Okhotsk Sea opposite Northern Sakhalin. This vast territory attracted different tribes over an enormous period of time, from the Neolithic to the present. In the Middle Ages (1413) several ethnic groups were registered on the Amur banks by Chinese travellers: *Ku-i* (Ainu), *Ji-le-mi* (Jurchen *gilemi* – Nivkh), and *Ye-ren* (Jurchen *udigen nyarma*, lit. 'wild people'). In the 19th century eight small nationalities lived in the Lower Amur basin and on the Okhotsk Sea shore: Nanay, Ulcha, Oroch, Udege, Negidal, Evenki, Even, and Nivkh. Nowadays, this territory is still inhabited by the same nationalities. Russian scholars call them aborigines as opposed to Russians who began to inhabit the Far East in the middle of the 19th century.

The Lower Amur basin usually refers to the territory between Khabarovsk and Nikolayevsk-na-Amure, which is situated near the Amur Liman, where the Amur mouth is. In this area the following minorities live: Nanays (ca.12,000), Ulchas (ca. 3,500), Oroch (ca. 500), Negidals (ca. 400), Evenkis (ca. 4,000 – the total number of Evenkis is about 30,000) and Nivkh (the total number is ca. 4,500: in the Lower Amur there are ca. 2,500 people and on Sakhalin island ca. 2,000).

The Lower Amur region is inhabited by different aborigines whose languages belong to two linguistic groups: Manchu-Tungusic languages and so-called Paleo-Siberian languages. The first group is represented by Nanay, Ulcha, Oroch, Negidal, and Evenki, whereas the second one is represented by the Nivkh.

The Lower Amur basin has always been the arena of various ethnic and cultural contacts. Manchurian, Mongolian, and Korean influences can be traced in the aboriginal cultures. The annexation of the Far Eastern region by the Russian Empire played a very important role in the destiny of the Amur basin natives.

The earliest contacts between aborigines and Russians date back to the 17th century when the Cossack Khabarov and his detachment came to conquer the Amur region. A number of stories about Khabarov's cruel voyage are still told among the Nanay people. However, there is also a Nanay story about general N.

Murav'ëv, who saved the Nanay from the Manchu yoke and offered them the protection of the Russian Empire.

It should be mentioned that the Amur aborigines were still not subject to any authority when they were found by the Russian Cossacks in the 17th century. In 1689 Russia was forced to sign the treaty with the Qing Empire. According to this treaty the Amur basin area came under the Qing protection, although there were no clear borders between the two empires. It was only in 1858 when general N. Murav'ëv signed the Aygun agreement, in which the line of demarcation was determined and the Lower Amur region was returned to Russia.

Even before the Aygun agreement Russians undertook some expeditions down the Amur. The most famous one was by admiral G. Nevel'skoj, who believed that only respect and good treatment of the Lower Amur natives would make the Far East a real part of the Russian Empire. He did his best to learn the differences between the Lower Amur cultures and peoples, and also located the specific territories of their inhabitance. He and his friends were the first who gave a description of the Sakhalin Oroks (Uiltas), Nivkh (Gilyaks), and Negidals. G. Nevel'skoj paid much attention to Nivkh: he proved that the Russian Cossacks were right when they called the Amur mouth and Sakhalin island "Gilyak territory", whereas A. Kruzenštern mistakenly called it "Tatar territory". The expedition of Nevel'-skoj marked the beginning of Russian settlements in the Lower Amur. Before that time contacts were irregular. So in fact, close interaction between aborigines and Russians began in the region in the middle of the 19th century and lasted about 150 years. The most intensive contacts were during the Soviet period.

It is well-known that for a very long time small groups of northern native people lived in small villages. Their main occupation was fishing, hunting, and gathering. This was also the case in the Lower Amur region. The Soviet authorities, however, decided to "improve" the life of the aborigines. First of all, they gathered the natives in big villages. Certainly, this action intensified the influence of the Russian language and culture. The forced migrations eventually resulted in almost complete disappearance of traditional aboriginal cultures.

Language indicates the ethnic identification, i.e. somebody's belonging to a group of people. Thus, it is the most important component of every national culture. Language shift often leads to abrupt changes in the original culture.

After the Second World War the Soviet government enforced Russian in every sphere of life. Nationalities and ethnic groups (especially minorities) were rapidly losing their cultures and languages. As for northern aborigines, the special boarding-school system of educating aboriginal children (*internat* in Russian) played a tragic role in this process. Of course, one can explain the introduction of this system by the hard living conditions of the natives. However, it should be pointed out that the *internat* system caused the destruction of family ties and accelerated the disappearance of a number of ethnic groups.

The problem of "aboriginal Russian" (i.e. the Russian language of the aboriginal population) has not attracted much attention so far. The entire population of the former USSR was considered to speak good Russian. However, this was not the case. Here I shall try to survey some of my recent data on the subject.

First of all, the natives' knowledge of Russian depends on the age of the speakers. The representatives of the oldest generation who were born in the beginning of the 20th century had a very peculiar kind of spoken Russian. In the eighties I recorded in the Lower Amur region astonishing examples of pidginized Russian, e.g. *nasa takoj netu* 'we have no such [things]' (lit. 'our such no'); *nasa saman čo bylo* 'we have almost no shamans' (lit. 'our shaman what was'); *nasa negidales* 'we are Negidals' (lit. 'our Negidals'); *nasa ne pakasyvaet* '[men] do not show it to us [women]' (lit. 'our not shows'); *nasa ne kusaet sabak* 'we do not eat dogs' (lit. 'our not eats dogs'); *deti taskaet sebe gorbu* '[seal] carries it's young ones on it's back' (lit. 'children drags itself back'); *ryba koža delali* '[it] was fish skin made [thing]' (lit. 'fish skin made-they'); *tajga brosat'* 'to leave in the tajga' (lit. 'tajga throw'); *oxota taskajut* '[they] bring [something] to the hunting' (lit. 'hunting carry-they'); *sivinsa atlivali* '[they] cast [it] from the lead' (lit. 'lead cast-they'); *bagul'nik topit* '[he] burns up the bagul'nik grass' (lit. 'bagul'nik heats'); *Kapa xodil', čaj popil', ryba potaščil'* 'Kapa came, had some tea, took the fish' (lit. 'Kapa went, tea drank, fish dragged'). The typical features of this kind of pidginized Russian are: the absence of Russian case markers and prepositions, special sentence structure (SOV), and the position of the attribute before the main (determined) word. Sometimes, however, case markers in "aboriginal Russian" sentences can come from the native language: *ryba kuravan malen'ko varjat* 'one must boil a little the fish skin' (the word *kuravan* < Russian *škura* 'skin' includes the Tungusic accusative case suffix); *bjut palkad'i* '[they] drum by the stick' (the word *palkad'i* includes the Tungusic instrumental case suffix); *Kal'madu byla saman* 'there was a shaman in Kal'ma [village]' (the name of the village *Kal'madu* includes the Tungusic dative case suffix).

The limited Russian lexicon of the older people caused semantic extensions of many words, especially some frequent verbs: *taščit'* 'to drag', also meaning 'to carry, to take, to wear'; *topit'* 'to heat', also meaning 'to set fire, to burn'; *gonjat'* 'to drive', also meaning 'to pursue, to hunt, to hunt down'; *idti* 'to go', also meaning 'to move, to approach, to suit', etc. Cases of separating different meanings of lexemes are also due to the poor Russian lexicon. For example: *veter xočet načinat'* 'the wind begins to blow' (lit. 'wind wants to begin').

As for phonetics, it should be pointed out that the pronunciation of Russian sounds by the oldest generation of the Lower Amur natives was identical to that of their own native languages. They did not distinguish in particular Russian *č'* and *t'*; *d'* and *z*, *ž*; *š*, *šč*, and *s'*. Very old Lower Amur natives did not hear and pronounce Russian *t'*: they perceived it as their own palatalized *č'*, thus not distinguishing Russian words such as *veter* 'wind' and *večer* 'evening'; *tëtka* 'aunt' and *čëtko* 'clearly'; *Pet'ka* (name) and *pečka* 'stove'; *test'* 'father-in-law' and *čest'* 'honour'; *tesno* 'narrow' and *čestno* 'honestly'.

In Manchu-Tungusic languages there is a phonetic rule: two or more consonants in *anlaut* are prohibited. This rule applies also to "aboriginal Russian". The natives either drop the "unnecessary" consonants or insert certain prothetic vowels: *s'o* (Russian *vsë*) 'the whole, all, everything'; *remja* (Russian *vremja*) 'time'; *kura* (Russian *škura*) 'skin'; *čera* (Russian *včera*) 'yesterday'; *sida* (Russian *vsegda*) 'always'; *mesto* or *namesto* (Russian *vmesto*) 'instead'; *aran'če* (Russian *ran'še*) 'before'; *arasnaj* (Russian *raznyj*) 'different'; *kilep* (Russian *xleb*) 'bread'; *isnait* (Russian *znaet*) '[he] knows', etc.

As for pronouns, there is only one pidgin form preserved, i.e. the 1st person plural form *nasa* 'we'. Other forms (e.g. *tebe, tvoja* 'you', *mine, maja* 'I') were not recorded.

It is easy to find similarities between our examples and some well-known models of the so-called Far Eastern pidgin (also *Kjaxta* or *Majmačin* pidgin) that have been studied by V.K. Arsen'ev, A.G. Šprincin, and others: *maja ni magu* 'I cannot' (lit. 'my not can'; Šprincin 1968: 90); *duoja madamu jesi* 'are you married?' (lit. 'yours madam is'; Šprincin 1968: 90); *Naša tut nado dožidaj* 'we have to wait here' (lit. 'our here must wait'; Arsen'ev 1986: 23); *Moja doma netu* 'I have no house' (lit. 'my house no'; Arsen'ev 1986: 15); *tebe ponimaj netu* 'you do not understand' (lit. 'to you understand no'; Arsen'ev 1986: 23); *nis'iwo ni delai iwo* 'he does nothing' (lit. 'nothing not do his'; Eloeva and Perexval'skaja 1986: 56), etc. Although we are dealing with the same type of examples, they are of a different origin.

The Far Eastern pidgin originated near the Russian-Chinese border in the second half of the 19th century when the Russian-speaking population began to settle the south of the territory. Soon there was a convergence area in which the new variety of Russian-Chinese pidgin started to develop. Unfortunately, we have no sufficient data on the Far Eastern pidgin. Although a few preliminary studies have been carried out (A.G. Šprincin, V.I. Belikov, F. Eloeva and E. Perexval'skaja), there are no detailed descriptions available.

In the Lower Amur region there were no intensive Russian-Chinese contacts. In my opinion, some models and elements of the Far Eastern pidgin must have been introduced into "aboriginal Russian" by Russian pioneers in the 19th century. The settlers came to the Lower Amur from the south of the Far East where the Russian-Chinese pidgin was widespread. They thought that this type of language was more intelligible for the natives. Actually, I think that the first aborigine's contact with Russian in the 19th century was through the Far Eastern pidgin. Thus, modern Lower Amur pidginized Russian is based on the Russian-Chinese pidgin of the 19th century. Of course, in more recent times it has been influenced by spoken Russian (especially southern Russian dialects).

An interesting question is how the pidginized Russian developed. At the moment this issue can be discussed only in theoretical terms because all speakers whose first language was aboriginal have died in the course of time. In the eighties there was only the possibility to study pidginized Russian that had been preserved by Lower Amur natives. The structure of this pidginized Russian, so-called *Govorka* (pidgin of Taymyr), is typologically similar to *Kjaxta* pidgin and some other Russian-based pidgins.

The present old-aged generation was born at the end of the twenties or the beginning of the thirties. They were educated in schools and can be regarded, to a certain extent, as bilingual. At the same time the Russian of the older people reveals some idiosyncracies that are partly due to their native articulatory base. Also interesting is the fact that they have more than one speech variety. They can speak Russian rather well with Russians, minimizing under these circumstances grammatical mistakes. Another variety is when they know that the listener understands a little bit of the aboriginal language. In this case they bother less to speak Russian correctly and mix Russian and aboriginal words and grammatical forms. The third variety applies to conversations with adolescents, in which a peculiar language mixture reveals the mutual penetration of the two languages.

At this point I would like to give some examples. In fieldwork expeditions I observed that the old people's main language is the language of their ethnic group. Even in their "good Russian" (when they try to minimize grammatical mistakes) they usually have a number of calques: *varëna malako* 'boiled milk' (there is no difference in the Manchu-Tungusic languages between the notions 'to cook' and 'to boil', whereas Russian has two different words: *varit'* and *kipjatit'*); *my svoi slova snaim* 'we know our [native] language' (there is no difference in Manchu-Tungusic and in Nivkh between the notions 'language' and 'word'), etc.

When a speaker knows that the conversation partner understands his native language he will put native words and forms here and there in his speech: *listja-haltin* 'big leaves' (the root *listja* is Russian, whereas the suffixes -ha-, -l-, -tin are Tungusic); *potom d'igge melko-melko* 'then cut [it] in very small pieces' (the word *d'igge* is Tungusic); *umgu ola govorit* 'the girl says' (the words *umgu ola* are Nivkh); *fitis upal* 'the blanket fell' (the word *fitis* is Nivkh), etc.

If older people know that the listener understands their native language rather well, they will use a peculiar mixture of languages: *kasdy ras kusivatča* '[they are] fighting every time' (*kusivatča* is a Tungusic word); *sit'as ongkud'ap* 'now [we'll] pour out [the water]' (*ongkud'ap* is a Tungusic word); *tomkod'i činili* '[they] mended [their boots] by the sinew' (*tomkod'i* is a Tungusic word); *Na temkevun palkad'i bili* '[they] drummed the *temkevun* [a musical log] by the stick' (*temkevun* is a Tungusic word, *palkad'i* is a Russian word with the Tungusic instrumental case suffix); *amim soktojihin – zdët selyj den'* 'if my father is drinking, [his dog] is waiting all day long' (the first part of the phrase is Tungusic); *palo-čofski* 'in Russian' (here we have a Russian prefix + a Nivkh root + a Russian suffix), etc. As I have already mentioned, this kind of language mixture is often used by parents when they talk to their children. (By the way, parents normally use 'hear' instead of 'understand' in phrases like 'my children hear our native language'.)

I would like to stress that there are many similar features and at the same time differences between Russian that is spoken by the old Nivkhs and by the old Tunguses. Certainly, there are substantial differences between Nivkh and the Manchu-Tungusic languages that influence the "aboriginal Russian".

The representatives of the middle-aged generation have a good command of Russian. Nevertheless, some features of aboriginal grammar can be observed in their speech. Sometimes they transfer elements of their native grammar and lexical system into Russian: *v vodu molitsja* 'to apply to water' < Nivkh *tolyzdox mehrynyd'*; *biserom narisovanyj* 'embroidered with beads' (lit. 'painted with beads') < Negidal *elga* = 'to paint, to embroider'. A characteristic feature of Russian spoken by the middle-aged generation is the preservation of palatalized *n', d', č'*. The main difference between the oldest and the middle generation is the fact that middle-aged people rarely speak their mother tongue although they understand it rather well.

For the younger people who grew up in the Soviet boarding-schools Russian became their native language. They do not speak standard Russian but one of the local dialects. However, this generation still preserves a few aboriginal articulation peculiarities, the most striking one being palatalized *n', d', č'*. At the moment children know at best only a few aboriginal words. Their only language is Russian.

The linguistic data presented in this article exemplify the gradual disappearance of the aboriginal languages due to the pressure of Russian. It is quite clear that the language shift is more intensive among the smallest communities (e.g. Orochs, Negidals) and will eventually lead to language death. Other peoples, like the Nanays and Evenkis, preserve their native languages better (the middle generation speak the aboriginal language).

The relations between Russian and the aboriginal languages in the Lower Amur region cannot be considered as real contact. The problem is more complicated. To my opinion, the phenomenon can be characterized as the pressure of Russian on the endangered and unwritten minor languages. During the Soviet period it was intense Russian cultural expansion supported by the authorities that finally led to the partial or even complete loss of the native languages in the Lower Amur region.

Russian Academy of Sciences,
Peter the Great Museum of Anthropology and Ethnography,
St. Petersburg

REFERENCES

Arsen'ev, V.K.
1986   *Po Ussurijskomu kraju*. Vladivostok.
Belikov, V.I.
1994   "Russko-kitajskij pidžin", in: *Kontaktologičeskij ènciklopedičeskij slovar'-spra-vočnik*, 294-298. Moskva.
Eloeva, F., and E. Perexval'skaja
1986   "K xarakteristike dal'nevostočnogo kontaktnogo jazyka", in: *Istoriko-kul'turnye kontakty narodov altajskoj jazykovoj obščnosti, 29 sessija PIAC*, 54-56. Taš-kent.
Šprincin, A.G.
1968   "O russko-kitajskom dialekte na Dal'nem Vostoke", in: *Strany i narody Vostoka* 6, 86-100. Moskva.

Languages in Contact, edited by D.G. Gilbers, J. Nerbonne, and J. Schaeken (= *Studies in Slavic and General Linguistics*, vol. 28), 187-191. Amsterdam - Atlanta, GA: Rodopi, 2000.

VARIETIES IN CONTACT AND THEIR IMPACT ON LANGUAGE PLANNING IN YIDDISH

ANE KLEINE

1. Introduction

This study is primarily the result of linguistic interests and is meant to give a bird's-eye survey of the impact contact situations have had and continue to have in Yiddish language planning. Little research has been done on the standardization of modern Yiddish and almost nothing in regard to its pronunciation (Kleine 1998: 201ff.). In this paper I would like to point out in which ways various kinds of language contact may have contributed to establishing a supra-regional, standard Yiddish language.

Central in the discussion of Standard Yiddish is the differentiation of two types of language contact, INTER-LANGUAGE CONTACT and INTRA-LANGUAGE CONTACT, which must be considered in their respective (socio-)historical contexts. Inter-language contact means the co-existence of different languages in one territory. Intra-language contact, in contrast, designates both the coming together of Yiddish speakers with different dialectal backgrounds, and contact situations in which different social groups meet.

2. Impact of inter-language contact

From its beginnings in the late ninth century based on middle- and high-German dialects, the language of Ashkenazic Jewry has been a fusion language, incorporating Hebrew-Aramaic as well as Romance elements into its German component.

With the continuing spread of the language, Yiddish was increasingly shaped by numerous co-territorial languages. First it was influenced by local varieties of the surrounding German. With the great migratory movements to Eastern Europe during the "Black Death" and the Crusades, the Slavic languages of the new home countries were potential sources for language innovation, affecting vocabulary as well as grammar, syntactic features, and the system of phonemes. Unlike other languages in Europe, Yiddish always had to survive in a situation where its speakers not only lived next to other vernacular languages but right in the middle of them (without doubt in need of acquiring at least a smattering of those languages). As a result Eastern Yiddish began to develop differently from the Western variety.

At its maximum extension, Yiddish was a language of communication and literature in Germany, Switzerland, Austria, North Italy, Poland, Hungary, Romania, the Baltic countries, Western Russia, Ukraine, and Belarus, with more than 12 million speakers.

While it is true that this situation gave rise to distinct dialects, unifying tendencies can be observed at any time in the development of Yiddish. How can this be explained?

3. Impact of intra-language contact before World War II

First we have to reflect on the fact that Jews were frequently forced to migrate and were limited to special occupations. One of them was the occupation of itinerant trader. Consequently, speakers of different dialects often met and had to communicate. Furthermore, as Katz (1993: 52ff.) points out, the necessity of written communication over long distances in a diasporic situation was a major factor leading to the development of a cross-dialectal, written Yiddish.[1]

In this paper I shall focus on the modern Yiddish language, from the period starting in the late 19th and early 20th century. When modern linguists at the beginning of the 20th century started to recognize Yiddish as a language of its own, language families were investigated using diachronic and synchronic methods (Kleine 1999: 60f.). As a reaction to the undeniably close relationship between Yiddish and German, which came into focus at that time, a need for clear distinction and differentiation arose. Dialectal differences were pushed into the background while focusing on supraregional common features. In this situation phenomena such as LANGUAGE LOYALTY – as Uriel Weinreich (1970: 99) calls it – spread, inducing the speakers to concentrate on the standardization of the language.

Moreover, at the end of the 19th century the famous Yiddish writers Mendele Mokher Seforim, Shalom Aleichem, and I.L. Peretz had created a widely acknowledged modern written Yiddish, the so called SHRAYBSHPRAKH B (Max Weinreich, cf. note 1), which gave its name to the corresponding pronunciation, known as the LITERAL PRONUNCIATION. The intellectuals of Lithuania were the most vocal advocates of this form, since its more or less conservative representation of the vowel system closely resembled the Lithuanian Yiddish dialect (Mark 1951: 7f.).

Despite the demographic dominance of Southern Yiddish speakers, the higher prestige of Northern Jewish communities in Eastern Europe made their dialect more likely to subdue all others. This was the case on the stage and in Yiddish film production (Uriel Weinreich 1951: 28f.), even though the southern oriented

---

[1] Max Weinreich (1973 II: 397 / 1980: 733 and passim) lists various characteristics of this early form of 'literary' Yiddish and refers to it as SHRAYBSHPRAKH A.

Bine-Oysshprakh (another functional and regional variety of a general norm) had been accepted. Thus, its use in such prestigious functions as the language of schools and public discussion contributed to the acceptance of this supraregional variety (Katz 1993: 48), since the training of teachers took place in Lithuania where the initiative of a secular school system was born.[2]

Another factor that contributed to a northern oriented standard Yiddish was the founding of YIVO, the 'Institute for Jewish Research', in Vilna in 1925, as a result of rising linguistic interest in Yiddish. Vilna had been the home of many standardizing efforts, where several conventions (e.g. orthographic conventions with the *Takones fun yidishn oysleyg* 1937) were fixed.[3]

4. Impact of intra-language contact after World War II

The socio-cultural setting of language contact and its linguistic effects were radically different in the war time and post war exile communities. After the YIVO's migration to New York in 1941 it was again highly involved in promoting the development and spread of this new standard, especially the Standard Yiddish pronunciation. The best known textbook, *College Yiddish* (Uriel Weinreich 1949), was printed under the aegis of YIVO; it has already been reprinted in more than 20 editions. It provided the first teaching material for Yiddish as a foreign language and therefore devoted a full chapter to the proper pronunciation of a form of Yiddish, which undoubtedly can be traced back to earlier discussions on Yiddish language planning. As far as I can tell, to this day nearly all descriptions of modern Yiddish pronunciation in other textbooks are based on *College Yiddish*. The migration overseas both at the turn of the century and as a response to the Nazi-crimes in Europe all but extinguished the language in its historical territory, and the new Yiddish speaking centers around the world were marked by dialect multiplicity. In the new communities speakers of different dialectal backgrounds suddenly lived next to each other.

Before the destruction of the Jewish communities in Eastern Europe by the German Nazis, the inter-language contact had reached its peak, with interferences from numerous Slavic languages. Jewish centers with a dense Jewish population, like Warsaw (31%), Białystok (76%) or Berdichev (80%) and many others, could indulge in speaking exclusively local variants. Enough people spoke exactly this specific dialect and were able to preserve it. It was, therefore, not essential for the speech community to level local differences. But in the overseas communities no cohesive forces strengthened any local variety and no cohesive hinterland sup-

---

[2] The impact of the Yiddish secular school in Eastern Europe on Yiddish as a high language is discussed in several articles in Fishman (1981).

[3] However, Russian Yiddish adhered to a completely different spelling system, called SOVYETI-SHER OYSLEYG 'Soviet spelling' and undermined the efforts made in order to establish a writing system of universal validity.

ported any dialect.[4] It was only after the war that the impact of intra-language contact was at its peak. In this situation the Yiddish speaking community rallied to draw attention to its means of communication, and, as a matter of course, Yiddish speakers ended up at yielding a standardized variety.

Language shift is a phenomenon often observed in (partly) Yiddish speaking families.[5] The new generation learns Yiddish as a second or even as a foreign language, which leads to a breakdown into subgroups using various languages as their predominant idiom. In response to an impending language shift, priority is given to the preservation of the threatened language, which is obviously vanishing from everyday life. The incorporation of Yiddish in academic programs promotes the standardized version of the language, i.e. the language of teaching.

University of Trier

REFERENCES

Fishman, Joshua A. (ed.)
1981   *Never Say Die! A Thousand Years of Jewish Life and Letters* (*Contributions to the Sociology of Language* 30). The Hague: Mouton.

Katz, Dovid
1993   *tikney takones. fragn fun a yidisher stilistik* [*Amended Amendments. Issues in Yiddish stylistics*]. Oxford: *Oksforder yidish*.

Kleine, Ane
1998   "Toward a 'Standard Yiddish Pronunciation'. An Instrumentally Aided Phonetic Analysis", in: M.S. Schmid, J.R. Austin, and D. Stein (eds.), *Historical Linguistics 1997. Selected papers from the 13th International Conference on Historical Linguistics, Düsseldorf, 10-17 August 1997*, 201-211. Amsterdam: John Benjamins.
1999   "Florilegium zur jiddischen Phonetik. Eine Zeitreise", in: W. Röll and S. Neuberg (eds.), *Jiddische Philologie. Festschrift für Erika Timm*, 51-63. Tübingen: Niemeyer.

Mark, Yudl
1951   *"vegn a klalishn aroysreyd"* ["On the Standard Pronunciation of Yiddish"], *yidishe shprakh* XI, 1-25.

Takones fun yidishn oysleyg
1937   *Takones fun yidishn oysleyg. Yidisher visnshaftlekher institut*. Vilne.

---

[4] New exile varieties, bearing a mixture of the original dialects, were also rapidly evolving in these new centers and gained more importance. The effects can easily be perceived in the speech behavior of many Yiddish speakers today.

[5] This language shift had already started in the former Eastern European Jewish communities, where the trend to secularization was accompanied by a language shift which did not lead to the total loss of the Yiddish mother tongue in a family or a whole generation. However, it is reported that vernacular Russian or Polish was used even in groups consisting of Yiddish speakers only.

Weinreich, Max [Vaynraykh, Maks]

1973   *Geshikhte fun der yidisher shprakh. bagrifn, faktn, metodn.* New York: YIVO (= Weinreich, Max: 1980, *History of the Yiddish Language.* Transl. by Sh. Noble and J.A. Fishman. Chicago-London: University of Chicago).

Weinreich, Uriel

1949   *College Yiddish. An Introduction to the Yiddish Language and to Jewish Life and Culture.* New York: YIVO.

1951   *"Tsu der frage vegn a normirter oysshprakh"* ["How to Standardize Yiddish Pronunciation"], *yidishe shprakh* XI, 26-29.

1970   *Languages in Contact. Findings and Problems.* The Hague-Paris: Mouton (first edition: New York 1953).

Languages in Contact, edited by D.G. Gilbers, J. Nerbonne, and J. Schaeken (= *Studies in Slavic and General Linguistics*, vol. 28), 193-197. Amsterdam - Atlanta, GA: Rodopi, 2000.

QUANTITY LOSS IN YIDDISH: A SLAVIC FEATURE?

YURI KLEINER AND NATALIA SVETOZAROVA

From the point of view of quantity, the dialects of Yiddish can be divided into two major groups, viz. (a) those that have the opposition of vowel length and (b) those that do not have it. The Western and Mid-Eastern dialects, on the one hand, and the North-Eastern dialects, on the other, represent groups (a) and (b), respectively.

According to most dialectologists, the South-Eastern dialects have not retained the opposition of length, thus belonging to the (b)-group dialects. Yet, there are those who argue that in some of the SE dialects this opposition is still present, although it is less manifest than in (a) (e.g. covering some of the vowels only). If this group exists in reality, it belongs to an intermediary type that may or may not reflect the general tendency, but itself is not indicative of the mechanism of quantity loss.

According to Ulrike Kiefer,[1] the tendency to lose the "systematische Opposition zwischen Lang- und Kurzvokalen" becomes stronger towards the East (Kiefer 1995: 158), leading to North-Eastern Yiddish which is "der am meisten neuernde [Dialekt] (weil Längenunterschiede völlig abgeschafft sind)", as Dovid Katz has put it (Katz 1983: 1030).

Since the loss of quantity distinctions is regarded as indicative of the advanced state of the language, it follows that the opposite (i.e. length distinctions, as in Western Yiddish) must be typical of its most archaic state. The latter must have coincided with the earliest period of the history of Yiddish, most probably from its origin (between the 11th and 13th c.) to the time of the migration of the Jews to the East (15th-16th c.). In other words, the earliest state of Yiddish is the period when Yiddish was a German(ic) dialect. In this capacity, it must have been characterized by an admixture of Hebrew elements only.

According to Neil G. Jacobs, the Hebrew component in Yiddish had a certain specificity with respect to quantity. Thus, Hebrew words show reflexes coinciding with those of long vowels in some forms, but not in others, cf. *sojdes* 'secrets' and

---

[1] Kiefer's conclusion is based on and corroborated by the data of *LCAAJ*: "Distinctive vowel length occurs in WY,CY, and SEY (only i-i), although it is utilized unevenly. It may occur also along the westernmost fringes of NEY. In some northeastern border varieties of CY length seems to be absent" (*LCAAJ* 1992: 19).

sod 'secret', respectively. On the basis of this, Jacobs reconstructs long vowels in Tiberian Hebrew (TH) that "did not record vowel length as distinctive" (Jacobs 1993: 193), suggesting that in *sojdes*, etc. the evolution of the vowels was similar to that of the Germanic long-vowel words, cf. *brojt* 'bread', with /oj/ < /o:/, while in *sod* the vowel had undergone shortening and therefore was not diphthongized (Jacobs 1993: 194). Jacobs explains both the diphthongizaton of the vowels and the lack of it as resulting from the type of syllable, to which the vowels belonged, open and closed, respectively. This implies that, in the Hebrew component, vowels were subject to open-syllable lengthening (OSL) and closed-syllable shortening (CSS), as in Germanic words. Comparing *sod* and *brojt* (MHG /bro:t/) on the one hand, and *sod* and Germanic /(C)VCC/ words on the other, Jacobs concludes that the development of quantity in Germanic and Semitic words in Yiddish was not absolutely parallel, for "in the TH component, a single consonant is generally enough to close a syllable; in the German-component CSS, two consonants were generally needed" (Jacobs 1993: 203). In this context, Jacobs suggests a pre-Yiddish stage, in which the Hebrew component words adjusted themselves to the German(ic) quantitative pattern and to which vowel shortening in the *sod*-type words belonged. Consequently, he dates vowel shortening "as pre-Yiddish, and diphthongization later than it" (Jacobs 1993: 195).

A conclusion similar in some respects was made, concerning borrowings, on a much greater scale, during the Anglo-French contacts after 1066. It was suggested, for example, that *arriver* 'arrive' and *doute* 'doubt' had had long vowels in French (Keller 1920: 112-113; Bliss 1952: 121-122, 125-126). This would imply that French had quantitative distinctions, which has no other corroboration than the behavior of the borrowings in English. Even there, however, the same French vowel could be long and later diphthongized in *bacon*, but short and monophthongal in *baron*.

Likewise, words with /i/ and /u/, allegedly long in TH, e.g. [di:ni:m] 'laws', [gəvu:rɔ:] 'heroism' and pre-Yiddish */di:nəm/, */gvu:rə/, show no diphthongization in Yiddish, unlike the respective vowels in *dajn* 'your' and *mojer* 'wall', originally long, cf. OHG /di:n/, /mu:r/ (> NHG *dein, Mauer*) (Jacobs 1993: 195). But does this mean that OSL and CSS were distinct from the similar Germanic processes at least chronologically, as Jacobs (1993: 210) has suggested?

The earliest quantitative change in the Germanic languages was from phonemic length in vowels to syllable levelling of the Scandinavian type: /V:C/ ~ /VC:/. The presence of long consonants in English (cf. consonant doubling in ME *Or-mulum*) and German (cf. Zinder and Stroeva 1965: 79, note) suggests that the same was typical of the Middle period of the Germanic languages in general. In this situation, both lengthening and shortening are accounted for by the shift of the quantitative peak, on /V/ and /C/ respectively. This means that they are but two aspects of one and the same process, and for this reason, they could not be separated chronologically.

It should be noted that (a) shortness of the vowel requires a long consonant, rather than two consonants, and (b) the shift of the peak may take place within the same morpheme, resulting either in variation within the paradigm, as in Swedish *vit* /vi:t/ ~ *vitt* /vit:/ 'white' (m., n.), or in doublets, as English *black* ~ *Blake* (ME *blaku*). The diphthong in the latter is the result of another change, viz. from syllable levelling to the correlation of syllable cut typical of the West Germanic languages. Here, too, different reflexes of vowels suggest either the variation in their quantity/quality or, more probably, in the syllable structure at an earlier stage. Characteristically, *bread* has a short vowel in standard English, whereas /e:/, /i:/, /ei/, /iə/ are attested in English dialects.

The same applies to pairs like *sod - sojdes* that belong to the Swedish /vi:t/ ~ /vit:/ or English *black* ~ *Blake* type. Likewise, disyllabic forms, such as /šoləm/ 'peace', that according to Jacobs (1993: 195) had a long vowel in pre-Yiddish, can be compared with *baron* and *city* (< OF), where the vowels may have behaved as in *body*, that is, probably having various manifestations (cf. ME *boody*), but eventually developing into short nuclei of closed syllables.

In this context, C. Heck's once pioneering conclusion that vowels in borrowings retain their original quantity (Heck 1906: 245) looks naïve. Indeed, whatever the specificity of TH vowels, they must have adjusted to the quantitative pattern that, through the history of Yiddish on the Germanic territory, was based on the same principle and underwent the same changes as in German.

As Uriel Weinreich has suggested with reference to Sapir (1915: 236), the loss of quantity in Yiddish "has probably received regional encouragement from contact with East Slavic" (Weinreich 1958: 4). This suggestion would have been flawless, if only quantity had not been regarded as *Ding an sich*, as it often is, not connected with other elements of the phonological system of Yiddish or, for that matter, systems of Yiddish and the languages it was in contact with.

Since the opposition of quantity is in reality that of two types of syllable, viz. open and closed, the only explanation of the loss of quantitative distinctions in Standard Yiddish can be a change in the syllable structure. The standard variety of Yiddish was formed on the basis of the Eastern dialects. Therefore, it will not be a mistake to conclude that so considerable a change was due to the influence of the languages, with which Yiddish had been in contact after migration, in particular the Slavic languages, where the original (Proto-Slavic) three types of syllables (**ru:ba* 'fish', **ronka* 'hand', **voda* 'water'), similar to Germanic /V:-/, /VC-/, /VCV-/ (Kleiner 1999) were replaced by one (pleophonic) type (/VCV/), presupposing an (actually or potentially) open-syllable as the only structure.

Besides a considerable portion of lexical borrowings (or together with these), Yiddish has adopted certain grammatical and phonological Slavic traits. One of them could be the open syllable (or rather the absence of the closed syllable), which is one of the most characteristic features of Slavic phonology, distinguishing it from the phonology of the Germanic languages other than Yiddish.

It should be noted that it is the closed syllable (= close cut), rather than length as such that has been lost in language contacts. This clarifies Weinreich's doubt concerning the Slavic role in quantity loss. As he points out "quantity has been eliminated in NE Yiddish not only on the territory of Belorussian, which indeed lacks the feature, but also on the territory of Lithuanian, which has it" (Weinreich 1958: 4). The Baltic languages (Latvian, Lithuanian) indeed have quantity distinctions, although at the time the contacts began it must have been based on mora counting that does not exclude the open syllable.

The question arises why quantity (i.e. syllable cut) distinctions have been retained in the Mid-Eastern variety of Yiddish spoken on the territory of Poland, although Polish is also a Slavic language that does not have this opposition. As an explanation, we can assume that extra-linguistic factors were at work, namely, the limited nature of contacts with the neighbors and their language.

St. Petersburg State University

REFERENCES

Bliss, A.J.
1952   "Vowel quantity in Middle English borrowings from Anglo-Norman", *Archivum Linguisticum* 4 (2), 121-143.

Heck, C.
1906   "Die Quantitäten der Akzentvokale in ne. offenen Silben mehrsilbiger Wörter", *Anglia* 29, 55-119.

Jacobs, N.G.
1993   "On pre-Yiddish standardization of quantity", *Diachronica* 10, 191-214.

Katz, D.
1983   "Zur Dialektologie des Jiddischen", in: W. Besch, U. Knoop, W. Putschke, H.E. Wiegand (eds.), *Dialektologie. Ein Handbuch zur deutschen und allgemeinen Dialektforschung*, 2. Halbband, 1018-1041. Berlin.

Keller, W.
1920   "Mittelenglische lange Vokale und die altfranzösische Quantität", *Englische Studien* 54 (1), 111-116.

Kiefer, U.
1995   *Gesprochenes Jiddisch. Textzeugen einer europäischen Kultur*. Tübingen.

Kleiner, Ju.A.
1999   "Moroščitanie: germanskij, slavjanskij...", in: *Problemy fonetiki i akcentologii baltijskix jazykov*, 20-22. Sankt-Peterburg.

LCAAJ
1992   M. Herzog, U. Weinreich, V.Baviskar (eds.), *The Language and Culture Atlas of Ashkenazic Jewry*. Tübingen.

Sapir, E.
1915   "Notes on Judeo-German Phonology", *Jewish Quarterly Review* 6 (n.s.), 231-266.
Weinreich, U.
1958   "Yiddish and colonial German in Eastern Europe: The differential Impact of Slavic", in: *American contributions to the Fourth International Congress of Slavists*, 1-53. 's-Gravenhage.
Zinder, L.R., and T.V. Stroeva
1965   *Istoričeskaja fonetika nemeckogo jazyka*. Moskva-Leningrad.

Languages in Contact, edited by D.G. Gilbers, J. Nerbonne, and J. Schaeken (= *Studies in Slavic and General Linguistics*, vol. 28), 199-207. Amsterdam - Atlanta, GA: Rodopi, 2000.

THE ISOLATED RUSSIAN DIALECTAL SYSTEM IN CONTACT WITH TUNGUS LANGUAGES IN SIBERIA AND THE FAR EAST

ALEKSANDR KRASOVICKY AND CHRISTIAN SAPPOK

The language varieties we are presenting here have their historical origin in a migration process taking place in the early 17th century. From that time on these language communities have been isolated from the Russian homeland, but in intense contact with several non-Russian languages, mainly Even. Before the linguistic facts (mostly phonemic) are presented indicating far-reaching contact between Russian and Tungus languages, a short overview of the present situation shall be given, restricted to the following information:

- Do we have names for these isolated communities that will make it possible to ask for more detailed information and not to have them mixed with other communities of Russian origin?
- Do we have official statistics counting the number of the members of these communities, which are informative about their societies and the tendencies of development?
- The third aim is to give a first subjective auditory impression that makes it possible to discriminate the specific features of the varieties as compared to standard Russian and to Russian dialects in the proper sense. This auditory demonstration can be heard on the Internet:

    http://www.ruhr-uni-bochum.de/LiLab/Landeskunde

At the beginning a look at Picture 1 will be helpful, a map prepared by Ozerova and Petrova (1979), depicting the situation as it was a hundred years ago but still valid. Old settlers (*starožily*) with a strong influence from Tungus are presented as Nrs. 13, 14, 15, and 16. The first group, Nr. 13, are the *Russkoustincy* on the upper Indigirka River, settling in Russkoye Ust'ye (intermediately called *Poljarnyj*) and in Chokurdakh. Farther East there are the Kolymchane (Nr. 14) on the Kolyma River, now to be found mostly in Pokhodsk. Bogoraz (1901) describes their *sladkojazyčie*, i. e. their replacing /r/ and /l/ by the glide /j/. Nr. 15 is farther to the East, in the Chukotka district, in a settlement called Markovo, where the *Markovcy* (or, as they call themselves now, the *Čuvancy* 'Chuvans') are living. Nr. 16, the Kamchadals, is to be found in several places, not only on the Kamchatka peninsula, but also on the shore of the Okhotsk Sea, in Okhotsk, Tauysk, and in Gizhiga.

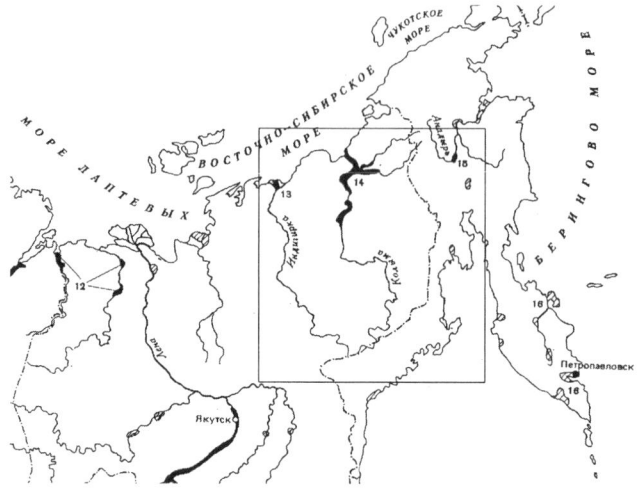

полехи, *3* — горюны, *4* — саяны, *5* — мещера, *6* — однодворцы, в Азиатской части России: *7* — уральцы, *8* — поляки, *9* — каменщики, *10* — семейские, *11* — якутяне, *12* — затундрен-ские крестьяне, *13* — русскоустинцы, *14* — колымчане, *15* — марковцы, *16* — камчадалы;

Picture 1 is from Ozerova and Petrova 1979, showing the places where old Russian settlers (*starožily*) were to be found at about 1900.

The first statistical information on Russian colonists was given by Ataman Kol'co when he visited Moscow in 1622. The data he reported to Czar Mikhail Romanov were approximate; he spoke of 4,000 Cossacks, 1,000 people of the transporting business (*jamščiki*), and so on. As to women, he continues (cited after Ščeglov 1893), they are very few, so that Russian Cossacks and traders are forced to choose foreign partners, Tatar, Tungus and others. Patriarch Filaret criticizes this practice, not because of the foreign origin, but because of those women not being baptized. This is interesting information as to the ethnic mixture of standard families. The father was, as a rule, of Slavic origin and of orthodox faith, the mother non-Russian and non-orthodox.

What is the statistical situation today? The last census was done in 1989, cf. Goskomstat Rossii 1992, where one can find quantitative information about the Kamchadals and the Chuvans, mostly qualified as 'Russian speaking'. So the old Russian settlers have inherited the names of non-Russian ethnic unities which have almost disappeared. Kamchadals are russified Itelmens, Chuvans are russified Yukagirs. There is no statistical information available as to the *Kolymchane* and the *Russkoustincy*.

In June 1997 we made an expedition to Russkoye Ust'ye, and we made about 20 hours of high quality tape recordings. Samples of the material, together with background information, are presented on our homepage (address above), and an auditory anthology will come out in the near future. The first auditory impression will reveal a striking intonation, possibly stemming from the North Russian dialects spoken by some of the forefathers of the present community (cf. Kasatkina 1996). This intonation can be described as an extra high rise. This contour could be attributed to an extra degree of emotionality, but evidently this is not the case, as was shown elsewhere, cf. Sappok 1999 with an interpretation of this and numerous other examples as verification and explanation. Speakers of an oral type of culture tend not to focus on the informational content of their utterances to oppose old and new. They tend to emphasize things that are regarded as common knowledge to all partners within the discourse situation.

We now come to a more detailed analysis of the phoneme system of the *Russkoustincy*. It may be assumed that the language of Russkoye Ust'ye was strongly affected by the language of the Even, who were the nearest neighbors of Russian colonists there. The focus of our research was the consonantal system, which went through considerable modification. The following most significant features distinguish the consonantal system of Russkoye Ust'ye from its mother (Arkhangel'sk) dialect:

– Destruction of the original distribution of soft and hard consonants and the merging of phonemes – members of contrastive sets. This type of modification covers labials and trills.
– Regular replacements of consonants by those of an adjacent place of articulation and displacement of old distinctive features. Sibilants and hushing fricatives are involved in this process.
– Collapse of some 'soft-hard' distinctions as a result of merger with Even consonants and restructuring of phonological relations as a consequence of this phonetic change. For example, the transition [t'] → [č] destroyed the correlation /t/ - /t'/ since the right member of the phonological opposition merged with another phoneme.

There were presumably 11 contrastive sets in the mother dialect based on the feature 'soft-hard' (Table 1).

/b/	/p/	/v/	/m/	/n/	/l/	/s/	/z/	/t/	/d/	/r/
↕	↕	↕	↕	↕	↕	↕	↕	↕	↕	↕
/b'/	/p'/	/v'/	/m'/	/n'/	/l'/	/s'/	/z'/	/t'/	/d'/	/r'/

Table 1. Oppositions of hard and soft phonemes in the mother dialect.

As a result of various sound changes in the language of Russkoye Ust'ye nine of the eleven sets (leaving only the two pairs /l/ - /l'/ and /n/ - /n'/) were either lost or they acquired new distinctive features. Hereby one of the basic Russian phonological categories – pairing of soft and hard phonemes – was almost destroyed.

Labials and trills

Sound changes: [C] → [C'] (before /i/)
              [C'] → [C] (in final and prevocalic positions, except for /i/)
Phonemic change: /C'/   /C/

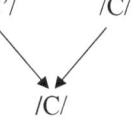

                        /C/
Phonological contrast lost: 'soft-hard'
Phonological contrast acquired: none

For the labials and trills this process resulted in the merger of phonemes opposed as soft and hard. The mother dialect should have 4 pairs of labials: /p - p'/, /b - b'/, /v - v'/, /m - m'/ and a pair of trills /r - r'/. They were opposed in final position (except for /v/ - /v'/ that apparently were not presented in this position) and in four prevocalic positions (Table 2) – before phonemes /a/, /o/, /u/ and /i/ (the phoneme /i/ is presented by the allophone [ɨ] after hard consonants and by the allophone [i] in the rest of the positions): [͡tsep] 'beater' - [͡tsep'] 'chain', [spor] 'argument' - [spor'] 'argue (imperat.)', [zabɨt] 'to forget' - [zab'ít] 'to bang down', [zavál] 'abatis' - [zav'ál] 'miff off', [mal] 'small' - [m'al] 'creased', [post] 'post' - [p'os] 'dog', [górɨ] 'hills' - [gor'ít] 'burns', [v'éru] 'credence (acc.)' - [v'ér'u] 'I believe'.

CA	CO	CU	Cɨ
↕	↕	↕	↕
C'A	C'O	C'U	C'I

Table 2. The system of oppositions of labials and trills, based on the distinctive feature 'soft-hard', in the mother dialect.

In the language of RU soft labials and trills were replaced in final position by their hard counterparts: [glup'] 'depth' → [glup], [dver'] 'door' → [dver]. This sound shift destroyed one of the two positions of maximum differentiation for the two groups of the consonants. At once the language began eliminating a number of combinations which conflicted with the interfering (i.e. Even) phonetic system. The process of elimination of inadmissible combinations covered all the four prevocalic positions (Table 3). As a result soft labials and trills could no longer stand before /a/, /o/ and /u/. This determined transitions like [upr'áʃka] → [upráʃka], 'rig, span', [k mór'u] → [k móru] 'to the sea', [vir'ófka] → [virófka] 'cord', [teb'á] → [tebá] 'you (acc.)'.

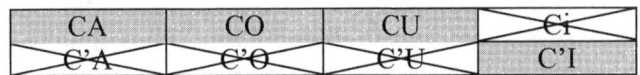

CA	CO	CU	~~Cɨ~~
~~C'A~~	~~C'O~~	~~C'U~~	C'I

Table 3. Lost (in crossed squares) and remaining combinations
of labials and trills with vowels in the language of Russkoye Ust'ye.

Of the two combinations – Cɨ and C'I – the choice was to the advantage of the latter, that was apparently a consequence of the [ɨ] - [i] merger and the displacement of [ɨ]: [mɨ] → [m'i] 'we', [lápɨ] → [láp'i] 'feet, paws', [golubɨe] → [golub'íe] 'blue (pl.)', [rɨba] → [r'íba] 'fish'. Hereby the language lost all of the distinctions in which soft and hard labials and trills were opposed. The feature 'soft-hard' stopped being phonologically relevant and turned to be a context-sensitive characteristic in these two groups of the consonants. A new phoneme which emerged in accordance with each of the correlative pairs is presented by soft allophones before front vowels and by hard allophones in the rest of the positions.

Stops /t - t'/ and /d - d'/

Sound change: [t'']¹ → $\widehat{[tʃ]}$
                         [d''] → $\widehat{[dʒ]}$
Phonemic change: /t'/ → $/\widehat{tʃ}/$
                         /d'/ → $/\widehat{dʒ}/$
Phonological contrast lost: 'soft-hard'
Phonological contrast acquired: 'stops-affricates'

Sometimes a soft consonant could find a counterpart in the Even language. Then it acquired a new phonological quality and formed a new opposition with its correlate based on another phonological characteristic. This type of modification covers stops /t/ - /t'/ and /d/ - /d'/.

In the language of Russkoye Ust'ye palatal stops [t''] and [d''] were replaced by palatal affricates $\widehat{[tʃ]}$ and $\widehat{[dʒ]}$. To date palatal [t''] and [d''] occur in the Arkhangel'sk dialects as allophones of /t/ and /d/ (*Russkie narodnye govory* 1991: 198), and it is likely that they were even more common earlier. It may be also assumed that originally the soft members in each pair had more or less distinctive hushing fricative element in the release. According to the Dialectological Atlas of the Russian Language (*Dialektologičeskij atlas* 1986, map 56) this type of articu-

---

¹ The double apostroph in our paper is used to denote a palatal (not a palatalized) sound, as is common practice in Russian phonetics.

lation of soft stops is presented in small districts diffused all over the Russian speaking territory. The nearest counterpart of this type of [t"] in the Even system is palatal [t͡ʃ] as well as palatal [d͡ʒ] is nearest to [d"]. The Even sounds [t͡ʃ] and [d͡ʒ] may be characterized as affricates or "close to affricates" (*Jazyki narodov SSSR* 1968: 90). However, the difference between the Russian soft stops and the Even afrricates was not significant enough to become an obstacle to the sound shifts [t"] → [t͡ʃ] and [d"] → [d͡ʒ] (Tables 4 and 5).

Parent form		Derived form
ʒ ' í t " e l ' i	'inhabitants'	ʒ í t͡ʃ i l ' i
d o p ' i t " í	'till five'	d o p ' i t͡ʃ í
t " á n u t	'drag (3ʳᵈ pers. pl.)'	t͡ʃ á n u t
k a r t " í n a	'picture'	k a r t͡ʃ í n a
t " u r ' m á	'jail'	t͡ʃ u r ' m á
t " ó p l ə j	'warm'	t͡ʃ ó p l ə j
o t m ' é t " i t "	'to celebrate'	o t m ' é t͡ʃ i t͡ʃ
ʒ ' i t "	'to live'	ʒ ' i t͡ʃ
t " é x n ' i k a	'mechanism'	t͡ʃ é x n ' i k a

Table 4. The [t"] → [t͡ʃ] transition.

Parent form		Derived form
r o d " í t ' i l ' i	'parents'	r o d͡ʒ í t͡ʃ i l ' i
m o l o d " ó ʃ	'young people'	m o l o d͡ʒ ó ʃ
x o d " í l i	'walked'	x o d͡ʒ í l i
u g o d " í t '	'to win favour'	u g o d͡ʒ í t͡ʃ
p o b ' e d " í l	'overcame'	p o b ' e d͡ʒ í l
d " á d " a	'uncle'	d͡ʒ á d͡ʒ a
l ' u d " m ' í	'people (instr.)'	l ' u d͡ʒ m ' í

Table 5. The [d"] → [d͡ʒ] transition.

The result of the [t"] → [t͡ʃ] transition concurs with the original phoneme /č/ which was also presented by the palatal affricate [t͡ʃ]: [t͡ʃásto] 'often', [t͡ʃístaja] 'clean', [t͡ʃuʒój] 'alien', [t͡ʃórnɨj] 'black', [not͡ʃ] 'night', [pé t͡ʃka] 'stove'. The [d"] → [d͡ʒ] transition gave a new phoneme /d͡ʒ/ which did not exist in the mother dialect. The phonological opposition 'soft-hard' was displaced by the opposition 'stops-affricates'.

Fricatives /s/ - /s'/ and /z/ - /z'/

Sound change: [s"] →   [ʃ"]
                  [s]   →   [ʃ]

[z"] → [ʒ"]
[z] → [ʒ]
Phonemic change: /s'/ → /ʃ/
/z'/ → /ʒ/
Phonological contrast lost: 'soft-hard'
Phonological contrast acquired: 'alveolar - post-alveolar'

There is a strong tendency in the language of Russkoye Ust'ye to replace soft (palatal) sibilants [s"], [z"] with hushing sounds, soft and hard according to the position. The general rule of this sound change is the following: soft hushing sounds are pronounced instead of soft sibilants if the position provides palatalization (for example before front vowels or palatal consonants); hard hushing sounds may appear in accordance with soft sibilants in positions which do not support palatalization (for example before back vowels or in final position). Table 5 presents transitions [s"] → [ʃ"] and [z"] → [ʒ"].

Parent form		Derived form
p é s " e n k a	'song'	p é ʃ " e n k a
s " í n ' i j	'blue'	ʃ " í n ' i j
p ' í s " m a	'letters'	p ' í ʃ " m a
z " i m á	'winter'	ʒ " i m á
z " e l ' ó n ə j	'green'	ʒ " e l ' ó n ə j
p r ' i v ' e z " ó n ə j	'brought'	p r ' i v ' e ʒ " ó n ə j

Table 6. Examples of the phonetic change [s"] → [ʃ"], [z"] → [ʒ"].

It should be pointed out that in a number of Russian dialects phonemes /s'/ and /z'/ have allophones with lisping or even more or less distinctive hushing quality (*Dialectologičeskij atlas* 1986, map 56). Sound systems with lisping or hushing allophones for /s'/ and /z'/ are found all over the Russian speaking territory and in the Arkhangel'sk region in particular (*Russkie narodnye govory* 1991: 36-39). On the other side the only Even sibilant /s/ is also presented by the lisping allophone (*Jazyki mira* 1997: 286). Hence this feature in the language of Russkoye Ust'ye could be inherited from the mother dialect and supported by the affecting system. Palatal [ʃ"] and [ʒ"] represent soft members of oppositions /s/ - /s'/ and /z/ - /z'/. These oppositions were realized in prevocalic positions and voiceless consonants were also opposed in final position (normally voiced consonants do not occur there): [sáxar] 'sugar' - [ʃ"ádu] 'sit (1st pers. sing.)', [ʒárko] 'hot' - [ʒ"ábko] 'chilly', [nos] 'nose' - [broʃ"] 'drop (imperat.)'. On the contrary, the sound shift [s"] → [ʃ] and [z"] → [ʒ] (Table 7) may be interpreted neither as an old, original feature, nor as a result of an internal self-supporting process since this change comes in conflict with one of the most significant categories of the Russian phonological system – correlation of soft and hard consonants.

Parent form		Derived form
p o s " ó l ə k	'township'	p o ʃ ó l ə k
p o - f s " á k o m u	'in any way'	p o - f ʃ á k o m u
u n ó s " a t	'they take away'	u n ó ʃ a t
v ' e r n ú s "	'will come back'	v ' e r n ú ʃ
p r i v ó z " a t	'they bring'	p r i v ó ʒ ə t
v z " a l á	'took, past, fem.'	(v) ʒ ə l á
p r á z " n i k	'holiday'	p r á ʒ n i k

Table 7. Examples of the phonetic change [s"] → [ʃ], [z"] → [ʒ].

It is quite evident that the change [s"] → [ʃ] and [z"] → [ʒ] (with [ʃ"] and [ʒ"] as an intermediate step, i. e. [z"] → [ʃ"] → [ʃ] and [z"] → [ʒ"] → [ʒ]) was initiated by the Even system, which did not demand positions of differentiation for soft and hard phonemes. Soft [ʃ"] and [ʒ"] were displaced if they were not supported by the context (by front vowels for example). The 'new' [ʃ"]/[ʃ] and [ʒ"]/[ʒ] merged with the original [ʃ"]/[ʃ] and [ʒ"]/[ʒ] that represented the phonemes /ʃ/ and /ʒ/ respectively. These two phonemes did not participate in the pairing of soft and hard phonemes since soft and hard hushing sounds did not occur in the same context. After the phoneme /s'/ merged with /ʃ/ and /z'/ merged with /ʒ/ the phonological contrast between hard and soft sibilants was lost. It was replaced by a contrast based on the feature 'place of articulation'. Alveolar /s/, /z/ formed oppositions with post-alveolar /ʃ/, /ʒ/: /s/ - /ʃ/ and /z/ - /ʒ/.

Conclusion

Durable contacts between the Russian and the Even languages resulted in considerable modification of the phonological system in the language of Russkoye Ust'ye. Ignoring the two pairs /l/ - /l'/ and /n/ - /n'/, the contrastive sets based on the feature 'soft-hard' were destroyed. The opposed phonemes either merged or acquired new distinctive features, and formed new contrastive sets. The correlation of hard and soft consonants is one of the highly marked features in Russian. It covers the majority of Russian consonants. Regular alternations and neutralizations of hard and soft consonants make the bond between members in each set particularly strong.

The fact that the language of Russian colonists underwent such fundamental changes should be interpreted as evidence of the strong cultural influence of the neighboring Even population over the Russian community at the mouth of the Indigirka.

Institute of Russian Language at the Russian Academy of Sciences
Ruhr Universität Bochum

REFERENCES

Bogoraz, V.G.
1901   *Oblastnoj slovar' kolymskago russkago narečija.* Sankt-Peterburg.
Dialektologičeskij atlas
1986   *Dialektologičeskij atlas russkogo jazyka. Fonetika.* Moskva.
Goskomstat Rossii
1992   *Čislennost' naselenija otdel'nyx etničeskix grupp.* Moskva.
Jazyki mira
1997   *Jazyki mira. Mongolskie.jazyki. Tunguso-man'čžurskie jazyki. Japonskij jazyk.*
              Korejskij jazyk. Moskva.
Jazyki narodov SSSR
1968   *Jazyki narodov SSSR. 5: Mongolskie, tunguso-man'čžurskie i paleoaziatskie ja-*
              zyki. Leningrad.
Kasatkina, R.F.
1996   "Prosodija russkix govorov", in: T.M. Nikolaeva (ed.), *Prosodičeskij stroj rus-*
              skoj reči, 207-235. Moskva.
Ozerova, G.N., and T.M. Petrova
1979   "O kartografirovanii grupp russkogo naroda na načalo XX v.", *Sovetskaja ètno-*
              grafija 1979/1, 72-79.
Russkie narodnye govory
1991   *Russkie narodnye govory. Zvučaščaja xrestomatija. Severnorusskie govory.*
              Moskva-Bochum.
Sappok, Ch.
1999   "Beobachtungen zur Intonation und Informationsstruktur in russischen Dia-
              lekttexten", in: R. Rathmayr and W. Weitlaner (eds.), *Slavistische Linguistik*
              1998, 233-256. München.
Ščeglov, I.V.
1893   *Xronologičeskij perečen' važnejšix dannyx iz istorii Sibiri* (1032-1882). Surgut.

Languages in Contact, edited by D.G. Gilbers, J. Nerbonne, and J. Schaeken (= *Studies in Slavic and General Linguistics*, vol. 28), 209-224. Amsterdam - Atlanta, GA: Rodopi, 2000.

TRACES OF SÁMI-SCANDINAVIAN CONTACT IN SCANDINAVIAN DIALECTS

JURIJ KUSMENKO AND MICHAEL RIESSLER

1. Introduction

The present Sámi region spans westward from the Kola Peninsula in northern Russia to Dalarna in Sweden and Hedmark in Norway. Loan word studies show that the contact between Sámi and Scandinavian began in the Proto-Scandinavian period (200-500 A.D.) (cf. Sköld 1992). Such long contact can be traced in both languages. Common Sámi-Scandinavian isoglosses were usually interpreted either as a heritage of a common non-Scandinavian and non-Sámi substratum (Wagner 1964; Kylstra 1983) or as a result of Scandinavian influence on the Sámi dialects (Posti 1954; Schlachter 1991). Influence the other way round is mostly neglected because of Scandinavian dominance (cf. Jahr 1997: 943). However, some Scandinavian dialectologists take into consideration the possibility of Sámi influence in some northernmost Swedish and Norwegian vernaculars, contacting present-day Sámi. But, this influence is regarded as restricted to marginal phonological features (cf. Wallström 1943: 24; Dahlstedt 1950: 1; Bull 1992).

In fact, the social dominance of Scandinavian is clearly reflected in the lexicon of the respective languages. During the last 1500 years more than 2000 Scandinavian words have been borrowed into the neighbouring Sámi dialects, and the process is continuing. In Scandinavian dialects, however, there are no Sámi loan words other than a few related to Sámi matters. Under these circumstances one might expect constant Scandinavian influence on Sámi phonology and grammar as well. But, this is not what one finds because we are dealing with the Scandinavization of the Sámi. We can thus expect the formation of Scandinavian dialects with Sámi interference. Therefore, Sámi substratum features should occur just where the Sámi have 'disappeared', i.e. where they were assimilated by their Scandinavian surroundings.

Sámi Scandinavization did not begin with the Scandinavian colonisation in the North. Though there is clear evidence of contact, mainly in loanwords from the 2nd century on, the relations between Sámi and Scandinavians were still rather of a "'peaceful co-existence' of both ethnic groups differently exploiting natural resources and inhabiting different zones" (Urbanczyk 1992: 62; cf. Zachrisson 1997). The Sámi in Sweden and Norway became object of a strong national assimilation policy first during the last centuries. The Scandinavization of the Sámi proceeded most rapidly in the southern Sámi region. The differences between southern and northern Sámi in their degree of assimilation is still important.

The southern Sámi - central Scandinavian area, especially Trøndelag in Norway, must be regarded as the historical centre of Sámi-Scandinavian contacts. Loan words and place names suggest early Sámi activity in Trøndelag and Hålogaland before the Viking Age (Bergsland 1964, 1983: 74). Historians point out the special relationship between the Scandinavian settlers and southern Sámi in north-central Scandinavia (cf. Hallan 1976; especially Nesheim 1967: 104-105, fig. 2, 5, 8-15). Until a few decades ago, all southern Sámi were active speakers of Sámi. Some of them were also fluent speakers of the Scandinavian dialect of their respective neighbourhood. Documents from the 16th century on show that local authorities dealt with the Sámi in Norwegian and Swedish (Bergsland 1992: 7).

Before the Middle Ages the Sámi probably reached even much further south than has been assumed until recently. The present southern Sámi boundary is not likely the result of late Sámi expansion. It probably moved as a result of the expansion of Scandinavian agriculturists (Sammallahti 1990: 441). Archaeological findings give evidence of a Sámi population that possibly reached as far south as the Mälardal-region in present central Sweden (cf. Zachrisson 1997). The Swedish ethnologist Svanberg (1986) finds evidence for a nomadic Forest Sámi culture in central Sweden that had been assimilated by the 19th century. Even anthropometrical and serological features, characteristic of Sámi population, are found in the districts that lie much further south than the present boundary of the Sámi area in Norway and Sweden (cf. Beckman 1959). The increase of Scandinavian population in northeastern Scandinavia probably occurred at the expense of the Sámi population.

In this paper we shall try to show that the Sámi interference in Swedish and Norwegian involves some of the most important features of a large Swedish and Norwegian dialect area. The northeastern Scandinavian dialects (eastern Norwegian and north-central Swedish dialects) differ both from West Scandinavian (western Norwegian dialects, Icelandic, Faeroese) and from southern Scandinavian (southwestern Norwegian, southern Swedish and Danish dialects). The dialect area of northeastern Scandinavia is characterised by VOWEL BALANCE, LEVEL STRESS, METAPHONY, and CONSONANT LENGTHENING in original short syllable words. All these features indicate the close cohesion between the elements of a word. A close cohesion between the elements of a word is also characteristic of all Sámi dialects (Bartens 1989: 42). The strongest interdependence can be found in South Sámi (Hasselbrink 1965: 32). It manifests itself in the contrasting quantity correlation, in interdependence of the quantity of the unstressed syllable and the quantity of the stressed syllable, and in metaphony (regressive vowel assimilation).

We shall try to show that such northeastern Scandinavian isoglosses as vowel balance, metaphony, and consonant lengthening can be explained as due to Sámi-Scandinavian interference, which was caused by the Scandinavization of the southern Sámi during the second half of the last millennium.

2. Vowel balance

2.1 Vowel balance in Swedish and Norwegian dialects

Vowel balance means the dependence of quantity and quality of the second syllable upon the quantity of the first syllable. Vowel balance is characteristic of all eastern Norwegian vernaculars (strongest in Trøndelag), of the northern Norwegian vernaculars of Helgeland and Rana (Christiansen 1954: 32-33), as well as of central and northern Swedish vernaculars (Hesselman 1905: 16).

In the most archaic Scandinavian dialects vowel balance is manifested in the Law of Three Moras: A disyllabic word consists always of three moras: Either the first syllable is bimoric and the second monomoric as in /kas(2)-ta(1)/ and /bi:(2)-ta(1)/ (OIc. *kasta*, *bíta* 'to cast', 'to bite') or the first syllable is monomoric and the second bimoric as /vi(1)-ku:(2)/, /vu(1)-ku:(2)/ (OIc. *viku* 'week' casus obl.) The second mora in the original disyllabic short syllable words is in this case always lengthened, as in /viku/ > /viku:/ (OIc. *viku*), /stugu/ > /stugu:/ (OIc. *stugu* 'cabin'), /næva/ > /næva:/ (OIc. *nefa* 'fist'), /læsa/ > /læsa:/ (OIc. *lesa* 'to read') in some Norwegian dialects (Storm 1908: 62-63; Kolsrud 1974: 10-11). The same development is characteristic of the most archaic Swedish dialects with vowel balance (Wessén 1970: 69).

In the case of threemoric bisyllabic quantity we are dealing with the rule of prosodic neutralisation of the opposition monomoric vowel ~ bimoric vowel in the second syllable. In the position of neutralisation we have either a phonological long vowel (after a short syllable /læsa:/) or a phonological short vowel (after a long syllable /bi:ta/).

In the majority of the modern Swedish and Norwegian dialects with vowel balance, the vowel balance has another form: in the original disyllabic trimoric words such as *bíta* and *kasta* the first two moras (/bi:-/, /kas-/) are stressed, but the third mora (/-ta/) is reduced (/kasta/, /bi:ta/) or even apocopated (/kâst/, /bî:t/). In the disyllabic bimoric words both moras have stress, i.e. 'level stress', as in /vuku/ 'week', /tålå/ 'to talk' /tå(1)-lå(1)/ (OIc. *tala*). In most of the dialects one finds prosodically determined allophonic variation [a] ~ [ə] (as in [kastə] ~ [vata] (< *vita* 'to know'). Otherwise there is no opposition /a/ ~ /ə/.

The original short syllable words may look as if they had preserved their original bimoric quantity. But forms like /tålå/, /livå/ 'to live', /såvå/ 'to sleep' (cf. OIc. *tala*, *liva*, *sofa*) with /å/ in the second syllable show that even these dialects had once lengthening of the second mora in the original CVCV-words, because only a long /a:/ developed into /å/ (cf. OIc. *ár*, Sw./Nw. *år* 'year'). The development in this case was /liva/ > /liva:/ > /livå:/ > /livå/.

Vowel balance is found as early as in Swedish manuscripts from the 14th century (Kopparbergsprivilegier and Codex Bureanus [Noreen 1904: 128-129]). In some Old Swedish manuscripts one can find sure evidence for lengthening of the ending /-a/ > /-a:/ in short syllable words (with the later development /-a:/ > /-o/, e.g. *bära* > *bäro* 'to bear', *koma* > *komo* 'to come' [Wessén 1970: 70]). The first examples of vowel balance in eastern Norway (Trøndelag) are from the same time (Seip and Saltveit 1971: 274, 375-376). However, vowel balance is assumed to reach its peak in the 16th century (Hovda 1954: 109).

2.2 Vowel balance in Sámi

In Sámi the dependence between quantity of the first stressed syllable and quantity of the second syllable is characteristic of northern and eastern dialects (cf. Korhonen 1981: 354-355). In East Sámi, this feature is found most completely. Itkonen describes the trend in East Sámi (which has no direct contact with Scandinavian dialects) to hold the total quantity of the speech act more or less constant (Itkonen 1946: 49). Kola Sámi has an absolute word length isochrony: The length of the unstressed vowel depends on the length of the root syllable. The unstressed vowel is strongly reduced in the words with a long geminate, [pal'lə] illat. sg. 'polar fox', it is weakened in words with a shorter geminate (respectively a long consonant), [pallʌ] nom. sg., and it preserves its quantity in words with a short consonant, [pala] gen.-acc. sg. (Senkevič-Gudkova 1966: 369-371). In these forms we have the rule of prosodically determined allophonic variation [ə]-[ʌ]-[a]. In North Sámi the vowels /á, a, i, u, o/ are long if the preceding syllable has a short vowel, e.g. /ala:s/ 'high upwards', /ola:n/ 'I reach out', /mana:n/ 'I go' (Bartens 1989: 41-42; cf. Nickel 1990: 13-14). In this case we have prosodically determined quantity neutralisation after a short syllable, with preservation of the opposition short vs. long after a long syllable. Interdependence between latus and consonant centre and the duration of the vowel centre is characteristic of the Kautokeino dialect of North Sámi (cf. Magga 1984). Here the CVCV-type is possible only in imperative forms. In all other words after short vowel + short consonant only a long vowel is possible, e.g. *mana* /mana/ 'go!', *bahá* /paha:/ 'bad' (ibid.: 23).

The interdependence of the quantity of the first and the second syllable in Sámi is considered to be as old as the consonant gradation (Lagercrantz 1927: 25). Wiklund (1896) and Lagercrantz (1927) assume it to be as old as the Fennic-Sámi proto-language. The short syllable lengthening in South Sámi is dated back to the 17th century. But, before that time the same interdependence could have been characteristic of South Sámi as well.

2.3 Connection between Scandinavian vowel balance and Sámi CVCV:-type

The similarities between the Sámi and the Scandinavian interdependence of first and second syllable in a disyllabic word could be assumed to be typologically parallel developments. But, both the geographical spreading of vowel balance in Scandinavian, whose core area coincides with the southern Sámi-Scandinavian contact area, the similar course of this innovation coinciding up to details both in northeastern Scandinavian and Sámi (cf. Sc. /viku:/, /neva:/ - Sa. /mana:/), and the age of vowel balance, which is at least three to four centuries older in Sámi more likely suggest Sámi influence on Scandinavian. Last but not least spreading of vowel balance into Scandinavian dialects and Scandinavization of the southern Sámi occupy the same period.

Referring to Wiik's (1995) hypothesis of a Finno-Ugric substratum in Proto-Germanic, Elert (1997: 79f.) connects the northeastern Scandinavian vowel balance with Finnic 'foot isochrony'. Actually, this connection is plausible. But, Wiik's substratum hypothesis concerns only the West Germanic balance apocope (OHG *sunu* 'son', *hant* 'hand') which affects only /i/ and /u/ (cf. Wiik 1997: 270). In Old Scandinavian there was no such a 'foot isochrony'. The northeastern Scandinavian vowel balance (which affects not only /i/ and /u/, but even /a/) is not be found until the 14th century. Thus vowel balance is not likely an ancient Finno-Ugric substratum in Scandinavian, as Elert (1997) assumes. It is caused by the Scandinavization and the language shift of the southern Sámi from the late Middle Ages on.

3. Metaphony

3.1 Metaphony in Scandinavian dialects

Metaphony is a regressive vowel assimilation where the quality of the second syllable vowel affects the quality of the first syllable vowel in original short syllable words. Metaphony in dialects that preserve the original short syllables results in regular alternations of the root syllable, e.g. Nederkalix (Sweden) *drepa* inf. 'to kill', *dripi* sup. (OIc. *drepa*, *drepit*); Trøndelag *tælær* pres. 'to talk', *tålå* inf. (OIc. *talar*, *tala*). The metaphony can be complete or partial. In Trøndelag one can find forms both with a complete assimilation, e.g. *vuku*, *vukku* (OIc. *viku* obl. casus from *vika* 'week'); *våtå*, *våttå* (OIc. *vita*), or a partial one, e.g. *væka*, *vækka* (OIc. *vika*); *væta*, *vætta* (OIc. *vita*) (Borg 1973). Partial metaphony mostly affects the degree of opening (*vætta*, Ic. *vita*), as in Sámi. But there are other directions of assimilation too, for example rounding or tongue-position (front/back) just as in South Sámi, e.g. /vø:tå/ < /vita/ in eastern Telemark (Norway) (ibid.)

Metaphony is spread over eastern Norwegian and north-central Swedish dialects. In western Norwegian, southern Swedish, and Danish dialects as well as in Icelandic and Faeroese metaphony is absent. Metaphony is especially strong in

Trøndelag, mainly in north Østerdalen (where the metaphony is complete), and in the Swedish vernaculars in southern Norrbotten and Västerbotten. Traces of metaphony can also be found in vernaculars where it has disappeared today (Hovda 1954: 112-114; Borg 1973: 86-87). In Sweden there are traces of metaphony in southern Dalarna, Östergötland, Västmanland, Gästrikland, Uppland, and Södermanland, e.g. *ladu > lädu* 'barn', *galin > gälin* 'mad', *gättu* (< *gatu*) 'street' (Hesselman 1905: 15, 32; Borg 1973).

Metaphony is characteristic only of dialects with vowel balance. Because of the reduction of the unstressed vowel after an original long syllable the assimilation occurs only in original short syllable words VCV(C). At the same time words preserving their original quantity (as bimoric CVCV-words) are characterised by level stress. Here stress and quantity are evenly spread on the root syllable and the following syllable. The prosodic correspondence CVCV=CV: or CVC(C) that manifests itself mainly in vowel balance (see above) is the precondition for the merger of the two vocalic moras in CVCV(C)-words into one qualitative complex. Metaphony is a practical way for the qualitative connection of two vowels, forming together one peak of a bimoric stress in CVCV(C)-words (Kuz'menko 1983). At partial metaphony, the vowels are connected by their common feature (*væta < vita*); at complete metaphony the vowels become identical (*vuku < viku*).

The first examples of metaphony were found in 15th century manuscripts in spellings like *skada* instead of *skoda* 'loss, damage' (Larsen 1913: 29). However, they give no clear evidence for metaphony, because spelling with *a* could show a merger of original short /o/ and /å/ < /a:/ at this time as well. Clear evidence of metaphony can be observed first in the 16th-18th century (Hovda 1954). In relative chronology, metaphony is older than the consonant gemination. The latter occurs just in the area of metaphony. Some vernaculars with metaphony still preserve the original short syllables.

3.2 Metaphony in Sámi

Most Finno-Ugric languages have progressive vowel assimilation (vowel harmony). But, characteristic of Sámi is a regressive assimilation (metaphony), where the vowel quality of the following syllable affects the vowel quality of the root syllable.

The Sámi dialects differ in the extent of the metaphony rule: Metaphony is relatively weak in North Sámi, where it concerns only opening diphthongs, i.e. narrow monophthong before *i* or *u* but opening diphthong before an open vowel, e.g. *nuorra* nom. sg. 'young', *nurrii* illat. sg. (Bartens 1989: 147). Metaphony is much stronger in East and South Sámi (Korhonen 1969), e.g. ESa. (Babino) /mann/ 3.pres. sg. 'to go', /mɛnam/ 1.pres. sg., /minnim/ 1.pret. sg. (Zajkov 1987: 108). Metaphony in South Sámi is even stronger. Here in a polysyllabic word the first syllable is always affected by 'Umlaut' (Hasselbrink 1944: 218), e.g.

/jæ:mɛt/ 'to die'; /ja:ma/ 3.pres. sg.; /jɛ:mi/ 3.pret. sg., where the alternation /æ/-/a/-/ɛ/ in the first syllable is conditioned by the alternation /ɛ/-/a/-/i/ in the second syllable (Lagercrantz 1923: 119). In South Sámi one finds not only assimilation according to the degree of opening (open/closed) – as in North Sámi – but assimilation according to rounding and tongue-position (front/back) as well, e.g. *bissieh!* imperative 'roast!', *bæssam* 1.pres. sg., *byssove* pres. part. (Bergsland 1992: 9; Hasselbrink 1981: 80-83).

The regular metaphony in South Sámi has the same function as vowel harmony in other Finno-Ugric languages: It serves mainly as marker of the word boundary in polysyllabic words. The phonemic feature (palatal/velar, open/closed, rounded/unrounded) goes through the entire polysyllabic word. In accordance with Firth's theory Hasselbrink looks at metaphony as a suprasegmental feature (Hasselbrink 1965: 47). Together with vowel balance, metaphony belongs to the features ensuring the coherence of a word.

Finno-Ugrists place the Sámi metaphony into the Proto-Sámi period, i.e. 1000 BC. - 800 AD. (cf. Korhonen 1988: 265). Steinitz assumes its inner-Sámi origin (Steinitz 1964: 111-112). According to this the innovation must have occurred during the first period of the development of Proto-Sámi (Korhonen 1988: 269). In all Sámi dialects there was a trend to further development of the Proto-Sámi metaphony (Wickman 1960: 25). This trend shows its extreme effects in South Sámi. Even if the occurrence of metaphony in South Sámi belongs to later times, as Bergsland (1992) assumes, it is much older than the metaphony in Scandinavian dialects.

3.3 Connection between the Scandinavian and the Sámi metaphony

Because of the similarities in their mechanisms, Kylstra compared Sámi metaphony and Germanic Umlaut and explained their affinity with help of the terms 'Sprachbund' and 'Areallinguistik' (Kylstra 1983: 173). The processes behind these terms, however, do not become clear: A common substratum (that he assumes even for other cases [Kylstra 1972; cf. Wagner 1964]), borrowing from Sámi into Germanic, or vice versa. The geographical spreading of Umlaut in the Germanic languages (it is strongest in German and in West Scandinavian) as well as time of its occurrence (Umlaut is much older than the northeastern Scandinavian metaphony) are reasons to argue against all three assumptions. On the other hand, the connection between Sámi and Scandinavian metaphony is plausible with respect to geographical spreading, mechanism and time. In 1983 Kusmenko argued, that the Scandinavian metaphony was borrowed from Sámi in the process of Sámi Scandinavization in northeastern Scandinavia (Kuz'menko 1983: 44-50). The paper was written in Russian and did not attract any attention among Scandinavists. In 1992 Bergsland noted that metaphony in Sámi "recalls the Scandinavian metaphony" (Bergsland 1992: 8), but just as in his argumentation about quantity shift (Bergsland 1983; see below) he only wants to prove it was not bor-rowed from Scandinavian. The occurrence of metaphony in East Sámi, where Scandinavian influence is impossible, prevent him from assuming the Scandina-vian origin of the Sámi metaphony (Bergsland 1992: 8-9). We should consider borrowing from Sámi into Scandinavian – which is quite out of the question for Bergsland – as much more plausible. Some cases of Scandinavian metaphony, e.g. *dripi* < *drepit*, *lisi* < *lesit*, repeat completely the Sámi metaphony. In particu-lar cases of metaphony where /u/ does not cause rounding (as the Proto-Scandinavian Umlaut), but only raising as in Sámi, this connection becomes clear. In many northeastern Scandinavian vernaculars /i/ and /u/ have just the same ef-fect as in the Sámi metaphony, e.g. *lädu* < *ladu*, *gälin* < *galin* in northern and central Swedish vernaculars cf. /æluk/ < /aluk/ 'high', /æviin/ < /aviin/ comit. from /avve:/ 'belt' in Sámi vernaculars in Sweden (Collinder 1938: 57-63).

First, the South Sámi metaphony was characteristic of Swedish or Norwegian dialects of the Scandinavized southern Sámi. The functional necessity of meta-phony in Swedish and Norwegian vernaculars with vowel balance explains the penetration of metaphony into genuine Scandinavian dialects.

4. Quantity shift and consonant gemination

4.1 Consonant gemination in Scandinavian

In a great part of the Scandinavian area short syllables have been abolished by lengthening of the original short vowel or by gemination of the short consonant, cf. OIc. *vita*, *vika* ~ Ic. /viːta/, /viːka/; Sw. *veta* /veːta/, *vecka* /vekːa/. In western and southern Scandinavia the vowel was lengthened (Ic. *vita*, Da. *vide*). The ver-naculars in Trøndelag show regular gemination of the consonant, e.g. *vatta*, *våttå*, *vætta* (< *vita*) or *vukku*, *vokko*, *vækka* (< *viku*, *vika*) (Reitan 1922: 3). Often con-sonant gemination as result of the quantity shift occurs also in eastern Norwegian, central and northern Swedish dialects, e.g. North Sw. *vætta*, *vækka*; Central Sw. *vikku*, *bitti* (Hesselman 1905: 19).

In some vernaculars the original CVCV-pattern and the new CVCCV-pattern are optional variants, as for example in Senjen in North Norway with a mixed Sámi and Scandinavian population (Iversen 1913: 3), e.g. *leve/levve* 'to live', *bete/bette* 'tusk', *bore/borre* 'to drill' (ibid.: 26) or in Solør, e.g. *tapa/tappa* (< *tapa*) 'to loose', *tåkå/tåkkå* (Ic. *þoka*) 'fog', *gamel/gammel* 'old' (Larsen 1894: 46, 49), where no Sámi population can be found today. Some eastern Norwegian as well as some northern and central Swedish vernaculars still preserve the CVCV-pattern (at least partly), especially in disyllabic words.

Although the first evidence for consonant gemination is from the 14th century, e.g. ONw. *konno*, *gerra* ~ OIc. *kona* 'wife', *gera* 'to do' (Seip and Saltveit 1971: 171), it occurred later than vowel lengthening. Consonant gemination is often considered as indication of late quantity shift (Söderström 1972: 89). In most

Swedish and Norwegian dialects the development CVCV > CVCCV took place between the 17th and 20th century. In Trøndelag and Østerdal in Norway and in Uppland in Sweden, for example, the original short syllable forms weren't abolished until the beginning of the 20th century (Kolsrud 1944: 20; 1974: 19; Lindroth 1911-12: 134). Here in many cases one still can find the alternation CVCV/CVCCV.

4.2 Consonant gemination in Sámi

In North Sámi a short stressed vowel can be followed by a short consonant, *basam* 'I roast', a short geminate *massam* 1. pres. sg. 'I loose', and a long geminate *mas'sam* part. perf. (Bergsland 1983: 73). In cases of quantitative consonant gradation, usually two of these consonant grades alternate in different morphological forms: VC~VCC (*basam* pres. ~ *bassam* part. perf, *bœsse* 'nest' nom. sg. ~ *bœse* gen.-acc. sg.); VCC~VC'C (*bœsse* gen.-acc. sg. 'birch bark' ~ *bœs'se* nom. sg.) Some roots can even show all three possible consonant grades.

In South Sámi there are no short syllable words. All stressed root syllables are long. After a short vowel only a long consonant is possible, NSa. *basam* - SSa. *bissav* 'I roast'. As in the Scandinavian languages, the root syllables are lengthened either by lengthening of the vowel or lengthening of the consonant. In South Sámi there is no consonant gradation and the root is qualitatively unchanged through inflexion.

The strong interdependence of phonological elements in the word, characteristic of all Sámi dialects, manifests itself in the so-called Law of Contrasting Quantity Correlation. It concerns, among others, the distribution of quantity amongst the vowel and the following consonant. The contrasting quantity correlation is characteristic of the whole Sámi area, though it is not equally strong. In its entire consequence the Law of Contrasting Quantity Correlation is present in some eastern and southern Sámi vernaculars (Lagercrantz 1927: 24-25). Lagercrantz notes, that in the South Sámi Vefsn-vernacular "jedes betonte Wort einen langen Laut als Träger der Quantitätsstruktur enthalten muß. Dieser ist entweder der Stammvokal oder der Stammkonsonant. Beide können niemals gleichzeitig kurz oder gleichzeitig lang sein" (Lagercrantz 1923: 147). South Sámi, however, has not only two prosodic types, as V:C and VC: in Scandinavian. Here there are three isochronal types with mutual dependence of vowel and consonant quantity. (ibid.: 148-152). The South Sámi rule, the longer the vowel the shorter the consonant, is only partially valid in North Sámi. But the same rule is found in East Sámi, which unlike South Sámi has consonant gradation. In the Skolt Sámi vernacular of Notozero the mutual dependence of vowel and consonant quantity becomes obvious at the consonant gradation, [pallʌ] short vowel + long consonant, [pal'lə] overshort vowel + long geminate, [paːla] long vowel + short consonant (Senkevič-Gudkova 1966: 368-369, cf. Zajkov 1987: 44).

According to Lagercrantz the Law of Contrasting Quantity Correlation is as old as the consonant gradation, i.e. from the Proto-Sámi period (Lagercrantz 1927: 25). However, the disappearance of consonant gradation and generalisation of long consonants after a short vowel in South Sámi occurred later, but not later than up to the 17th century (Bergsland 1967: 47).

4.3 Connection between Sámi and Scandinavian consonant gemination

The quantity shift in South Sámi, where consonant gradation is abolished and consonant lengthening generalised, is considered to be either directly borrowed from Scandinavian (cf. Ravila 1960: 303; Schlachter 1991: 117; Bergsland 1945: 17) or to be the result of the same trend, i.e. strengthening of the root syllable. In South Sámi, however, the quantity shift occurred earlier than in neighbouring Scandinavian dialects. The latter often still preserve the VC-pattern in disyllabic words. In the Scandinavian areas with predominant development CVCV > CVCCV (Trøndelag, Uppland), consonant gemination occurred not earlier than in the 19th and the beginning of the 20th century. The independence of the South Sámi quantity shift and consonant gemination from the corresponding Scandinavian development is convincingly demonstrated by Bergsland (1967: 47; 1983: 85; 1992: 8). On the other hand, consonant gradation in all Sámi dialects is much older than the optional variants C/CC (*tapa/tappa*, *borre/bore*) in modern Scandinavian dialects. The CVCV/CVCCV-alternations, especially in those dialects that are still in contact with Sámi, correspond completely to the alternations in Sámi consonant gradation (NSa. *nama/namma* 'name', *livva/liva* 'a reindeer's rest period', *gurra/gura* 'gap').

The development CVCV > CVCCV can also be observed in West Germanic (e.g. OHG. *site* > Ger. *Sitte*), but this was rather an exception. The main rule here was vowel lengthening in the open syllable as in Icelandic and Danish. The unique development of regular consonant lengthening (*vækka*, *våttå* < *vika*, *vita*) in northeastern Scandinavian dialects which can be observed neither in other Germanic nor even in other Indo-European languages with short syllable lengthening, can be explained as the result of Sámi interference. In nearly every Sámi word at consonant gradation a simple consonant is alternating with a long consonant or with a geminate (*nama/namma*). The Scandinavian loan words in Sámi show what the Scandinavian short syllable words in the language of the Scandinavized Sámi looked like: Almost all of them have geminated consonants, e.g. Sa. *smiddo* < Sc. *smid* 'smith'; Sa. *konno* < Sc. *kona* 'wife' (cf. Qvigstad 1893). Precisely the form *konno* is one of the first examples of consonant lengthening in Old Norwegian (see above).

5. Form of substantivized adjectives

In Sámi nominal inflection there is no difference between nouns and adjectives. The so-called predicative form of an adjective can be used as a noun. It can be declined in all cases in singular and plural; declension types and consonant gradation rules are the same for nouns and adjectives (cf. Nickel 1990: 84; Bartens 1989: 105).

As in the other Germanic languages substantivized adjectives in the Scandinavian standard languages are formed with the prepositional definite article (so called 'adjective article'), e.g. Sw. *den gamla* (cf. Ger. *die Alte*). The same model is valid for the western and southern Scandinavian dialects. The form of definite adjectives (with the prepositional article) in Scandinavian differs from the form of definite nouns. The latter have a suffixed article ('noun article'), cf. Sw. *mannen* ~ Ger. *der Mann*. However, in the northeastern Scandinavian dialects the substantivized adjectives get the suffixed noun article, e.g. *gamlen* 'the old (man)', *gamla* 'the old (woman)' instead of *den gamle*, *den gamla* (cf. *stolen* 'the chair', *bordet* 'the table'). Substantivized adjectives get thus the same form as nouns.

In Scandinavian dialects that retain or partly retain noun declension, substantivized adjectives are even declined as nouns, e.g. in the vernacular of Älvdalen (northern Dalarna) *gambla* def. nom. sg. fem. 'old', *gamblun* def. dat. sg. fem., *gamblu* def. acc. sg. fem., *gamblar* def. nom. fem. pl. (Levander 1909: 52-53). Such use of substantivized adjectives is recorded in nearly all vernaculars of north-central Sweden and eastern Norway (cf. Delsing 1996). The spreading of this feature into vernaculars of the Sámi-Scandinavian contact area – especially its occurrence in Trøndelag where substantivized adjectives with suffixed article are used even in comparative and superlative (Kolsrud 1974: 48) – can be attributed to Sámi influence.

In this case we are not dealing with a substantial borrowing into Scandinavian but with borrowing of a model (no difference between nouns and adjectives in morphology both in Sámi and in northeastern Scandinavian dialects). Shift-induced functional change that represents borrowing of structure without form seems not to be that unusual even for other cases of language contact (cf. Thomason and Kaufman 1988).

There are some other features in phonology and grammar common to northeastern Scandinavian and Sámi dialects, as for example high tone word stress, preaspiration, consonant shift, different forms of attributive and predicative adjectives, topic-emphasising constructions, which could also be explained by the Sámi Scandinavization. These features can not be unequivocally attributed as a consequence of Sámi-Scandinavian contacts, because they can be found in Scandinavian dialects distant from the Sámi-Scandinavian contact zone. However, this does not exclude the Sámi influence on the preservation or development of these features in the contact area.

6. Conclusion

Some important northeastern Scandinavian isoglosses, first of all vowel balance, metaphony, and consonant gemination can be explained as the result of the language shift of the southern Sámi. The spreading of these features coincides almost completely with the southern Sámi-Scandinavian contact area during the Middle Ages (cf. Zachrisson 1997: fig. 139). The epicentre of this contact area was the Norwegian province of Trøndelag, where the interference features appear as strongest. Some features of Sámi interference in Scandinavian dialects disappeared, but those corresponding to the trends of the Scandinavian language development were not only preserved, but penetrated into the neighbouring genuine Scandinavian dialects. Jakobson (1938) noted, that firstly elements are borrowed that fit into the language's inner trends. In our case it is the Two Moras Prominence Law in Scandinavian (which led to vowel balance and metaphony) and the trend to merge syllable boundaries and morpheme boundaries in all Germanic languages (which led to consonant gemination). The spreading of these features shows that there was no 'neighbour opposition' (term of Larsen [1916]) between the speakers of the dialects of the Scandinavized Sámi and those of the genuine Scandinavian dialects.

Model of the Sámi-Scandinavian contacts: (1) Subordinative Sámi-Scandinavian bilingualism; (2) Formation of Scandinavian dialects on Sámi substratum; (3) Loss of features which did not correspond to the Scandinavian internal trends; (4) Penetration of original Sámi features into genuine Scandinavian dialects.

Humboldt-Universität zu Berlin

REFERENCES

Bartens, Hans Hermann
  1989   *Lehrbuch der saamischen (lappischen) Sprache.* Hamburg: Buske.
Beckman, Lars
  1959   *A contribution to the physical anthropology and population genetics of Sweden.* Lund.
Bergsland, Knut
  1945   "L'alternance consonantique date-t-elle du lapon commun?", *Studia Septentrionalia* 2, 1-53.
  1964   "To Samiske navn på Namsen lånt fra norsk", *Maal og Minne* 3-4, 136-147.
  1967   "Lapp dialectal groups and problems of history", in: *Lapps and Norsemen in Olden Times (Institutt for Sammenlignende Kulturforskning* A: 26), 32-53. Oslo.

1983   "Southern Lapp and Scandinavian quantity patterns", in: *Symposium Saeculare Societatis Fenno-Ugricae* (*Mémoires de la Société Finno-ougrienne* 185), 73-87. Helsinki.

1992   "Language contacts between Southern Sami and Scandinavian", in: Ernst Håkon Jahr (ed.), *Language Contact. Theoretical and Empirical Studies*, 5-15. Berlin: Mouton de Gruyter.

Borg, Arve
1973   "Jamning", *Svenska landsmål och svenskt folkliv* 298, 82-100.

Bull, Tove
1992   "A contact feature in the phonology of a northern Norwegian dialect", in: Ernst Håkon Jahr (ed.), *Language Contact. Theoretical and Empirical Studies*, 17-36. Berlin: Mouton de Gruyter.

Christiansen, Hallfrid
1954   "Hovedinndelingen av norske dialekter", *Maal og Minne*, 30-41.

Collinder, Björn
1938   *Lautlehre des waldlappischen Dialektes von Gällivare* (*Mémoires de la Société Finno-ougrienne* 74). Helsinki.

Dahlstedt, Karl-Hampus
1950   *Det svenska Vilhelminamålet* 1 (*Skrifter utgivna genom Landsmåls- och folkminnesarkivet i Uppsala* A: 72). Uppsala.

Delsing, Lars-Olof
1996   "Nominalfrassyntax i skandinaviska dialekter", *Nordica Bergensia* 9, 24-74.

Elert, Claes-Christian
1997   "Språket i södra Skandinavien under bronsåldern: finsk-ugriskt, baltiskt, germanskt eller ...?", in: Patrik Åström (ed.), *Studier i svensk språkhistoria* 4, 77-86. Stockholm: Institutionen för nordiska språk.

Hallan, Nils
1976   "Annermannen i norsk og sørsamisk", *Arkiv för nordisk filologi* 91, 192-201.

Hasselbrink, Gustav
1944   *Vilhelminalapskans ljudlära med särskild hänsyn till de första stavelsens vokaler.* Uppsala: Almqvist & Wiksell.

1965   *Alternative Analysis of the Phonemic Systems in Central South-Lappish* (*Indiana University Uralic and Altaic Series* 49). Bloomington: Indiana University.

1981   *Südlappisches Wörterbuch* 1 (*Schriften des Instituts für Dialektforschung und Volkskunde in Uppsala* C: 4). Uppsala.

Hesselman, Bengt
1905   *Sveamålen och de svenska dialekternas indelning.* Uppsala: K. W. Appelberg.

Hovda, Per
1954   "Ymist kring jamvektlovi", *Maal og Minne*, 109-114.

Itkonen, Erkki
1946   *Struktur und Entwicklung der ostlappischen Quantitätssysteme* (*Mémoires de la Société Finno-ougrienne* 88). Helsinki.

Iversen, Ragnvald
1913   *Senjenmålet. Lydverket i hoveddrag.* Kristiania.

Jahr, Ernst Håkon
1997   "Norway", in: Hans Goebl et al. (eds.), *Kontaktlinguistik.* (*Handbücher zur Sprach- und Kommunikationswissenschaft* 12: 2), 937-948. Berlin: de Gruyter.

Jakobsen, Roman
1962 [1938]   "Sur la théorie des affinités phonologiques entre des langues", *Selected writings* 1, 234-246. The Hague: Mouton. (Reprint from *Actes de Quatrième Congrès International de Linguistes*, 48-59. Copenhagen: Einar Munksgaard.)

Kolsrud, Sigurd
1944   *Utsyn över målet i Øysterdalane og Solørbygdene*. Bergen.
1974   *Nynorsken i sine målføre*. Oslo: Universitetsforlaget.

Korhonen, Mikko
1969   "Lapin metafoniasta", in: *Juhlakirja Paavo Siron täyttäessä 60 vuotta 2.8.1969* (*Acta Universitatis Tamperensis* A: 26), 79-89. Tampere.
1981   *Johdatus lapin kielen historiaan* (*Suomalaisen Kirjallisuuden Seuran toimituksia* 370). Helsinki.
1988   "The History of the Lapp Language", in: Denis Sinor (ed.), *The Uralic languages. Description, history and foreign influences* (*Handbook of Uralic studies* 1), 264-287. Leiden: Brill.

Kuz'menko, Jurij K.
1983   "Istoki skandinavskoj metafonii (o saamskom vlijanii na skandinavskie dialekty", in: N.K. Tolstoj (ed.), *Areal'nye issledovanie v jazykoznanii i ètnografii*, 44-50. Leningrad.

Kylstra, Andries Dirk
1972   "Die Präaspiration im Westskandinavischen und im Lappischen", *Orbis* XXI: 2, 367-382.
1983   "Skandinavisch-lappische Parallelen", in: *Symposium Saeculare Societatis Fenno-Ugricae* (*Mémoires de la Société Finno-ougrienne* 185), 159-177. Helsinki.

Lagercrantz, Eliel
1923   *Sprachlehre des Südlappischen nach der Mundart von Wefsen* (*Bulletin* 1). Kristiania: Kristiania Etnografiske Museum.
1927   *Strukturtypen und Gestaltwechsel im Lappischen* (*Mémoires de la Société Finno-ougrienne* 57). Helsinki.

Larsen, Amund Bredesen
1894   *Lydlæren i den solørske dialekt især i dens forhold til oldsproget*. Kristiania.

Larsen, Amund Bredesen
1913   *Om vokalharmoni, vokalbalangse og vokaltiljevning i de norske bygdemål*. Kristiania.
1993 [1916]   "Nabooposition – knot", in: Ernst Håkon Jahr, Ove Lorenz (eds.), *Historisk Språkvetenskap* (*Studier i norsk språkvetenskap* 5), 97-109. Oslo: Novus. (Reprint from *Maal og Minne 1916-1917*, 34-46.)

Levander, Lars
1909   *Älvdalsmålet i Dalarna. Ordböjning och syntax* (*Nyare bidrag till svenska landsmål och svenskt folkliv* 4: 3). Stockholm.

Lindroth, Hjalmar
1911-1912   *J. Th. Bureus, den svenska grammatikens fader*. Lund.

Magga, Tuomas
1984   *Duration in the quantity of bisyllabics in the Guovdageaidnu dialect of North Lappish* (*Acta Universitatis Ouluensis* B: 11). Oulu.

Nesheim, Asbjørn
1967   "Eastern and western elements in Lapp culture", in: *Lapps and Norsemen in Olden Times* (*Instituttet for Sammenlignende Kulturforskning* A: 26), 104-167. Oslo.

Nickel, Klaus Peter
1990   *Samisk grammatikk*. Oslo: Universitetsforlaget.

Noreen, Adolf
1904   *Altschwedische Grammatik mit Einschluß des Altgutnischen*. Halle.

Posti, Lauri
1954   "On the Origin of the Voiceless Vowel in Lapp", in: Dag Strömbeck (ed.), *Scandinavica et Fenno-Ugrica. Studier tillägnade Björn Collinder*, 199-209. Stockholm: Almqvist & Wiksell.

Qvigstad, Just Knut
1893   *Nordische Lehnwörter im Lappischen* (*Videnskaps-Selskabs Forhandlingar* 1893: 1). Christiania.

Ravila, Paavo
1960   "Probleme des Stufenwechsels im Lappischen", *Finno-ugrische Forschungen* 33, 285-325.

Reitan, Jørgen
1922   *Nytrøndsk ordforkorting og betoning*. Kristiania.

Sammallahti, Pekka
1990   "The Sámi Language: Past and Present", in: Dirmid R. F. Collins (ed.), *Arctic languages*, 437-458. Paris.

Schlachter, Wolfgang
1991   *Stufenwechselstörungen im Malålappischen* (*Veröffentlichungen der Societas Uralo-Altaica* 33). Wiesbaden: Harrassowitz.

Seip, Didrik Arup, and Laurits Saltveit
1971   *Norwegische Sprachgeschichte* (*Grundriß der germanischen Philologie* 19). Berlin: de Gruyter.

Senkevič-Gudkova, B.B.
1966   "Zakon kontrastnoi korreljacii količestva i ego vlijanie na sistemu fonem notozerskogo dialekta saamskogo jazyka", in: S. K. Šaumjan (ed.), *Issledovanija po fonologii*, 368-375. Moskva.

Sköld, Tryggve
1992   "The earliest linguistic contacts between Lapps and Scandinavians", in: Axel Groundström et al. (eds.), *Wortstudien. Festschrift Tryggve Sköld zum 70. Geburtstag* (*Umeå studies in the humanities* 109), 99-110. Stockholm: Almqvist & Wiksell.

Söderström, Sven
1972   *Om kvantitetsutvecklingen i norrländska folkmål. Gammal kort stavelse i Kalix- och Pitemålen i Nordmalings och Ragunda socknar* (*Studier till en svensk dialektgeografisk atlas* 5). Uppsala: Almqvist & Wiksell.

Steinitz, Wolfgang
1964   *Geschichte des finnisch-ugrischen Vokalismus* (*Finnisch-ugrische Studien* 4). Berlin: Akademie-Verlag (2nd edition).

Storm, Johan
1908   "Norsk Lydskrift med Omrids af Fonetiken", *Norvegia* 1, 19-132.

Svanberg, Ingvar
1986   "A Forest Lapp Culture in Central Sweden in the 17th and 18th centuries", *Svenska landsmål och svenskt folkliv* 109, 61-75.

Thomason, Sarah Grey, and Terrence Kaufmann
1988   *Language contact, creolization, and genetic linguistics*. Berkeley: University of California Press.

Urbanczyk, Przemyslaw
1992   *Medieval Arctic Norway*. Warszawa: Semper.
Wagner, Heinrich
1964   "Nordeuropäische Lautgeographie", *Zeitschrift für celtische Philologie* 29, 225-298.
Wallström, Sigvard
1943   *Studier i Övre Norrlands språkgeografi med utgångspunkt från Arjeplogsmålet.* Uppsala: Almqvist & Wiksell.
Wessén, Elias
1970   *Schwedische Sprachgeschichte (Grundriß der germanischen Philologie* 18). Berlin: de Gruyter.
Wickman, Bo
1960   "Some remarks concerning metaphony, especially in Livonian", in: *Språkvetenskapliga Sällskapets i Uppsala Förhandlingar 1958-1960,* 25-48. Uppsala: Lundequist.
Wiik, Kalevi
1995   "The Baltic Sea Prosodic Area Revisited", in: Seppo Suhonen (ed.), *Itämerensuomalainen kultuurialue – The Fenno-Baltic Cultural Area (Castrenianumin toimitteita* 49), 75-90. Helsinki.
1997   "The Uralic and Finno-Ugric Phonetic Substratum in Proto-Germanic", *Linguistica Uralica* XXXIII: 4, 258-280.
Wiklund, Karl Bernhard
1896   *Entwurf einer urlappischen Lautlehre* 1 (*Mémoires de la Société Finnoougrienne* 1). Helsinki.
Zachrisson, Inger
1997   *Möten i gränsland: samer och germaner i Mellanskandinavien (Monographs* 4). Stockholm: Statens historiska museum.
Zajkov, Petr M.
1987   *Babinskij dialekt saamskogo jazyka.* Petrozavodsk: Karelija.

Languages in Contact, edited by D.G. Gilbers, J. Nerbonne, and J. Schaeken (= *Studies in Slavic and General Linguistics*, vol. 28), 225-230. Amsterdam - Atlanta, GA: Rodopi, 2000.

MORPHOLOGICAL SIMPLIFICATION: MORE THAN EROSION?

WOUTER KUSTERS

In studies into language change and contact, a concept frequently used is "simplification" with respect to inflectional morphology (cf. for example, Thomason and Kaufman 1988: 129; Meillet 1917: 112). Although its exact definition is seldom discussed, the following principles[1] characterise simplification:

- TRANSPARENCY PRINCIPLE: There should be a one-to-one relationship between meaning and form. This principle leads to the avoidance of allomorphy, fusion, fission and syncretism.
- MIRROR PRINCIPLE: The order of morphemes should mirror the order of the syntactic or semantic operations.
- ECONOMY PRINCIPLE: As few categories as possible should be expressed.

This characterisation is based on a priori considerations, noticeable in terms such as "ideal language" and "deviations" (cf. Carstairs 1987: 12ff.), but also on empirical evidence from language acquisition and language processing.

The interplay of these Principles makes a wide range of scenarios possible. However, the most widely discussed example of simplification in inflectional morphology is the one of the Indo-European (IE) and especially the Germanic languages, where the following developments concurred:

- a stress shift leading to disharmony between phonological and morphological prominence;
- a general tendency towards erosion and consequent renewal;
- a sharp reduction of morpho-syntactic categories;
- a moderate reduction of allomorphy.

It is commonly assumed that these developments could only take place in a social environment with much dialect/language variation and contact. Now I will first discuss the IE situation further. Then, I will present a case of simplification in

---

[1] These principles are not to be understood in terms of the Principle-and-Parameter model. In fact, they are more closely related to 'Constraints' in Optimality Theory. However, since I do not provide explicit tableaux, I will refrain from using the term 'constraint'.

Quechua, with a view to showing that the developments listed above are not intrinsically related to one another, and that these developments represent only one case of several possible mixtures of Principles.

1. Morphological Simplification in Indo-European

Here I will discuss morphological simplification as it happened in Scandinavian because that language group is representative for Indo-European with respect to variation in inflectional complexity, and variation in factors causing the change.

Until 1200 AD, a wealth of noun and verb classes, also called declension and conjugation classes, existed in Scandinavian, which triggered extensive allomorphy. In nouns, four cases and two numbers were expressed, while in verbs, tense, mood, number and person were expressed. In contrast to the conservative insular Faroese and Icelandic, this system has been simplified in modern continental Scandinavian varieties[2] as follows:

– There is no morphological case anymore, except in some pronouns.
– Number is only expressed in noun phrases, with less allomorphy than before.
– Instead of three, there are only two genders in most varieties.
– There are still noun and verb classes, but since there are fewer nominal and verbal categories, these do not trigger such extensive allomorphy anymore.
– In verbs, tense is still expressed, but with less allomorphy. In most varieties there are no number or person distinctions anymore and no subjunctive mood.

This process of simplification was initially of a phonetic nature; that is, it was continuous, and it involved phonetic reductions such as final consonant loss and vowel reduction. This led to the reductions mentioned above, which means that especially the Economy Principle has become more important in modern continental Scandinavian, while the Transparency Principle is also a little better complied with. Compare, for instance, the following verbal paradigms of 12th century Old Norse (ON) with modern Norwegian:

Past.indic.	12th c. ON	Mod.Nw.		12th c. ON	Mod.Nw.
1 pers.sg.	beit 'bit'	bet	1 pers.pl.	bitum	bet
2 pers.sg.	beitst	bet	2 pers.pl.	bituð	bet
3 pers.sg.	beit	bet	3 pers.pl.	bitu	bet

The period in which these changes took place was one of intensive language/ dialect contact with Low German traders, dialect variation in the Scandinavian languages, and an open attitude of Scandinavian speakers to other varieties (cf. Haugen 1976: 253). Precisely in places with less intensive contact (Northern

---

[2] However, in the more remote inland parts of Scandinavia the system has been less simplified.

Scandinavia[3]), or where the society was less open to other varieties and language change (Iceland), there was less simplification. Language/dialect contact is therefore an important factor in Scandinavian language change. This contact occurred between closely related languages, involving much accommodation, interference, and borrowing, without however the rise of a pidgin or a standardised lingua franca.

According to several authors (e.g. Meillet 1917; Haugen 1976), these social factors do not suffice to explain the simplification, because they do not explain why this process started before the contact period and still lasted until after this period. Furthermore, morphological simplification also occurs in languages less influenced by the kind of contact as mentioned above, such as the Celtic languages. Therefore, it is often claimed that these social factors only accelerated the changes that were already on their way for independent reasons. Now I will turn to these other reasons.

Meillet (1917: 113) and Haugen (1976: 285) state that the morphological simplification resulted from a change in the prosodic system in Germanic. In their opinion, Germanic was set apart from other IE languages, because of the rigorous shift from a pitch accent system to an initial stress system. Under influence of this new system, vowels in non-stressed syllables would tend to be abbreviated and eventually to disappear. As a result of this change inflectional endings would disappear automatically. Social factors would then only boost a tendency that was already there. Evidence for this view, is that most Germanic languages show this vanishing of word-final inflection.

However, this explanation is not fully satisfactory as there are other languages with non-initial stress, like French, which have also been simplified. To explain this, sometimes a third factor is referred to, namely a natural tendency in language to erode word-finally (cf. Meillet 1917: 84). This tendency would constitute a larger historical cycle, in which on the one hand forms continue to erode and conflate, as a result of articulatory pressures, while on the other hand new forms are introduced, as a result of the motivation to be expressive. When a morphological system as a whole is on a certain point on this cycle, as Proto-Indo-European was, it can only move in one direction, which would be in this case initially towards a more fusional (Old Norse), and then towards a more isolating structure. But the exact speed of this change would be determined by other factors. Evidence for this view comes from the fact that all IE languages have simplified their inflections to a certain extent. A problem for this view are languages in which there is

---

[3] Actually, in Northern Scandinavia, there was language contact with speakers of the unrelated Sámi language (cf. Kusmenko and Rießler 2000). The kind of contact was, however, of a quite different nature in comparison to the contact situations discussed here.

no such tendency to erosion of complex word forms, such as the Athabaskan languages.

2. Morphological Simplification in Quechua

With about ten million speakers, Quechua is the largest indigenous language group in South America, and consists of several quite diverse varieties. I will discuss Ecuadorian Quechua here, the only variety of Quechua which has extensively simplified its inflectional morphology, and I will compare this variety to its closest well-described relative, Ayacucho Quechua.

In Ayacucho Quechua verbal inflectional morphology consists of the suffixal expression of object agreement, tense, subject agreement and number, usually in that order. The number suffix refers to the number of the subject or the object and varies with respect to inclusivity, for example:

(1) *Riku-wa-rqa-nki-ku*
     See-1st-past-2nd-Plur.exc.
     You (sg.) saw us.

There is, however, a port-manteau morpheme for 1st person subject, 2nd person object agreement, which hinders this order, e.g.:

(2) *Riku-rqa-yki*
     See-Past-1stSub.2ndObj.
     I saw you (sg.).

Furthermore, for agreement with a 3rd person subject and a 2nd person object, there is an affix combination which is non-compositional with respect to the positions of these affixes and their meanings. For example:

(3) *Riku-su-rqa-nki-cik*
     See-3rd-Past-2nd-Plur.incl.
     He saw you (pl.).

Now, in Ecuadorian Quechua there is no port-manteau subject-object agreement morpheme anymore and also the '-su-nki-' combination no longer exists, thereby precluding structures as in (2) and (3). The Transparency Principle is thus better complied with. Furthermore, only one obligatory number affix has remained, which can only pluralise the adjacent subject agreement affix, thereby precluding structures as in (1). This means that also the Mirror Principle has become more dominant. As a result of this, the variety of morpho-syntactic categories has declined in Ecuadorian Quechua, which entails that the Economy Principle is better complied with. In Ecuadorian Quechua, meanings as in (1), (2) and (3) are no longer expressed with only morphological means.

As in Indo-European, language contact has also played an important role in Quechua simplification. Quechua was brought from Peru to Ecuador by traders, after which it spread quite rapidly over large parts of Ecuador. During this dispersal Quechua was massively learned as a second language by non-Quechua speakers, who initially used Quechua as a lingua franca. Consequently Quechua changed and developed into a new Ecuadorian variety. In contrast to the Scandinavian case, Quechua changed after it had been adopted by speakers of an *unrelated* language, in a country where originally no Quechua speakers lived.

In Ecuadorian Quechua there are no phonological or prosodic changes, as in the case of Scandinavian, which could explain the simplification. Furthermore, the tendency towards natural erosion is not attested in Quechua. Even if there were such a tendency to shorten words, then still this does not relate to the peculiar way of simplification in Ecuadorian, which occurs discretely and non-word-finally, as in the disappearance of *riku-su-rqa-nki*, but not *riku-wa-rqa-nki*.

3. Conclusion

In Scandinavian the simplification process initially had a phonetic character, leading to homonymies and loss of categories, which implies a better compliance with the Economy Principle. This resulted eventually also in a better compliance with the Transparency Principle, although some non-transparent allomorphies still remain.

In Quechua the changes were motivated primarily by the Transparency and the Mirror Principles, which entails a different simplification path. Furthermore, the simplification process had a strictly morphological character, that is, it was not continuous and there was no phonetic erosion.

Both ways of simplification are typical of a language situation in which the most easily processable forms are selected to optimize an otherwise problematic communication. That is a language contact situation in which language shift and second language learning are prominent. Whereas this is a plausible scenario for Quechua, in Scandinavian language-internal factors may also have played a role.

The differences between the ways of simplification in Scandinavian and Quechua may point to the importance of the structure of the original languages, in which some Principles already ranked high or low. On the other hand, the different kinds of language contact situations – especially the closeness of the linguistic relationship – may also have been of influence on differences in specific demotions and promotions of Principles.

CNWS, Leiden University

REFERENCES

Carstairs, A.
 1987 *Allomorphy in inflexion*. London: Croom Helm.
Haugen, E.
 1976 *The Scandinavian languages*. Londen: Faber & Faber.
Kusmenko, J., and M. Rießler
 2000 "Traces of Sámi-Scandinavian contact in Scandinavian dialects". This volume, 209-224.
Meillet, A.
 1917 *Caractères généraux des Langues Germaniques*. Paris: Librairie Hachette et Cie.
Thomason, S.G., and T. Kaufman
 1988 *Language contact, creolization, and genetic linguistics*. Berkeley: University of California Press.

Languages in Contact, edited by D.G. Gilbers, J. Nerbonne, and J. Schaeken (= *Studies in Slavic and General Linguistics*, vol. 28), 231-246. Amsterdam - Atlanta, GA: Rodopi, 2000.

LINGUISTIC BALKANIZATION:
CONTACT-INDUCED CHANGE BY MUTUAL REINFORCEMENT

JOUKO LINDSTEDT

1. Introduction

The Balkan Sprachbund was the first linguistic area discovered by modern scholarship. According to Kopitar's (1829: 86) famous statement about Albanian, Wallachian, and Bulgarian (in modern terms: Albanian, Balkan Romance, and Balkan Slavic), in the Balkans "nur *eine* Sprach*form* herrscht, aber mit dreyerley Sprach*materie*". The main features of the Sprachbund were described in Sandfeld's (1926, 1930) masterpiece and subsequent research by others (see Schaller 1975, Solta 1980, Asenova 1989). But we still lack an overall description of the historical development of this linguistic area. Especially the question of the origins and causation of the main areal features of the Balkans, the linguistic Balkanisms, is notoriously difficult.

In this paper I shall discuss the typological characteristics of grammatical Balkanisms, as well as the nature of the sociolinguistic contact situation which gave rise to the convergence that can be observed among the languages of the area. I shall argue that the origins of most grammatical Balkanisms are not to be sought in the internal development of any one of these languages, but rather in the multilingual contact situation itself, to the extent that the traditional notions of "source language" and "target language" may not always be applicable.

The languages or language groups of the Sprachbund are Albanian, Greek, Balkan Romance, Balkan Slavic, and Balkan Romani. Balkan Romance comprises the (Daco-)Romanian language spoken in Romania and Moldova, as well as Aromanian (Arumanian) and Megleno-Romanian spoken in the Central Balkans. Balkan Slavic means Bulgarian, Macedonian, and the so-called Torlak dialects of Serbian; Muslim speakers of Bulgarian and Macedonian are ofted referred to as Pomaks. Balkan Romani should be understood as an areal term comprising both Balkan dialects proper and those Vlax dialects spoken in the Balkan area. In addition to these five language groups, Ladino (Judezmo) and various forms of Balkan Turkic (such as Rumelian Turkish and Gagauz) have adopted some areal features; I will have to take them into account at a later stage of exploration.

2. Grammatical Balkanisms

The areal features of the Balkans can be divided into lexical (including phrase-ological), phonological, and grammatical. A Balkanism need not occur in all Bal-kan languages, but those with the widest distribution are theoretically also the most interesting. I shall concentrate upon morphosyntactic features, for grammat-ical innovations attest to more radical contact influence than mere loanwords or phonological traits do.

Table 1 presents the distribution of twelve shared grammatical innovations in the five language groups of the Sprachbund. A plus sign + means that the feature in question is dominant.in most of the group. Of course this way of presentation requires some simplification: object reduplication, for instance, is subject to dif-ferent grammatical rules even in such closely related languages as Bulgarian and Macedonian. A plus sign in parentheses (+) indicates that the feature is present as a tendency only or that it only occurs in some contact varieties.

	Greek	Albanian	Balkan Slavic	Balkan Romance	Balkan Romani
Argument marking					
ENCLITIC ARTICLES	(+)	+	+	+	(+)
OBJECT REDUPLICATION	+	+	+	+	+
PREPOSITIONS INSTEAD OF CASES	(+)	(+)	+	(+)	(+)
DATIVE / POSSESSIVE MERGER	+	+	+	+	–
GOAL / LOCATION MERGER	+	+	+	+	(+)
RELATIVUM GENERALE	+	+	+	+	+
Verb system					
AUX (+ COMP) + FINITE VERB	+	(+)	+	(+)	+
VOLO FUTURE	+	(+)	+	+	+
PAST FUTURE AS CONDITIONAL	+	+	+	(+)	(+)
HABEO PERFECT	+	+	(+)	(+)	–
EVIDENTIALS	–	+	+	(+)	(+)
Other					
ANALYTIC COMPARISON	(+)	+	+	+	+

Table 1. Shared grammatical innovations in the Balkans.

Notes on the twelve features chosen:

ENCLITIC ARTICLES: Instead of the classical Balkanism of "postpositive definite article", I propose this cover term for different articles taking the second position in the NP. (For discussion, see sect. 3 below.)

OBJECT REDUPLICATION: Direct and indirect objects receive head-marking by clitic pronouns attached to the verb. The actual rules are different in each language (Aronson 1997), which is why a plus sign in parentheses is not applicable here.

PREPOSITIONS INSTEAD OF CASES: A tendency away from inflectional case marking (except the vocative case). Albanian is the most difficult to assess here, since we do not know whether and when it might have had more cases; but some conclusions can be drawn by means of internal reconstruction (Asenova 1989: 58, citing Demiraj).

DATIVE / POSSESSIVE MERGER: The use of the same inflectional case marking, the same preposition, or the same series of enclitic pronouns for marking the indirect object at the verb or the possessor at a noun. Notice that this feature does not fully coincide with "dative / genitive merger" even when there is a genitive case (Tzitzilis, in press): cf. Greek *tus gráfi éna grámma káthe méra* '(s)he writes them a letter every day' and *to spíti tus* 'their house', where *tus* 'them, their' is an accusative.

GOAL / LOCATION MERGER: The same prepositions and adverbs, including the interrogative adverb 'where', are used to express both going somewhere and being somewhere.

RELATIVUM GENERALE: Relative clauses are introduced by an uninflected marker which does not distinguish number, gender, or syntactic role (the latter is often marked with a clitic pronoun at the verb). Especially the standard languages may also use an inflected pronoun at this position. Since the impact of literary traditions is difficult to assess, I have not made use of a plus sign in parentheses at this feature.

AUX (+COMP) + FINITE VERB: Modal auxiliaries are followed by a finite verb, not an infinitive. This is traditionally known as the "Balkan infinitive loss", but we do not really know what kind of an infinitive Albanian might have lost; we only know that it has grammaticalized a new infinitive, though finite complements are still widely used (Joseph 1983: 85-100).

VOLO FUTURE: The future tense is marked with an auxiliary that has grammaticalized from a verb meaning 'to want' (cf. English *will*).

PAST FUTURE AS CONDITIONAL: A past tense marking attached to the *volo* future indicates the conditional mood (for an overview, see Gołąb 1964). The past marking may be attached either to the future marker (cf. English *would*) or to the main verb.

HABEO PERFECT: A perfect (anterior) tense formed with the auxiliary 'to have' and either a past participle passive or a special perfect participle of the main verb.

EVIDENTIALS: Grammaticalized evidential distinctions (Friedman 1986, 1998; for Romani, see Matras 1995). This is a wider Eurasian areal feature (Haarmann 1970).

ANALYTIC COMPARISON: Adjectives form their comparative and superlative with particles instead of suffixes.

If we calculate the indices of Balkanization of different language groups from Table 1, giving a whole point for each plus sign and half a point for a plus sign in parentheses, we receive the following scores: Balkan Slavic 11.5 – Albanian 10.5 – Balkan Romance and Greek 9.5 – Romani 7.5 points. To be sure, the differences are small, and the exact scores are dependent on the set of features chosen, but this ranking of the languages does seem to agree with the overall impression their grammars make. Balkan Slavic is grammatically more Balkanized than the other languages; actually, Macedonian would score full a 12.0 points. Romani is less Balkanized than the other four groups. In sect. 4 below I shall discuss the possible sociolinguistic reasons for these differences.

An interesting detail is that in linguistics, "Balkanization" refers to convergent development – more or less the opposite of the notions attached to the Balkans and Balkanization in common language (cf. Todorova 1997). The peculiar combination of contact and boundary maintenance (Friedman, in press) is one of the keys for understanding the Balkan linguistic situation, at least in the past centuries when the Sprachbund took its form.

It should also be pointed out that the five language groups are partly coterritorial, and they were more so in the past. Thus, there may be no differences as to the extent to which the contacting dialects of different languages have been Balkanized. The epicentre of Balkanisms seems to be somewhere south of the lakes Ohrid and Prespa, where the Greek, Albanian, Macedonian, Aromanian, and Romani languages meet (see the map in the first volume of Weigand 1894-95), their local forms being clearly more similar to each other than the five language groups taken as wholes. In addition, Turkish and Ladino/Judezmo were spoken in the area.

What unites most grammatical Balkanisms structurally is a tendency towards explicit marking of grammatical functions with particles, prepositions, and other uninflected function words that are identifiable across the languages (cf. Hinrichs 1997: 20). The main uses of several frequent prepositions in them are also remarkably similar (Asenova 1989: 72-76). But each language realizes the parallelisms with its own material. The borrowing of grammatical morphemes is not common and neighbouring languages easily tolerate direct cross-language clash between their phonological forms in the same semantic fields: compare 'yes' : 'no' = Bulgarian /da/ : /ne/ = Greek /ne/ : /óxi/; 'and' : 'or' = Bulgarian /i/ : /íli/ = Greek /ke/ : /i/; 'my' : 'his' = Bulgarian /mi/ : /mu/ = Greek /mu/ : /tu/.

3. The Elusive Origins

According to Kopitar (1829), whom I quoted in the introduction to this paper, Albanian preserves its original linguistic form, but "Wallachian" and "Bulgarian" adopted it only after their speakers arrived in the Balkans. In the 19th century, the Balkanization of Romance and Slavic was supposed to have taken place by substratal influence, Albanian representing the structure of the original languages of the arca.

The theory of the substratal origins of the Balkanisms has now largely been abandoned. We do not know what the grammars of Thracian, Dacian, Illyrian, and other ancient languages of the Balkans looked like (Katičić 1976), which means that even in principle it would be impossible to prove the hypothesis to be correct. Moreover, the theory is directly disproved by the fact that in the Old Church Slavonic texts from the 10th century onwards, Balkan Slavic definitely does not appear as a Balkanized language, though the shift from the substratal languages into Slavic had already largely taken place; the index of OCS in Table 1 would only be 0.5. Finally, the traditional substrate theories do not explain the Balkanisms of Greek, which is known to have been spoken in the southern Balkans for more than 3,500 years.

There is, however, another version of substrate theory that must be seriously considered, namely the hypothesis that most Balkanisms are internal developments in Balkan Romance, later adopted by other languages (cf. Sandfeld 1930: 170-173). Since Romance languages are still spoken in the Balkans, some would classify this as an adstratal theory. However, owing to the low social status of Daco-Romanian in the past, and of other forms of Balkan Romance even today, only language shift of an originally Romance-speaking population would explain the diffusion of Balkanisms, and in this sense this is a substrate theory.

Gołąb (1984, 1997) argues that the high degree of Balkanization of Macedonian is due to a language shift from Aromanian into Slavic. As noted above, the geographical centre of Balkanisms on dialect maps would be in Macedonia. We also know that Balkan Romance, or Balkan Vulgar Latin, used to be the most important language of the Balkans west and north of the so-called Jireček line (Jireček 1901), and even east of it along the Via Egnatia. It is tempting to see Romance, or more specifically Aromanian, substrate as the main source of Balkanisms in this area.

There are problems in this hypothesis, though. It rests on the fact that Balkan Slavic has several features that are not typical of other Slavic languages and, Gołąb argues, are therefore likely to have been borrowed from a non-Slavic source. However, the problem is that several Balkanisms, such as the postpositive article and the loss of the infinitive, are not typical of all of Romance, either. As a result, there is nothing to prove that their source must have been in the spontaneous development of Balkan Romance.

Gołąb's Romance substrate theory does not fully explain the Balkanisms of Greek, either. The Aromanian population of Northern and Central Greece is of course known to have been larger than it is today (Weigand 1888, 1894-95; Gołąb 1984: 11). However, for demographic reasons the gradual and still on-going shift of the Aromanian population into Greek could hardly have radically changed the Greek language, whose centre of gravity was farther south. Notice that even the Slavic population in mainland Greece did not leave any significant traces in Greek, though it was presumably larger than the Romance-speaking population ever was (Vasmer 1941; cf. Weithmann 1994).

However, a case can be made for an earlier Romance, or rather Latin, influence upon Greek, through an adstratal relation in late Antiquity. Horrocks (1997: 73-78) points out some possibly Latin-influenced changes in the Greek of the time, such as the extension of finite subjunctive clauses at the expense of the infinitive, the rise of the periphrastic future, and the merger of the aorist and the synthetic perfect. But from the vantage point of other Balkan languages, such changes should still be counted as originating in Greek.

We thus come to the explanation that Greek, the most influential language among the Christian population of the Balkans, was the primary source of Balkanisms. This was Sandfeld's (1930: 213) opinion, though he admitted that at least the postpositive article must have had another source. Another frequently cited exception is the formation of the numerals from eleven to nineteen on the model "one-upon-ten" and so on; here Slavic, which is generally not seriously considered as the originator of other significant Balkanisms, is the obvious source.

Tzitzilis (in press) has recently collected lots of interesting material from Greek dialects and old written sources in an effort to show that many Balkanisms in Greek are older than has been assumed in Balkan linguistics, and that Greek, as the official language of the Byzantine Empire, would have been an obvious source of contact-induced change in other languages of the peninsula. His material pertains to such fundamental Balkanisms as the periphrastic *volo* future, the replacement of the infinitive with finite constructions, object reduplication, analytic comparison, and the merger of dative and possessive constructions. Their earlier dating in Greek makes Sandfeld's assumption of Greek primacy in building the Balkan Sprachbund more convincing.

There are, however, two fundamental shortcomings in explanations of this kind. First, Greek is the best-documented language of the Balkans, with the longest historical record; if Balkanisms are due to a typological drift that has been taking place in the area for a long time (somewhat in the spirit of Nichols 1992), the fact that a given change is attested in Greek at an early date does not show that it could not also have been attested in some other Balkan language, notably Albanian, if we had comparable records of it at our disposal. It should be remembered that nothing that we know prevents assuming an equally long prehistory in the Balkans for Albanian as for Greek.

Second, thought should be given to the fact that all Balkanisms supposed to have originated mainly in Greek are post-classical innovations in this language, too. This situation is unlikely to have arisen by chance: if Greek had indeed been the primary source of the contact-induced changes in other Balkan languages, we would expect it to have contributed old and new features alike. There is no certain example of a significant grammatical feature which has been stable in Greek ever since Antiquity and which has been borrowed by several other Balkan languages. The explanation for this fact must be that even in Greek, Balkanisms were innovations that it shared with other languages of the area to begin with, though we lack direct historical evidence for this.

The loss of the infinitive has been considered a Greek-based Balkanism par excellence. The gradual replacement of Greek infinitival constructions with subordinate clauses introduced by the final conjunction *na* < *hína* is well-documented. However, Joseph's (1983) detailed study showed that in various Balkan languages a complex interplay of contact-induced change and language-internal causes must be assumed (cf. also the survey in Asenova 1989: 150-155).

On the other hand, Greek cannot be wholly excluded when the history of the Balkan article system is described, though this is often done because Greek does not have a postposed article (neither does Romani, whose article system, at least in the Vlax dialects, is closely modelled upon Greek). Greek is the first Balkan language known to have possessed a definite article, though it was, and is, preposed. But it is also the first language known to have possessed a linking article between the head of NP and the following modifiers (e.g. *i giortés i megáles* "the-feasts-the-big" = 'the great festivals'), a phenomenon that can be connected to the linking articles in Albanian and Balkan Romance (cf. Solta 1980: 193-194). That is why the linking and postposed articles have been subsumed under the heading "enclitic article" in Table 1.

It is possible that such enclitic determinants represent a very old areal feature of the Balkans (see Hamp 1982 on possible toponymic evidence for the postposed article in the ancestor language of modern Albanian). This feature is most grammaticalized in Albanian, which has both a postposed and linking article and whose linking article does not require the NP to be definite. Romanian has both article types, too, but its linking article used with adjectives does require a definite NP. However, this is not the case with the link used in possessive constructions:

(1) *imitaţii   perfecte   ale   celor   originale*
    imitation.PL   perfect.PL.FEM   LINK.PL.FEM   DEF.PL.DAT   original.PL.FEM
    'perfect imitations of the original ones'

The *a*- link is used to introduce a second NP in the dative-possessive case, but it does not presuppose the definiteness of the preceding NP, with which it agrees. The *ce*- link agrees with the following NP, which should be definite; it is here required because the head noun that would carry the postposed article with dative-possessive marking is missing.

Balkan Slavic does not possess the linking article; moreover, its postposed article is more agglutinative than its Romance counterpart. The Slavic article can, however, attract the primary stress of the phonological word in dialects with mobile stress, which is not possible with the preposed article of Greek. In all, it seems as if Greek has borrowed part of an enclitic article system by adopting the linking use of its preposed article; this use is now obligatory when modifiers follow the head. On the other hand, Balkan Slavic has adopted a postposed article which is structurally based on a demonstrative (cf. Bulgarian *knigata* 'the book' with Polish *książka ta* 'this book') and which has an enclitic second position in the NP (Bulgarian *goljamata kniga* 'the big book').

Albanian looks most like the prototype of the Balkan article system, but it is a NA language, whereas Slavic and Greek are AN languages. Thus, every language has a unique combination of article types and NP structures, and no one (except, perhaps, Romani) is actually calquing any other. The languages seem to be participating in a common drift towards a second-position article, with different realizations in each.

I believe that the impossibility of finding a single source language for this and other grammatical Balkanisms is not due to our limited knowledge of the history of the Balkan languages taken separately; indeed, Greek and Balkan Slavic, for instance, are sufficiently documented in the relevant period. The source language simply does not exist in the traditional sense: the sociolinguistic contact situation has caused changes that would not have occurred in any of the Balkan languages by internal drift. I shall try to develop this thesis in the remaining part of the paper.

4. The Sociolinguistic Situation

During the five centuries of Ottoman rule in the Balkans, the administration of the Empire was based not on geographical or ethnic units, but upon the division of the population into religious groups (millets). The founding of nation states slowly took place during the 19th century, ending the prerequisites for linguistic convergence in the whole area. After that, contact-influenced changes have mainly concerned the numerous ethnic minorities that were left inside each country.

During Ottoman rule, there was no single lingua franca among the Christian population, which is why no large-scale unidirectional borrowing or large-scale language shift took place, though the prestige of Greek cannot be denied. Turkish was the language of the State, but not a prestigious language among the Christians. As the history of Albania and Bosnia shows, even conversion to Islam did not necessarily mean linguistic shift to Turkish. The Balkans were characterized by stable multilingualism, with stable prestige relations among the languages.

Gumperz and Wilson's (1971) classical study shows how stable multilingualism in the Indian village of Kupwar has led to radical convergence that they call "intertranslatability": a single syntactic surface structure can be filled in with words from different languages. At the grammatical level there exists a kind of blueprint for a contact language, but it has several distinct lexica, so that people are still perceived as speaking different languages. This is a compromise between intense inter-group contacts and strong in-group identities in Kupwar, and the sociolinguistic situation in the Balkans seems to have been largely similar. I find the following common conditions to be the most important:

a) Speakers of different languages live closely together, often in the same villages.
b) There is no single dominant lingua franca.
c) Speakers of each language have sufficient access to the other languages they need.
d) Native languages are important symbols of group identity.

Because of population mixture – as well as such specifically Balkan phenomena as transhumance – speakers of different languages must often communicate with each other. There is no single lingua franca they could resort to, but different multilingual strategies are adopted. Since speakers of each language have sufficient access to other languages they need in order to communicate, no pidginized varieties arise; individuals acquire various degrees of bilingualism and multilingualism.[1] The multilingual situation gradually leads to structural convergence between the languages, but as languages remain important symbols of group identity, they all retain their distinct lexica.

Ross (1996) describes some Papua New Guinea cases in which bilingualism without language shift has led to structural convergence of genetically unrelated languages. Each language has retained the inherited form of its functional morphemes, but their use is often modelled upon those of another language. In the New Guinea of the past there were no wide-spread lingua francas, but from their

---

[1] Gustav Weigend writes about the town of Monastir [= Bitola] in Macedonia 110 years ago: "Es ist klar, daß in einer Stadt mit so verschiedenen Nationalitäten auch eine große Vielsprachigkeit herrscht; das Türkische und Bulgarische [= Macedonian] ist [sic] fast gleich verbreitet, die Aromunen, wenigstens die Männer, können außer ihrer Muttersprache bulgarisch und griechisch, die meisten auch türkisch und albanisch; viele verstehen selbst das Spanische [= Ladino/Judezmo], das, wie sie wohl fühlen, viele Wörter mit ihrer Sprache gleich oder ähnlich hat. Daß in Gesellschaften zugleich mehrere Sprachen gesprochen werden, ist ganz gewöhnlich" (Weigand 1894-95, p. 6 in vol. 1).

childhood people must have been bilingual in the "emblematic", in-group language of their own ethnic group and the intergroup language used with the neighbouring villages, as is still the case today in this area.

Friedman (1997: 32-35) sees two main features in the Balkan folk ideology concerning language. The first is the identification of language and religion with ethnicity; this is the boundary-maintaining function of the language. The second is the identification of language with wealth in the sense that "the knowledge of many languages is an asset", though not all languages have the same prestige. Multilingualism is, or used to be, valued, but language shift less so.

The prerequisites for the special sociolinguistic situation in the Balkans date back at least to the Slavic and Avar invasion of the Byzantine territory, from the sixth century onwards (Vasmer 1941: 11-19; Tăpkova-Zaimova 1966; Fine 1983: 59ff.), which resulted in the weakening of the cities and central administration and the radical ruralization of society (Weithmann 1994). Later, under Ottoman rule, there were no administrative boundaries to prevent large-scale population movements and population mixtures caused by the weak and at times brutal and arbitrary local administration (Sugar 1977). Ethnic groups were associated not with territories, but with languages, religions, and even livelihoods, the Slavs being mostly farmers and many Albanians and Aromanians being transhumant shepherds. Thus, economic exchange relations presupposed much cross-linguistic communication.

The formation of nation states in the Balkans during the 19th and 20th centuries has meant the creation of new units that attempt to be as self-sufficient as possible both economically and culturally. The period of linguistic convergence in this area has ended, though some Balkanisms may in principle still spread inside each individual language owing to a typological drift called the "snowball effect" by Joseph (1983: 210-212).

Civ'jan's (1965: 14ff., 183ff.) theory of an abstract intermediary langue (jazyk-posrednik) in the Balkans is based on sociolinguistic premises that somewhat resemble those I am proposing. However, she assumes an unconscious attempt of the speaker of Balkan language A to speak in structures that would be maximally comprehensible for the speaker of another Balkan language B; Rozencvejg's (1969, 1972, 1976) model is partly similar. In my view, this theory appears too speculative. It does not explain why language A would permanently change owing to such encounters. It also presumes the existence of a special kind of Balkan "foreigner talk" that does not show much similarity to actually observed cases of foreigner talk (Romaine 1988: 72-84). I think it is safer to base assumptions on the interference phenomena that are present in every bilingual speech community (Romaine 1995: 51ff.). A strong second language of a bilingual individual may and does influence the first language even when it is used in a monolingual setting. This is in accordance with the mechanism proposed by Ross (1996: 202-206) to explain convergent change in New Guinea.

Influence through shift can nevertheless be a partial explanation for convergence. The situation was different for each language, depending on its relative social status. For the Balkanization of Romani, the language least valued by other ethnic groups, the reasons must be sought in the multilingualism of its native speakers. On the other hand, for the prestigious Greek language substratal effects may have been relatively stronger. Tsitsipis (1998) describes how hellenization is positively valued among the Albanian-speaking minority of Greece. Weigand's (1888, 1894-95) classical works abundantly testify to how a hundred years ago whole Aromanian villages saw no problems in supporting a Greek school for children and adopting the Greek literary culture. But nowhere in the Balkans can we assume language shift and concomitant substratal influence to have been the decisive factor for contact-induced change of whole languages. The main mechanism of change must have been interference phenomena in the minds of multilingual individuals.

5. Mutual Reinforcement of Change

Linguistic Balkanization does not mean straightforward simplification. Even complicated subsystems, such as the Balkan verb system with several past tenses, can be retained if there is sufficient structural overlap between the languages.

I propose that linguistic Balkanization was initiated by speakers who were bilingual or multilingual to such an extent that in their speech there were transfers not only from, but also into their native languages and who for that reason favoured features that made it easier to identify structures across languages. In language contact, such syntactic features as word order and different particles are easier to transfer from one language to another than inflectional categories are (Thomason and Kaufman 1988: 72 ff.). This is why the contact situation itself has favoured explicit syntactic marking in the Balkan languages: structural conflicts between the languages are solved analytically, by syntactic means, because cross-language identification between analytic structures is easier than between inflectional categories. Multilingual speakers may favour even such structures that were not common in any of the contacting languages to begin with (cf. Thomason and Kaufman 1988: 96).

Romaine (1988: 80-81) notes that Gumperz and Wilson's Kupwar case of "intertranslatable" languages (or "isogrammatism", Gołąb's term for the same phenomenon in the Balkans) does not resemble the relexification typical of pidgins or, as it should rather be said, of mixed languages proper (Bakker and Muysken 1995). Instead, Romaine proposes the term "re-syntactification". But at least in the Balkans, this does not mean that language A has adopted the syntax of language B; rather, all the languages were converging towards complete cross-linguistic identifiability of syntactic structures in terms of function words and word order. A complete intertranslatability or isogrammatism was of course never reached, nor will it be ever attained in the present conditions of the Balkans. But structures common to the Balkan languages are far more numerous than many nationalistically minded local linguists are willing to admit (Friedman 1997).

By the term "mutual reinforcement of change" I want to emphasize that the origins of most Balkanisms cannot be found in the internal drift of any of the languages of the Sprachbund. None of them would have developed those features outside the contact situation, since it is this situation itself that favoured certain grammatical structures (Friedman, in press, speaks of "interactive interference"). In this scenario, the notions of source language and target language, thought to be necessary in describing contact-induced change, become relative or even super-fluous.

Notice that at any rate, finding the absolute origins of an areal feature would hardly count as an explanation for it. The earliest attestation of *hína* instead of an infinitival complement does not explain why it gained so much ground in Greek – still less does it explain why the other Balkan languages borrowed it, if it indeed first appeared in Greek. In fact, all the languages of the area have produced countless linguistic changes over the centuries, but only some of these became features of the Sprachbund. We should ask why some changes were more successful than others and what the sociolinguistic situation was like that made them successful. This is a kind of evolutionary model in which the particular contact situation forms the environment to which certain mutations are better adapted than others.

In terms of pidgin and creole linguistics we can perhaps say that although no pidgins or creoles arose in the Balkans, a blueprint existed for a contact language that was realized with different lexica in the concrete languages that participated in a common areal drift.

The particular cross-linguistic contacts in the Balkans have seldom been symmetrical, and despite numerous changes in the status and prestige of particular languages (Friedman 1977: 33-35) the overall power relations among them have not changed radically over the centuries. In terms of prestige, Greek has always been close to the top, while Romani has been near the bottom ever since its speakers first arrived in the Balkans in the 13th century (Hancock 1995: 18). It is interesting to note that in Table 1, Greek and Romani are among the less Balkanized languages. For Romani, its shorter age as a Balkan language may be part of the explanation, but both Romani and Greek were characterized by the least amount of mutual bilingualism with other languages. Romani speakers were multilingual,[2] but the speakers of other languages did not learn Romani. Greek was

---

[2] Until recently, Balkan scholars have mostly neglected the Roma, but cf.: "Unter den umherwandernden Zigeunern [in Berat, Albania], wie Kesselflickern, Schmieden, Bärentreibern findet man

learnt by many speakers of other languages and a certain amount of language shift took place, but its speakers were in turn less motivated to learn other languages. On the other hand, the most Balkanized languages, viz. Macedonian, Bulgarian, Albanian, and Aromanian were near the middle of the prestige scale. Their speakers learnt Greek, but there was also a fair amount of mutual multilingualism among them. The most Balkanized language, Macedonian, was not only geographically in the centre, but also socially in the middle. There is a Macedonian saying, *nie sme krotok narod* 'we are meek people' (Friedman, p.c.). In Balkan conditions, the Slavic Macedonians have been relatively pragmatic in their relations with other ethnic groups. They have also borrowed grammatical features from other languages, to which a certain amount of substratal influence of Aromanian can be added. This is an example of the kind of historical sociolinguistics that Balkan linguistics is in need of.[3]

University of Helsinki

REFERENCES

Arends, Jacques, Pieter Muysken, and Norval Smith (eds.)
1995   *Pidgins and creoles: An introduction* (*Creole Language Library* 15). Amsterdam-Philadelphia: John Benjamins.
Aronson, Howard I.
1997   "Transitivity, reduplication, and clitics in the Balkan languages", *Balkanistica* 10, 20-45.
Asenova, Petja
1989   *Balkansko ezikoznanie: Osnovni problemi na balkanskija ezikov săjuz*. Sofija: Nauka i izkustvo.
Bakker, Peter, and Pieter Muysken
1995   "Mixed languages and language intertwining", pp. 41-52 in Arends et al. (eds.) 1995.
Civ'jan, T[at'jana] V[ladimirovna]
1965   *Imja suščestvitel'noe v balkanskix jazykax. K strukturo-tipologičeskoj xarakteristike balkanskogo jazykovogo sojuza*. Moskva: Nauka
1979   *Sintaksičeskaja struktura balkanskogo jazykovogo sojuza*. Moskva: Nauka.
1990   *Lingvističeskie osnovy balkanskoj modeli mira*. Moskva: Nauka.
Fine, John V. A., Jr.
1983   *The early medieval Balkans: A critical survey from the sixth to the late twelfth century*. Ann Arbor: The University of Michigan Press.

---

viele, die, aus Rumänien stammend, sich auch der rumänischen Sprache als Muttersprache bedienen, während die Einheimischen außer der Zigeunersprache meist aller Balkansprachen mächtig sind" (Weigand 1894-95, p. 78 in vol. 1).

[3] Victor Friedman, Johanna Nichols, Juhani Nuorluoto, and Sarah Thomason read earlier versions of this paper and suggested several improvements.

1987   *The late medieval Balkans: A critical survey from the late twelfth century to the Ottoman conquest.* Ann Arbor: The University of Michigan Press.
Friedman, Victor A.
1986   "Evidentiality in the Balkans: Bulgarian, Macedonian, and Albanian", in: Wallace Chafe and Johanna Nichols (eds.), *Evidentiality: The linguistic coding of epistemology*, 168-187. Norwood, New Jersey: Ablex.
1997   "One grammar, three lexicons: Ideological overtones and underpinnings in the Balkan *Sprachbund*", in: *Papers from the Panels on Linguistic Ideologies in Contact [...]*, 23-44. Chicago, Illinois: Chicago Linguistic Society.
1998   "The grammatical expression of presumption and related concepts in Balkan Slavic and Balkan Romance", in: Robert A. Maguire and Alan Timberlake (eds.), *American contributions to the Twelfth International Congress of Slavists: Literature. Linguistics. Poetics*, 392-406. Slavica.
(in press)   "Romani in the Balkan linguistic league", to appear in: *Synchrony and diachrony: Proceedings of an International Conference on Balkan linguistics 1997.* University of Thessaloniki.
Gołąb, Zbigniew
1964   *Conditionalis typu bałkańskiego w językach południowosłowiańskich, ze szczególnym uwzględnieniem macedońskiego (Polska Akademia Nauk, Oddział w Krakowie, Prace Komisji Językoznawstwa* 2). Wrocław-Kraków-Warszawa.
1984   *The Arumanian dialect of Kruševo in SR Macedonia, SFR Yugoslavia.* Skopje: Macedonian Academy of Sciences and Arts, Section of Linguistics and Literary Sciences.
1990   "The ethnic background and internal linguistic mechanism of the so-called Balkanization of Macedonian", *Balkanistica* 10, 13-19.
Gumperz, John J., and Robert Wilson
1971   "Convergence and creolization: A case from the Indo-Aryan / Dravidian border in India", in: Dell Hymes (ed.), *Pidginization and creolization of languges*, 151-167. Cambridge: Cambridge University Press.
Haarmann, Harald
1970   *Die indirekte Erlebnisform als grammatische Kategorie. Eine eurasische Isoglosse (Veröffentlichungen der Societas Uralo-Altaica* 2). Wiesbaden: Otto Harrassowitz.
Hamp, Eric P.
1982   "The oldest Albanian syntagma", *Balkansko ezikoznanie – Linguistique balkanique* 25, 77-79.
Hancock, Ian
1995   *A handbook of Vlax Romani.* Columbus, Ohio: Slavica Publishers.
Hinrichs, Uwe
1997   "Südslavische Sprachwissenschaft und Südosteuropa-Linguistik", *Zeitschrift für Balkanologie* 33: 1, 9-25.
Horrocks, Geoffrey
1997   *Greek: A history of the language and its speakers (Longman Linguistics Library).* London-New York: Longman.
Hymes, Dell
1971   "Introduction [to Sect. III]", in: Dell Hymes (ed.), *Pidginization and creolization of languges*, 65-90. Cambridge: Cambridge University Press.
Jireček, Konstantin
1901   *Die Romanen in den Städten Dalmatiens während des Mittelalters.* Wien.

Joseph, Brian D.
1983   *The synchrony and diachrony of the Balkan infinitive. A study in areal, general, and historical linguistics (Cambridge Studies in Linguistics, supplementary volume).* Cambridge: Cambridge University Press.

Katičić, Radoslav
1976   *Ancient Languages of the Balkans* 1-2 (*Trends in Linguistics, State-of-the-Art Reports* 4). The Hague-Paris: Mouton.

Katsánis, N., and K. Ntínas
1990   *Grammatikí tis Koinís Koutsovlachikis (Archeío Koutsovlachikón Meletón* 1). Thessaloníki.

[Kopitar, Jernej.] K.
1829   "Albanische, walachische u. bulgarische Sprache", *Jahrbücher der Literatur* (Wien) 46, 59-106.

Lindstedt, Jouko
1998a   "Torlak narrative systems as illustrated by Olaf Broch's material", in: J.I. Bjørnflaten, G. Kjetsaa, and T. Mathiassen (eds.), *A centenary of Slavic studies in Norway: The Olaf Broch Symposium*, 178-185. Olso: The Norwegian Academy of Science and Letters.

1998b   "On the Balkan linguistic type", *Studia Slavica Finlandensia* 15, 91-103.

Matras, Yaron
1995   "Verb evidentials and their discourse function in Vlach Romani narratives", pp. 95-123 in Matras (ed.) 1995.

Matras, Yaron (ed.)
1995   *Romani in contact: The history, structure and sociology of language (Amsterdam Studies in the Theory and History of Linguistic Science* IV: 126). Amsterdam-Philadelphia: John Benjamins.

Nichols, Johanna
1992   *Linguistic diversity in space and time.* Chicago-London: The University of Chicago Press.

1994 (MS)   *Europe as a linguistic area.*

Romaine, Suzanne
1988   *Pidgin and creole languages.* London-New York: Longman.

1995   *Bilingualism.* Oxford-Cambridge: Blackwell (2nd edition; 1st edition 1989).

Ross, Malcolm D.
1996   "Contact-induced change and the comparative method: Cases from Papua New Guinea", in: Mark Durie and Malcolm Ross (eds.), *The comparative method reviewed*, 180-217. New York-Oxford: Oxford University Press.

Rozencvejg, Viktor Jul'evič
1969   "Infinitivnye konstrukcii i balkanskie jazykovye kontakti", *Slavia* 38, 189-209.

1972   *Jazykovye kontakty: Lingvističeskaja problematika.* Leningrad: Nauka.

1976   *Linguistic interference and convergent change (Janua Linguarum*, Series Maior 99). The Hague-Paris: Mouton.

Sandfeld, Kristian
1926   *Balkanfilologien. En oversigt over dens resultater og problemer.* København: Bianco Lunos.

1930   *Linguistique balkanique. Problèmes et résultats (Collection linguistique publiée par la Société de Linguistique de Paris* 31). Paris: Klincksieck (noveau tirage 1968).

Schaller, Helmut Wilhelm
1975   *Die Balkansprachen: Eine Einführung in die Balkanphilologie.* Heidelberg: Carl Winter.
Solta, Georg Renatus
1980   *Einführung in die Balkanlinguistik mit besonderer Berücksichtigung des Substrats und des Balkanlateinischen.* Darmstadt: Wissenschaftliche Buchgesellschaft.
Sugar, Peter F.
1977   *Southeastern Europe under Ottoman rule, 1354-1804 (A History of East Central Europe* 5). Seattle-London: University of Washington Press.
Tăpkova-Zaimova, Vasilka
1966   *Našestvija i etničeski promeni na Balkanite prez VI-VII v.* Sofija: Izdatelstvo na Bălgarskata akademija na naukite.
Thomason, Sarah Grey, and Terence Kaufman
1988   *Language contact, creolization, and genetic linguistics.* Berkeley: University of California Press.
Todorova, Maria
1997   *Imagining the Balkans.* New York-Oxford: Oxford University Press.
Tsitsipis, Lukas D.
1998   *A linguistic anthropology of praxis and language shift: Arvanitika (Albanian) and Greek in contact (Oxford Studies in Language Contact).* Oxford: Clarendon Press.
Tutunović, Drita
1992   *Diksionario ladino serbo. Ladino srpski rečnik.* Beograd: Nova.
Tzitzilis, Christos
(in press)   "Das Mittelgriechische im Lichte der Balkanlinguistik", to appear in: *Synchrony and diachrony: Proceedings of an International Conference on Balkan linguistics 1997.* University of Thessaloniki.
Vasmer, Max
1941   *Die Slaven in Griechenland (Abhandlungen der Preußischen Akademie der Wissenschaften,* Jahrgang 1941, *Philosophisch-historische Klasse* 12). Berlin: Verlag der Akademie der Wissenschaften.
Weigand, Gustav
1888   *Die Sprache der Olympo-Walachen nebst einer Einleitung über Land und Leute.* Leipzig: Johann Ambrosius Barth. (Reprint: Vivliopoleio Dionysiou Noti Karavia, Athina 1988.)
1894-95   *Die Aromunen: Ethnographisch-philologisch-historische Untersuchungen über das Volk der sogenannten Makedo-Romanen oder Zinzaren* I-II. Leipzig: Johann Ambrosius Barth (Arthur Meiner).
Weithmann, Michael W.
1994   "Interdisziplinäre Diskrepanzen in der 'Slavenfrage' Griechenlands", *Zeitschrift für Balkanologie* 30: 1, 85-111.

Languages in Contact, edited by D.G. Gilbers, J. Nerbonne, and J. Schaeken (= *Studies in Slavic and General Linguistics*, vol. 28), 247-261. Amsterdam - Atlanta, GA: Rodopi, 2000.

CREOLE GENESIS: EVIDENCE FROM WEST AFRICAN L2 FRENCH

PATRICK-ANDRÉ MATHER

1. Introduction

A pidgin is traditionally defined as a simple code which "evolves as a response to a limited need for communication" and which encodes only "the most basic functions of communication (...) the result being impoverished or absent morphology (...) limited lexical stock; a constrained number of adpositions; non-expression of the copula; and lack of sentential embedding" (Hymes 1971: 65-90). Creoles were long thought to be nativized pidgins that had become increasingly complex to meet all the requirements of a native language.

There are, of course, many examples of pidgins corresponding to the general definition above: Russenorsk and Chinese Pidgin English are two well-documented cases, and there are others. However, if one looks at the history of European-lexifier creoles, in particular the exogenous varieties spoken today in the Caribbean and Indian Ocean, there is little direct evidence of a pidgin stage in the development of these languages. In addition to the absence of any written attestation of Pidgin English or Pidgin French which may have been spoken on European plantation colonies in the 17th century, Chaudenson (1979, 1995), Singler (1996) and others have shown that, at least in French plantation colonies, the African/European ratio in the early stages of colonization was very low, and that both groups lived in close contact on isolated homesteads, before the shift to large-scale sugar plantations required the import of massive numbers of slaves by the early 18th century. Finally, some authors have shown (e.g., Chaudenson 1981) that the earliest recorded creole texts are much closer to their respective European lexifier texts, than contemporary creoles.

The evidence would indicate that, in many European plantation colonies, there never was a pidgin stage per se, but rather the gradual development of increasingly basilectal varieties of French or English, based on increasingly divergent L2 interlanguage varieties of the lexifier language spoken by successive waves of African slaves. In a sense, one could say that creolization in these circumstances is like second language acquisition in reverse, i.e., the successive interlanguage stages are increasingly "off-target".[1] While it is probably true that the earliest creole varieties spoken in the 17th century were L2 varieties, they were only "pidgins" in the sense that they were spoken as a second language, not because of their linguistic structure.

Three kinds of evidence help support the SLA/gradualist model of creole genesis. First, current research in second language acquisition has yielded valuable insights into the mechanisms of creolization, in particular L1 transfer. Second, case studies on West African L2 French and other interlanguages can give us an idea of the initial stages of creolization. Third, the creole continua that exist to this day on several former plantation colonies, including Réunion and Martinique, may very well represent a survival of the successive stages of creole genesis in the 17th and 18th centuries, with the acrolectal varieties being the oldest, and the mesolectal and basilectal varieties representing more recent developments.

2. The case for gradual creolization

Chaudenson (1989, 1995) provides sociohistorical evidence that creolization only occurred after the shift from small-scale farms to large-scale sugar plantations, which significantly reduced access by slaves to the European language. Furthermore, Singler (1996) provides detailed historical and demographic evidence showing that creolization in Haiti and Martinique must have taken at least three generations, based on the fact that Haitian is a more radical creole than Martinican, even though during the first half century of colonization there was a higher proportion of Africans in Martinique than in Haiti. In addition, based on the ethnolinguistic origin of the African slaves and the slow rate of nativization, Arends (1995a) argues that creolization in Surinam must have spread over as much as 100 years as a result of sustained substratum interference from speakers of Gbe and Kikongo languages. The demographic evidence provided by Singler (1996) for Martinique and Arends (1995a) for Surinam finds further support in Baker's (1995) linguistic analysis of 12 morphosyntactic features found in a variety of pidgins and creoles, including Martinican (Antillais), Mauritian and Sranan. In particular, he calculates the following rates of development starting from the initial settlement of the colonies: 56 years for Antillais, 84 years for Mauritian and 92 years for Sranan, based on the first attestation of seven major creole features.

In fact, the sociohistorical, demographic, ethnolinguistic and linguistic evidence summarized here, based on independent studies of several English and French plantation creoles, all point to the same conclusion: most plantation creoles emerged over several generations as successive waves of African slaves acquired

---

[1] If one considers the European lexifier to be the target. Some have argued (e.g., Baker 1990) that the creators of creoles never really had the superstrate as a target.

increasingly basilectal varieties of, and introduced new substratum features into, the emerging contact languages. As such, contrary to the bioprogram hypothesis, creolization is mainly a process of second language acquisition by adults, and it is a gradual, rather than sudden process, spanning over a period of 50 to 100 years, depending on the specific demographic history of each plantation colony. Given that during the formative years of creole genesis, African-born slaves outnumbered locally born slaves, it is reasonable to assume that the former introduced substratum features into the emerging contact language. Evidence from Singler (1996) and Arends (1995a) suggests that the new slaves were reasonably homogenous linguistically, which further increases the likelihood of substratum interference.

The linguistic evidence provided by Lefebvre (1986, 1998b) for Haitian Creole, far from disconfirming the gradualist hypothesis, reinforces it since this evidence supports the hypothesis that creolization was largely done by adult speakers of West African languages, and that these speakers introduced many features of their respective L1s into the emerging creoles. Even if one disagrees with the mechanism of relexification (which is indeed highly controversial), the detailed linguistic comparison in Lefebvre (1986, 1998a, 1998b) leaves little doubt about the major role played by substratum languages in the genesis of Haitian. This of course does not rule out other SLA strategies, including simplification and morphological leveling, and in some cases structures can be accounted for by various factors, all of which involve L2 acquisition. In the following section, I will provide evidence that many creole features are also attested in L2 varieties of European languages, in particular in West African L2 French.

3. Features found in creoles and in L2 varieties of European languages

3.1 Within the noun phrase

The position of the specifier, adjectives and complements within the noun phrase is a very salient syntactic feature, and is readily identifiable in both creoles and in L2 varieties of European languages.

As noted by Lefebvre (1998: 94), the definite article is post-nominal in both Haitian and FonGbe:

(1)   *M*   *manje*   *krab*   ***la***   (Haitian Creole)
(2)   *N*   *du*   *ason*   ***o***   (FonGbe)
     I   eat   crab   Det
     'I ate the crab (in question/that we know of)'

Interestingly, in the L2 French of speakers of Ewe (a language spoken in southern Togo and closely related to FonGbe), there are also many examples of post-posed determiners:

(3)   *nyɔnu - à*   (Ewe; Lafage 1985: 242)
        woman - the(SING)

(4)   *nyɔnu - wo*
        woman - the(PLUR)

(5)   *N'y a qu'à pousser auto-là*   (L2 French, L1 Ewe; Lafage 1985: 409)
        'All you need to do is to push the car'

It should be noted that, in Ewe, the plural marker *wò* is homophonous with the 3rd person plural pronoun. The same is true for the plural marker *yo* in Haitian, suggesting transfer from the West African substrate:

(6)   *Jina ap   sèvi-yo*
        Jina PROG   serve them
        'Jina is serving them'

(7)   *Tab-yo*
        'The tables'

In standard French, by contrast, the article precedes the noun (compare with example 5):

(8)   *Il n'y a qu'à pousser l'auto*

According to Lafage (1985: 251), "*l'article français n'a pas véritablement d'équivalent en éwé*", in particular because of the absence of an indefinite article. However, there is a post-posed, emphatic definite particle (*-o* in Fon, *-à* in Ewe), as we saw above, as well as a post-nominal plural marker, *wo* (Ewe). Note that one of the variants of *-la* in Haitian, *-a*, is homophonous with its Ewe counterpart.

Given that articles are always postponed in Ewe and Fon, and that indefiniteness in both languages is usually expressed by a bare noun, Ewe learners of French tend to omit the article, as in the following examples (Lafage 1985: 256):

(9)   *C'est pas poulet*   Standard French: *C'est pas **un** poulet*
        It is not   chicken

(10)   *Il a tué pintade*   Standard French: *Il a tué **une** pintade*
        He has killed guinea-fowl

(11)   *Donner cadeau*   Standard French: *Donner **un** cadeau*
        Give   present

(12)   *Faire effort*   Standard French: *Faire **un** effort*
        Make   effort

In Standard French, most examples above take a preposed indefinite article. This interference feature of West African L2 French is also found in Haitian, since according to Lefebvre (1986: 293) there is no indefinite article in Haitian:

(13) *da*   *o*   (Fon)
      sepa   *a*   (Haitian)
      snake   the   [+definite]

(14) *da*   (Fon)
      sepa   (Haitian)
      snake   (generic or [- definite])

While it is true that the French demonstrative *là* can be suffixed to a noun (especially in overseas French varieties like Quebec French), it must be used in addition to the pre-posed definite article, and it has a demonstrative meaning which is absent in both Haitian, FonGbe and in the L2 French example above. This suggests that the position of the specifier in the L1 can be transferred into the L2 interlanguage, as evidenced by the Haitian and L2 French data. Further evidence is found in Lafage (1985: 409) who provides examples of numerals following the noun (as they do in Ewe, and contrary to the French order):

(15) *J'ai frères **quatre***   Standard French: *J'ai **quatre** frères*
      I have brothers four   (Lafage 1985: 409)

(16) *Y en a chien **deux***   Standard French: *Il y a **deux** chiens*
      There are dog   two   (Lafage 1985: 417)

Ewe and Fon do not have an indefinite article, indefiniteness being expressed by a bare noun. The post-posed definite article in Ewe is translated by Lafage (1985) as 'the (person/thing) in question', so it has an emphatic meaning not found in the English or French definite article. It is worth noting that, in all French Caribbean creoles, the definite article is postposed (D'Ans 1968: 115; Bernabé 1983: 18), whereas the indefinite article, **when present**, is preposed and seems to have been inherited from French, as in the following examples from Haitian:

(17) *nu tab*
      'a table'

(18) *tab la*
      'the table'

(19) *nu pje tab*   (D'Ans 1968: 115)
      'a table foot'

(20) *Man konnet **an** moun ki ka rété Chelchie*   (Bernabé 1983: 18)
      'I know a person who lives in Schoelcher'

In addition to articles, Lafage found other examples of post-posed determiners in the L2 French of L1 Ewe speakers, including possessive pronouns:

(21) *Père-**lui** c'est mort*   Standard French: ***Son** père est mort*
      Father-him it's dead   (Lafage 1985: 417; L2 French, L1 Ewe)
      'His father is dead'

(22) *Père-**moi***   Standard French: ***Mon** père*
      Father-me   (Lafage 1985: 411)
      'My father'

As shown in the two examples above, instead of using the French preposed possessive pronoun (*mon, ton, son...*), L1 Ewe speakers post-pose the 3rd person singular pronoun to express possession. What is striking here is that this is exactly the pattern found in several French-based creoles, including Haitian. According to Lefebvre (1986: 131), "in nominal structures, personal pronouns are used to indicate possession":

(23) *Liv*   ***mwen***   /u   /li   /....   /yo   (Haitian; ibid.: 131)
      Book   I   /you   /he   /...   /they
      'My / your / his / ... / their book'

(24) *Liv*   ***li***   *yo*   (Haitian; ibid.: 131)
      Book   he   PL
      'His books'

In Ewe, Fon and Haitian, proximity and distance are expressed through suffixed demonstrative pronouns:

(25) *Dèví - ya sè nú*   (Ewe; Lafage 1985)
      Child-this heard thing
      'This child heard'

(26) *Dèvi- ma mé - sè nú ò*   (Ewe; Lafage 1985)
      Child-that NEG heard NEG
      'That child did not hear'

(27) *àso   é   lo   léé*   (Fon)   (Lefebvre 1986: 293)
      krab   sa   a   yo   (Haitian)
      Crab   Dem Det Pl
      'These crabs'

Ewe speakers of French tend to avoid pre-posed French demonstrative determiners, and instead combine a determiner with a demonstrative pronoun, following Ewe and Fon patterns:

(28) *Appelle les enfants ceux-ci*   Standard French: *Appelle ces enfants-ci*
      Call   the children here/these

(29) *Appelle les enfants ceux-là*   Standard French: *Appelle ces enfants-là*
      Call   the children there/those   (Lafage 1985)

3.2 Within the verb phrase

Lafage (1985: 417) notes that the order of constituents in L2 French in Togo closely follows the strict word order of the L1, Ewe: "*L'ordre des mots est généralement stable. C'est celui de l'éwé...: SVO, que l'objet soit un nom ou un pronom*". Here is the linear order of personal pronouns in Ewe, according to Lafage (1985: 290):

Subj. pronoun   Verb   1st compl. pronoun   '*nà*'   2nd compl. pron.

This is illustrated by the following examples of L2 French, influenced by the strict Ewe SVO order:

(30) *La femme a reproché **lui***   Standard French: *La femme l'a grondé*
      The woman has reproached him (Lafage 1985: 417)

(31) *On a volé **lui** tout*   Standard French: *On **lui** a tout volé*
      One has stolen him everything (Lafage 1985: 413)
      'Everything was stolen from him'

In French, while complements follow the verb when they are full NPs, pronominal complements are pre-verbal clitics:

(32) *La femme **lui** a reproché (quelque chose)*
      The woman him has reproached (something)

Again, French-based creoles follow the strict SVO pattern found in both West African substrata and in L2 French in Togo, i.e. with full NPs, strong personal pronouns and even weak personal pronouns, as in Haitian:

(33) *l   wè   l*   (Haitian; Koopman 1986: 237)
      3 sg. saw   3 sg.
      'He saw himself'

(34) *Mari pòte l / li / ti-mounn   nan*   (Haitian; Lefebvre 1998b: 152)
      Mary carry him/him/child   DET
      'Mary carried him / the child'

The "misplacement" of object pronouns in L2 French is not limited to West African French: Véronique (1984: 207-208) also noted this type of error in both oral and written data produced by North African learners of French (Arabic L1):

(35)   *J'ai **lui** raconté*   Standard French: *Je **lui** ai raconté*
        I have him told
        'I told him'

(36)   *Nous avons **le** porter*   Standard French: *Nous **l'**avons porté*
        We have   him carried
        'We carried him'

(37)   *Les animaux n'ont pas **me** manger*
        The animals   have not   me   eaten
        'The animals did not eat me'
        Standard French: *Les animaux ne **m'**ont pas mangé*

(38)   *Il a vu   **lui** tout de suite*   Standard French: *Il **l'**a vu tout de suite*
        He has seen   him right away
        'He saw him right away'

(39)   *Il licencie **nous** sans préavis*
        He fired us without notice
        Standard French: *Il **nous** licencie sans préavis*

(40)   *J'attaque **lui***   Standard French: *Je **l'**attaque*
        I attack him

Note that all examples above would be grammatical in Standard French if the pronoun were a full NP. In other words, L2 learners of French do not automatically cliticize pronouns onto the verb, placing them instead in the canonical, postverbal object position.

Zobl (1980) showed that French learners of English never place pronouns before the verb (**I her see*), but English learners of French often place pronoun after V: **Je vois elle*. The reason is that the pre-verbal positioning of a pronoun is marked, and French speakers don't transfer it into English. Thus, the French L2 and creole patterns may represent an unmarked UG option, rather than L1 transfer, though again both may be complementary.

Lefebvre (1998a) has shown that, in addition to TMA particles, the heads of the intermediate phrases (above VP) in Haitian creole can be filled by determiners, the very same ones found in the noun phrase. Lefebvre (1998a) concludes that, in both Haitian and FonGbe, determiners are multifunctional heads which can appear as the heads of several functional category projections, namely DP (determiner phrase), MoodP (mood phrase), TP (tense phrase) and AspP (aspect phrase). Furthermore, the determiner is post-nominal in both Haitian and FonGbe, so it always appears at the end of the phrase, whether an NP, a TP, etc. Clausal determiners do not exist in European languages, but are present in both Haitian Creole and in several West African languages (including FonGbe and Ewe), which provides a strong case for L1 transfer. Indeed, "in both Haitian and Fon-Gbe, the determiner also plays a central role in the structure of simple clauses" (Lefebvre 1998a: 95). There is also evidence of clausal determiners in West African L2 French. One possible example is the *là*, which Lafage calls a phrasal article: "*Le là...joue en français local un rôle assez difficile à déterminer auquel nous attribuons la dénomination approximative d'article de phrase*".

(41)   *Son   argent   n'a   pas   suffi   **là***   (Lafage 1985: 407)
      His   money   Aux   Neg   suffice   Det
      'His money was not enough'

3.3 The absence of copula

The absence of copula is often cited as a characteristic feature of pidgins and creoles (e.g. Bickerton 1981: chapter 2), especially the most basilectal varieties. For example, Bickerton (1975) shows that speakers of basilectal Guyanese creole start with zero forms, and only introduce the copula in the mesolect. Though Bickerton does not attribute the absence of the copula to an African substrate, Holm (1984) argues that the zero forms of the copula do have their origins in African substrata, and that Black English for instance has inherited an African pattern from creoles where the following predicate determines the form (and presence or absence) of the copula. For example, the presence or absence of the copula may depend on whether it is followed by a **predicate noun** (equative copula), a **predicate adjective**, a **locative** or a progressive form. In Hawaiian English Creole, the copula is only present in decreolized varieties, so that both forms exist as alternatives:

(42)   *mai dada stei/Ø in da haus*   (Romaine 1988: 172)
      'My mother is in the house'

It should be noted here that *stei* is the copula only for locatives (as well as being the nonpunctual aspect marker), and is used in basilectal varieties along with zero copula.

In Haitian Creole (which consists of a basilect, with no mesolectal or acrolectal varieties), no copula is used with **locatives** or **predicate adjectives**, as shown in the following examples:

(43)   *Koku   aba   tab   la*   (Lefebvre 1986: 287)
      Koku   under   table   Det
      'Koku is under the table'

(44)   *Silvya   nan   klas   la*   (Savain 1993: 76)
      Sylvia   in   classroom   Det
      'Sylvia is in the classroom'

(45)   *Jina ansent*   (Savain 1993: 75)
        Jina   pregnant
        'Jina is pregnant'

(46)   *Eliza bel   bel*   (Bernabé 1983: 187)
        Eliza   pretty   pretty
        'Eliza is very pretty'

However, with a **predicate noun**, a copula is used (*se*, from French *c'est*) if the NP has a determiner, though not with a bare noun:

(47)   *Se yon doktè*   (Savain 1993: 75)
        It's a doctor

(48)   *Pyè sé an doktè*   (Guadeloupean; Bernabé 1983: 104)
        Pierre is a doctor

(49)   *Pyè doktè*   (Bernabé 1983: 105)
        Pierre doctor

In Ewe, most adjectives are reduplicated verbal roots, and no copula is used with predicate adjectives (Lafage 1985: 270), just as in Haitian. Thus, the sentence

(50)   *ati lolo*
        tree big

has two possible interpretations: 'the big tree', or 'the tree is big', depending on the context of the utterance. Presumably, in the first case it is simply an NP. whereas in the second we have a sentence with a null copula.

Here is an other example of a zero equative copula in Ewe:

(51)   *nyɔnu-à lolo*   (Lafage 1985: 355)
        woman-this fat

In FonGbe, a language related to Ewe, there is a copula for locative predicates, contrary to Haitian:

(52)   *Koku do   tavo   o   glwe*
        Koku Cop.   table Det. under
        'Koku is under the table'

The absence of a copula with attributive predicates is also found in some examples of oral L2 French in Togo, suggesting Ewe L1 interference (although it may equally be attributed to simplification):

(53) *Lui grand*   (Lafage 1985: 270)
      him big
      'He is big'

(54) *Ça, gâté*   (Lafage 1985: 270)
      that rotten
      'That is rotten'

(55) *Koffi maigre avec une courte taille*   (Lafage 1985: 355)
      Koffi skinny with a   short height
      'Koffi is skinny and short'

3.4 Reduplication

Many languages use reduplication to modify the meaning of a particular word, for example to intensify the meaning of adjectives and adverbs, as in the following examples from Ewe and West African L2 French:

(56) *É-zo   blewu-blewu*   (Ewe; Lafage 1985)
      He walked softly-softly
      'He walked very softly'

(57) *Il m'a giflé bien-bien*   (L2 French; Lafage 1985)
      He me slapped well-well
      'He slapped me hard'

(58) *Il est venu vite-vite*   (L2 French; Lafage 1985: 106)
      He came   quickly-quickly

(59) *Il m'a battu bien-bien*   (L2 French; Lafage 1985: 106)
      He beat me   well-well

Lafage (1985: 106) recognizes the influence of the Ewe substrate in these constructions: "*Quand à la tendance métropolitaine du redoublement de l'adverbe de quantité dans l'expression superlative, elle est localement modifiée en fonction d'un schéma de l'éwé*". Not surprisingly, reduplication of the adjective is also common in French-based creoles claimed to have a strong Kwa substrate, as in the following examples from Haitian:

(60) *Eliza bel bel*   (Bernabé 1983: 187)
      'Eliza is very beautiful'

(61) *Eliza bel bel bel bel*   (Bernabé 1983: 187)

There are also examples of reduplication in L2 varieties of English, in particular South African Indian English:

(62)   *Waiting-waiting we got so fed up*

(63)   *I'm running-running, but I can't catch him*   (Mesthrie 1992: 53)

Interestingly, Mesthrie (1992: 159) notes that the use of reduplication has spread from Dravidian speakers (whose L1s have reduplication) to Indic speakers (whose L1s have no reduplication), which strengthens the case of substratum influence, since speakers of L1s with no reduplication do not independently introduce such constructions in their L2.

4. The mystery of TMA markers

In this paper, I have argued that many of the features found in French lexifier plantation creoles have been shown to occur in L2 French and other interlanguages, as a result of L1 transfer or other SLA strategies, including the position of specifiers and adjectives within the noun phrase, the position of verbs, pronouns and full NP complements within the verb phrase, serial verb constructions, copula deletion, reduplication of adjectives, absence of gender marking and pre-verbal negation. The most notable absence is the tense-mood-aspect markers found in virtually all plantation creoles: there is very little evidence of TMA markers in any French or other European interlanguage variety. How can this be accounted for?

We know that verbal inflection is often the first casualty in the initial stages of second language acquisition. If auxiliaries and modals lost their agreement features in the initial stages of creolization, then it is conceivable that they were re-interpreted as invariant verbal particles. It would seem to be the case for past markers such as *te* in Reunionese and other French creoles. Similarly, if periphrastic verb constructions such as *je suis après* are reduced to *apr(e)*, then their verbal origin cannot be retrieved by learners of creoles. But again, why is there little evidence of TMA markers in any L2 varieties of European lexifiers? Following DeGraff (1999a) and Lightfoot (1999a, 1999b), I would argue that the I-grammar of a language is recreated in the minds of each new generation of speakers, and that children acquiring a language create a grammar based on the input. Perhaps it is children who "created" the TMA markers found in most plantation creoles, as they interpreted their parents' inflectionless auxiliaries and modals as bare verbal markers. After all, even though it is probably adults who introduced most grammatical features into the incipient creoles, children too may have played a role, and TMA markers may be a case in point. Furthermore, given that substratum languages were probably spoken for some time before being replaced by the creoles, the first generations of children were bilingual, so they may also have introduced some substratum features into the incipient creoles.

As Lefebvre (1998b: 113) points out, the phonetic forms of Haitian TMA markers are derived from French periphrastic constructions. As for Haitian, these periphrastic constructions can be used to encode tense, mood or aspect as illustrated in the examples below from Lefebvre (1998b: 113):

(64)   *Jean va manger*
       'John will eat (in the near future)' (see Haitian indefinite future marker *a-va*)

(65)   *Jean est pour partir*
       'John is about to go' (see Haitian subjunctive marker *pou*)

(66)   *Jean est après manger*
       'John is eating' (see Haitian imperfective marker *ap*)

(67)   *Jean a été malade*
       'John has been sick' (see Haitian past marker *te*)

Chaudenson (1995) sees this as evidence that Haitian TMA markers are derived from colloquial French periphrastic constructions, rather than from FonGbe TMA markers. Indeed, the French constructions do appear before the lexical verb, as in Haitian. But does the superstratist explanation rule out the substratist/relexification account? I think not. In second language acquisition, inflectional morphology is the first element of the target language *not* to be acquired by shifting speakers, probably because it is neither acoustically salient nor semantically useful. Once the French periphrastic constructions were stripped of their inflectional endings by the first generation of creole speakers, then they could more easily be reinterpreted as preverbal TMA markers by adult and children speakers of Kwa languages, who identified them with their own L1 TMA markers. The "missing link" is not available for Haitian, but the reanalysis of invariant auxiliaries as preverbal TMA markers can be seen in Reunionese, where the various lects of the creole continuum reflect, to a large extent, the gradual creolization process.

The first known sentence in RC was recorded ca. 1722 by a local intellectual who reported a decision made by the *Conseil Provincial de Bourbon* (Chaudenson 1981: 3):

(68)   *Moin la parti   marron   parce qu'Alexis   l'homme de jardin*
       I   past-perf. leave maroon   because Alexis   the gardener
       l'était qui fait à moin   trop l'amour   (Chaudenson 1974: 444)
       past-impf. make to me   too-much love
       'I ran away because Alexis the Gardener was always making love to me'

This sentence already displays some features of Reunionese:

1) substandard form of the 1st person pronoun (*muê, amuê*);
2) past perfect: aux. *la* + past part. *parti* (Standard French uses the auxiliary *être*, not *avoir*);
3) past imperfect tense: *lete ki* (presumably from *l'était qui*?).

5. Conclusion

In this paper I have made three arguments concerning Caribbean and Indian Ocean plantation creoles: (1) that creole genesis is a kind of SLA "in reverse", where the acrolectal varieties pre-date the mesolectal and basilectal varieties, reflecting what Chaudenson (1989, 1995) described as a "centrifugal" development of creoles away from the superstrate; (2) that creole genesis was a gradual process over several generations; (3) that SLA processes (especially transfer and simplification) were responsible for creoles features.

Of course, (1) depends on (2) and (3), but (2) and (3) don't depend on (1). Thus, while the evidence provided for (2) and (3) doesn't prove (1), at least it illustrates that the necessary conditions for (1) occur.

McGill University, Montreal

REFERENCES

Arends, Jacques
    1995a   "Demographic Factors in the Formation of Sranan", in: Arends (1995b), 233-277.
Arends, Jacques (ed.)
    1995b   *The Early Stages of Creolization.* Amsterdam: Benjamins.
Baker, Phillip
    1990   "Off target?", *Journal of Pidgin and Creole Languages* 5:1, 107-119.
    1995   "Some Developmental Inferences from Historical Studies of Pidgins and Creoles", in: Arends (1995b), 1-24.
Bernabé, Jean
    1983   *Grammaire créole. Fondas kréyol-la.* Paris: L'Harmattan.
Bickerton, Derek
    1975   *Dynamics of a creole system.* London: Cambridge University Press.
    1981   *Roots of Language.* Ann Arbor: Karoma.
Chaudenson, Robert
    1974   *Le lexique du parler créole de la Réunion.* Paris: Champion (2 volumes).
    1979   "Le français dans les îles de l'Océan Indien", in: Albert Valdman (ed.), *Le français hors de France*, 543-620. Paris: Editions Honoré Champion.
    1981   *Textes créoles anciens (La Réunion et Ile Maurice).* Hamburg: Helmut Buske Verlag.
    1989   *Créoles et enseignement du français.* Paris: L'Harmattan.
    1995   *Les Créoles.* Paris: Presses Universitaires de France.
D'Ans, André-Marcel
    1968   *Le créole français d'Haïti: Étude des unités d'articulation, d'expansion et de communication.* The Hague: Mouton.
DeGraff, Michel
    1999a   "Creolization, Language Change, and Language Acquisition: A Prolegomenon", in: DeGraff (1999b), 1-46.

DeGraff, Michel (ed.)
1999b   *Language Creation and Language Change: Creolization, Diachrony, and De-velopment.* Cambridge: The MIT Press.
Holm, John A.
1984   "Variability of the Copula in Black English and its Creole Kin", *American Speech* 59:4, 291-309.
Hymes, Dell (ed.)
1971   *Pidginization and creolization of languages. Proceedings of a conference held at the University of the West Indies, Mona, Jamaica, April 1968.* Cambridge: Cambridge University Press.
Koopman, Hilda
1986   "The Genesis of Haitian: Implications of a Comparison of Some Features of the Syntax of Haitian, French and West African Languages", in: Muysken and Smith (1986), 231-258.
Lafage, Suzanne
1985   *Français écrit et parlé en pays Éwé (Sud-Togo)* (Université de Nice Doctoral dissertation 1976). Paris: Société d'études linguistiques et anthropologiques de France.
Lefebvre, Claire
1986   "Relexification in creole genesis revisited: The case of Haitian Creole", in: Muysken and Smith (1986), 279-300.
1998a   "Multifunctionality and variation among grammars: the case of the determiner in Haitian and in FonGbe", *Journal of Pidgin and Creole Languages* 13:1, 93-150.
1998b   *Creole genesis and the acquisition of grammar: The case of Haitian creole.* Cambridge: Cambridge University Press.
Lightfoot, David
1999a   "Creoles and Cues", in DeGraff (1999b), 431-452.
1999b   *The Development of Language: Acquisition, Change and Evolution.* Oxford: Blackwell.
Mesthrie, Rajend
1992   *English in language shift: The history, structure and sociolinguistics of South African Indian English.* Cambridge, UK: Cambridge University Press.
Muysken, Pieter, and Norval Smith (eds.)
1986   *Substrata versus Universals in Creole Genesis.* Amsterdam: Benjamins.
Romaine, Suzanne
1988   *Pidgin & Creole Languages.* London-New York: Longman.
Singler, John Victor
1996   "Theories of creole genesis, sociohistorical considerations, and the evaluation of evidence: the case of Haitian creole and the relexification hypothesis", *Journal of Pidgin and Creole Languages* 11:2, 185-230.
Véronique, Daniel
1984   "The acquisition and use of aspects of French morphosyntax by native speakers of Arabic dialects", in: Roger Andersen (ed.), *Second languages: a cross-linguistic perspective*, 191-213. Rowley, Mass.: Newbury House.

Languages in Contact, edited by D.G. Gilbers, J. Nerbonne, and J. Schaeken (= *Studies in Slavic and General Linguistics*, vol. 28), 263-275. Amsterdam - Atlanta, GA: Rodopi, 2000.

FROM LINGUISTIC AREAS TO AREAL LINGUISTICS:
A RESEARCH PROPOSAL

PIETER MUYSKEN

Three approaches to the grouping and comparison of languages have emerged:

- *Areal*: similarities between the languages of a specific region are explored, similarities possibly due to mutual influence or convergence (such a region is also termed a Sprachbund or linguistic area);
- *Genetic*: similarities between languages due to common ancestry are explored, and language families are reconstructed;
- *Typological*: similarities between languages due to common design features and general properties of communicative systems are studied.

It is clear that logically these three approaches are independent, even if they were often confused in the earliest stages of the discipline of Comparative Linguistics. Indeed, the three approaches have developed quite separately.

Genetic linguistics for a long time has taken the lead, and been responsible for some of the more spectacular successes of the linguistic disciplines as a whole. At present, over one hundred language families all over the world are being studied. The most original forms of these language families, termed the proto-languages, are being reconstructed, and these efforts are accompanied by ethnological and archeological research attempting to establish the external history of these languages.

Areal linguistics is an outgrowth of genetic linguistics. It emerged as a field, now part of language contact studies, when it was discovered that in certain regions, e.g. the Balkan, India, and the Baltic region, there were similarities between languages that could not be explained genetically. Now a number of "linguistic areas" are being discovered, ranging from Meso-America to central Australia, and well-established linguistic areas are being further explored.

Typological linguistics has its roots in the early nineteenth century, but received its major impetus from the pioneering work of Joseph Greenberg, who in the mid-sixties discovered a number of linguistic universals based on typological comparisons of languages. There is now a flourishing school of typological linguistics, and increasing sets of data are being assembled and theoretical conclusions drawn.

1. Recent developments in the field

A number of recent developments in the field have brought these three approaches much closer to each other, making the traditional lines between them less clearly demarcated. The paradigm shift, leading to the need for more intensive collaboration, if not integration, is apparent in a number of recent publications and discussions.

Joseph Greenberg (1987) has claimed that there are only three language families in the Americas, among which the huge and highly controversial Amerind family. While he has been (rightly) criticized for his imprecision and over-general claims, his work has left most researchers with the feeling that the traditional genetic approach will only yield part of the picture, and that new frameworks are called for.

Furthermore, Johanna Nichols (1992) has brought new impulses to the field of areal linguistics by claiming that there are very large areal distribution patterns worldwide, related to long-range migration and settlement patterns. Again, many details are not well-established, but the role of long term language contact and diffusion has received renewed attention.

Third, the ESF activity in language typology EUROTYP has brought to light a large number of highly abstract areal features in western Europe, again underlining the need for areal studies in regions where so far these had not been considered relevant.

In a recent essay Bob Dixon (1998) has proposed that the differentiation between languages (the traditional subject of genetic linguistics) only exceptionally takes the form that leads to the establishment of clear language families, and that more often we get more diffuse areal relationships and typological resemblances as the result of language split.

In several parts of the world the generally very succesful paradigm of genetic comparative linguistics has not yielded very clear results. In part this is due to lack of adequate descriptions, in part to complex interactions between genetic and contact-induced similarities in the languages involved. Thus we need to study the relation between areal and genetic linguistics in more detail.

Genetic, areal and typological linguistics form a kind of triangle. The three comparative approaches in linguistics, though logically independent, depend on each other for their results: the typological approach gives insight into common and uncommon, marked and unmarked features of language, and their interdependence. A language sample of the type used in typological research depends on genetically unrelated and geographically dispersed languages. The genetic approach explains similarities and differences through postulating historical relationships, based on correspondences which cannot be explained areally or typologically. The areal approach, finally, approaches similarities and differences from the perspective of local contiguity, and needs to filter out genetic and typological resemblances.

2. Some questions surrounding linguistic areas

There is a large literature on linguistic areas. A useful summary of some core properties of these areas is given in Campbell (1998: 299-310). I will first consider the types of linguistic areas that might be encountered, and then the types of features we expect to be shared in these scenarios. Finally I will try to give a systematic list of features provided by Campbell for different linguistic areas and attempt to relate these to the types of areas found.

2.1 Types of areas

Campbell (1998: 300) distinguishes between *circumstancialist* and *historicist* accounts of linguistic areas. Circumstancialist accounts simply note the existence of a number of shared traits. Historicist accounts try to give an explicit explanation of the historical circumstances of language contact that produced the linguistic area.

When we turn to general historical accounts proposed for the type of language contact process leading to linguistic areas, a good place to begin is Thomason and Kaufman (1988). These authors assume there to be two main processes: borrowing and shift. Borrowing involves an asymmetric adoption by one language of features from another one, first of some words, then more words, then affixes, then finally grammar. Shift involves the adoption by a speech community of an imposed language. Traces of the original language may remain in pronunciation, some lexicon, and some grammatical constructions.

On the basis of these processes, a number of scenarios come to mind when we try to establish the background of a given linguistic area.

A. All languages in the area may have been influenced by one dominant language, that has now disappeared (Thomason and Kaufman's 1987 *maintenance and borrowing* scenario).
B. Idem, with the dominant language still present.
C. All languages in the area may have been acquired as second languages by speakers of one non-dominant language, now disappeared (Thomason and Kaufman's *shift and transfer* scenario).
D. Idem, with the non-dominant language still present.

However, there may be other possibilities, not covered by the two principal scenarios developed in Thomason and Kaufman's work. Since neither borrowing nor shift are always adequate in explaining the areal patterns and historical developments concerned, we will discuss two other possible scenarios or contact processes: surface convergence and relexification. Surface convergence takes place in two speech communities where several languages are in frequent use. Since speakers will try to employ the same sentence production strategies for both languages, particularly surface word order will be affected. Since bilingualism has been documented among many small groups all over the world, word order convergence among otherwise unrelated and dissimilar languages can be explained.

E. Convergence between several coexisting languages towards each other (we may term this the *coexistence and convergence* scenario).

A further pattern I want to discuss is relexification: the word for word and even morpheme for morpheme modelling of one language upon another, so that roughly the structure comes from the one and at least the content lexicon from the other language. This process occurs:

(a) In ethnically mixed communities (that were constituted through intermarriage) the language structures of the mothers are combined with content lexicon of the fathers' language.
(b) In language innovation due to migration the home language structures are combined with lexicon from the community towards which migration took place.
(c) In secret languages the structure of the language of wider communication is combined with an ingroup lexicon.
(d) In situations of reversal of language shift the structures of the "new" language are combined with the remembered lexicon of the "old" language.

F. Relefixication of the patterns of one language with words from a different language.

Finally, we can imagine that parallel linguistic changes could be at the root of a linguistic area:

G. Set of shared language changes.

2.2 Types of shared features

These different scenarios will necessarily lead to different types of shared features. We will adopt the same order as used in the list of types of areas in the previous section to discuss these. Crucial here are the distinctions between the different components of language: discourse, lexicon, and syntax – and between Humboldt's Inner Form (the underlying organization of language structure) and Outer Form (the outwardly visible shapes). These distinctions yield the following range, if we assume that each component has both an inner form and an outer form:

particles	word forms	word order & morpho-syntax	OUTER FORM
|	|	|	
principles	word meanings	abstract organization	INNER FORM
DISCOURSE	LEXICON	SYNTAX	

When all languages in the area may have been influenced by one dominant language (maintenance and borrowing scenarios A and B), we expect rather outer form shared features such as shared non-core lexicon, and perhaps shared word order of phrases, shared discourse particles and some derivational morphology.

When all languages in the area may have been acquired as second languages by speakers of one non-dominant language (shift and transfer scenarios C and D), we may find more inner form syntactic and discourse features, in addition to phonological features and retained word meanings.

In the case of coexistence and convergence between several languages or of a set of shared language changes (scenarios E and G), we may particularly expect more complex shared features, both internal and external, shared word order patterns, phonological alternations, etc.

Relexification will lead to shared structural patterns and possibly shared phonetic features, but divergent lexical elements.

2.3 Areal features in the literature

Campbell (1998: 300-306) contains a useful summary of a number of language areas with their features. It can be summarized in Table 1, where *phon* refers to phonological features, *lexi* to lexical and derivational morphology features, *mosy* to morphosyntactic features, and *synt* to purely syntactic features:

Balkan		phon	lexi	mosy	synt
1	central vowel	+			
2	syncretism dative and genitive		+		
3	postposed articles				+
4	periphrastic future			+	
5	periphrastic perfect			+	
6	absence of infinitives			+	
7	clitic doubling for objects		+	+	

South Asia		phon	lexi	mosy	synt
1	retroflex consonants	+			
2	absence of prefixes		+		
3	dative-subject construction		+	+	
4	SOV and NP/P order				+
5	absence of verb 'to have'		+	+	
6	conjunctive/absolutive participle			+	+
7	morphological causatives		+	+	
8	explicator compound verbs		+		
9	sound-symbolic reduplication	+	+		
Mesoamerica		**phon**	**lexi**	**mosy**	**synt**
1	PoD-agr/PoS possession		+	+	
2	relational nouns		+		
3	vigesimal numeral systems		+		
4	non-SOV order				+
5	shared loan translations		+		
Northwest Coast		**phon**	**lexi**	**mosy**	**synt**
1	elaborate consonant systems	+			
2	extensive use of suffixes		+		
3	few prefixes		+		
4	complex reduplications		+		
5	numeral classifiers		+		
6	alienable/inalienable in nouns		+		
7	pronominal plural			+	
8	nominal plural			+	
9	masculine/feminine in nouns		+		
10	visible/invisible in demonstratives		+		
11	evidential markers on the verb			+	
12	passive constructions				+
13	negation initial			+	
(14)	*k > č	+			
(15)	tones	+			
(16)	ergative			+	
(17)	lexical suffixes		+		
(18)	weak noun/verb contrast		+	+	+

Baltic		phon	lexi	mosy	synt
1	first syllable stress	+			
2	consonant palatalisation	+			
3	tonal contrast	+			
4	partititive case			+	
5	evidential voice			+	
6	particlc + verb combinations		+		
7	SVO order				+
8	adjective/noun agreement			+	
Ethiopia		phon	lexi	mosy	synt
1	SOV and NP/P order				+
2	subordinate clause / main clause				+
3	gerund			+	
4	quoting construction		+	+	
5	light verbs		+	+	
6	negative copula		+		
7	plurals of nouns not after numbers		+	+	
8	2nd and 3rd pronoun gender			+	
9	reduplicated intensives		+		
10	different present tense in main/sub clause			+	
11	fem sing used in plural concord			+	
12	singulative affixes		+	+	

Table 1. Linguistic features of six linguistic areas (based on Campbell 1998).

It is a bit too early to convincingly link these different settings to different scenarios. The Ethiopian and South Asian cases have often been argued to be examples of a shift and transfer scenario and indeed many of the relevant features are relatively internal in nature. Some of the other areas represent such a wide array of types of features shared that only a coexistence and convergence scenario seems likely.

3. Language contact and the construct of linguistic areas: the Andean/Amazonian transition area

In this section I will consider areal features in a region which so far has not really been discussed in these terms: the Andean/Amazon transition area. Andean languages such as Quechua and Aymara, although probably not directly related, share a great many typological features, as is well known, and thus represent the core of the Andean linguistic area. In accounting for the phenomena encountered, I want to take up the challenge posed by Terrence Kaufman in a recent article when he states in conclusion (1990: 32):

> "Thus recognition and identification of language contact phenomena will be among the steps required to unravel the tangled skein of South American linguistic relationships."

Similarly, many researchers have pointed to a set of quite distinct linguistic features that characterize many Amazonian languages, thus defining another linguistic area. The question is how to characterize the languages at the fringe of the Quechua-Aymara area on the eastern slopes (*montaña*) of the Andes. Are they a continuation of the Andean core linguistic area? Do they represent a mixed type (as has been assumed in some sources)? But what does that mean: can we assign a structural anteriority to either their Andean or their Amazonian features? Are they clearly Amazonian? To what extent does it make sense at all to use labels such as Amazonian and Andean?

Of course, no general answer can be given at present. It is meaningless to talk about Andean, Amazonian, Montaña languages as linguistic types. Rather, we could loosely talk of eastern and western Amerindian languages, from an areal perspective, following Doris Payne (1990). The Andean languages can only be understood in an Amazonian context. We will try to provide additional support here for Payne's assumption that there are two large groups, an eastern and a western group. The western group includes not only many of the eastern slope languages, but also the central Andean languages. Tessman (1930) claims that Cholón is the only case where a mixed language has developed from Quechua and the Montaña languages ("der einzige Fall, dass sich eine Mischsprache zwischen Ketchua und Waldlandsprachen gebildet hat"). This is not true, in our opinion. It simply shares a number of features with Quechua, as well as with eastern slope languages. One of the problems here concerns the fact that a supposed "areal" feature may be characteristic of the Amerindian language family as a whole.

Doris Payne (1990: 214) claims that the western group of Amazonian languages is characterized by polysynthesis, directionals with TMA functions, and some noun classification. It includes Pano-Tacanan, Maipuran/Arawakan, Saliban, Zaparoan, Yaguan, Huitotoan, and Cahuapanan. The eastern group, in contrast, is more isolating, has very few or no minimal / no directionals, and no noun classification. It includes Jê-Bororo, Tupian, Cariban, and Makú.

It is too early to provide an overall evaluation of Payne's proposal and its ramifications for our view of Amerindian areal linguistics. At present we are engaged in studying the whole region in more detail, through the systematic comparison of language data. I begin by presenting some exploratory data on word order patterns. A more thorough study will be needed to flesh out the picture. There are a number of languages with an SOV pattern like Quechua and Aymara:

Quechua	OV	GEN N	AN	postP
Jivaroan	OV	GEN N	AN	postP
Cholon-Hibito	OV	GEN N	AN	postP
Harakmbet	OV		AN	postP
Bora-Huitoto	OV	GEN N	AN	postP
Chayahuita	OV	GEN N	AN	postP
Candoshi	OV	GEN N	AN	postP
Tucanoan	OV			postP
Leco	OV			postP
Chipaya	OV			
Guarayu	OV			
Cofán	OV			
Waorani	OV			postP
Cocama	OV			
Pano-Tacanan	OV	GEN N	AN/NA	postP
Zaparoan	OV/VSO			?preP
Tupian	OV		NA	preP
Maipuran	OV/VSO			preP
Cayuvava	VOS			
Itonama	VO	N GEN	NA	preP
Móvima	VO/VS	N GEN	AN	preP
Chiquitano	V(S)O	N GEN	–	preP
Yagua	VSO			postP
Taushiro	VSO			postP
Urarina	OVS	GEN N	NA	postP

Table 2. Word order patterns in the languages of the eastern slopes.

However, the number of languages marking agreement with suffixes is considerably less:

	nominal	verbal
Quechua	suffix	suffix
Jivaroan	suffix	suffix
Pano-Tacanan		suffix
Zaparoan		prefix
Cholon-Hibito	prefix	prefix

	nominal	verbal
Chiquitano	prefix	prefix
Harakmbet	prefix	prefix
Urarina		suffix
Bora-Huitoto	proclitic	suffix
Chayahuita		prefix
Leco		prefix

Table 3: Agreement patterns of the languages of the eastern slopes.

Doris Payne (1990: 214) classifies a number of the languages in the area (including Pano-Tacanan, Maipuran, Arawakan, Tucanoan, Saliban, Zaparoan, Yaguan, Huitotoan, and Cahuapana) as typologically similar in their morphology. Shared features are (a) a high degree of polysynthesis, (b) directionals in the verb which may have tense/aspect/mode functions, and (c) "western Amazonian" noun classification systems. It should be noted that features (a) and (b) are shared by Quechua and Aymara. Similarly, agglutinative patterns are dominant.

As noted by Doris Payne, many of the western languages share complex verbal morphology, including polysynthesis, as can be seen from Table 4:

Quechua	many suffixes
Jivaroan	many suffixes
Pano-Tacanan	some derivational suffixes
Cholon-Hibito	many suffixes
Chiquitano	inflectional prefixes / many suffixes
Harakmbet	some suffixes
Urarina	inflection / some derivational suffixes
Bora-Huitoto	derivational suffixes
Leco	many suffixes

Table 4: Verb morphology of the languages of the eastern slopes.

First, we will compare pronoun and person marking systems, to see whether they show similarities both in their organization and morpho-syntactic properties, and in the forms used for reference to specific grammatical persons. The aim here is mainly comparative and typological.

Then we will see whether the generalization proposed by Derbyshire (1987) for the Carib-Ge-Tupi cluster, namely that we are dealing with a group of originally ergative SOV languages, can be extended to the eastern slopes languages more generally:

Quechua	0 / accusative / genitive / oblique
Jivaroan	0 / 0 (accusative)
Cholon-Hibito	?tup / accusative / genitive / oblique
Chiquitano	none
Harakmbet	oblique marked with suffix
Urarina	0 / 0 / oblique
Bora-Huitoto	0 / accusative / 0 / oblique
Leco	0 / accusative

Table 5. Case marking of the languages of the eastern slopes.

There are a number of other shared features to be considered here which characterize different subsets of the languages of the region. Quechua, Yamara, Jivaroan, Pano-Tacanan and possibly Cholon-Hibito show switch reference intersecting with tense. Quechua, Aymara, Jivaroan, Pano-Tacanan, probably Cholon-Hibito, Urarina, and Bora-Huitoto use validator elements, often in final position. Quechua, Aymara, Chiquitano, Itonama, Sirionó, and Móvima have inclusive plural person marking and/or pronouns. Móvima, Harakmbet, Panoan, Cayuvava, and Tupí-Guaraní show patterns of noun incorporation.

Thus there are a great many shared features among the languages in the region. The main issue now is how to reconcile the lack of lexical-genetic relationships among the languages in the area with their strong typological resemblance. How come there are so many apparent isolates without the ensuing typological diversity?

There certainly has been borrowing in the area concerned, as in the adoption of Quechua items already mentioned above. However, this influence has never been very profound, except possibly in the case of Amuesha (Wise 1976). In any case, since borrowing always involves extensive lexical influence, the situation to be explained – structural similarities without lexical similarities – cannot be due to Thomason and Kaufman's borrowing scenario.

Shift has occurred on the eastern slopes. Thus lowland Ecuadorian Quechua has replaced Shuar and Záparo in some areas, and retains vocabulary from lowland languages, as well as grammatical and possibly also phonological features. The overextension of the lowland Ecuadorian clause boundary marker *nisha* 'saying' from declarative to desiderative complements could be due to Shuar substrate influence. Whatever the role of shift may have been in the western Amazon area, it cannot explain the pattern encountered, since shift is only useful to explain structural divergence within a genetically established family (cf. "substrate" in Romance).

Of the four possible patterns of relexification, it is not clear which one would be best suited to fit the case of the western Amazon. It is clear that there have been many cases of ethnic restructuring in recent years, and we may assume this was also the case in the past. Patterns (c) and (d) lead to the situation we want to account for: shared structure without shared lexicon. Relexification may well have been less frequent than surface convergence, but it explains a more specific structural resemblance between two varieties. To give just one example, assume that there was originally at least one language with a strong suffixing system and a tendency towards bi-syllabic roots. Then other languages could be modelled upon it and profoundly restructured. Person prefixes could be reinterpreted as suffixes, and compounds of mono-syllabic roots could start functioning as new bi-syllabic roots.

4. From linguistic areas to areal linguistics

In the previous sections I have drawn up a tentative typology of linguistic areas and offered some initial data on the languages in the eastern slopes of the Andes and the adjacent Andean mountain ranges and Amazon basin. This paper is premature in that neither the typology of linguistic areas nor the Amerindian data have been sufficiently well-explored, let alone the fit between them. However, it is important to break new terrain in this complicated field, which will need the cooperation of many researchers. This is the reason to present these observations at this moment.

In the study of the Balkan as a linguistic area, often a distinction is drawn between the core Balkan Sprachbund and more peripheral Balkanesque regions. This suggests the image of concentric circles, with the core Balkan Sprachbund at the center. However, in addition, many other models for linguistic areas are imaginable, such as the Olympic chain of rings. Here area A shares features with B, and B with C, but A not necessarily with C. This chain of circles is probably a more fitting image for the situation in South America, where the Quechua-Aymara complex constitutes one center of gravity, the western Amazonian languages discussed by Doris Payne another one, and other languages in between are more like the one or more like the other type. Further research will have to indicate whether a more fine-grained analysis is called for, combining perhaps the representation in terms of concentric circles with the one in terms of interlocking circles. In all cases, the perspective needed constitutes a shift from linguistic areas as fixed entities to areal linguistics, the study of the distribution of linguistic features in space and time.

Leiden University

REFERENCES

Adelaar, Willem F.H., and Pieter Muysken
   in prep.   *The languages of the Andes.* Cambridge: Cambridge University Press.
Campbell, Lyle
   1998   *Historical Linguistics. An Introduction.* Edinburgh: Edinburgh University Press.
Derbyshire, Desmond C.
   1987   "Morphosyntactic areal characteristics of Amazonian languages", *International Journal of American Linguistics* 53, 311-326.
Dixon, Robert M.W.
   1998   *The rise and fall of languages.* Cambridge: Cambridge University Press.
Greenberg, Joseph H.
   1987   *Language in the Americas.* Stanford: Stanford University Press.
Kaufman, Terrence
   1990   "Language history in South America. What we know and how to know more", in: Doris Payne (ed.), *Amazonian Linguistics. Studies in Lowland South American Languages*, 13-33. Austin: University of Texas Press.
Nichols, Johanna
   1992   *Linguistic diversity in space and time.* Chicago: The University of Chicago Press.
Payne, Dorris
   1990   "Morphological characteristics of lowland South American languages", in: Doris Payne (ed.), *Amazonian Linguistics. Studies in Lowland South American Languages*, 213-241. Austin: University of Texas Press.
Tessman, Günter
   1930   *Die Indianer Nord-Ost Perus.* Stuttgart.
Thomason, Sarah Grey, and Terrence Kaufman
   1988   *Language contact, creolization, and genetic linguistics.* Berkeley: University of California Press.
Wise, Mary Ruth
   1976   "Apuntes sobre la influencia inca entre los amuesha: Factor que obscurece la clasificación de su idioma", *Revista del Museo Nacional* 42, 355-366.

Languages in Contact, edited by D.G. Gilbers, J. Nerbonne, and J. Schaeken (= *Studies in Slavic and General Linguistics*, vol. 28), 277-282. Amsterdam - Atlanta, GA: Rodopi, 2000.

CODE-SWITCHING AND -MIXING
IN RUSSIAN-HEBREW BILINGUALS

LARISSA NAIDITCH

1. Background

In the last decades there has been an increasing interest in the problems of contact linguistics. The phenomena of interference of languages and, more concretely, of alternative use of different languages – code-switching – have been described for several languages. The present paper focuses on the case of Russian in Israel (RI) and on the influence of Hebrew on Russian.

Since the year 1989, over 900,000 persons were repatriated to Israel, more than 84% of them from the countries of the former USSR. Practically all of them know Russian, and for most it constitutes a mother tongue. The motivation for the preservation of Russian as a language of conversation at home and sometimes in the working place, and as a language of culture in the Russian community in Israel is still very strong and has even been enhanced during the last decades. Its use is implemented, on the one hand, by the access to Russian sources (TV, libraries, book shops, guest performances of Russian actors) and by relatively convenient communication with native speakers in the metropolis and, on the other hand, by a tendency towards cultural autonomy in Israel. Many examples collected by us demonstrate a contrary situation to the well-known conservatism usually ascribed to languages spoken in foreign-speaking environments. Thus, the traditional notion of a Sprachinsel is challenged. Several peculiarities of RI have led to the development of a specific variety of Russian as a minority language in Israel (Moskovich 1978; Orel 1994). The degree of interference varies depending on linguistic proficiency of speaker and interlocutor, subject of conversation, and register of speech.

2. Linguistic interference. The notion and classification of mixes

The influence of Hebrew manifests itself in shifts in intonation contours, in several syntactic changes, and especially in the broad use of Hebrew words. Whether the latter are Hebrew words interwoven into the Russian speech or loan words, i.e., a part of the Russian vocabulary, or something else, is difficult to determine unambiguously. The criteria that can clarify this problem include: 1) the regularity of use of the word; 2) its use only by speakers of low proficiency in the host language (in our case Russian) and high proficiency in the guest language (Hebrew) or by all speakers; 3) the degree of integration of corresponding lexemes into the phonetic, grammatical and lexical system of Russian; 4) its stylistic markedness (as foreign, unusual, etc.) or neutrality; 5) an additional criterion, which does not always apply, concerning the possibility of replacement of the word by its correspondent in the host language. For instance, the words /kart'is/ 'ticket', /mazgan/ 'air conditioner', /t'ijul'/ 'excursion' are regularly used by all Russian speakers in Israel and are integrated into the phonological and grammatical system of Russian. The word /xaver/ 'boyfriend' is not only regularly used, but also does not have a Russian correspondent. Thus, these words have become an integral part of the vocabulary of RI; they can be considered as loan words; but there are a lot of intermediate cases that are difficult to interpret. A few decades ago, E. Vereščagin (1968) proposed the term "vključennaja leksema" ("an included lexeme") to designate words of one language used in another, that possess several peculiarities of each and do not belong to either. Similarly, Elite Olshtain and Shoshana Blum-Kulka (1990: 61) used the term code-mixing (mixes), referring to "smaller units, usually words or idiomatic expressions, which are borrowed from one language and inserted into the sentence of another language". The latter term will be used hereafter. Thus, mixes border on loan words on the one hand and on situational switches on the other, the boundaries being rather fluent. In most cases they are very close to loan words, being broadly used and well integrated into the morphological system.

Several classes of mixes can be singled out in RI: 1) nouns and noun phrases; 2) verbs; 3) discourse markers. Nouns, which are the most frequent category of mixes, are predominantly (but not always) culturally bound semantic units that reflect Israeli life: /pk'ida/ 'clerk (fem.)', /šuk/ 'market', /tekes/ 'ceremony'. Some of them belong to a professional vocabulary, used, for instance, in schools, at universities and in working places: /m'ifxan/ 'exam', /boxan/ 'test (in school)', /maabada/ 'laboratory', or to everyday life: /m'ištara/ 'police', /n'ikajon/ 'cleaning'. In several cases a semantic shift of loan words takes place: specialization of word meaning – /s'ifrut/ in Hebrew 'literature', in RI 'literature as a subject in school', /xaver/ in Hebrew 'friend', in RI 'boyfriend'; change of meaning because of ellipsis – /teuda/ in Hebrew 'document', in RI 'identity card' (ellipsis of *teudat zehut*), /taxana/ 'station', also used in the meaning 'central bus station' (ellipsis of *tachana merkazit*). More profound and hidden shifts in the semantic structure of lexemes in RI, distinguishing them from both Russian in the metropolis and Hebrew, manifest themselves in psycholinguistic experiments, e.g. word association tests.

3. Morphological adaptation of loan words and mixes

Several morphological types of Russian nouns are generally reduced to two or three in RI: 1) words ending in /a/ are treated as Russian feminines of the corresponding class, e.g., *tachana* like *storona*; *švita* like *plita*; in most of the cases the nominative has an end stress, the *-á* being interpreted as flexion; examples with stress on the stem, like *maškánta*, are rare; 2) words ending in a consonant are treated as masculines of the corresponding type: *mivchan* /m'ifxan/ like *tuman*; 3) a few nouns ending in stressed *-e* remain unchanged: *chozé* [xaze] 'contract' as *šossé*.

The rules above show that the gender of the words is generally dictated by its auslaut in nom.sg. in RI. Thus, in several cases the gender of the Hebrew words is changed, most examples of this type being words ending in /t/, that are feminines in Hebrew and become masculines in RI: /xanut/ 'shop', /persomet/ 'advertisement', etc. The gender of the words designating animate objects, especially persons, are in most cases treated according to their sense: /on byl mumxe/ 'he was a specialist'. In type 1 mentioned above, the declension in the singular generally obeys that of the corresponding group in Russian, whereas the formation of the plural is problematic. Sometimes the plural is avoided; in many cases hybrid forms (a Hebrew plural marker plus a Russian one) or the Hebrew plural are used: /sadnaoty/ 'workshops', /xadašoty/ or /xadašot/ 'news', etc. For the former cf. such Russian loan words, as /džinsy/ 'jeans' with double marking of the plural. To explain this phenomenon the trend in the development of the corresponding morphological noun group should be kept in mind. According to the most frequent morphonological pattern of this type for Modern Standard Russian, the stress in the plural is shifted from the flexion to the word stem: cf. plitá - plíty, travá - trávy, golová - gólovy. The non-movable stress in the flexion survives only in a few nouns of this type: mečtá - mečtý (Zaliznjak 1967: 166). The latter morphonological pattern became obsolete, because of the long lasting process of maximal accentual differentiation between singular and plural in nouns ending in *-á* (Zaliznjak 1967: 164-166). Hebrew mixes used in RI demonstrate a reluctance for stress shift, explained by a tendency to fix stress in non-integrated foreign lexemes in Modern Standard Russian. The latter is confirmed by the declension of foreign family names: nom. /bal'zák/ - gen. /bal'záka/ Balzac in contrast with /kazák/ - /kazaká/ 'Cossack'. The plural forms of class 2 mixes generally correspond to the Russian pattern: /bagruty/ 'high-school matriculation exams', /t'ijul'i/ 'excursions', etc. To sum up the plural formation in mixes, it should be noted, that in Russian it is part of the declension, the flexion being synthetic and denoting number and case simultaneously, whereas in the morphology of mixes different principles can be used.

Here are some examples of code-mixing: *Ja ètu sugiju uže rešil* 'I have already solved this problem', *Segodnja tri raza ošiblas'. Kakaja buša!* 'I have made a mistake three times today. What a shame!', *Kakie xadašoty? – Xadašotov nikakix* 'What's new? – No news', *Kupila brjuki po mivce* 'I have bought trousers in a sale', *Priexali na tachanu* 'We came to the (Central) bus station', *Čto so švitoj?* 'What about the strike?', *U nas ešče ne bylo matkoneta po sifrutu* 'We haven't had a preliminary exam in literature yet'.

Hebrew compound nouns consisting of two parts, one in the form of status constructus, are also used as mixes. Many of them are declined as regular nouns; only their second part changes, e.g., *Prišlos' exat' domoj iz misrad apnima* 'I had to go home from the Ministry of Interior' (nom.sg.: *misrad a pnim*), *U menja ne bylo s soboj teudat zeuta* 'I have not taken my identity card' (nom.sg. *teudat zeut*). Sometimes only the first part is used because of ellipsis (*teudat* = *teudat zeut* 'identity card'). All these compounds are pronounced as one lexical unit, the accentual structure of which corresponds to that of Hebrew words: the chief stress lies on the second word (the attribute), predominantly on the last syllable, with an additional, weaker, stress on the first part. It may be assumed that the morphonological structure of the examples discussed above represents a new type of composite, in which only the second element is declined (cf. examples like *stop-kadr, marš-brosok, krem-pudra*) (Comrie, Stone, and Polinsky 1996: 113).

Switches or loan words occur much more seldom in verb forms than in nouns, a universal rule, for which Weinreich (1963: 37) provided lexico-semantic, rather than grammatical and structural reasons. They are predominantly used in a rather low register of speech, in contrast to nouns, which often belong to a neutral style, e.g., *otciljumit'* 'to copy' (from *ciljum* 'copy'), *nikajonit'* 'to clean (professionally)' (from *nikajon* 'cleaning'), *švitovat'* 'to strike' (from *švita* 'strike'), *metape-lit'* 'to treat, to nurse' (from the present form or participle of the corresponding verb), *bitljanut'* 'to cancel' (from the past stem of the corresponding Hebrew verb). The first two examples are adnominal forms, in which analogy with the Russian word formation can be seen: *švitovat'* like *bastovat'* 'to strike' or *bunto-vat'* 'to rebel'; *nikajonit'* like colloquial *inženerit', šoferit'* 'to work as an engineer, as a driver', or *kalamburit'* 'to make a pun', *bazarit'* 'to make noise, to quarrel'. The Russian aktionsart is expressed in these verbs by means of the presence/absence of prefixes: *otciljumit'/pereciljumit'* vs. *ciljumit', metapelit'* vs. *pro-metapelit'*, etc. Cf. an example from Russian in the USA: *Mašinu zalokala* 'I have locked the car'. Besides these examples of morphological adaptation of verbs, switching of the whole verb in a form corresponding to that of Hebrew can be observed, especially in the students' slang: *Ja tak ictamcamti v etoj rabote, čto basof vyšlo po reva-amud* 'I shortened this work in such a way, that finally it became a quarter of page each', *U menja minimal'nyj sikuj lefateach skarlatinu. Skoree vsego, daže esli ja efateach mašehu, ničego ne budet* 'I have a minimal chance of developing scarlatina. Most probably, even if I'll develop, nothing will happen'.

The examples demonstrate code-switching, often a situational one, to be distinct from mixing in the sense mentioned above.

Word formation from Hebrew nouns and adjectives with the help of Russian formatives, resulting in nouns, adjectives and verbs is possible: *betachonščik* 'security policeman' (derived from the noun *betachon* 'security' by means of the suffix *-ščik*), *mesibucha* 'party'(derived from *mesiba* 'party' by an "emotive" suffix), etc. Especially interesting are the adjectives *olimovskij* 'belonging to new repatriates' and *datišnyj* /dat'išnyj/ 'religious'. The first one is derived from *olim*, the plural form of the word 'repatriate', which became a basis for further derivations, probably because of the "inconvenience" of the singular form *olé* and by its frequent use in the plural. Cf. several cases of reinterpretation of plural form as singular: *miluim* 'army reserve', *picuim* 'compensation'. Compare also the old loan words *serafim* and *cheruvim* (Moskovič 1978: 169). The adjective *datišnyj*, as well as the noun *datišnik* 'religious person', reflect the new processes in word formation in Russian, the usage of the infix *š* after the stem ending in vowel; cf. such examples, as *kinošnyj*, *kinošnik*, *kegebešnyj*, *kegebešnik*. This type of word formation, which has been considered as non-standard, is obviously productive (Panov 1968: 48-49); cf. also *pisiška* from PC 'personal computer' in the professional jargon of Russian speaking software engineers.

Because of the structural differences between Russian and Hebrew (the discontinuous pattern of the root and specific prefixes in the latter [Ephratt 1997]), morphological restructuring takes place in mixes, e.g., the word /m'ištara/ 'police' containing the root *š-t-r* and the prefix *mi-* in Hebrew is perceived in RI as consisting of the root /m'ištar/ plus the flexion /a/ (the latter like in Hebrew).

Another class of mixes constitute discourse markers that are unchangeable and are used in the host language without constraints, e.g., /be seder/ 'OK', /beemet/ 'really'. The communicative function of these discourse markers as well as their phatic function are obvious.

4. Conclusions and outlook

The observations above generally correspond to what we know of code-switching and -mixing, and contribute to a typology of these phenomena. Another aspect of this study, which seems to be interesting, concerns the trends in the development of code-mixing in Russian. Several of them have been pointed out: 1) the unproductivity of the fixed stress pattern in feminine words ending in *-á* (unproductive *mečtá* vs. productive *golová*, *straná*); 2) the avoidance of stress shift in declension paradigms of foreign words that are not fully integrated into the Russian morphological system; 3) the productivity of the infix *š*; 4) the possibility of integration of composita with an unchangeable first part into the Russian grammatical system. These data experimentally confirm what is already known about the trends in the development of some morphological patterns in Modern Standard Russian.

Thus, the situation of language contact can become a linguistic laboratory. The linguistic experiments, the importance of which has been stressed by many linguists, especially by Lev V. Ščerba and his school, are provided by daily experience.[1]

The Hebrew University of Jerusalem

REFERENCES

Comrie, Bernard, Gerald Stone, and Maria Polinsky
1996   *The Russian Language in the Twentieth Century*. Oxford.
Ephratt, Michal
1997   "The Psycholinguistic Status of the Root in Modern Hebrew", *Folia Linguistica* XXXI/1-2, 77-103.
Moskovich, Wolf
1978   "Interference of Hebrew and Russian in Israel", *Slavica Hierosolimitana* 2, 215-234.
Olshtain, Elite, and Shoshana Blum-Kulka
1990   "Happy Hebrish: Mixing and switching in American-Israeli family interaction", in: S. Gass, C. Madden, L. Selinker (eds.), *Variation in Second Language Acquisition: Discourse and Pragmatics*, 59-83. Clevedon.
Orel, Vladimir
1994   "Russkij jazyk v Izraile", *Slavjanovedenie* 4, 35-43.
Panov, M.V. (ed.)
1968   *Russkij jazyk i sovetskoe obščestvo. Sociologo-lingvističeskoe issledovanie. Slovoobrazovanie sovremennogo russkogo literaturnogo jazyka*. Moskva.
Vereščagin, E.M.
1968   "O probleme zaimstvovanija fonem", *Jazyk i obščestvo*, 160-170. Moskva.
Weinreich, Uriel
1963   *Languages in Contact. Findings and Problems*. The Hague (second edition).
Zaliznjak, A.A.
1967   *Russkoe imennoe slovoizmenenie*. Moskva.

---

[1] The research was supported by the Ministry of Science and Arts of Israel and by the Franz Rosenzweig Research Center for German-Jewish Literature and Cultural History (the Hebrew University of Jerusalem). I am grateful to the students Rene Perelmuter and Miriam Weingarten for assistance in collecting and interpreting material.

Languages in Contact, edited by D.G. Gilbers, J. Nerbonne, and J. Schaeken (= *Studies in Slavic and General Linguistics*, vol. 28), 283-298. Amsterdam - Atlanta, GA: Rodopi, 2000.

SHOR-RUSSIAN CONTACT FEATURES

IRINA NEVSKAJA

1. Introduction

The territory of South Siberia has always been a melting pot of cultures, peoples and languages. The Shor people, an indigenous Turkic people of the area, are no exception: Ob'-Ugric, Mongolian and later Russian had their turn in playing a prominent role in the development of the Shor language; the genetically and are-ally close languages Khakas, Altay, Kumandy, Teleut have been in contact with Shor for centuries and contributed to its areal features.

Contacts with Russian, a language of a completely different system, episodic in the earlier periods of the Shor language history, got more and more intense be-ginning with the seventeenth century, when the area was joined to the Russian Empire, and became a decisive factor in the Shor language development since the 1930s. One of the first Russian fortresses in South Siberia was built in Mountain Shoriya in 1618; it grew into the town of Novokuznetsk, today one of the most important industrial and cultural centers. Early Russian speaking migrants had to adopt a number of Shor traditional life patterns in order to survive in the severe Siberian climate; they also shared their own skills and knowledge with the Shors. This period is characterized by lexical borrowing processes between the Shor and the Russian languages. In the beginning of the nineteenth century, the Altay mis-sionaries started propagating Christianity to the native population of South Sibe-ria; they organized primary schools, published religious and educational literature and preached in the languages of indigenous peoples. In the time of the Stolypin reform at the end of the nineteenth century, the territory absorbed a considerable number of Russian settlers. But it was not until the 1930s that the Shor-Russian interaction became one-sided and menacing for the Shor language and culture. The cultural revolution of the early 1930s, which can be defined as the most flourishing period in the history of the Shor language, was followed by a long pe-riod of its neglect. This turn took place in the late 1930s when the industrial de-velopment of the region began. The mass influx of migrants for whom Russian was a *lingua franca* initiated assimilation processes, which created a threat to the very existence of the Shor nation. The long period (1942-1988) when Shor was neither written, nor taught at schools lowered the social status of the language as compared to Russian even more. As a result, the people began to give up their own language. Within the last thirty years the number of speakers has diminished, all of them are bilingual, language transmission to younger generations has almost stopped, all the systems of the language appear to be open to influences coming from Russian. In spite of the nascent attempts to revive the literary language (Nevskaja 1998), Shor remains strongly endangered. However, it has proven its vitality and the will of the people to keep it alive in spite of all the unfavourable circumstances. It has accomodated to the modern sociolinguistic situation by developing new ways of expression, including copies of Russian structures and even of morphological categories with the Shor language means.

Strange as it might seem, contact determined Shor language phenomena are still an untouched field for Shor linguistics: there has been no research on language contacts and code-copying processes instigated by these contacts. One can only find some information on contact factors that might have played a prominent role in the historical development of Shor in publications devoted to other topics. Linguistic, ethnological and anthropological research of the Shors gives evidence of their Ob'-Ugric substratum; the toponymy of Mountain Shoriya proves former Shor-Ket contacts. Our research on how the Shor language changed in time and space has recently started in the framework of a cooperative German-Russian project involving the creation of a computer data base of the Shor language.[1]

In section 2 of our paper, we delineate the Shor language systems showing code-copying from Russian. In section 3, we describe the Shor infinitive whose functions have obviously been broadened to match those of the Russian infinitive, thus giving one example of the Russian influence on the Shor morphology, a language level which is, as a rule, copied last. Describing Shor contact determined features we will use the terminology proposed by Lars Johanson and will refer to his understanding of the types of code-copying processes reflected in the monograph *Strukturelle Faktoren in türkischen Sprachkontakten* (1992).

2. Code-copying processes in the Shor vocabulary and grammar

Although there is an opinion that only elements of the lexical level can be copied, and that "languages do not borrow grammar" (Givón 1979), the Turkic language material disproves these restrictions (Johanson 1992). Shor can add examples of deep structural changes prompted by Shor-Russian language contacts involving all the language levels. Plenty of loaned words from or through Russian, among them conjunctions and other functional words, deep changes in the language syntax, e.g. loosened scrambling processes and signs of transition from SOV to SVO word order, development of the analytical type of clause combining instead of the

---

[1] The cooperative project "A Shor language electronic text corpus" is carried out at Frankfurt University and at Novokuznetsk State Pedagogical Institute; it is supported by the German Research Society (DFG) and by the Russian Foundation of Research in the Humanities (RGNF).

synthetic or asyndetic ones are features characteristic of modern Shor, especially of its spoken variety.[2]

A few examples of Shor-Russian contact features are listed below. The phenomena given under 2.1 (a) and 2.2 may be defined as *global copying* in the sense of Johanson 1992: 177-195, i.e. the copying of both the material form and the function of a source language entity; 2.3, 2.4 and 2.5 (b) illustrate *partial structural copying*, i.e. the copying of a functional, semantic or structural entity of the source by the means of a recipient language; 2.1 (b) and 2.5 (a) illustrate *mixed copying* when a copying entity contains a globally copied element of the source language.

2.1 Recent lexical borrowings from Russian or through Russian

As opposed to earlier loans, borrowings now preserve the phonetic and graphic shape of the Russian source; we give them in transliteration:

(a) *televizor* 'a TV-set', *japonskij* 'Japanese', *stiral'nyj mašina* 'a washing machine' – these can be defined as *global copies* of the corresponding Russian entities although they show traces of their adoptation to the Shor language system, e.g. note the affix of the masculine gender on the attribute *stiral'nyj* that is not congruent with the feminine gender of the head noun *mašina*, violating Russian grammar rules;

(b) *besedovat' et-* 'to speak to each other', *centrifugalyg* < *centrifuga* +LIG[3] offer examples of *mixed copying* where the Shor verb *et-* 'to do' and the adjectivizing affix +*LIG* are used for the integration of foreign lexemes into the Shor language system.

---

[2] Written Shor is normalized according to the literary rules based on the only academic grammar of Shor published more than half a century ago (Dyrenkova 1941) when Shor did not show so many features copied from Russian; this work may already be regarded as a historic source.

[3] Turkic languages belong to the agglutinative type. Their morphonology is characterized by so-called synharmonism, i. e. progressive assimilation processes affecting both consonants and vowels, mainly in affixes. Consequently, Turkic affixes may have up to 16 morphonological variants. Therefore, we use an archimorphemic representation of Turkic formants which is a tradition in Turkology. *A* denotes *a* after stems with back vowels and *e* after stems with front vowels. *I* denotes *ï* in words with back vowels and *i* in words with front vowels. *X* has the same values as *I* in words with unrounded vowels, but it denotes *ü* in words with front rounded vowels and *u* in words with back rounded vowels. *G* denotes *g* after stems with front vowels ending in a vowel or a sonorous consonant, *γ* after stems with back vowels ending in a vowel or a sonorous consonant, *k* after stems with front vowels ending in a voiceless consonant, *q* after stems with back vowels ending in a voiceless consonant. *S* denotes *s* after stems ending in a voiceless consonant and otherwise *z*. *K* denotes *q* in words with back vowels and otherwise *k*. *B* denotes *m* after nasals, *p* after unvoiced consonants and otherwise *b*. *L* has the value of *l* after vowels and sonorants except nasals in which case *n*, and *t* after voiceless consonants. Vowels in brackets *()* appear only after stems ending in consonants. Consonants in brackets *()* appear only after stems ending in vowels.

2.2 Borrowed functional words

These include borrowed discourse particles, modal words and aspect adverbs, conjunctions: *odnako* 'well, really, as a matter of fact', *i* 'and', a coordinative conjunction, *ili* 'or', a disjunctive conjunction, *no* 'but', an adversative conjunction, *a* 'while', a disjunctive conjunction, *a to* 'otherwise', a conjunction of an alternative state of affairs harmful for the subject of the main clause, *a to i tak* 'anyway', a conjunction of undesired consequences which may aggrevate the existing state of affairs already characterized by similar problems, *iščo < eščo* 'also', *a iščo* 'besides', *mož, možet* 'maybe', *navernoe* 'probably', *uže* 'already'. These are *global copies*.

2.3 Scrambling and postposition of attributes and objects

Among recent developments in Shor, one finds scrambling and postposition of attributes and objects as compared to the normal preposition of dependent components to their heads:

Qarï kiži-ni ŋ čüreg-ež-i čïda-baan andïɣ nebe-ni,
old man-GEN heart-DEMIN-POSS.3.SG bear-CONV:neg such thing-ACC
'The poor heart of the old man could not bear such a thing,

and-oq infarkt pol par-dï i apčïɣ ando-q öl-büs-tü.
then-PARTC heart attack be go:aux.-PAST and then-PARTC die-PERF-PAST
he got a heart attack and died at the same moment.'

2.4 Analytical clause combining

A globally copied conjunction is used along with the copying of the Russian syntactic structure:

(a) *Ili a ŋ qulaɣ-ïn-ɣa uɣ-ul par-dï,*
    either:Russ. his ear-POSS.3.SG-DAT hear-PASS go:aux.-PAST
    'Either it seems to him that he heard,

   ili čïnap kiži ün-ü uɣ-ul-ča.
   or:Russ. really man voice-POSS.3.SG hear-PASS-PRES
   or a human voice can really be heard.';

(b) *Sïn-ïn-ɣa čet par-ïp, ebire kör-dü,*
    backbone-POSS.3.SG-DAT reach go:aux.-CONV, around see-PAST
    'Having reached the middle part (of the cedar tree), he looked around,

   no pir da torum körü-n-meen-ča.
   but:Russ. one PARTC cone see-REFL-CONV:neg-PRES
   but no cone was visible.'

2.5 Multiple expression of semantic relations

Among newly attested and, apparently, contact determined syntactic features one can find syntactic synthetic constructions of a complex sentence whose dependent clause contains a conjunction denoting the same semantic relation as the dependent predicate. A conjunction may either be borrowed from Russian (a), or it may have developed from internal language sources, e.g. interrogative pronouns, non-finite forms of auxiliary verbs, etc. (b):

(a) *Kogda kel-ze-ŋ / Kel-ze-ŋ, čoqta-ž-ar-ïs.*
    when:Russ. come-CONV-POSS.2.SG, speak-RECIPR-FUT-1.PL
    'When you come, we will speak.'

(b) *Qačan kel-ze-ŋ / Kel-ze-ŋ, čoqta-ž-ar-ïs.*
    when:Shor come-CONV-POSS.2.SG, speak-RECIPR-FUT-1.PL
    'When you come, we will speak.'

2.6 Code-copying processes in Shor morphology

Finer and less obvious traces of the Russian influence can be observed in Shor morphology. Contacts with Russian may have faciliated some recent developments, e.g. a rapid rise of some morphological categories like the *infinitive* and the perfective and imperfective *Aktionsart* categories.

The infinitive in Shor is formed on the basis of the future tense participle in the dative case. For Turkic in general, the infinitive is considered to be a rather young category. We suppose that its rise in Shor was determined by certain language internal factors having much in common in many Turkic languages (since they have developed their infinitives using similar sources), and was fostered by external ones. The infinitive functions in Shor are strikingly similar to those of the Indo-European infinitive, especially of the Russian infinitive. The infinitive in Shor (as in Khakas) has replaced other non-finite forms in many positions still occupied by them in Siberian Turkic languages. This refers even to some analytical phasal and modal constructions that are otherwise pretty stable.

3. The Shor infinitive as an example of a copying of the functional sphere of the Russian infinitive

3.1 The category of the infinitive

Infinitive properties and functions may differ throughout languages distinguishing this category. Therefore, it is not quite clear when and why this or that form of a language can be defined as an infinitive. Nevertheless, linguists appear to have a certain set of criteria which allow them either to speak of infinitive forms in some languages, e.g. Russian, German, English, French, Turkmen, Altay, Khakas, Shor, Kazakh, Bashkir or Tatar, or to state the absence of such forms in Tuva, Tofa, Mongolian, Evenki or Khanty. A most common set of infinitive features, un-doubtedly based on the properties and functions of Indo-European infinitives, seems to be as follows.

The infinitive is a non-finite verb form; hence it does not express absolute tense or mood distinctions. It usually denotes an anticipatory or potential action, often seen as the purpose of a head action. It easily combines with phasal, modal (emotive, intentional, desiderative) and propositional attitude (evaluative, com-mentative) predicates.[4] It does not usually accept personal markers,[5] although its action can be assigned to an agent expressed in a sentence by a nominal phrase with the dative case marker unless its agent is shared with the host predicate. With this exception, the infinitive preserves the valency pattern of a verb stem. It can also be modified by adverbs and entities used in adverbial functions (e.g. certain nominal groups, converbs, dependent adverbial clauses). The infinitive has all the other verb categories: those of voice, causality, reflexivity, reciprocity, frequenta-tivity, actionality, modality, negation, etc. (a set of verbal categories is language specific). Consequently, it can be formed from all kinds of derived stems, along with various compound and complex stems. Thus, in Turkic languages it is formed from passive, causative, reciprocal and reflexive stems, from so-called analytical verbs including lexical compounds as well as compounds of a phasal, modal or *Aktionsart* semantics, and from negative stems. Moreover, Indo-European infinitives often participate in various aspect and temporal verb forms.

The infinitive names an action. It can represent it in general, without referring it to its agent (*to speak, to go, to smoke*). Thus, it often serves as the dictionary form of verbs, but not in Turkic languages where the most common dictionary verb form is that of the 2nd person singular of the imperative mood consisting of a bare verb stem. Several infinitives sharing the above-mentioned functions and propertiers might be distinguished in a language, but, as a rule, only one form has the nominating function.

3.2 Infinitive forms in Turkic languages

In Turkic languages, the category of the infinitive is considered to have been formed relatively recently from different sources (Gadžieva 1973), or it was not formed at all, e.g. there is no infinitive in Tuva (Isxakov and Pal'mbax 1968). However, the form *-mAk* is attested already in Old Uygur in the infinitive func-tions. It could be a pretender to the role of a Common Turkic infinitive. It still

---

[4] The semantic types of predicates combining with action nominals are analysed in Koptevskaja-Tamm 1988.

[5] This restriction is not absolute even for Indo-European languages: the Portuguese infinitive does accept a personal marking. Quite a number of Turkic infinitives certainly do (Jusupov 1985: 114; Clark 1998). However, it seems to be necessary that a candidate for the infinitive status can be used without a personal marking, thus representing an action in general.

functions as an infinitive in Oghuz Turkic. In Siberian Turkic, it has moved into the sphere of derivation: the corresponding Shor affix *-BAK+* derives deverbal nouns: *čar-baq* 'a saw' from *čar-* 'to cut' (instruments), cf. the infinitive form *-mAk* in Turkish and Turkmen.

Nevertheless, it is true that modern Turkic languages show a great variety of infinitive forms. It is also characteristic of Turkic languages to have several competing forms found in the functions of the Indo-European infinitive. In Yakut, six infinitive forms are distinguished, they share traditional infinitive functions, but do not cover all of them: some typical infinitive functions are expressed by converbs (Ubrjatova 1976: 108-114). In Altay, Khakas and Shor, the infinitive has undoubtedly been formed (Tadykin 1971: 131; *Grammatika xakasskogo jazyka* 1975: 173-175; Dyrenkova 1941: 131; Nevskaja 1988). The specificity of Altay, Khakas and Shor is the fact that one form has established itself as the infinitive. They have analogous infinitive forms (found also in Tatar, Bashkir, Karachay, Balkar and Yakut). It is the future participle *-(A)r/-BAs* in the dative case: *-(A)rGA*, in the negative aspect *-BAsKA*. Native speakers of these languages perceive these formants as a fully fused whole. In Tofa, the form *-(A)rGA* is used very rarely, the infinitive functions are divided between future participles and converbs (Rassadin 1978: 198-200). The same holds for Chuvash.

The infinitive belongs to a class of verb forms functioning as event (or action) nominals (Comrie 1976). In Turkic languages, quite a number of forms can represent a nominalized action: infinitives, verbal nouns, participles and even, in some positions, converbs.[6] Verbal nouns are most close to infinitives. These two terms are often used as synonyms. Research on typology of verbal nouns has shown that in both cases a very similar set of properties is meant (Bondarenko 1980). However, some differences between these two classes can be found. They are especially relevant for languages having both categories: cf. a contrastive analysis of infinitive(s) and verbal noun(s) in Bashkir in *Grammatika baškirskogo jazyka* 1981: 318-323, in Tatar by Jusupov 1985: 203, in Turkish by Csató 1990 and Erdal 1998, in Turkmen by Clark 1998: 327-335.

Siberian Turkic does not have the category of verbal nouns, but a form recognized as the infinitive in a Turkic language can share some functions of Indo-European infinitives with other non-finite forms; this may lead to competition between them. Shor, Khakas and Altay give an example of an interaction between their infinitives, participles and converbs. Although materially identical, their infinitives have different scopes of functions due to the fact that the infinitive might be a more successful competitor in one of them. Thus, in Khakas and Shor, the infinitive is more active than in Altay: it is expanding its functions competing

---

[6] A more detailed analysis of action nominals in South Siberian Turkic can be found in Čeremisina and Nevskaja (in print).

against converbs and participles in some positions traditionally occupied by them. We may suppose that this happens under the influence of Russian.

In the following, we will describe infinitive functions in Shor and show the areas of interaction and competition between the infinitive and other non-finite verb forms.

Our first claim is that Shor infinitive functions are very similar to those of Indo-European infinitives, especially Russian: all the functions listed below can be performed by the Russian infinitive. The English infinitive also fulfils most of these functions, therefore we can almost always use an English infinitive translating phrases with the Shor or Russian infinitives. We are far from claiming that all of them were copied from Russian, although the Russian influence is obvious in quite a number of cases. Thus, our second statement is that some of the Shor infinitive functions are structural copies of the Russian infinitive.

3.3 The functions of the Shor infinitive

The Shor infinitive appears with phasal, emotive, intentional, desiderative, evaluative, commentative predicates in actant positions and as an adjunct with the semantics of purpose. It can be an attribute in a nominal phrase. It participates in analytical verb forms. It can also function without a head word. Consequently, we distinguish *independent* and *dependent* infinitives.

3.4 The functions of the independent infinitive

The *independent* infinitive, i.e. the infinitive without a head word a) gives a name to an action: "What is the Shor for 'to speak'?" – *čoqtažarɣa*; b) forms imperative constructions of explicit order: Shor *Parčazï turarɣa!* 'Stand up, all of you!', or invites to a joint action: *Čestek alarɣa!* 'Let's go to gather berries!'.

The latter use of the infinitive is attested in a number of Turkic languages (e.g. Khakas, Bashkir), all of them being in contact with Russian, which shows a similar infinitive function.

3.5 The functions of the dependent infinitive

The *dependent* infinitive a) occupies an attributive position; the head word is usually a noun of a very broad and abstract semantics, e.g. Shor *čer* 'land, earth, place', *kiži* 'person', *tem* 'time'; b) occupies complement or adjunct positions of predicates belonging to different syntactic and semantic types.

3.5.1 Infinitive as an attribute

The infinitive attribute denotes the destination of a head noun. If the head noun is animate, it denotes the agent of the infinitive action: *Pallarba odurarɣa kiži čoq polɣan* 'There was nobody to take care of the children'. If the head noun is inanimate, it cannot be the infinitive's agent: *čadarɣa čer* 'place where to live, place for living, for residing', *učuɣarɣa tem* 'time to fly'. Then, the infinitive agent can be expressed by a nominal phrase in the dative case: *Poɣuna čadarɣa čer tappadï* '(S)He has not found a place for (her)himself to live'. Thus, the infinitive forms relative clauses. It may also function as a headless relative clause as in *čiš par, ižerge teze čoq* 'There is food, but there is nothing to drink'.

The destination of a person or an object can also be expressed by the participles *-(A)r* and *-čAŋ* in Shor: *ižer/iščeŋ/ižerge suɣ* 'water to drink, for drinking'. The usage of the infinitive in this position is a modern development in Shor. It may also be instigated by Shor-Russian language contacts. In Altay, the participle *-(A)r* is preferred in such phrases.

Some combinations of the infinitive with head nouns may show a strong tendency to become grammaticalized due to the modal semantics of the head noun: Shor *saɣïš* 'thought, desire', *köŋnü* 'one's soul, desire', *tem* 'time', *küš* 'power, strength', etc.: *Aaŋ ürgenerge saɣïžï par* '(S)He wants to study', *Perilgen išti püdürerge küžibis alar ba?* 'Do we have enough power to do the work that we were given?'. The lexical verb may also have the form of the participle *-(A)r* or *-čAŋ*. Such combinations can be evaluated as phraseological intention constructions. They are found in other Turkic languages, but usually with a participle instead of the infinitive. Earlier Shor texts prefer participles in such constructions. Therefore, this construction is also a battlefield between the infinitive and the future participle in Shor.

Among all the infinitive functions, the most important ones are those fulfilled in combinations with head predicates.

3.5.2 The infinitive as a complement of a superordinate verbal predicate

3.5.2.1 Constructions of intention to fulfill an action

Dominating predicates have the semantics of mental perception or intention. The infinitive is their second actant: *Ol pararɣa sanaɣan* '(S)he wants to go (lit.: thinks to go)'. Existential verbs and verbs with the most abstract semantics of action (e.g. *et-* 'to do') can also head constructions of intention: *kelerge etken* '(s)he wanted to come'. Since they completely lose their lexical semantics and serve as auxiliaries, such combinations can be evaluated as analytical modal verb forms (Čeremisina and Nevskaja, in print).

3.5.2.2 Constructions of adaptation

Dominating predicates are verbs of knowledge and verbs of acquisition of knowledge, e.g. Shor *uŋna-, pil-* 'to know, to be able', *ürgen-* 'to study', *qïn-* 'to get used to, to come to love', etc. They express the modality of possibility of an action thanks to the inner abilities of its agent. Such combinations also tend to become grammaticalized. Some of them are very close to analytical modal forms, since the head verb has acquired a modal meaning, e.g. *Ol peš čašta qïrarγa ürgenip alγan* '(S)He learned to read when (s)he was five (= He could read)'.

In combination with the verbs *uŋna-* and *pil-*, the Shor infinitive gradually replaces the converb *-(I)p*, still used here by older Shor people and considered to be the norm: *Men nek saγarγa uŋnapčam* 'I know how to milk a cow (= I can milk a cow)' versus *Men nek saγïp uŋnapčam*. This is a new development in Shor found in the speech of younger informants. We consider such developments to be further examples of the Russian influence on Shor.

3.5.2.3 Emotive constructions

The infinitive is governed by an emotive or evaluative predicate, the components tend to have a unitary syntactic function – that of a compound modal predicate: Shor *kölen-* 'to love to do something', *qooruq-* 'to be afraid', *uya-* 'to be ashamed', *örün-* 'to be glad', *küčsün-* 'to find it hard to do something, to try', *egeniš-* 'to feel awkward about doing something', *arγastan-* 'to be lazy', etc. The head verb expresses an attitude to the infinitive action: *Aydarγa uyačir* '(S)He feels ashamed to say (that)'. The infinitive is its second actant: Shor *Arγas toolanarγa da argastanča* 'A lazy-bones is too lazy even to think'.

3.5.2.4 Prospective constructions

These are formed by prospective verbs: *to expect, to hope, to wait for*: *Men nanarγa iženčam* 'I hope to return'.

3.5.2.5 Preparatory constructions

They contain verbs of the type: *to get ready for, to prepare for, to be going to do something* (verbs of intention): *Men nanarγa tüqtünčam* 'I am getting ready to come back. I am going to come back'.

3.5.2.6 Combinations with phasal semantics

These combinations occupy a special place among constructions with a subordinate infinitive: on the one hand, the dominating phasal predicate (*to begin, to go on, to stop, to finish*, etc.) preserves its lexical semantics; on the other hand, such constructions refer to a certain stage of an action. The phasal meaning of these verbs is an auxiliary one in itself. Such verbs are always used together with a lexical one.[7] In Turkic languages, where such combinations are grammaticalized no less than in Russian (to say the least), the lexical component usually gets a converbial form *-(I)p*. However, in this position, one can often find the infinitive.

---

[7] The latter may be omitted by pragmatic reasons: Russian *ja načala koftu* 'lit.: I started a pullover' means *Ja načala vjazat' (ili šit') koftu* 'I started to knit (or to saw) a pullover'.

Since almost all Turkic speakers in South Siberia are bilingual, it may be assumed that the infinitive is penetrating this sphere under Russian influence.

Phasal constructions in Siberian Turkic can denote the *starting point* of an action: Shor *pašta-, paža-, šïq-, kir-* 'to begin, to start'. In Shor, the infinitive competes with the converb *-(I)p* in combinations with the verbs *šïq-* and *pašta-*: *Pis on častaŋ ala išterge pažadïbïs* 'We began to work when we were ten (lit.: since ten years)', *Kün am ne šïqqanda, pis palïqtarγa / palïqtap šïqtïbïs* 'As soon as the sun rose, we started fishing'.

Phasal constructions with the infinitive can denote the *finishing point* of an action. An action can be finished because it has reached its terminate point, or it can be interrupted. In Siberian Turkic languages, the first semantic variant is expressed by analytical constructions with the converb *-(I)p*. Such constructions usually combine the terminative meaning with that of the *Aktionsart* type: in Shor *paγlap aldïm* 'I have knit', the form *-(I)p al-* expressed an action performed to benefit its agent: 'I have knit something for myself'. The second semantic variant, that of an interrupted action, is expressed by infinitive constructions with the verbs *toqta-* 'to stop, to interrupt', *tašta-* 'to stop, to give up'; the gerund *-(I)p* is also possible in this position: Shor *Ol kelgen poyubïla, ižerge / ižip taštadï* 'He came back and gave up drinking'.

3.5.2.7 Causative constructions

In these constructions, the subject of the matrix clause causes the subject of the embedded clause to fulfill the infinitive action. In Turkic languages, there are special voice forms expressing causation. Constructions with the dependent infinitive represent an analytical way of expressing the causative diathesis. The host predicates are as follows:

a) causative verbs of adaptation: *üret-* 'to teach' (causative), cf. *üren-* 'to study' (non-causative), *sal-* 'to predetermine': *Saγa uluγ quday salγan iygi qolunaŋ alïp čayalarγa!* 'The great God predestined that you should create brave warriors from both hands of yours!';

b) verbs of positive or negative influence on the infinitive action: *poluš-* 'to help', *aarlïš-* 'to interfere', *požat-* 'to allow to go', *al-* 'to accept somebody for a joint action': *Meni oynarγa alzaar!* 'Let me play with you (lit.: take me to play)!';

c) causative verbs of saying: *sura-* 'to ask', *ayt-* 'to say, to order', *per-* 'to allow', *qïïr-* 'to call, to invite to come (in the direction to the speaker)', *ïs-* 'to send, to cause to go (from the speaker)': *Qïs qarïndažïm aγa pararγa maγa ayčir* 'My friend advises me to marry him'.

3.5.3 The infinitive in the complement position of a nominal predicate

It usually occupies the position of the first actant of such predicates. A copula is needed to refer the situation to the past or to the future, to present it as a desired or possible one or to negate it. The agent of the infinitive action can be introduced by a nominal phrase in the dative case.

3.5.3.1 Evaluative constructions

Infinitives may be headed by propositional attitude predicates, i.e. nominal predicates with evaluative semantics: Shor *čaqšï* 'good, right', *čabal* 'bad', *uyat* 'shame, shameful'. The infinitive denotes a situation which is evaluated: Shor *Andïɣ nebeni aydarɣa da uyat* 'It is shameful even to say such a thing', *Sooq kün kebege čiilinarɣa čaqšï polar edi* 'It would be good to get warm by the stove on a cold day'.

3.5.3.2 Commentative constructions

They are formed by commentative predicates: Shor *küš* 'difficult', *nïŋnaq* 'easy', etc. The infinitive denotes a situation which is commented upon: *Pararɣa raq* 'It is far to go', *Qazarɣa küš polɣan* 'It was difficult to dig'.

3.5.3.3 Expressive constructions

These are rhetoric questions with interrogative pronouns: Shor *qayde* 'how', *qayaɣa* 'where', *qačan* 'when', etc.: *Aydarɣa qayde!* 'How to say (that)! (= It is impossible to say that!)', *Pararɣa qayaɣa!* 'Where to go! (= There is nowhere to go!)'.

3.5.3.4 Modal constructions

Such constructions are formed by nominal predicates: Shor *kerek* 'it is necessary', *čarabas* 'it is impossible, it is prohibited, it does not go', *kelišpes* 'it is not suitable': *Eede išpeske kereksiŋ noo!* 'It is impossible for you to drink so much!', *šïɣarɣa kelišpes* 'It is not suitable to go out', *Seeŋ adïŋdï maɣa adarɣa čarabas* 'I am not allowed to call you by name'. The participle *-(A)r* is also used in this construction. Dyrenkova 1941 evaluates it in this position as a contracted infinitive form, but we doubt that this is the case: The future participle is found in this construction throughout Siberian Turkic languages, while the infinitive appears only in Shor and Khakas. Therefore, the participle can be considered to be primary here. This is another conflict position for the infinitive and the future participle.

3.5.4 The infinitive as an adjunct of a superordinated predicate

3.5.4.1 Constructions expressing the purpose of motion.

These are combinations of a subordinate infinitive with a verb of motion. The infinitive occupies an adjunct position: *Mus parïsqan soonda, pis suɣ töbere palïqtarɣa eneris* 'After the ice has flown away, we will go fishing (lit.: to fish) down the river'.

The Common Turkic converb *-(I)p* can fulfill the same function. In South Siberian Turkic, it has the purpose meaning in a very restricted surrounding: the head verb should be that of movement, the verb in the converbial form should be that of obtaining an object: *aŋnap parɣam* 'I went hunting'. Verbs of obtaining an object are usually derived by the affix *+LA-* from nouns denoting those objects: Shor *aŋ-na* 'to hunt' from *aŋ* 'a wild animal', *quš-ta-* 'to hunt birds' from *quš* 'a bird', *palïq-ta-* 'to fish' from *palïq* 'fish', *örtekte-* 'to hunt ducks' from *örtek* 'a duck', *qïs-ta-* 'to court girls' from *qïs* 'a girl'. Only a few verbs of differing derivational patterns can be found as converbs of purpose in this position: *tile-* 'to look for', *aal-a-* 'to stay at some place as a guest' from *aal* 'a village', *sura-* 'to ask for'. One might gain the impression that these combinations have already been lexicalized. However, they still allow other lexical words to get between the two components: *Taŋda aŋnap erte pararïm* 'I will go hunting early in the morning tomorrow'.

3.5.4.2 Constructions of the purpose of a voluntary action

The infinitive combines with a wide range of verbs denoting a voluntary action occupying an adjunct position and expressing the purpose of the action of a superordinate verb. Such constructions are mostly same-subject ones: *amzarɣa sadïp alɣan* 'He bought (it) to taste'. In a different-subject construction of purpose, the predicate of the subordinated clause is usually not an infinitive, but the imperative form of the 3rd person along with the conjunction *dep/tep* (an *-(I)p* converb of the verb of saying *te-* 'to say, to speak'): *amzazïn dep sadïp alɣan* '(S)he[1] bought it for her/him[2] to taste'. In exceptional cases, the infinitive can appear in a different-subject construction with the semantics of purpose. In Shor, the agent of the action expressed by the infinitive can appear in the sentence as a nominal phrase in the dative or, very rarely, in the nominative case: *Pis qïšqïda sooqqa toɣbasqaɣa, ičem ödük tïq pergen* 'So as we would not get cold in winter, my mother sew boots' or *Qïšqïda sooqqa toɣbasqaɣa, ičem piske ödük tïq pergen*.

3.5.4.3 Constructions of the consequences of an involuntary action

Verbs of an involuntary action do not have a component of purpose in their semantics. Therefore, the infinitive can only express consequences of such actions: Shor *Anï čolap pararɣa, arɣa moynuŋ tïŋïɣalaq* 'You are not strong enough, to follow him (lit.: Your spine and your neck have not yet got strong enough, (for you) to follow him)'.

In our survey, we have not dealt with the topic of analytical verb forms in Siberian Turkic or the role of the infinitive in them. This should be a subject of a special research. We would like to note that Turkic converbs and participles play a most prominent role in building aspect and tense verb forms, while the infinitive participates in numerous analytical forms of modality (Čeremisina and Nevskaja, in print).

4. Conclusion

1) Shor shows deep structural changes in the language systems that could be initiated or fostered by contacts with Russian. All the language systems including morphology appear to be open to influences coming from Russian. It is a natural experimental laboratory of language contacts.

2) Contrary to other Turkic languages that possess several infinitives or/and verbal nouns sharing different functions of the Indo-European infinitives, Shor, Altay and Khakas have one infinitive form, which is similar to the situation in Indo-European languages.

3) The modern category of the Shor infinitive is, to a certain extent, a structural copy of the Russian infinitive: the Shor infinitive is broadening its functions to match those of the Russian infinitive, it is pushing away other infinite forms from the positions traditionaly occupied by them in Shor and in other languages that are genetically and areally closely related (Khakas, Altay). Similar developments can be observed in Khakas, another Siberian Turkic language that is heavily influenced by Russian.[8]

Johann Wolfgang Goethe-University, Frankfurt am Main
Novokuznetsk State Pedagogical Institute, Novokuznetsk

REFERENCES

Anon.
   1884   *Grammatika altajskogo jazyka, sostavlennaja členami altajskoj missii.* Kazan'.
Baskakov, N.A.
   1947   "Očerk grammatiki ojrotskogo jazyka", in: *Ojrotsko-russkij slovar'*, 219-312. Moskva.

---

[8] I express my heartiest gratitude to Prof. Lars Johanson whom I owe so much, including the fact that he attracted my attention to this field of research during my stay at his Institute as a Humboldt fellow. I would like to thank the Alexander von Humboldt Foundation that fosters the research work of its fellows in an exemplary way.

Bondarenko, I.V.
1980   "Sintaksičeskie funkcii 'infinitivov' v tjurkskix jazykax", in: *Polipredikativnye konstrukcii i ix morfologičeskaja baza*, 47-60. Novosibirsk.
Clark, L.
1998   *Turkmen Reference Grammar.* Wiesbaden: Harrassowitz.
Comrie, B.
1976   "The syntax of action nominals: a cross-language study", *Lingua* 40, 177-201.
Csató, É.Á.
1990   "Non-finite verbal constructions in Turkish", in: B. Brendemoen (ed.), *Proceedings from the 32nd Meeting of the Permanent International Altaistic Conference. Oslo, June 12-16, 1989*, 75-88. Oslo.
Čeremisina, M.I., L.M. Brodskaja, L.M. Gorelova, et al.
1984   *Predikativnoe sklonenie pričastij v altajskix jazykax.* Novosibirsk: Nauka.
Čeremisina, M.I., L.M. Brodskaja, L. M., E.K. Skribnik, et al.
1986   *Strukturnye tipy sintetičeskix polipredikativnyx konstrukcij v jazykax raznyx sistem.* Novosibirsk: Nauka.
Čeremisina, M.I., and I.A. Nevskaja
in print   "'I stood to lie down' and 'I sat to leave': infinitive constructions of intention in South Siberian Turkic languages", to be published in: *Turkic Languages.* Wiesbaden: Harrassowitz.
Dyrenkova, N.D.
1941   *Grammatika šorskogo jazyka.* Moskva-Leningrad: Izdatel'stvo AN SSSR.
Dyrenkova, N.P.
1948   *Grammatika xakasskogo jazyka. Fonetika i morfologija.* Moskva.
Erdal, M.
1998   "On the verbal noun in -(Y)Iš", in: *Doğan Aksan Armağanı*, 53-68. Ankara.
Fundamenta 1
1959   Jean Deny, Kaare Grönbech, Helmuth Scheel, and Zeki Validi Togan (eds.), *Fundamenta 1* (*Philologiae Turcicae Fundamenta 1*). Aquis Mattiacis: Steiner.
Gadžieva, N.Z.
1973   *Osnovnye puti razvitija sintaksičeskoj struktury tjurkskix jazykov.* Moskva: Nauka.
Givón, T.
1971   "Historical syntax and synchronic morphology: an archaeologist's field trip", *Chicago Linguistic Society* 7, 349-415.
Grammatika sovremennogo baškirskogo literaturnogo jazyka
1981   A.A. Juldašev (ed.), *Grammatika sovremennogo baškirskogo literaturnogo jazyka.* Moskva.
Grammatika sovremennogo jakutskogo literaturnogo jazyka
1982   E.I. Ubrjatova (ed.), *Grammatika sovremennogo jakutskogo literaturnogo jazyka* (AN SSSR, Sibirskoe otdelenie, Jakutskij filial, Institut jazyka, literatury i istorii). Moskva.
Grammatika xakasskogo jazyka
1975   N.A. Baskakov (ed.), *Grammatika xakasskogo jazyka.* Moskva: Nauka.
Isxakov, F.G., and A.A. Pal'mbax
1961   *Grammatika tuvinskogo jazyka.* Moskva.

Johanson, L.
1992   *Strukturelle Faktoren in türkischen Sprachkontakten* (*Sitzungsberichte der Wissenschaftlichen Gesellschaft an der J. W. Goethe-Universität, Frankfurt am Main* 29, 5). Stuttgart.
Juldašev, A.A.
1977   *Sootnošenie deepričastnyx i ličnyx form glagola v tjurkskix jazykax.* Moskva.
Jusupov, F.Ju.
1981   *Neličnye formy glagola v dialektax tatarskogo jazyka.* Kazan': Izdatel'stvo Kazanskogo Universiteta.
Koptevskaja-Tamm, M.
1988   *A typology of action nominal constructions.* Department of Linguistics. Stockholm University.
Lyons, J.
1977   *Semantics* I-II. Cambridge: University Press.
Nevskaja, I.A.
1988   "Upotreblenie formy na -*rga* v šorskom jazyke", in: E.I. Ubrjatova et al. (eds.), *Grammatičeskie issledovanija po tjurkskim jazykam*, 43-67. Novosibirsk.
1993   *Formy deepričastnogo tipa v šorskom jazyke.* Novosibirsk: Izdatel'stvo NGU.
1998   "The revival of literary Shor", *Turkic Languages* 2/2, 253-270.
Pritsak, O.
1959   "Das Abakan- und Chulymtürkische und das Schorische", in: *Fundamenta I* (1959), 598-640.
Rassadin, V.I.
1978   *Morfologija tofalarskogo jazyka v sravnitel'nom osveščenii.* Moskva.
Tadykin, V.N.
1971   *Pričastija v altajskom jazyke.* Gorno-Altajsk.
Ubrjatova, E.I.
1976   *Issledovanija po sintaksisu jakutskogo jazyka. Složnoe predloženie* I. Novosibirsk: Nauka.

Languages in Contact, edited by D.G. Gilbers, J. Nerbonne, and J. Schaeken (= *Studies in Slavic and General Linguistics*, vol. 28), 299-304. Amsterdam - Atlanta, GA: Rodopi, 2000.

SOME NOTES ON PROSODY IN MPUR AND LOCAL INDONESIAN

CECILIA ODÉ

Introduction

Mpur (West Papuan Phylum) is a Non-Austronesian language with approximately 5,000 speakers in the Northeast Bird's Head Area, Irian Jaya, Indonesia. In the literature Mpur is sometimes referred to as Kebar or Amberbaken, which are geographic names for the two regions where it is spoken.

Mpur is a phylum-level isolate with dialectal differences in at least lexicon and prosody between speakers in the Kebar valley, in the mountains and on the coast, respectively. Mpur has three lexical tones: high, mid and low. The analysis of the results of some perception and production experiments on tone is still in progress: the issue is whether a fourth, midrising tone is phonologically significant. In polysyllabic words, syllables can be more prominent than their surrounding syllables, especially under the influence of high tone; yet there is no evidence for lexical stress in Mpur. The lexicon is of Papuan origin, but morphology and syntax show Austronesian features (Reesink 1998: 603ff.), such as subject-verb-object word order and the absence of heavy verb morphology. For a discussion of features of Austronesian and Non-Austronesian languages, the reader is referred to Foley (1998). Many loans, predominantly from neighbouring languages, entered Mpur from Numforese, Irianese Malay, Standard Indonesian, and also from Dutch. Indonesian is taught in village schools mainly by non-Mpur teachers, but they play truant as much as Mpur children do. In town Mpur children learn Indonesian more properly and only they are fairly able to distinguish between Indonesian and Mpur words. Mpur is an unwritten language. Apart from my work, texts have been collected by Greg and Carol Kalmbacher (Summer Institute of Linguistics) and are written down in Indonesian orthography. A phonology of Mpur is forthcoming (Kalmbacher 1996). A brief description of Mpur morphology will appear (Odé).

The prosodic phenomena discussed below are analysed by means of an analysis-by-resynthesis method, using GIPOS (Graphical Interactive Processing of Speech), developed at the Institute for Perception Research, Eindhoven, The Netherlands, by E. Gigi and L. Vogten, in which the PSOLA (Pitch Synchronous Overlap and Add) technique for speech synthesis based on waveform editing is implemented.

Loans from Dutch, Indonesian and Numforese in Mpur

Though the topic of this article is prosody, I will nonetheless present some examples of lexical loans that entered Mpur. In the Mpur examples, tones are marked on syllable vowels as follows: ´ high, ` low; mid tone is not marked.

Not surprisingly, many loans are of Indonesian origin. It is hard to distinguish between loans from Standard Indonesian and variants of Irianese Malay. Instead I will use the term 'Local Indonesian' (henceforth LI) for the variant spoken in the Bird's Head Area, examples of which will be indicated in bold face. Though interesting enough, the issue of tracing the loans is beyond the scope of this article. Loans from LI are increasingly used, also when original Mpur words are available, from all word classes, but especially adverbs (**terus** 'continually', 'then', **biasa** 'usually'), fillers (**apa** 'what', 'eh'), conjunctions (**jadi** 'so', **atau** 'or') and quantifiers. In the analysed Mpur texts no code-switching has been observed. Loans can occur in inflected forms, as for example in *m-bi-**paksa*** 3SF-VB-force 'she forces', **buka**-*an-ám* open-2S-eye 'open your eyes'. There are also combinations of Mpur and Indonesian, for example *bi-**jadi** ntón* VB-be.born child 'to give birth'. Loans from Numforese are numerous. For example *sànsun* 'clothes', *bi-ànkar* VB-tell.lies 'to lie', *kàku* 'very'. Morphemes of Numforese origin entered Mpur, like for instance the causative verbal prefix *fa-* as in *jik* 'kill' *fà-ji(k)-ém* 'argue (lit. to make each other dead)' and *brek* 'turn' *fà-brek* 'turn.around, capsize'. Some loans of Dutch origin are still being used: *pempum* 'squash' from Dutch *pompoen*, *prei* 'green onions' from Dutch *prei*, *bi-skop* 'kick' from Dutch *schoppen* 'kick' with verbalizer *bi-*. An Indonesian-Dutch combination is *àri-màndak* 'Monday' from Indonesian **hari** 'day' and Dutch *maandag* 'Monday'.

Prosody in Mpur and prosodic loans in Local Indonesian

In the languages of Irian Jaya and (part of) Eastern Indonesia, prosodic phenomena occur that are characteristic of narratives and the oral tradition (see also below). In this section I will present examples of three prosodic phenomena as a means to lend prominence and to express emotive emphasis, that are characteristic of storytelling of the Mpur speaking community (Odé 1997, 1998), and that have entered LI: 1) large pitch movements in and lengthening of final vowels at a prosodic boundary, 2) words repeated from two up to ten times, 3) an upward or downward jump in the fundamental frequency course in tail-head constructions. A prosodic boundary occurs at a pause, silence, hesitation, reset in the fundamental frequency course, as a result of the temporal organization of an utterance, at the end of a stream of thought. A tail-head construction is defined as a lexical repetition of the tail of an utterance in the head of the immediately following utterance. Linking utterances, the constructions are used as a means to keep the flow of a narrative going.

For the present analysis I conducted a pilot production experiment during fieldwork in 1998. Three speakers participated who understand to some extent, but do not speak their mother tongue and who were born in Irian Jaya and educated in LI only: a woman (29) and a man (37) from Yapen and a man (43) from Ambon. I asked them to tell about some recent event in their village Anjai, Kebar valley, and I recorded them on digital tape. The five examples from LI discussed below are taken from this experiment; the six examples from Mpur are from earlier recordings (Odé 1997; to appear). The examples are numbered 1-11, six of which indicated with an asterisk are illustrated in figures 1-6 at the end of this article.

1) Large pitch movements in and extreme lengthening of final vowels at prosodic boundaries. For instance, in Mpur (1) *À-kon té* 3SM-sleep until 'He sleeps all the time', *té* is pronounced with a long sustained vowel (600ms). Likewise, in the Indonesian utterance (2) **Mereka tidak lapor sampai** 3PL not report until 'They didn't report at all', the final syllable *-pai* shows a sustained vowel of 500ms. Another example in Mpur is (3*) *Wár-(d)ùkwa kutut-é* river-take along-EMPH 'The river took (the plate) all along' with a long sustained final vowel of 1010ms and a falling movement of -5 semitones. This intonation, very characteristic of LI, is in fact a prosodic loan from, geographically speaking, Bird's Head languages, but also from Tidore (West Papuan Phylum, M. van Staden (p.c.)). Compare the LI utterance (4*) ... **tapi karena angin** ... but because wind '... but because of the wind ...', where the final syllable shows a long sustained falling pitch movement (-4 semitones, 870 ms).

2) Words repeated from two up to ten times. Two examples in Mpur both with rising intonation during the repetition are (5) *À-fo ombrá ka si-jùn si-jùn si-jùn míntàki mim kú arwàr fràru-i* 3SM-go.up slow there to-top to-top to-top like.this till at stairs middle-CL 'He went slowly upwards and upwards, like this he arrived at the middle of the stairs'; (6*) *N-aw n-aw n-aw n-aw n-aw n-aw n-aw* 3SF-run 'She ran and ran and ran'. An example in LI, with level pitch in the repeated word, is (7*) **Saya sudah pikir kenapa ada asap asap asap** 1S already think why there.is smoke smoke smoke 'I was already thinking: why is there all that smoke?'. The examples in Mpur express a continuing action and in LI emotive emphasis, but note that both uses occur in both languages.

3) Jumps in the fundamental frequency course in tail-head constructions. There is a difference between the realization of the tail and the head in intonation and temporal organization. At the boundary between tail and head, a jump upward or downward occurs in the fundamental frequency course of a speaker. That is, if the tail is high, the head is low, or the reverse. Also, the duration of vowels in tail and head can be different. Examples of the two vari-

ants in Mpur are the following. Low tail and high head: (8*) *N-un na n-sí njèp, n-sí njèp maw-i* 3SF-go to 3SF-cut firewood 3SF-cut firewood finished-CL 'She went to cut firewood, she cut firewood till it was enough'. High tail and low head with longer vowel *-ò-* in the tail: (9) *À-ret ntón-à à-ret ntón-à maw* 3SM-eat child-3SM 3SM-eat child-3SM finished 'He ate the child, he ate the child up'. An example in LI with low tail and high head is: (10*) *Kita tusuk jarum, jarum (di) tangan. Jarum (di) tangan, (terus jadi...)* 1PL.INCL prick needle needle (into) hand needle (into) hand (then thus ...) 'We prick a needle into her finger. A needle into her finger, (and then ...)'. An example with high tail and low head is: (11) *Itu ada satu ibu. Dia masak. Dia masak di komfor yang pakai sumbu* that there.is one woman 3SF cook 3SF cook on stove that use wick 'There was a woman, she was cooking. She was cooking on a stove with a wick'.

The Mpur and LI utterances presented above are just a few examples showing that in LI spoken in the Bird's Head Area, prosodic loans occur from indigenous languages. The observations made in storytelling are confirmed in my other recordings of Mpur, consisting of myths of origin and daily-life narratives, and clearly recognized by my colleagues who work both on Austronesian and Non-Austronesian languages of Irian Jaya and Eastern Indonesia, as far as Tidore and the Moluccas. A detailed study of tail-head constructions in Abun (West Papuan Phylum), the only other Non-Austronesian tone language in the Bird's Head Area, can be found in Berry (1998).

In figures 1-6 below, produced with GIPOS, waveforms and pitch contours are presented of the six examples marked with an asterisk. Pitch contours are given on an ERB-rate scale (Equivalent Rectangular Bandwidth rate), between 50 and 400 hertz on the y-axis; this scale expresses the perception of melodic intervals in speech more adequately than a logarithmic scale does, used for the perception of melodic intervals in music (Hermes and van Gestel 1991); however, in the discussion above, pitch values are given in the more familiar semitones. In the waveform the text is indicated, labelled at the beginning of words or syllables. Note that since the utterances have different durations, the time scale of the pictures is also different.[1]

---

[1] This research is part of ISIR (Irian Jaya Studies: a programme for interdisciplinary research), a priority programme of NWO (Netherlands Organization for Scientific Research) which is financed by WOTRO (Netherlands Foundation for the Advancement of Tropical Research). The programme is carried out in cooperation with LIPI (*Lembaga Ilmu Pengetahuan Indonesia*). I wish to express my gratitude to Dr Hasan Alwi, head of the *Pusat Pembinaan dan Pembangunan Bahasa*, for his willingness to be my sponsor. I am greatly indebted to the storytellers from the Mpur and Local Indonesian speaking community in Kebar and Amberbaken, with special thanks to the speakers of the present examples, in alphabetical order: Joël Lesnusa, Mada Sapari, Markus Wabia, Seppy Wabia, Mika Waroi.

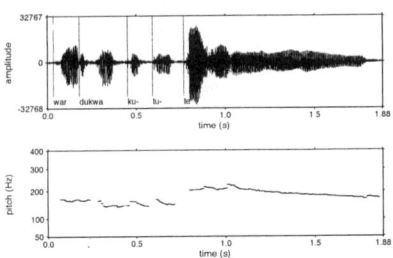

Figure 1. Example 3*: final vowel lengthening in Mpur in the word *kutute* 'all along'. 'The river took (the plate) all along'.

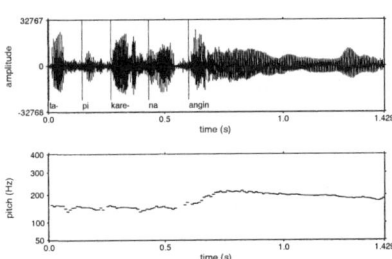

Figure 2. Example 4*: final vowel lengthening in LI in the word ***angin*** 'wind'. '... but because of the wind ...'.

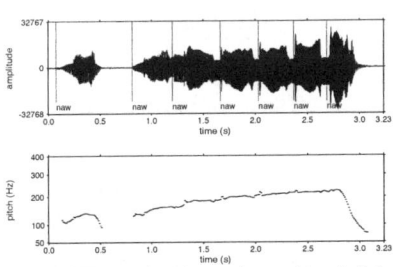

Figure 3. Example 6*: word repetition in Mpur of the word *naw* 'she ran'. 'She ran and ran and ran'.

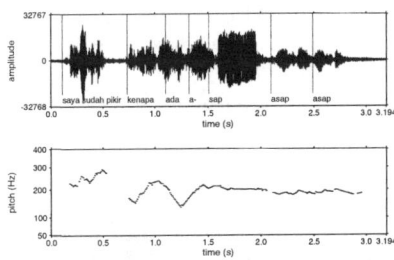

Figure 4. Example 7*: word repetition in LI of the word ***asap*** 'smoke'. 'I was already thinking: why is there all that smoke'.

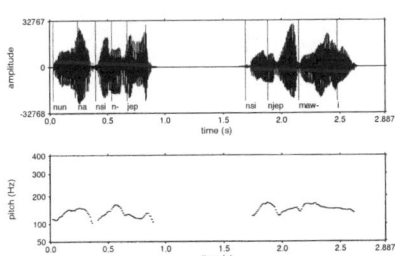

Figure 5. Example 8*: tail-head construction in Mpur. 'She went to cut firewood, she cut firewood till it was enough'.

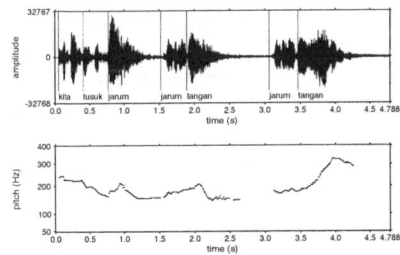

Figure 6. Example 10*: tail-head construction in LI. 'We prick a needle into her finger. A needle into her finger (and then ...)'.

Irian Jaya Studies, Leiden University

ABBREVIATIONS

CL	clitic	INCL	inclusive	NF	Numforese
CONT	continuation	NL	Dutch	S	singular
EMPH	emphasis	PL	plural	VB	verbalizer
F	feminine	M	masculine	1, 2, 3	first, second, third person

REFERENCES

Berry, Christine
  1998   "The art of storytelling in Abun society", in: Jelle Miedema, Cecilia Odé, Rien
              C. Dam (eds.), *Perspectives on the Bird's Head of Irian Jaya, Indonesia*, 519-
              534. Amsterdam: Rodopi.
Foley, William A.
  1998   "Toward understanding Papuan languages", in: Jelle Miedema, Cecilia Odé,
              Rien C. Dam (eds.), *Perspectives on the Bird's Head of Irian Jaya, Indonesia*,
              504-517. Amsterdam: Rodopi.
Hermes, D.J., and J.C. van Gestel
  1991   "The frequency scale of speech intonation", *Journal of the Acoustic Society of
              America* 90/1, 97-102.
Kalmbacher, J. Gregory Jr.
  1996   *Mpur Phonology*. Unpublished manuscript (47 pp.). Irian Jaya Bethany Foun-
              dation and Summer Institute of Linguistics.
Odé, Cecilia
  1997   "A descriptive study of prosodic phenomena in Mpur", in: *Eurospeech 1997,
              Proceedings* 1 (with the corrected version in the volume *Abstracts/Addendum*),
              183-186. Rhodes-Greece: Eurospeech.
  1998   "The bird said 'I am here': a prosodic study of the *waimon* story in Mpur", in:
              Jelle Miedema, Cecilia Odé, Rien C. Dam (eds.), *Perspectives on the Bird's
              Head of Irian Jaya, Indonesia*, 575-602. Amsterdam: Rodopi.
  To appear   "Mpur morphology", in: Ger P. Reesink (ed.), *Languages of the eastern Bird's
              Head*. Canberra: Pacific Linguistics (70 pp.).
Reesink, Ger P.
  1998   "The Bird's Head as Sprachbund", in: Jelle Miedema, Cecilia Odé, Rien C.
              Dam (eds.), *Perspectives on the Bird's Head of Irian Jaya, Indonesia*, 603-642.
              Amsterdam: Rodopi.

Languages in Contact, edited by D.G. Gilbers, J. Nerbonne, and J. Schaeken (= *Studies in Slavic and General Linguistics*, vol. 28), 305-309. Amsterdam - Atlanta, GA: Rodopi, 2000.

SOUND DATABASES IN THE STUDY OF PHONETIC INTERFERENCE

PAVEL A. SKRELIN

1. Introduction

A sound database is a comfortable means for organizing and storing digitized sound material. Two types of sound databases developed at the Department of Phonetics of St. Petersburg State University make it possible to handle various types of sound material used in phonetic research of the interference between languages. Their structural differences are defined by the differences of the units chosen for storage and description.

Databases of the first type (Sound Archives) are designed for big corpora. The description of such storage unit refers to the whole text. The database of the second type (Speech Corpus) is designed for the storage of phonetically balanced material (text). The storage unit in this case is the text, the description units are syllables and phrases.

2. Sound Archive

For the last ten years work has been under way at the Department of Phonetics of St. Petersburg University on the use of the computer for the organization of speech material. In 1995-97 within the framework of the INTAS project the first Sound Database for old recordings was developed. The facilities of this database were used for the organization and study of Žirmunskij's collection of old recordings from the Sound Archive of the Institute of Russian Literature (Pushkinsky Dom). This archive contains recordings of German folklore, made in the twenties and thirties in Russia (Skrelin and Volskaja 1996).

In collaboration with the Sound Archive of the Institute of Russian Literature Žirmunskij's collection of old recordings has been published on CD ROM, as well as other materials from the Sound Archive that are included in the Database, such as "Tales of the Russian North" and "Poetic Folklore of the Russian North (lamentations)". Thus, the invaluable archival sound material was transferred on modern sound carriers and made accessible for research.

At present, the Database is used in the NWO project "Voices from the Shtetl" and in the INTAS project "Sound Archives on the World Wide Web with Sound Recordings from Saint Petersburg Collections" (Project Nr. 1705). The INTAS project aims at the use of the developed technology for the organization of the archival recordings of speakers of the Russian, Nenets and Komi languages who inhabit the Northern territories of Russia. The storage and description unit in this system is the whole text, the minimal access unit is a word.

The first version of the Sound Archive on the Internet is available at: http://www.speech.nw.ru/phonetics/homepage.html

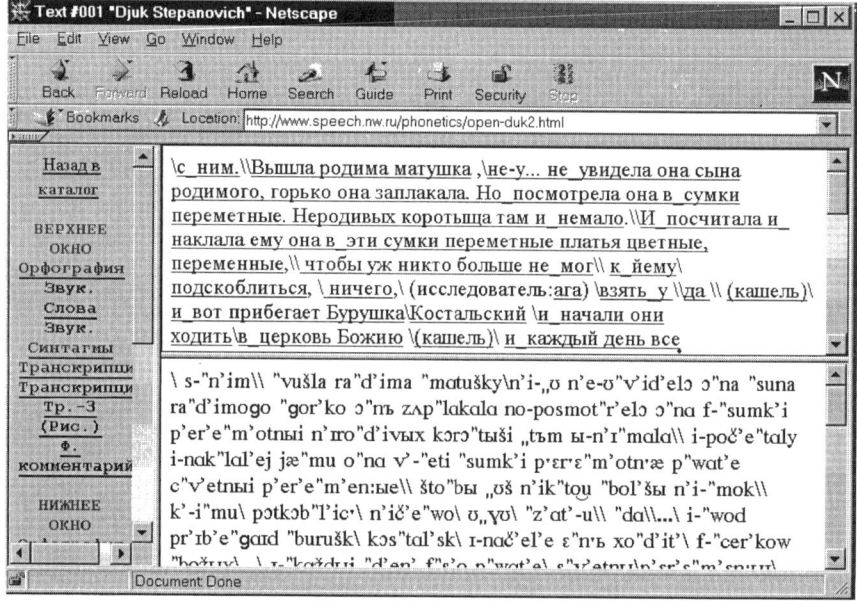

Fig. 1. View of the Internet version of the Sound Database.

The user will find information about the project participants: the Sound Archive of the Institute of Russian Literature, the Department of Phonetics of St. Petersburg State University, and the University of Groningen. There are links to the INTAS and Groningen servers (Bondarko et al. 1999).

The version of the database provides information on parts of the Sound Archive material that are devoted to the former Archangelsk region (collections of Gippius and Evald). Two texts in their orthographic form and in transcription are available with sound files attached to them. They provide the audio output of selected words and phrases and can be used for testing the means of sound transfer on the Internet. In the future, users will get access to all facilities provided by the CD ROM version.

The following facilities should be provided to meet these requirements:

– simple on-line registration of the user;
– search of the sound fragments which the user wishes to hear;

– conversion of the sound fragments into Real Audio format before transferring them to the user.

The second type of the Database is designed for the storage of phonetically balanced sound material (the text). The storage and the description unit in this case is the syllable (Skrelin and Talanov 1999).

The sound material, illustrating phonetic interference, is now being introduced into the Database: a Russian phonetically balanced text in the realization of Bulgarian, Finnish, American English, Korean, etc. speakers of Russian.

3. Speech Corpus

At present, the Phonetics Department is working on a new project aimed at the development of the Sound Database with text as the storage unit. This type of database will use both an isolated sound segment and a phrase (or an intonation phrase) as description units. The Database provides access to phonetically balanced texts recorded in the seventies and eighties in various regions of the former USSR.

The sound material recorded during field work has been transcribed; the transcription reflects the peculiarities of each regional pronunciation variant of Russian (Bondarko and Verbickaja 1987). All specific phonetic features represented in the form of tables of phonetic features, are being organized into a computer database.

The introduction of the digitalized sound material into the database provides access to the audio illustration of each regional pronunciation feature. The Database developed as a result of the project will be adapted for the use on the Internet. Specialists in the field of regional variants of Russian pronunciation will have on-line access to the Database.

The use of description units varying in size allows the user to access information about phonetic peculiarities of segmental and suprasegmental units. The tables of phonetic features characterizing regional pronunciation variants will be linked to the Database. It is possible to search for the pronunciation variant in the text and the audio feedback that provide illustrations of each phonetic feature described by phoneticians.

In order to carry out a comparative study the user should have the following options to access the research material:

1) Select from the menu the required pronunciation variant and get on a visual display its orthographic record and transcription; listen to the whole fragment or parts of it and follow the phonetic features indicated in the text or in the transcription; access the table of phonetic features and phonetic commentaries.

2) Select from the menu the required pronunciation variant, access the table of phonetic features and listen to their sound illustrations.
3) Search the database for the required phonetic feature in the regional pronunciation variant (or variants) in which this feature is described.

The requirement of automatic discrimination of segmentation of the sound signal into units of different levels should be fulfilled in order to provide access to the segmental and suprasegmental characteristics of regional variants of Russian. Segmental features can be demonstrated using a syllable or a group of words (in case of their realization at word boundaries). The problem of selecting a syllable or a number of syllables which constitute the required sound string has already been solved, i.e. in the process of the development of the Acoustic Database for Russian standard pronunciation (Skrelin and Talanov 1999). This method allows the formation of a sound stream of any length – from a syllable to a phrase or a group of phrases. In the study of the suprasegmental characteristics of an utterance it is desirable to provide not only its phonetic realization, but also the F0 curve of the selected fragment. This requirement can be met by introducing means for automatic F0 extraction into the Database. The software developed at the Department of Phonetics allows fairly quick and precise F0 extraction, but like most of the programs of this type it is not free from drawbacks and can therefore only be used at the initial step of the analysis, i.e. for the segmentation of the sound stream into F0 periods, with an afterward manual correction of the segmentation where necessary. The corrected segmentation will be stored in the same description file of the sound signal as the results of the segmentation into syllables, words, phrases and utterances.

Software for speech processing developed at the Department of Phonetics and the structure of the description file make it possible to use the same bit of a sound signal for several labels, indicating boundaries of different phenomena – from the F0 period to a phrase or a sentence. Thus, this bit is the first both in a phrase (sentence), in the word and in the syllable; besides, it can indicate the beginning of the F0 period.

After the user has selected a particular string of language units for listening, the program defines its physical boundaries on the basis of the information from the description file; it makes it possible to present the F0 curve of the signal within the physical boundaries that are indicated.

The description file contains information:

– about the position of labels inside the physical signal;
– the name of the label (text or transcription of the sound fragment; labels indicating F0 boundaries, are marked as 'noname');
– the intensity data of the fragment between two neighboring labels (required only for segmentation into F0 periods);

- the label function and number;
- the position of the label (in ms) with regard to the beginning of the signal;
- the duration values of the fragment between two neighboring labels;
- the fundamental frequency values (required only for fundamental frequency extraction).

Using the information about the required segmentation labels, the program provides the audio output of any text fragment together with the fundamental frequency curve of the selected part as well as information about the realization of certain phonetic features.[1]

Department of Phonetics, St. Petersburg State University

REFERENCES

Bondarko, Lija V., and Ljudmila A. Verbickaja (eds.)
1987   *Interferencija zvukovyx sistem.* Leningrad.
Bondarko, Lija V., Nina B. Volskaja, Pavel A. Skrelin, Tat'jana Ju. Šerstinova, and Aleksandr Ju. Kastrov
1999   "Koncepcija i struktura Web-sajta 'Katalog zvukozapisej Sankt-Peterburgskix kollekcij'", in: *Èlektronnye biblioteki: Perspektivnye metody i texnologii, èlektronnye kollekcii* (*Materialy Pervoj Vserossijskoj konferencii, Sankt-Peterburg, 19-22 oktjabrja 1999 g.*), 216-218. Sankt-Peterburg.
Skrelin, Pavel A., and Andrej O. Talanov
1999   "Sound Databases in the Phonetic Studies", in: *Proceedings of the 14th International Congress of Phonetic Sciences, San Francisco, 1-7 August, 1999*, 1213-1216. San Francisco.
Skrelin, Pavel A., and Nina B. Volskaja
1996   "The Structure of an Acoustic Database for the Old Recordings", in: *Archives of the Languages of Russia*, 82-85. St. Petersburg-Groningen.

---

[1] This project is supported by the Russian Foundation for Humanitarian Research grant (N 99-04-12015b) "Russian Regional Pronunciation Variants in the Internet".

Languages in Contact, edited by D.G. Gilbers, J. Nerbonne, and J. Schaeken (= *Studies in Slavic and General Linguistics*, vol. 28), 311-327. Amsterdam - Atlanta, GA: Rodopi, 2000.

LINGUISTIC AREAS AND LANGUAGE HISTORY

SARAH GREY THOMASON

Linguistic areas, or Sprachbünde, have been the topic of a very large amount of research for more than a century.[1] But although there are numerous valuable studies of particular linguistic areas and of particular features within certain linguistic areas, there is still little consensus on the general nature of the phenomenon. This paper is a preliminary attempt to characterize the notion 'linguistic area'. Section §1 below begins with a definition of the term and a justification of the definition. I will also state my position, with reasons, on several controversial issues in this domain, and then articulate what seem to me to be the most important historical questions about linguistic areas: How do linguistic areas arise? And how do the areal structural features originate and diffuse through the area? The section concludes with an outline of the crucial requisites for determining that contact-induced change has occurred; this outline sets the stage for the attempt, in §2, to interpret the areal features of five representative Sprachbünde historically. Section 3 is a brief conclusion. Not surprisingly, given the immense complexity and diversity one finds in the contact situations that comprise linguistic areas, no simple answers to the 'how' questions are possible; but comparing different linguistic areas at least shows what some of the many possibilities are. The most important (though not very neat) conclusion, however, is that attempts to find very general social and/or linguistic principles of convergence in a linguistic area are doomed – not only because every Sprachbund differs from every other one, but also because the conditions of contact in large Sprachbünde will inevitably vary over time and space. In other words, Sprachbund is not a uniform phenomenon linguistically, socially, or historically.

1. A definition and its ramifications

A linguistic area is a geographical region containing a group of three or more languages that share some structural features as a result of contact rather than as a result of accident or inheritance from a common ancestor. Three points in this

---

[1] This paper is a revised version of the one presented in November 1999 at the Conference on Language Contacts in Groningen. I am grateful to members of the audience there, and also to my students in a Language Contact course taught at the Linguistic Institute at the University of Illinois in July 1999, for helpful comments on earlier versions.

definition require some justification, because not all specialists would agree with them.

First, why must there be at least three languages before a region counts as a Sprachbund? Why not just two languages in contact? The most obvious reason is that subsuming two-language contact situations under the rubric 'linguistic area' would mean that almost every contact situation in the world that involves significant structural interference would be a linguistic area; and although there are important similarities between interference in two-language contact situations and interference in more complex contact situations, there are also important differences. Structural interference in many or most Sprachbünde is multidirectional, for instance, while structural interference in many or most two-language contacts is unidirectional: so, for instance, it is clear that the changes that formed the network of shared features in the Balkan Sprachbund did not all originate in the same language, while structural interference in the Romani-Russian contact situation is all from Romani to Russian, not vice versa (at least as far as Russian as a whole is concerned). But some linguistic areas, such as the Ethiopian highlands, seem to have unidirectional interference resulting from language shift (see discussion below); and in some two-language contacts, such as Uzbek and Tadzhik in the former USSR, structural interference can be found in both languages, though it didn't necessarily happen simultaneously or throughout the contact region (see Comrie 1981: 51, 163; for a broader view of Turkic-Iranian contacts, see e.g. Johanson 1992, 1998). From a historical linguist's viewpoint, perhaps the major reason for considering two-language contacts separately from Sprachbünde is that in the great majority of cases the source of a shared feature is easier to determine when only two languages are involved.

Second, why the insistence on **structural** features in the definition of a linguistic area? Again the motive is to avoid an all-inclusive definition: if shared vocabulary by itself were enough to establish a linguistic area, then the entire world would be one huge linguistic area, thanks to such widely shared words as *email*, *hamburger*, *democracy*, *pizza*, *Coca Cola*, and *television*. Using vocabulary as a sole criterion would therefore trivialize the notion of a linguistic area, and we'd need to invent a new term for those rather special contact situations that have traditionally been called linguistic areas.

Third, why must the shared features be due to contact? The answer to this question is that that's the whole point of the concept. Languages all over the world share numerous features that do not signal any kind of historical connection; "accidental similarity" is the usual cover term, though it must be used with caution because some shared features are due to linguistic universals of various kinds. Examples of features that are widely shared without having a common historical source are the existence of a phoneme /t/, the lack of click phonemes, a noun vs. verb distinction, SOV word order, exclusive use of suffixes (no prefixes or other affix types), and presence of subject agreement inflection on verbs. None of these features, with the possible exception of the noun vs. verb distinction, is found in every language in the world, but all are common in widely distant and unrelated languages. The other non-contact source of shared features is inheritance from a common ancestor. Shared structural features due to inheritance are found in the members of every language family in the world; to take just one of many examples, Salishan languages of the Pacific Northwest region of the US and neighboring Canadian provinces inherited such features as labialized dorsal stops, a glottalized lateral affricate, lexical suffixes, verb-initial word order, and a weak noun vs. verb distinction from Proto-Salish. The concept of the Sprachbund was put forward precisely in order to focus on shared structural features that arose out of contact rather than through inheritance.

The definition above includes all the contact situations traditionally considered to be Sprachbünde and excludes contact situations that are not generally considered to be Sprachbünde. In addition to these relatively uncontroversial definitional points, however, there are several general issues on which specialists disagree. I will discuss five of these questions briefly.

Do all the languages in a Sprachbund have to be **un**related to each other? The answer to this first question is clearly no. In a large Sprachbund it is virtually certain that some of the languages will be related to each other, and it's possible that all of them will be. It's easy to see why one might want to focus on changes in unrelated languages in a linguistic area: with related languages, distinguishing changes due to drift from changes due to contact may be very difficult. But methodological convenience cannot be a valid criterion for Sprachbund status, and the fact that related languages are most often spoken in contiguous territories makes their inclusion in the same linguistic area all too likely. One consequence of this is that, in a Sprachbund, demonstrably related languages will share features from all three possible sources – "accident", inheritance, and diffusion.

How many shared features are needed for a region to count as a linguistic area? The short answer to this question is that no figure can be given. But although a few scholars have argued that in principle a single shared feature is enough – Masica, for instance, refers to "the limiting case, the area defined by a single trait" (1976: 172) – most would agree that several features are needed. Campbell et al. (1986: 533) are certainly correct in asserting that there can be no specific limit that would permit us to distinguish putative linguistic areas "defined on the basis of several features from those based on a single shared trait"; but this surely doesn't mean that one is forced to accept a single feature as sufficient evidence for Sprachbund status. They refer (p. 532) to the old question of how many grains of sand it takes to make a heap, but the vital point is that it certainly takes more than one or two grains, though no precise number can be given. In other words, the problem is one of fuzzy boundaries, a familiar issue in historical linguistics:

one feature clearly does not make a Sprachbund, two dozen features clearly do, and the requisite number of features lies somewhere in between. Nor is the problem with a one-feature "Sprachbund" merely one of triviality, pace Campbell et al. (p. 532). The main problem is that a one-feature Sprachbund would be wildly unrealistic historically. It is difficult to imagine a process of diffusion that would spread exactly one structural feature from language to language within a large region; in all well-understood contact situations, diffusion of one structural feature is always accompanied by diffusion of at least a few others, even when just two languages are involved.

It is conceivable that a Sprachbund could develop with a sizable number of shared areal features and then, with loss of contact, all the diffused features but one could vanish from all the languages. But with such a historical scenario, and without evidence that there used to be more shared features, no responsible historical linguist would be likely to claim the area as a Sprachbund. Moreover, consider the single shared feature itself (again assuming that there is no old documentation to provide evidence that the languages of the proposed Sprachbund once shared more features). If it is a marked feature, why is it the **only** diffused innovation or relic? Most historical linguists would argue that marked features are less likely to diffuse and more likely to disappear than unmarked features. But if the single shared feature is unmarked, how could one possibly tell whether it's due to contact or not? It could easily have arisen via independent change in all the languages that have it.[2]

The next two questions concern the distribution of the areal features. First, do all the shared features have to be in all the languages of the Sprachbund? No, surely not: if the answer to this question were yes, the total number of the world's linguistic areas would immediately shrink from many to zero, because there is no Sprachbund in which all the areal features are found in all the languages. The reasons for this are easy to find. For one thing, innovations are sure to spread among the languages of a Sprachbund differentially – some changes spread farther than others, and if changes start in different places there will inevitably be different patterns of spread. And suppose that two languages in a Sprachbund acquire a certain feature by borrowing from a third language in the area, but that one of these languages subsequently loses the feature through internal change. It is likely to be impossible to prove that the feature ever existed in that language, and yet the language may otherwise be a definite member of the Sprachbund.

The next question is, do the shared structural features that characterize a particular linguistic area have to be confined to the area? Again the answer is clearly no. Suppose that a language X is both the source of an areal feature and a member

---

[2] It may be useful, as Campbell et al. suggest, to distinguish strong linguistic areas from weak ones. But I believe that, in practice as well as in principle, several shared features are needed even to establish a weak linguistic area.

of a language family that also has members outside the Sprachbund. If the feature is inherited in X and still present in its sister languages outside the area, then the feature is obviously not confined to the linguistic area; but if it spreads widely to other (unrelated) languages in the area, it would count as an areal feature too. In addition, speakers of some of the area's languages are likely to have some social contacts beyond the areal boundaries, and by that means there may be limited diffusion of areal features to outside languages. And finally, a feature may spread via contact within a Sprachbund and also occur in neighboring languages outside the area even without diffusion, especially if it's unmarked. So a criterion that insists on exclusivity of areal features is as worthless as a criterion that requires universality of areal features within the Sprachbund.

Taking all these distributional considerations into account, we would predict neither universality nor exclusivity of areal features within a Sprachbund. It is therefore hardly surprising that inspection of linguistic areas around the world support this prediction; for instance, as Campbell et al. observed with respect to the Balkan Sprachbund, "few Balkan isoglosses bundle at the [linguistic area's] borders; some fail to reach all the Balkan languages, while others extend beyond..." (1986: 561).

The final question concerns the nature of the link between language contact and contact-induced language change: is a Sprachbund inevitable when three or more languages are in intimate contact for a long time? Much of the literature assumes a 'yes' answer to this question; but in my opinion the question can't be answered with confidence at our present state of knowledge, because the only complex contact situations that have been studied intensively so far are those involving contact-induced changes. I doubt if a Sprachbund is inevitable even under long-term intimate contact, however. The main reason for this belief is that contact-induced change is demonstrably not inevitable in intense two-language contact situations, and I can see no reason why adding more languages to a contact situation should change the picture.[3] The basic problem with predicting that a Sprachbund must arise under certain contact conditions is that cultural attitudes may, and sometimes do, inhibit lexical and/or structural interference.

All the points of controversy discussed so far, though important issues, are ultimately less interesting than the two vital open historical questions about Sprachbünde: How do linguistic areas arise? And how are their linguistic features to be interpreted historically? The answer to the former question is that linguistic areas emerge through diverse social processes and institutions (e.g. trade relations, exogamy, and war); the answer to the second question is that the historical interpretations vary as much as linguistic areas vary. The next section illustrates this di-

---

[3] Montana Salish and at least some other languages of the US Northwest, for instance, have borrowed from each other, but have virtually no loanwords and little or no borrowed structure from English, in spite of well over a hundred years of intimate contact.

versity, and highlights the problems one encounters in trying to answer these two questions, through a survey of five linguistic areas.

Before beginning the survey, though, we need to set the stage by listing the requisites for establishing that contact-induced change has occurred. For simplicity's sake, the list below assumes just two languages in contact, X (the proposed receiving language) and Y (the proposed donor language), but the principle is the same for more complex contacts. There are four requirements:

(1) Establish that there was contact intimate enough to permit contact-induced structural change.
(2) Find several independent shared features in X and Y – ideally, features in different grammatical subsystems.
(3) Prove that the shared features were **not** present in pre-X.
(4) Prove that the shared features **were** present in pre-Y.

Note that requirement (1) is easy to satisfy if there are loanwords from Y in X. But there might not be any: if Y speakers shifted to X, interference features in X are more likely to be phonological and syntactic than lexical. Worse, if all Y speakers shifted to X, and if Y had no close relatives, it might be impossible to identify a source language for the suspected interference features. The crucial point to be made here is that if requirements (1)-(4) can't be satisfied, then it will be impossible to make a convincing case for contact-induced change. This does not mean that a given feature is **not** due to the influence of another language; but it won't be possible to distinguish between a contact origin for the feature and an ancient or recent internal origin (see Thomason 1986, 1993 for more detailed arguments in support of this claim).[4]

2. A survey of five "representative" linguistic areas

The word "representative" needs shudder quotes in this context because it isn't at all clear what would count as a truly representative Sprachbund. The ones outlined briefly in this section are diverse geographically and historically, but it may well be that choosing five different areas would result in quite a different conclusion (not that my conclusions will turn out to be very conclusive). Still, this survey at least suggests what sorts of factors need to be considered in the historical interpretation of linguistic areas. The five areas that will be discussed are the Balkans of southeastern Europe, the Sepik River Basin in New Guinea, The Pacific Northwest of North America, the Ethiopian highlands in Africa, and South Asia.

---

[4] Because of space limitations, I omit here discussion of MULTIPLE CAUSATION, in which an external source combines with an internal source to produce a particular change; in a more complete study of the changes that bring about Sprachbünde, multiple motivations must be considered.

2.1 The Balkan Sprachbund

The Balkan peninsula is the world's most famous linguistic area, and the one that has received the most attention from scholars over the longest period of time. Its major languages are Rumanian (a Romance language); Bulgarian, Macedonian, and southeastern dialects of Serbian (all are Slavic languages); Albanian; Greek; perhaps Balkan dialects of Romani (an Indic language); and dialects of Turkish that are spoken in the Balkans. All of these languages except for Turkish belong to the Indo-European language family.

Areal features are common in the Balkans, with, as noted above, varying distributions within the languages of the Sprachbund. Here are a few typical examples: there are many Turkish and Greek loanwords in (other) Balkan languages; among the more widespread structural Balkanisms are the presence of a high or mid central vowel, vowel harmony, the partial or total loss of the infinitive, postposed articles, pleonastic object markers, a merger of the dative and genitive cases, a future construction formed with the verb *want*, and a perfect construction formed with the verb *have*. Areal features with more limited distribution within the Sprachbund are a change of unstressed [o] to [u] (in Bulgarian, Rumanian, and Albanian), a Slavic diminutive suffix *-ica* (in Greek, Rumanian, and Albanian), a plural suffix borrowed into Arumanian from Greek, the replacement of dative feminine pronouns with dative masculine pronouns in Macedonian as a result of Albanian influence, and a vocative case in Rumanian as a result of Slavic influence.

The list of Balkanisms could easily be extended: it must be emphasized that these are only examples of the whole complex of areal features (see, for instance, Sandfeld 1930 and Lindstedt in this volume for more detail and further references). But it must also be emphasized that a complete list would not amount to massive restructuring in any of the Balkan languages: there has been significant, but by no means extreme, contact-induced structural change in the most-affected Balkan languages. For instance, the amount of change in Macedonian, which is generally believed to be the most Balkanized of all the languages in the Sprachbund, would probably fall into category 4, the second highest category of 'ordinary' structural interference, in the borrowing scale proposed in Thomason and Kaufman (1988: 74-76).

The crucial question is, what are the sources of the areal features in the Balkans? Several writers have argued for multiple causation (see especially Joseph 1983, in several passages listed under 'causation' in the index, and Lindstedt, this volume), but in the present context the focus is on the external motivations for the innovations. In spite of various proposals for source languages (e.g. Greek), there is little agreement among Balkanologists about the historical origins of most of the most famous Balkan features; but it is at least clear that the numerous area-wide and local contact situations were extraordinarily complex. The history of the

Balkans is famously turbulent. Most notoriously, five hundred years of Turkish invasion and conquest led directly and indirectly to large-scale multilingualism, promoted or at least facilitated by movements of small groups of people and even entire small communities from region to region and small-scale language shifts in certain regions and at different times. Multilingualism was presumably rather symmetrical over the area as a whole: with the possible exception of Turkish speakers during periods of Turkish rule, area-wide one-way bilingualism of the sort that often accompanies asymmetrical dominance relations is unlikely to have obtained.

The sources of lexical features are relatively easy to establish. We can be certain, for instance, about Greek and Turkish loanwords in the Balkan languages. The same is true of a few of the structural features; Latin had a perfect construction with *have*, for example, so Romance is a plausible source for that Balkan feature. Things are much less clear for most of the structural features, but it seems at best risky to assume a single source for them. It is much more likely, given the population movements and the resulting intimate contacts, that features arose in different places at different times and then, as is common in linguistic areas, spread differentially within the Sprachbund. It is also likely that most of the diffusion of features was via borrowing, i.e. incorporation of features from one language into another by bilingual speakers, rather than via imperfect learning during a process of group language shift, because apparently no large-scale language shifts took place during the relevant period (very roughly, 1000-1800 CE). But the non-lexical Balkanisms, especially, could in principle be due either to borrowing or to shift-induced interference, and the presence of numerous loanwords from languages that were very unlikely to be the source of most Balkanisms does not help to resolve the puzzle of origins.

2.2 The Sepik River Basin

Papua New Guinea has long been famous for areal phenomena: see, for instance, Arthur Capell's comment, with reference to the non-Austronesian languages of the central highlands, that although neighboring languages have different vocabularies, their grammatical features "recur with almost monotonous regularity from language to language" (cited in Wurm 1956: 451). William Foley, in his book on Papuan languages, observes that "Papuan languages are generally in a state of permanent intimate contact with each other" (1986: 210). Foley systematically explores the topic of contact-induced change in Papuan (non-Austronesian) languages of New Guinea and includes a very useful analysis of one small Sprachbund comprising three neighboring languages – Yimas, Alamblak, and Enga – which belong to three different language families, all spoken in the Sepik River Basin of northern Papua New Guinea (1986: 263-267). Foley's detailed study of the features shared by these languages makes it clear that the

Sprachbund is an old one and that, as in the Balkans, diffusion has been multi-directional. He also shows clearly that not all the shared features can be shown to have diffused at all.

All three languages have palatal consonants, with Enga as the presumed source because such consonants were demonstrably inherited by Enga but not by the other languages; and all three have complex tense systems (with at least a present, a future, and three pasts), a feature that seems to be old and perhaps inherited in both Enga and Alamblak but probably innovative in Yimas.

Yimas and Alamblak share the largest number of features. Four of these, a particular plural pronominal suffix, a type of temporal adverbial clause in which an oblique suffix -*n* is added to the inflected verb, an elaborate system of verb compounding, and a causative construction, have no detectable sources, though Foley believes that at least some of them are due to diffusion. One shared feature, bound adverbial forms in the verb, probably reflects diffusion from Alamblak to Yimas; and a sixth feature, the presence of more than one central vowel, seems to have been inherited by both languages.

Yimas and Enga share two features not found in Alamblak: one of these, a causative formed with -(*a*)*sa*, is an Enga interference feature in Yimas, but the source of the other one, an indirect causative formed with 'say', is obscure. Finally, Alamblak and Enga share a switch-reference construction that diffused from Enga to Alamblak.

In other words, it is possible to establish sources for some, but not all, of the features that are shared by two or all three languages in this small Sprachbund. It's noteworthy that Yimas is always a recipient language of non-inherited features that it shares with one or both of the other languages, never demonstrably the source language; beyond this, however, there appears to be no definite information about specific processes of diffusion. In the case of shared features inherited from the respective proto-languages, ancient diffusion is possible from one proto-language to the other; but the chances of establishing such ancient diffusion range from slim to none. The great virtue of Foley's study is that it lays out the difficulties with a historical analysis of a Sprachbund so clearly.

2.3 The Pacific Northwest

In the northwestern US states Washington and Oregon and in neighboring British Columbia, together with limited contiguous areas farther inland, there is a well-known but as yet understudied linguistic area. The three core language families of this Sprachbund are Salishan (about 21 languages), Wakashan (6 languages), and Chimakuan (2 languages). Smaller numbers of the areal features are also shared by other languages in the region: Tsimshian, Chinookan and Sahaptian languages, the isolate Kutenai, and to a slight extent nearby Athabaskan languages. As in the highlands of New Guinea, the level of multilingualism was apparently always high in the Northwest, so that here too one may reasonably speak of permanent intimate contact among neighboring languages.

From a historical viewpoint, the Pacific Northwest Sprachbund is the Sepik River Basin writ large. Most of the widespread areal features must be reconstructed for all three of the core proto-languages (Kinkade 1997). The most striking of these are labialized dorsal consonants, a velar/uvular distinction in dorsals, lateral obstruents such as lateral affricates and a voiceless lateral fricative, /ts/ affricates, a very common sound change from velars to alveopalatals, complex word structure with many suffixes but relatively few prefixes, minimal case systems, possessive pronominal affixes added to a possessed word, verb-initial sentential word order, sentence-initial negation, the presence of a yes/no question particle, a weak lexical noun/verb distinction, pairs of roots referring to singular vs. plural actions or states, optional plural marking, distributive plurals formed by reduplication, numeral classifiers (e.g. 'person' vs. 'non-person' categories), and a system of lexical suffixes (with concrete meanings like 'hand' and 'round object'). It seems very unlikely that all these features – which include many that are certainly independent of each other and several that are highly marked in terms of their distribution in the world's languages – are accidentally shared by all these language families; but if there was diffusion between two or more of the core families' parent languages, it cannot be established, at least not on the basis of current knowledge. That is: diffusion may be suspected, but there's no direct evidence to support a diffusional hypothesis.

Other areal features within the Sprachbund have limited distribution. Two of the most striking of these, striking because they are extremely rare cross-linguistically outside this area, are the presence of several pharyngeal consonants and a sound change that replaced nasal stops with voiced oral stops. What's especially startling about these two features is that they appear in non-contiguous areas, a fact that would stand in the way of a straightforward diffusion origin hypothesis even if we knew where each of the features appeared first. Most of the other limited areal features, which are quite numerous, also lack a clear source, though we know at least that they were not inherited from the respective proto-languages. Only a few, such as the lack of elaborate syllable-initial consonant clusters in the Salishan language Comox (due to interference from the Wakashan language Kwakwala) and a nonglottalized lateral affricate borrowed by the Chimakuan language Quileute from Wakashan, can be traced definitely to a particular source. And as with the Sepik River Basin Sprachbund, the processes of diffusion through which the Pacific Northwest Sprachbund arose cannot be determined.

2.4 The Ethiopian highlands

The African linguistic area that has received the most attention in the literature is the Ethiopian Sprachbund, more specifically the languages of the Ethiopian highlands (see e.g. Leslau 1945, 1952, Hetzron 1975, Moreno 1948, Little 1974, and Ferguson 1976). There are many languages in the region, three quarters of them members of two branches of the Afro-Asiatic language family; of these, the great majority belong to the Cushitic branch of the family (including the so-called Omotic languages), but there are also several Semitic languages. Besides the Afro-Asiatic languages, there are some languages in the region that belong to the proposed Nilo-Saharan family, but since these are not discussed in the literature on the linguistic area, I cannot comment on whether, or how, they fit into the Sprachbund.

The areal linguistic features have varying distributions, as is typical of linguistic areas: a few features are area-wide, but most have localized distributions. The languages spoken in the southern part of the area have significantly more of the features. Among the areal features are the presence of labialized dorsal stops, alveopalatal consonants, prothetic glides before mid vowels, a separate future tense, a causative formation with a double affix (prefixes in Ethiopic Semitic, suffixes in Cushitic), a negative perfect formation, lack of a dual number category, optional rather than obligatory plural marking on nouns, SOV word order with Verb-Auxiliary, Adjective-Noun, and Relative Clause-Noun word orders, postpositions, and subordination by means of non-finite gerund constructions. Besides these and other structural features, there are also shared lexical features – many words, including some quite basic terms (e.g. kin terms, numerals, and body parts), and also derivational suffixes and a vocative particle.

From a historical viewpoint, the Ethiopian Sprachbund differs strikingly from the other three areas we have examined: the major interference here seems to be unidirectional, from Cushitic to Semitic, and the process was apparently imperfect learning that occurred when some (groups of) Cushitic speakers shifted to the Semitic language(s) spoken by newcomers to the region. (This statement requires a hedge, because to date no systematic historical research has been carried out on the non-Semitic languages of the highlands; it may well be that some interference from Semitic to Cushitic will be found, and/or interference between the Afro-Asiatic and the non-Afro-Asiatic languages.) It is at least certain that Ethiopic Semitic has numerous lexical and structural features that are like Cushitic and unlike older Semitic. The age of the features in Cushitic is less clear, however; it's quite possible, for instance, that the Cushitic languages acquired the features from non-Afro-Asiatic languages rather than by inheritance from Proto-Cushitic. Still, the features are more widespread in the Cushitic languages of the area than in the Semitic languages, and this fact, together with specific structural considerations, makes an immediate Cushitic source likely. There is also sociolinguistic evidence that Cushitic speakers did shift in numbers to Semitic, a circumstance that supports the analysis of shift-induced interference.

2.5 South Asia

Like the Balkans, though to a lesser extent, South Asia is a well-known and much-studied linguistic area (see e.g. Emeneau 1980 and Masica 1976). Unlike the Balkans, however, its status as a linguistic area is a matter of considerable controversy; though few authors deny flatly that it should be classed as a Sprachbund, the areal status of several of the most famous features is vigorously disputed and, even more, the historical interpretation of the emergence of areal features in the subcontinent is disputed (in e.g. Hock 1975, 1984). I will not attempt to resolve this controversy here, but it should be noted that there are doubts about some of the features.

The Sprachbund comprises languages belonging to at least three different families: Dravidian, Indic (a sub-branch of Indo-European), and Munda (a branch of Austro-Asiatic). A few of the areal features are also shared by the isolate Burushaski and by some Iranian languages (Iranian and Indic together form a branch of Indo-European).

As is typical of linguistic areas, some features are more widespread than others, and some of the areal features are clearly older than others. Among the most prominent ancient areal features are the presence of retroflex consonants, agglutination in noun declension, a particular echo-word formation, a quotative construction, absolute constructions which differ from the typical Indo-European type, the syntax of a discourse particle (Indic *api*, Dravidian *-um*), SOV word order, morphological causatives, and a 'second causative' construction.

Language contact in the Indian subcontinent has a very long and a very complex history, dating back over three thousand years or more. Multilingualism is the norm today in some parts of the area, for instance in the village of Kupwar, where, according to Gumperz and Wilson 1971, grammatical convergence has been extreme. In Kupwar, the process by which the Indic languages Marathi and especially Urdu and the Dravidian language Kannaḍa have converged grammatically was apparently borrowing, not shift-induced interference. And it was certainly multidirectional: Kannaḍa is the source of some features and Marathi is the source of others. There is every reason to believe that this sort of convergence happened elsewhere in South Asia, so that Kupwar might be a miniature reflection of the Sprachbund as a whole.

However, the situation seems to have been different for the ancient areal features. The majority of those are reconstructable for Proto-Dravidian but not for Indic, which means that Dravidian has almost surely influenced Indic, not (in ancient times) vice versa. Significantly, there are very few old Dravidian loanwords in Indic languages; this, taken together with the structural interference, points to a process of shift-induced interference. There is good evidence that Dravidian speakers were in South Asia when Indic speakers arrived there, and it is at least very likely that many of them shifted to the Indic language(s) of the invaders. The South Asian Sprachbund therefore resembles the Ethiopian Sprachbund in presenting, for the earliest period of intimate contact, a picture of unidirectional interference via imperfect learning of a target language by shifting speakers.

3. Conclusion

As we have seen, it is often possible to establish a source language or language family for a particular areal structural feature in a Sprachbund, but very often no source can be established or, in many cases, even guessed at. For these features, the short answer to the question 'where do the features come from?', therefore, is a large question mark: we don't know. The best chances for establishing sources for areal features will be in linguistic areas that are relatively simple sociolinguistically, with (mostly) unidirectional rather than multidirectional interference. In practice, as far as I can tell from a review of numerous linguistic areas around the world, these are cases where there has been large-scale shift by speakers of one group of related languages to a different group of related languages – as (apparently) in the Ethiopian highlands and ancient South Asia – so that most interference features are due to imperfect learning of the target languages by the shifting speakers. Unfortunately for those who yearn for easy solutions to historical puzzles, Sprachbünde that are relatively simple sociolinguistically are much less common than the more complex kinds.

Even in socially more complex linguistic areas, however, a longer and more substantial answer can be given to the 'where from?' question. There are four obvious possible sources for areal features whose origin can't be traced to any of the languages of the Sprachbund. First, they could all have been inherited from a remote proto-language from which all the languages of the Sprachbund are descended. But if no genetic relationship can be established among some or all of the languages in the area, the putative all-encompassing proto-language must have been very remote indeed, beyond the reach of the Comparative Method; methodologically, therefore, this first possibility is worthless, and must be included under the second possibility.

The second possibility is that the areal features could be "accidentally" shared (and here we must remember that in this context the term includes the operation of various kinds of universal linguistic tendencies as well as genuine accident). This is unlikely for highly marked features like the Pacific Northwest pharyngeals and nasal-less consonant inventories, in spite of the fact that both features seem to be independent innovations in at least part of their present territory. The possibility of accident is much greater for universally unmarked features, which could easily arise as independent innovations in neighboring languages.

The other two possibilities both involve contact-induced change. One is that each feature arose through internal change in some language (or proto-language) in the area and then spread to some or all of the other languages (or proto-languages). This is of course possible even when, as in the Balkans, we know that the proto-language lacked the feature, because it could have arisen after the proto-language split into two or more daughter languages but before documentation of the daughter languages. If this happened in one of the proto-languages before any splits affected the languages in contact, contact-induced change could produce the situation we find in the Pacific Northwest: a number of areal features that must be reconstructed for all three core families' proto-languages. This possibility, unfortunately, is not amenable to testing or proof, unless further historical research permits the establishment of broader genetic relationships among an area's languages and hence earlier proto-language reconstructions.

The fourth and last possibility is that an areal feature may arise through a process of 'negotiation' – in this case, as a misperception by semi-bilinguals of an L2 structure. This misperception could then spread not only to the misperceivers' own language but also to the L2 and beyond. An example of this process in a two-language contact situation is the fixing of stress on the penult in a northern dialect of Serbo-Croatian – which like other Serbo-Croatian dialects originally had free stress – under the influence of Hungarian speakers who realized that Serbo-Croatian didn't have initial stress (as in Hungarian) but nevertheless assumed a fixed stress pattern and settled on the penult as its location (Ivić 1964; see Thomason 1997 for further discussion of negotiation as a mechanism of interference).

The problem, of course, is that in the vast majority of linguistic areas there is no hope of distinguishing between the third and fourth origin scenarios for historically mysterious areal features, even if "accident" can reasonably be considered relatively unlikely on grounds of plausibility. This is simply one more instance of an uncomfortable truth: historical linguists, like other historical scientists, are forced to deal with limitations on hypothesis testing that are imposed by gaps in the historical record. This does not mean that we should stop looking for solutions to puzzles; it does mean that we should be able to recognize when we've reached the limits of historical knowledge, so that we don't go beyond them into historical fantasy.

Specifically, the fact that we can list possible explanations for unsourced areal features is not an indication that we can expect to establish sources for all of them eventually. Ultimately, the reason for this is that we can't meet one or both of requisites (3) and (4) for proving that contact-induced change has occurred – that is, we can't prove the absence of a shared feature in one or more of the proto-languages and/or the presence of the feature in the other proto-language(s). Of course this happens in historical investigations of two-language contact situations as well, but it seems to be a worse problem for Sprachbünde (though this impression might be due to the fact that there is less research on linguistic areas than on two-language contacts).

A final concluding remark is in order. Even in the strongest Sprachbünde, the often-cited 'tendency toward isomorphism' rarely if ever leads to massive overall convergence. Even in the Kupwar case, a mini-Sprachbund within the larger South Asia linguistic area, only sixteen features, all of them morphosyntactic, are discussed in Gumperz and Wilson's famous 1971 article, and the total amount of change in any one of the languages is not all that radical (see Thomason and Kaufman 1988: 86-88 for discussion). There are probably many reasons for the lack of massive overall convergence in linguistic areas, all of them social rather than linguistic. But surely a major factor is that the 'other-directed' attitudes that promote convergence (presumably in conjunction with cognitive factors having to do with ease of processing of several languages) are counterbalanced by a 'self-directed' world view that promotes maintenance of one's own culture and language (Foley 1986: 27 et passim). Both of these attitudes are displayed in an old Croatian saying that celebrates multilingualism:

> Kulìko jezìkou člòvīg znâ,
> talìko člòvīg vaļâ.[5]

University of Michigan

REFERENCES

Campbell, Lyle, Terrence Kaufman, and Thomas C. Smith-Stark
  1986   "Meso-America as a linguistic area", *Language* 62, 530-570.
Comrie, Bernard
  1981   *The languages of the Soviet Union.* Cambridge: Cambridge University Press.
Emeneau, Murray B.
  1980   *Language and linguistic area* (ed. by Anwar Dil). Stanford: Stanford University Press.
Ferguson, Charles A.
  1976   "The Ethiopian language area", in: M. Lionel Bender, J. Donald Bowen, R.L. Cooper, and C.A. Ferguson (eds.), *Language in Ethiopia*, 63-76. Oxford: Oxford University Press.
Foley, William A.
  1986   *The Papuan languages of New Guinea.* Cambridge: Cambridge University Press.
Gumperz, John J., and Robert Wilson
  1971   "Convergence and creolization: a case from the Indo-Aryan/Dravidian border", in: Dell Hymes (ed.), *Pidginization and Creolization of Languages*, 151-167. Cambridge: Cambridge University Press.

---

[5] "However many languages a person knows, that's how much a person is worth."

Hetzron, Robert
1975   "Genetic classification and Ethiopic Semitic", in: James Bynon and Thodora Bynon (eds.), *Hamito-Semitica*, 103-127. The Hague: Mouton.

Hock, Hans Henrich
1975   "Substratum influence on (Rig-Vedic) Sanskrit?", *Studies in the Linguistic Sciences* 5/2, 76-125.
1984   "(Pre-)Rig-Vedic convergence of Indo-Aryan with Dravidian? Another look at the evidence", *Studies in the Linguistic Sciences* 14/1, 89-107.

Ivić, Pavle
1964   *Balkan linguistics*. Lecture course taught at the Linguistic Institute of the Linguistic Society of America, Indiana University, June-August 1964.

Johanson, Lars
1992   *Strukturelle Factoren in Türkischen Sprachkontakten*. Stuttgart: Franz Steiner Verlag.
1998   "Code-copying in Irano-Turkic", *Language Sciences* 20, 325-337.

Joseph, Brian D.
1983   *The synchrony and diachrony of the Balkan infinitive: a study in areal, general, and historical linguistics*. Cambridge: Cambridge University Press.

Kinkade, M. Dale
1997   "The emergence of shared features in languages of the Pacific Northwest". Paper presented at the symposium *The Pacific Northwest as a Linguistic and Cultural Area*, American Association for the Advancement of Science Annual Meeting, Seattle.

Leslau, Wolf
1945   "The influence of Cushitic on the Semitic languages of Ethiopia: a problem of substratum", *Word* 1, 59-82.
1952   "The influence of Sidamo on the Ethiopic languages of the Gurage", *Language* 28, 63-81.

Lindstedt, Jouko
2000   "Linguistic Balkanization: contact-induced change by mutual reinforcement". This volume, 231-246.

Little, Greta D.
1974   "Syntactic evidence of language contact: Cushitic influence in Amharic", in: Roger W. Shuy and Charles-James N. Bailey (eds.), *Towards tomorrow's linguistics*, 267-275. Washington, DC: Georgetown University Press.

Masica, Colin P.
1976   *Defining a linguistic area: South Asia*. Chicago: University of Chicago Press.

Moreno, Martino Mario
1948   "L'azione del cuscito sul sistema morfologico delle lingue semitiche dell'Ethiopia", *Rassegna di Studi Etiopici* 7, 121-130.

Sandfeld, Kristian.
1930   *Linguistique balkanique: problèmes et résultats*. Paris: Librairie C. Klincksieck.

Thomason, Sarah G.
1986   "On establishing external causes of language change", in: Soonja Choi et al. (eds.), *Proceedings of the Second Eastern States Conference on Linguistics*, 243-251. Columbus: The Ohio State University.
1993   "On identifying the sources of creole structures: Comments on the papers by Singler and Lefebvre", in: Salikoko Mufwene (ed.), *Africanisms in Afro-*

American Language Varieties, 280-295. Athens, GA: University of Georgia Press.

1997　　"On mechanisms of interference", in: Stig Eliasson and Ernst Håkon Jahr (eds.), *Language and its ecology: Essays in memory of Einar Haugen*, 181-207. Berlin: de Gruyter.

Thomason, Sarah G., and Terrence Kaufman

1988　　*Language contact, creolization, and genetic linguistics*. Berkeley: University of California Press.

Wurm, Stefan A.

1956　　"Comment on question: 'Are there areas of *affinité grammaticale* as well as of *affinité phonologique* cutting across genetic boundaries?'", in: F. Norman (ed.), *Proceedings of the 7th International Congress of Linguists*, 450-452. London: Permanent International Committee of Linguists, Section B4.

Languages in Contact, edited by D.G. Gilbers, J. Nerbonne, and J. Schaeken (= *Studies in Slavic and General Linguistics*, vol. 28), 329-334. Amsterdam - Atlanta, GA: Rodopi, 2000.

ON THE LOW GERMAN INFLUENCE ON KASHUBIAN DIALECTS

HANNA TOBY

1. Kashubian and its contact with Low German

Kashubian, spoken today in a small territory in North Poland, is the last non-Germanized remnant of Pomeranian dialects once spoken along the Baltic between the lower Vistula and the lower Elbe. The Kashubian speech area (Kashubia) suffered linguistic losses in the course of the centuries, resulting in language death of the western Kashubian periphery.[1] Although the German colonisation of Kashubia began as early as in the 12th century, the Kashubian-speaking territory contracted most rapidly in favour of German after its incorporation into West Prussia in 1772. The testimonies of, for example, Hilferding (Gil'ferding 1862) and Parczewski (1896) confirm the progressive language shift within the Kashubian population from their Slavonic vernacular to the local German dialect.

The language contact with German involved the three German varieties: Low German, Central German and High German. The majority of German inhabitants of Kashubia were speakers of the Low German colonial dialects: "Ostpommersch" (East Pomeranian) and "Niederpreussisch" (Low Prussian), the latter being spoken in the peripheral areas in the east. The period of the most intensive Kashubian-German language contact (1772-1945) was characterised by polyglossia and multilingualism. The different languages occupied different positions within the hierarchy of prestige, and were used in different linguistic situations in accordance with their function in society. Kashubian was mainly spoken at home and between local Kashubians, Polish in church, the local dialect of Low German

---

[1] According to toponymic evidence (Rzetelska-Feleszko 1973), Kashubian was once spoken as far west as the Parsęta River. The last Kashubian variety, Slovincian, became extinct at the beginning of the 20th century. It should be noted that there are discrepancies involving the designations "Kashubian", "Slovincian" and "Pomeranian". The latter is used in most scholarly literature (this view is also shared in the present paper) as being synonymous with Kashubian, and comprises Kashubian and Slovincian collectively. Slovincian is generally treated as a dialect of Kashubian, in accordance with the opinion held by Lorentz after 1903. For a typological classification of Slovincian as a separate Slavonic language, see earlier publications by Lorentz (1902: 44-45, 1903: 8-10).

with the members of the German community and High German in official institutions.[2]

Sociolinguistic factors such as duration, continuity and intensity of language contact, degree of proficiency, prestige and the social status of Kashubian and Low German (cf. Haugen 1950, Weinreich 1953), were all conducive to linguistic interference from the superstratum language (Low German) on Kashubian. The language contact situation changed abruptly in 1945, when the German population was expelled and Kashubia was in turn colonised by speakers of different Polish dialects. Polyglossia was gradually substituted by diglossia, with Polish as the high prestige variety. It is probable that since then the German linguistic influence on Kashubian has been in constant retreat. This issue has never been studied and merits further investigation.

2. Previous research on Low German linguistic influence on Kashubian

The issue of Low German linguistic influence on Kashubian has not yet been studied systematically. The first scholarly comments on the putative influence of German on Kashubian were made by Friedrich Lorentz (Lorentz, 1903: 10-12, 1925: 12, 77, 1958-1962 I: 40-42, 1958-1962 II: 452, 470-472, 695-696), who laid the foundation for further investigation. However, subsequent studies have not attempted to focus explicitly on Low German borrowings (for some exceptions, see Hinze 1993, Popowska-Taborska 1998). Many publications comprise very general studies on German influence which do not make distinctions between Low, Central and High German. None of these works are diachronic in their approach, nor are they embedded in a theoretical framework of language contact.

Until now, the most extensively investigated field of Kashubian-German linguistic interference has been that of lexical borrowings. Research has been done mainly by Friedhelm Hinze (e.g. Hinze 1963, 1965, 1967, 1993). His most exhaustive work – an investigation of the phonological integration of German loan words in Kashubian (Hinze 1965) – requires updating with regard to data sources and a solid theoretical framework.

Research on German grammatical interference (e.g. Hinze 1966, 1969, 1977, Piotrowski 1981) has mainly been devoted to Slovincian, an extinct Kashubian variety (cf. note 1).

---

[2] The role of Central German was more limited. Most Central German loanwords entered Kashubian via Polish (cf. Zabrocki 1956, Siatkowski 1967, Hinze 1963, 1965).

3. Towards a new approach to Kashubian-Low German interference

A new research project aims at making a detailed and diachronic analysis of the Low German linguistic influence on a single Kashubian dialect area. In contrast to previous research, which was mainly restricted to particular aspects of Kashubian-German language interference, my study will be:

1) geographically and dialectally delimited;
2) devoted explicitly to Low German language interference on Kashubian;[3]
3) an in-depth investigation of Low German influence on Kashubian in terms of different levels of interference;
4) diachronic in its approach;
5) embedded in the existing theories of language contact and contact-induced language change (cf. Haugen 1950, Weinreich 1953, Thomason and Kaufman 1988).

Ad 1: Dialect area

The dialect area in question is situated in northeastern Kashubia and comprises especially the so-called *l*-dialects. The main characteristic feature of the *l*-dialects is merger of /l/ and /ł/ into /l/, the so-called "bylaczenie".

The choice of the northeastern Kashubian dialect area is motivated by several factors:

– high intensity of language contact with Low German;
– in the course of history, less intensive language contact with Polish in comparison with other present-day Kashubian dialects;
– the existence of valuable dialect texts covering a considerable period of time (cf. below, ad 4);
– suitability of these dialects for the present-day fieldwork (a relatively compact area inhabited to a large extent by an autochthonous population).

Ad 3: Levels of interference

The study will elaborate on the complexity of interference phenomena in a defined Kashubian area and will involve phonetics/phonology, morphology, syntax, semantics and lexicon.

Some aspects of the phenomena of language interference, such as semantics, phonetics/phonology and morphology, are closely related to lexical borrowings. Accordingly, a detailed analysis of loan words (as defined by Haugen 1950: 213-214) will serve as a foundation for the investigation of the different linguistic lev-

---

[3] It should be noticed that some difficulties might arise in determining whether some linguistic features are diffused from High German or Low German, especially with respect to loan syntax.

els. The analysis of loan words will focus mainly on the manner and the extent to which they were adopted to fit into the phonological, morphological and semantic patterns of Kashubian. Further, the issue of the effect of loan words on the structure of the vernacular lexicon will be discussed.

The investigation of the remaining features of loan grammar will by and large draw on previous works, especially on the analysis of German loan syntax in Slovincian by Piotrowski (1981). It will include among others: verbal categories (such as participles, the perfect tense, the preterit tense, the pluperfect tense, passive constructions), word order and clause constructions. Attention will be paid to the question of whether the changes in the Kashubian grammar are internal developments triggered by contact with Low German, or whether they are borrowings (internal change vs. borrowing; cf. Thomason and Kaufman 1988).

Ad 4: Diachronic approach

The analysis will be based on dialect texts recorded in the same area over a period of a century, including contemporary recordings. A comparison of the linguistic data, especially from the period of the language contact situation and from the present day, will enable an evaluation of the rate of assimilation, evanescence or persistence of particular interference phenomena.

The analysis will be based on dialect texts excerpted from Bronisch (1898) and Lorentz (1924), on lexicographic material (mainly Lorentz 1959-83, Sychta 1967-76), as well as on more recent dialect data covering the area in question (*Atlas językowy kaszubszczyzny i dialektów sąsiednich* 1964-78, Topolińska 1967, 1968). The data will be supplemented by the results of my own fieldwork.[4]

The advantage of encompassing such an extensive data source is that it is representative and repetitive, thus yielding more reliable results. The drawback is the obvious difficulty in comparing a large amount of data collected by authors employing different transcriptions in their records.[5] A single systematic and consistent interpretation of these transcriptions will therefore be given.

University of Groningen

---

[4] Since the study of linguistic influence involves a comparison of linguistic structures of both the donor and the recipient language, relevant data on the Low German dialects will be scrutinised, including lexicographical material, monographs on Low German dialects spoken in Pomerania, German linguistic atlases and Low German texts.

[5] Compare different transcriptions of the Kashubian lexeme 'boy': *knωp* (Lorentz), *knôp* (Bronisch), *knöp* (Topolińska), *knåp* (Sychta).

REFERENCES

Atlas językowy kaszubszczyzny i dialektów sąsiednich
1964-78   *Atlas językowy kaszubszczyzny i dialektów sąsiednich* I-VI (ed. by Z. Stieber),
             VII-XV (ed. by H. Popowska-Taborska). Wrocław.
Bronisch, G.
1898   *Kaschubische Dialectstudien*. II. *Texte in der Sprache der Bëlöcë. Nebst An-
             hang: Proben aus einigen ł-Dialecten*. Leipzig.
Gil'ferding, A.
1862   *Ostatki slavjan na južnom beregu Baltijskago morja*. Sankt-Peterburg.
Haugen, E.
1950   "The analysis of linguistic borrowing", *Language* 26, 210-231.
Hinze, F.
1963   *Die deutschen Lehnwörter im Pomoranischen (Kaschubischen)*. Berlin.
1965   *Wörterbuch und Lautlehre der deutschen Lehnwörter im Pomoranischen (Ka-
             schubischen)*. Berlin.
1966   "Der Ausdruck des Passivs im Slovinzischen", *Zeitschrift für Slawistik* 11, 481-
             502.
1967   "Die Typen der Lehnprägungen nach deutschem Vorbild im Pomoranischen",
             Zeitschrift für Slawistik 12, 639-649.
1969   "Die Wiedergabe des deutschen Substantiv-Verbalabstrakt-Kompositums im
             Slovinzischen. Ein Beitrag zur deutschen Lehnsyntax im Slawischen", in: W.
             Krauss, Z. Stieber et al. (eds.), *Slawisch-Deutsche Wechselbeziehungen in Spra-
             che, Literatur und Kultur*, 63-68. Berlin.
1977   "Lehnadverb und Verbform als Ausdruck deutscher Distanzkomposita im Po-
             moranischen", *Zeitschrift für Slawistik* 22, 615-622.
1993   "Enige Lehnprägungstypen nach niederdeutschem Muster vornehmlich im
             Nordpomoranischen", *Zeitschrift für Slawistik* 38, 79-85.
Lorentz, F.
1902   "Das gegenseitige Verhältnis der sogenannten lechischen Sprachen", *Archiv für
             slavische Philologie* 24, 1-73.
1903   *Slovinzische Grammatik*. St. Petersburg.
1924   *Teksty pomorskie (kaszubskie)*. Kraków.
1925   *Geschichte der pomoranischen Sprache*. Berlin-Leipzig.
1958-62   *Gramatyka Pomorska* I-III. Poznań (2nd reprinted edition of 1927-37).
1959-83   *Pomoranisches Wörterbuch* I-V (vols. II-V continued by F. Hinze). Berlin.
Parczewski, A.
1896   *Szczątki kaszubskie w prowincji pomorskiej. Szkic historyczno-etnograficzny*.
             Poznań.
Piotrowski, J.
1981   *Składnia słowińska wobec wpływów języka niemieckiego*. Wrocław.
Popowska-Taborska, H.
1998   "Specyfika leksykalnych interferencji kaszubsko-dolnoniemieckich", *Z polskich
             studiów slawistycznych*. 9: *Językoznawstwo*, 225-230.
Rzetelska-Feleszko, E.
1973   *Dawne słowiańskie dialekty województwa koszalińskiego. Najstarsze zmiany fo-
             netyczne*. Wrocław.

Siatkowski, J.
1967   "Wpływ poszczególnych dialektów niemieckich na język polski", *Studia z filologii polskiej i słowiańskiej* 7, 33-46.
Sychta, B.
1967-76   *Słownik gwar kaszubskich na tle kultury ludowej* I-VII. Wrocław.
Thomason, S.G., and T. Kaufman
1988   *Language contact, creolization, and genetic linguistics*. Berkley.
Topolińska, Z.
1967   "Teksty gwarowe centralnokaszubskie z komentarzem fonologicznym", *Studia z filologii polskiej i słowiańskiej* 7, 87-124.
1968   "Teksty gwarowe północnokaszubskie z komentarzem fonologicznym", *Studia z filologii polskiej i słowiańskiej* 8, 67-93.
1974   *A historical phonology of the Kashubian dialects of Polish*. The Hague-Paris.
Weinreich, U.
1953   *Languages in contact. Findings and problems*. The Hague-Paris-New York.
Zabrocki, L.
1956   "Związki językowe niemiecko-pomorskie", *Konferencja pomorska (1954). Prace Językoznawcze*, 149-174. Warszawa.

Languages in Contact, edited by D.G. Gilbers, J. Nerbonne, and J. Schaeken (= *Studies in Slavic and General Linguistics*, vol. 28), 335-339. Amsterdam - Atlanta, GA: Rodopi, 2000.

TYPOLOGICAL AND LANGUAGE SPECIFIC FEATURES IN INTONATION QUESTIONS OF ARMENIAN AND ENGLISH

NINA B. VOLSKAYA AND ANNA S. GRIGORYAN

1. Introduction

Melodic patterns of so-called 'intonation questions' (IQ) reveal certain similarities in a number of languages: a rise in pitch on the tonic syllable or a high tone level of the whole utterance. Absence of lexical or syntactic markers of interrogativity is compensated by the intonation (Peškovskij 1930).

In this study pitch patterns of the IQs in Armenian will be investigated. The research includes listening experiments in which the effect of Armenian intonation question patterns on native English speakers was studied.

2. Description of the experiment

2.1 Experiment 1: Patterns of intonation questions in Armenian

The material on the Armenian language – 6-8 sentence-printed everyday conversations – was recorded from four native (two male and two female) speakers. The age of the speakers ranged from 18 to 21. Recordings were made onto DAT in a sound-proofed studio. The subjects were asked to speak the dialogues in a most natural way. 148 intonation questions were excerpted from the corpus, transcribed and put into the computer for further analysis. Most frequently used patterns of IQs in Armenian are presented in Table 1 below.

There are two distinct patterns of IQ that were used by the speakers, namely, a continuous rise within the tonic syllable in the final position, and a rise on the tonic syllable, followed by a fall on the post-tonic unstressed syllables. On-sets and off-sets of the rising movement on the tonic syllable differ: from low to upper-mid and from medium to the high level. It is not surprising that final rises are the most frequently observed patterns in Armenian IQ, as they are traditionally the canonical question markers used in many languages, including English, Dutch and Russian (Crystal 1969, Haan and van Heuven 1997, Bryzgunova 1980: 97-111). At the same time, bi-syllabic and polysyllabic words displayed a pattern in which a rise on the tonic syllable was followed by a fall in the post-tonic syllable(s).The choice of the pitch pattern here seems to be bound up with differences in the lexical stress pattern.

Number of syllables	Intonation patterns and frequency of their occurrence, %				
	Tonic Mid Rise	Post-tonic	Tonic High Rise	Post-tonic	Tonic Fall Rise
Monosyllabic words	33	–	58	–	9
Bi-syllabic words with a final tonic syllable	75	–	14	–	11
Bi-syllabic words with the first tonic syllable	50	Low	50	Low	
Polysyllabic words with unstressed pre-tonic syllables	62	High	38	High	
Polysyllabic words with unstressed post-tonic syllables	82	Low	18	Low	

Table 1. Intonation patterns of IQs with frequency of occurrence, %

2.2 Experiment 2: Perceptual identification of IQ patterns by English subjects

The material was presented over headphones to seven native English listeners. They were instructed to decide what sentence type they heard with forced choice from four alternatives: statement (.), non-finality (,), question (?), or exclamation (!), by putting a corresponding punctuation mark in a graphed chart. Sentences were presented in random order. Since a terminal rise is an almost sure sign of interrogativity, we expected useful information in the subtleties of phonetic realizations of IQs which should be reflected in the evaluation by the English listeners. Therefore, we introduced a graph in the chart where the subjects specified the neutral/emotional meaning of the utterances. None of the English subjects spoke Armenian or was familiar with its intonation system. Listeners' responses are presented in Tables 2 and 3.

2.3 Results

The analysis of the responses of the English listeners to different pitch patterns of Armenian IQ shows that the results differ from what we expected in the way that a great number of intended neutral questions were perceived as emotionally coloured questions or exclamations. This type of responses appeared for patterns with a fall in pitch in the post-tonic syllables and in patterns with low pitched pre-tonic syllables (Tables 2 and 3).

Sentence type	Intonation patterns					
	Tonic Mid Rise	Post-tonic	Tonic High Rise	Post-tonic	Tonic Rise	Post-tonic Low
1 Question	75		40		25	
2 Emotional question	25		40		25	
3 Exclamation			20		50	

Table 2. Percent responses to the suggested alternatives
for mono- and bisyllabic stimuli with a post-tonic syllable.

We also observed that the percentage of perceived neutral questions decreased with the increase of the number of low-pitched pre-tonic syllables (Table 4). The most frequently reported labels were surprise, incredulity.

Sentence type	Pre-tonic Low	Tonic Rising	Post-tonic Upper Mid	Pre-tonic Low	Tonic Upper Mid	Post-tonic Low
1 Question	30			57		
2 Emotional question	52			43		
3 Non-finality	5.5					
4 Statement	12.5					

Table 3. Percent responses to each of the alternatives for stimuli with pre-tonic syllables.

Number of low pre-tonic syllables	Percentage of perceived sentence types				
	Question	Emotional question	Excla-mation	Statement	Non-finality
One	61	28		5.5	5.5
Two	50	37.5		12.5	
Three	40	60			

Table 4. Percent responses as a function of the number of low-pitched pre-tonic syllables.

2.4 Experiment 3: Stimulus Analysis

The analysis of the waveforms (duration and F0 values) was performed with the help of a computer program developed at the Department of Phonetics. 21 stimuli perceived as neutral questions were put into the computer and digitized at 16 kHz. The parameters were extracted either automatically or by visual inspection of the signal. The acoustic data are presented in tables 5-7.

Mean values	Female speakers Tonic syllable	Male speakers Tonic syllable
F0, Hz	456	210
T, ms	189	174

Table 5. Mean F0 maxima and duration values for monosyllabic words.

	Female speakers		Male speakers	
	Pre-tonic Mean	Tonic Excursion	Pre-tonic Mean	Tonic Excursion
F0, Hz	219	380	112	222
T, ms		189		201

Table 6. Mean F0 and duration values for two-syllable words.

	Female speakers			Male speakers		
	Pre-tonic Mean	Tonic Excursion	Post-tonic Min	Pre-tonic Mean	Tonic Excursion	Post-tonic Min
F0, Hz	198	410	154	110	210	88
T, ms		157	161		136	180

Table 7. Mean F0 and duration values for polysyllabic words.

3. Conclusion

The experiment revealed a certain degree of similarity between pitch patterns of IQs in English and Armenian, since 50.2% of the presented stimuli were per-ceived as neutral questions. The pitch patterns used by our subjects, namely, Mid-Rise, High Rise and Rise + Fall on the post-tonic syllables, are similar to those included in the inventory of English question intonation (Crystal 1969). At the same time, specific patterns with low-pitched pre-tonic syllables, most frequent in Armenian questions, and low-pitched post-tonic syllables, induced English listen-ers to perceive emotion in questions, which are emotionally neutral to Armenian speakers.

Department of Phonetics, St. Petersburg State University

REFERENCES

Bryzgunova, Elena A.
  1980   *Russkaja grammatika 1.*
Crystal, David
  1969   *Prosodic Systems and Intonation in English.* Cambridge University Press.

Haan, J., and Vincent J. van Heuven
   1997   "Intonational characteristics of declarativity and interrogativity in Dutch: a comparison", *Proceedings of an ESCA Workshop on Intonation: Theory, Models and Applications, September 18-20, 1997*, 173-176. Athens.
Peškovskij, Aleksej M.
   1930   *Intonacija i grammatika.* Leningrad.